Liliana Sikorska
Nineteenth- and Twentieth-Century Readings of the Medieval Orient

Research in Medieval
and Early Modern Culture XXXII

Studies in Medieval
and Early Modern Culture LXXX

Liliana Sikorska

Nineteenth- and Twentieth-Century Readings of the Medieval Orient

—

Other Encounters

DE GRUYTER

ISBN 978-1-5015-2149-2
e-ISBN (PDF) 978-1-5015-1336-7
e-ISBN (EPUB) 978-1-5015-1310-7

Library of Congress Control Number: 2021948062

Bibliographic information published by the Deutsche Nationalbibliothek
The Deutsche Nationalbibliothek lists this publication in the Deutsche Nationalbibliografie;
detailed bibliographic data are available on the Internet at http://dnb.dnb.de.

© 2023 Walter de Gruyter GmbH, Berlin/Boston
This volume is text- and page-identical with the hardback published in 2021.
Cover image: Aleksander Laszenko (1883–1944). Brama w Sidibel Abbes [The Gate in Sidibel Abbes], color woodcut, 1932. From the author's own collection; 17th-c. Turkish brass plate. From the author's own collection; Translation into Arabic: Dr. Filip Andrzej Jakubowski; Preparatory cover version: Mr. Jakub Grabowski
Typesetting: Integra Software Services Pvt. Ltd.
Printing and binding: CPI books GmbH, Leck

www.degruyter.com

For Jacek, forever and beyond
and for my friends who were with me through thick and thin

Preface

In 1291, Acre, the last Christian settlement in the Crusader state of Outremer, was conquered by the Mamluk Turks.¹ Despite the Church's preaching, any effort to reclaim territory once held by crusaders was seriously hampered by the Hundred Years' War, which began in 1337. By the time it ended in 1453, Europe had been left ailing and weak, and it was about to witness an even more horrific event: the fall of Constantinople to the Turks in that same year. With this catastrophe perished Christendom's last remaining stronghold in the East and the remnants of the ancient Roman imperial might. The symbolic takeover of one of the oldest churches in Constantinople, the Christian basilica Hagia Sophia, which henceforth served as a mosque, solidified the Muslim presence at the borders of *respublica Christiana*.

By contrast, the ruins of the ancient city of Jerash in faraway Jordan, visited by the English writer and explorer Charles Montagu Doughty (1843–1926) during his wanderings through Arabia in the 1870s, testified to the glory of the Greco-Roman civilization and European cultural expansionism. Yet this seemingly ageless city in Arabia was also a memento of the destruction of the Roman Empire. Thus Doughty, like the medieval pilgrims traveling to the Holy Land, was exposed not only to an Old and New Testament site of sacred history but, first and foremost, to the overpowering presence of Islam. No wonder, then, that his account aligns with the earlier diaries and travel accounts of the post-Crusading period, as well as medieval – and for that matter, nineteenth-century – quest romances. Such works bear witness to the manifold confrontations with the culture of the past and the confluence of fascination and fear, or "fascination" in the Baconian sense of "hostile enchantment,"² which in turn engenders ever-present outrage.

For the past twenty years, we have been living in a world "where the 'Clash of Civilizations' is becoming a self-fulfilling prophecy," as Kamila Shamsie observes.³ The present study examines contact and conflict between the Christian West and Muslim East, analyzing the nineteenth- and twentieth-century cultural and literary works that narrate such confrontations. Misunderstanding, insult,

---

1 In 1095, Pope Urban II urged the faithful join a holy war, the First Crusade, which ultimately resulted in establishment of four crusader states: the County of Edessa, the Principality of Antioch, the Kingdom of Jerusalem, and the County of Tripoli. Christian dominance was constantly challenged, territories were lost, and succeeding popes preached subsequent crusades until 1291, when the City of Acre, the capital of the Kingdom of Jerusalem, fell.
2 See footnote 13 in page 16.
3 Shamsie, *Offence*, 15.

and terrorism – compounded by colonialism and religious differences – have contributed to the strained relations between and, simultaneously, the one-sided representations of, divergent cultures. The proliferation of works concerning ethnic conflict and terrorism in itself speaks to the ongoing relevance of the topic. Present-day terrorism, however, has to be read through the prism of discourses on Otherness. Race and ethnicity lie at the core of the construction of the stranger, the monstrous Other, in scientific as well as historical and cultural discourses of the nineteenth century, whose traces we can find in the contemporary juxtaposition of the East and the West. Nineteenth-century historical works and travel narratives, in turn, replicate earlier, medieval modes in their portrayal of the East, whereas contemporary texts, attempting to dislodge colonial accounts, inadvertently reproduce misconstrued, frequently racist images. The following overview of the literature on the topics discussed is intended to identify such ideologies in order to locate my arguments in existing critical practices and current approaches to the origins of these pervasive binary oppositions.

It comes as no surprise that the Crusades not only deepened the East–West divide, but also set us on a collision course thereafter. The habitual recurrence of the idea of European, or Western, unity against a common non-Christian enemy influenced the way in which twentieth- and twenty-first-century writers formed the so-called "war on terror" narrative. Yet, to understand the manifold impact of the Crusades in the late medieval period, we have to fathom the mechanisms of power in medieval Europe, in which the early enthusiasm of the universal call to arms was undermined by local baronial conflicts, so aptly described by the anonymous writer of the longest thirteenth-century Saracen romance of *Guy of Warwick*. The crusading spirit was further hampered by the Hundred Years' War, as England and France fought for succession and dominance. The loss of Acre, therefore, has to be seen as symptomatic of a much graver problem – the gradual defeat of the ideal *respublica Christiana*. By asserting the supremacy of the Mamluk Turks, the battle destabilized the hitherto cohesive European Christian identity that was the foundation of the initial ventures into the East. The first crusaders pledged their bodies and souls to the Christian cause above any national interests. Forty-six years after the fall of Acre, the Hundred Years' War[4] showed that this unity was an illusion. Dynastic and territorial disagreement took precedence over the Christian recapture of the Holy Land. Plagued by national and international antagonisms and mushrooming heretical movements such as the Cathars, the Waldensians, and the Lollards, Christian

---

4 Griffiths, *The Fourteenth and Fifteenth Centuries*.

Europe was the *respublica Christiana* in name only. The Great Schism between the Eastern and the Western Church in 1054 and the subsequent rise and establishment of the Protestant churches in the postmedieval period likewise contributed to the deterioration of doctrinal uniformity within Christianity.

Such instability and multiplicity is also evident in the case of Islam: the notion that Islam is a monolithic religion is untenable in the contemporary world. Consequently, a more feasible distinction, as Kamila Shamsie argues, can be made between "the hard-liners" and the "anti-hardliners."[5] Given the diversification of various Christian and Muslim groups, the reductionist and simplistic contrast of the Orient vs. the Occident will be challenged in the ensuing chapters. Still, one of the reasons for the constant disparagement of beliefs is the markedly different approach to individual freedoms. Undoubtedly, the concept of blasphemy exists in both Christianity and Islam, but the problem lies in the line that divides freedom of expression from transgression, and the resultant call for violence.[6] Shamsie discerns that "it is not merely Islam, but religions worldwide that carry with them demands for reverence and adherence to religious laws."[7] But it is Islamic leaders who issue death sentences for those who refuse to abide by their laws and, supposedly, offend the believers through their actions. Here the famous case of Rushdie's *Satanic Verses*[8] could serve as an example. The hostilities originating in the Middle Ages and echoing into the twentieth century not only fostered the emergence of the fundamentalist Muslim movements but also reawakened the need to understand the roots of existing divergences.

The matter of Araby, to use Dorothee Metlitzki's expression,[9] is thus not new. Early medieval Muslim imperialism, after centuries of skirmishes, was ended by Jan III Sobieski's victory at the Battle of Vienna in 1683. The fabled battle, immortalized in the large painting by the Polish painter Jan Matejko,[10] has always been perceived as the turning point in the Islamic invasion of Europe and as an indication of the superiority of Christianity. Sobieski's triumph generated a pro-Christian and anti-Turkish mood, as the threat of Islam was

---

5 Shamsie, *Offence*, 6.
6 Shamsie, *Offence*, 7.
7 Shamsie, *Offence*, 4.
8 Rushdie, *The Satanic Verses*. The fatwa pronounced on Salman Rushdie and everyone involved with the publication of the novel, as well as riots in Muslim communities in England and worldwide, were reported by all international newspapers. Shamsie also discusses a rally protesting the novel at the American Cultural Center in Islamabad. Shamsie, *Offence*, 59.
9 Metlitzki, *The Matter of Araby in Medieval England*.
10 Jan Matejko (1838–1893), currently on display in the Vatican Museums.

once again pushed back to the outskirts of Christian Europe. Strangely enough, the covert action of the US forces who tracked and killed Osama Bin Laden at his compound in Pakistan on May 2, 2011, flaunted a similar pro-Western and anti-Islam euphoria. Conflict is, and has always been (as I will argue in chapter 1) an essential part of the encounters between the East and the West and in recent years, as the so-called "terrorist novel"[11] and various non-fictional works have exposed religious divergence, this has received renewed attention.

The issue of terrorism itself has generated a wide range of works, not only concerning its literary incarnation but also tracing its origins, historical background, and psychological dimensions. While Margaret Scanlan scrutinizes literary texts with terrorist plots that were published before the 9/11 attacks, research by Andrew Silke, David Altheide, and Neil Smelser[12] is devoted to investigating the psychological traits of terrorists[13] in relation to group dynamics, responding to the need for definitions of fundamentalism and terrorism in the post-9/11 world. John Horgan, in turn, tries to establish the psychological profile of a terrorist through certain pathological disorders; he is, nonetheless, cautious about proclaiming that every terrorist is, in fact, displaying abnormal psychological features.[14] Joseph Soeters studies terrorism in connection with ethnic conflict and discusses the origins and dynamics of civil wars; his findings are essential for analyzing reading contemporary literature narrating the failure of multiculturalism.[15] None of these works, however, link medieval discourses on the Orient with contemporary literature as this present work seeks to do.

Only Bruce Hoffman's *Inside Terrorism* searches for the patterns of behavior encoded in texts written before the twentieth century and associates these modes with the more modern developments of extremism. Discussing the changing face of terrorism, Hoffman points to the fact that "terrorism in its original context was also closely associated with the ideals of virtue and democracy,"[16] and in the

---

11 Scanlan, *Plotting Terror*. Terrorism and how it is reflected in novels has been the subject of many critical works besides Scanlan's. One of the most interesting studies is Meenakshi Bharat's *Troubled Testimonies: Terrorism and the English Novel in India*, which charts the most contemporary literary responses to terrorism. Her *Shooting Terror. Terrorism in Hindi Films*, in turn, is devoted to the multifaceted home-bred and terror in contemporary India.
12 Silke, *Terrorists, Victims and Society*; Altheide, *Terrorism and the Politics of Fear*; Smelser, *The Faces of Terrorism*.
13 Silke's collection includes an article about the victims of terrorism; see Betty Pfefferbaum's contribution, 175–87.
14 Horgan, "Leaving Terrorism Behind."
15 Soeters, *Ethnic Conflict and Terrorism*.
16 Hoffman, *Inside Terrorism*, 3.

post-war period, in the 1960s and 1970s, it was still viewed as part of the revolutionary milieu.[17] Only in the 1990s did it became a warning to nation states by non-state actors.[18] Hoffman cites Maximilien Robespierre, the (in)famous French revolutionary who argued that terror is but justice, "prompt, severe and inflexible."[19] Violence and intimidation have been the only means to draw attention to the causes espoused by various anti-imperialist groups, and this is the main motif of Mohamed Laroussi El Metoui's *Halima*, discussed in part 2 of the present study. As modern-day terrorism subsumes ideas of freedom and liberation, the actions of armies and military organizations, and even self-defense movements, it is increasingly difficult to define its parameters and so to analyze it objectively. What transpires from Hoffman's enquiry is the connection between the emergence of modern-day international terrorism and the end of the British Empire.

This motif is further surveyed by Elleke Boehmer and Stephen Morton,[20] in a work that sketches theories of colonial and postcolonial terror[21] in their historical settings and inspects their manifold expressions in literature, theater, and film. Terrorism in literature refers to latent and manifest Orientalism, and it entails a discourse that shapes our ways of thinking through binary oppositions and hierarchies constructed by European empires. Edward Said suggested that there are two codependent "Orientalisms": "Orientalism as an innocent scholarly endeavor and Orientalism as an accomplice to empire, can never unilaterally be detached from the general imperial context that begins its modern global phase with Napoleon's invasion of Egypt in 1798."[22] Such a definition allowed him to argue that Orientalism is both the necessary precondition of imperialism and also its consequence. Criticizing nineteenth-century explorers, Said disregards the intellectual legacy of Antiquity and of medieval culture, and the religious heritage bequeathed in medieval romances, which initially divided the worlds of East and West into perpetually warring parties.[23] "Narrative progression

---

[17] Hoffman, *Inside Terrorism*, 16.
[18] Hoffman, *Inside Terrorism*, 18.
[19] Hoffman, *Inside Terrorism*, 4.
[20] Boehmer and Morton, *Terror and the Postcolonial*.
[21] Elleke Boehmer points to the necessity of distinguishing the term "post-colonial" from "postcolonial," as the former reflects the preoccupations with "the writing that 'came after' empire," while the latter "critically scrutinizes the colonial relationship." For her, "*postcoloniality* is defined as that condition in which colonized peoples seek to take their place, forcibly or otherwise, as historical subjects." *Colonial and Postcolonial*, 3.
[22] Said, *Orientalism*, 334.
[23] I have already written about the links between topography and the representations of non-European people in medieval romance of *Guy of Warwick* and Richard Burton's *First Footsteps in East Africa*. For more, see Sikorska, *Being (Non)Human*.

and triumphalism," as Simon Gikandi observes, "were all generated by unshakable confidence in the imperial enterprise."[24] In hindsight, Victorian exploration aided in the cultural construction of the myth of the Orient and accelerated economic exploitation.

There is an unquestionable correlation between knowledge and power handed down by Said via Michel Foucault, as the processes of conquest and colonization are always accompanied by cultural exemplifications aimed at the polarization of the superior and inferior subjects. Yet by de-essentializing the Orient, Said fossilized the Occident. While demonstrating how the discourse of Orientalism commodifies the colonized, depriving them of individuality, he disregarded the transformations of European scholarship from late eighteenth to the late twentieth century. By doing so, he refused the one aspect of contemporary critical practice he deemed indispensable in all scholarly pursuits – that is, the possibility of amendment. Said's oeuvre remains in the background of all debates on Orientalism, as it has brought to attention the politics of representation and the uncontested textuality of the recurrent images and metaphors through which it is described, but it is not under scrutiny here; I will therefore refer to his works but forgo the ongoing discussions concerning his arguments.[25] My purpose is to read nineteenth-century travel narratives and historical works, as well as lesser-known contemporary literary texts, through medieval tropes, in order to substantiate their shared ideological background and unearth the tenets of present-day islamophobia. There is no denying that militant Islam is a real, tangible threat in Europe, as evinced by the attacks in Paris in November 2015, in Brussels in March 2016, and in Berlin in December 2016, but such is also the case with the Russian separatist movement in Eastern Ukraine, which has been escalating since 2014 (though currently kept at bay), as well as the IRA and the Basque separatist movements, which are still dormant within the borders of the European Union. European Christian integrity, of which rightist governments nowadays like to repeatedly remind their citizens, is a product of both inclusion and exclusion; hence the troublesome status of modern Turkey, relegated to the rim of the enlightened world and left on the waiting list to join the European Union. There are many other dangerous flash points in the world, but it is the problem of current Islamic terrorism, whose image stems from the medieval Saracen

---

24 Gikandi *Maps of Englishness*, 161.
25 Said's assertions have been much debated, but the present book is not the place to engage in such. On the matter, see: Ahmad, *In Theory*, 159–219; Young, *Colonial Desire*, 159–66; Moore-Gilbert, *Postcolonial Theory*, 34–73. Walder, *Post-Colonial Literatures in English*, 70–72; Young *Postcolonial Criticism*, 383–98; and Lazarus, *The Postcolonial Unconscious*, 183–203.

Other, which continues to conceptualize the ultimate division between "us" and "them." The discords still hold sway in the Western imagination.

Otherness, therefore, lies at the core of contemporary cultural studies, underscoring the dynamics of cultural variance within relatively unified societies. The notion of the Other has been thoroughly explained in such diverse philosophical treatises as Emmanuel Levinas's *Totality and Infinity*[26] and Michel de Certeau's *Heterologies: Discourse on the Other*.[27] Levinas's work is a meditation on Otherness and sameness, seeing God as the absolute Other and the immanence of God's manifestation as a type of omnipresence. Levinas argued that the notion of truth relies upon the Other, as there exists a form of truth that is entirely alien to the speaking subject. An-Other is alternatively treated as an extension of the self, as well as wholly alien, but also manageable – an alien whom it is possible to manipulate to the advantage of an individual or the whole society.[28] In Levinas's thought, all ethics derive from a confrontation with an Other. This Other, with whom we interact, represents a gateway into the more abstract Otherness, which is as absolute as it is ineffable. The complete Other is strikingly similar to the monstrous stranger,[29] and that association with the inhuman is expounded in medieval romances. Analyzing the origins of the construction of Otherness, de Certeau, however, does not refer to the Saracens but cites Michel de Montaigne's "Of Cannibals" to show how a "cannibal" is "a figure on the fringe who leaves the premises, and in doing so jolts the entire topographical order of language."[30] In Western philosophical thought, the cannibal, much like the Saracen, is the emblem of an unenlightened past, consigned to the margins of civilization. By drawing attention to the perception of difference, de Certeau challenges the preconceived ideas on what constitutes the monster.

The widely established notion of the alien being articulated through bodily and cultural miscreation not only resurfaces in the work of Levinas and de Certeau but is likewise the basis of the rereading of medieval oriental tales. What is persistent in many oeuvres on the subject is the belief that cultural Otherness is

---

26 Levinas, *Totality and Infinity*. Alexa Wright links Levinas's thought with the discourse on monstrosity. In her view, his notion of the Other is "an absolute form of difference that cannot be known or articulated" and is therefore "very close to the concept of the monstrous." Alexa Wright, *Monstrosity*, 18.
27 De Certeau, *Heterologies*. Since the present study is devoted to the cultural constructions of the orient, I will not dwell on the *sensu stricto* philosophical and psychoanalytic readings.
28 Levinas, *Totality and Infinity*, 13.
29 Levinas, *Totality and Infinity*, 74–77.
30 De Certeau, *Heterologies*, 71.

both synchronic and diachronic and has to be seen within the framework of race and ethnicity. Here, Geraldine Heng's most recent work concerning the question of race in the European Middle Ages shows how Otherness labors against "the seductive promise of a triumphal pan-Christianity"[31] and can be seen through the lens not only of religion but also of color – that is, blackness – and cartographic deformity, linked with the Monstrous Races.[32] Today, the outsider is comprehended through the prism of mixophobia and mixophilia, so aptly expressed by Zygmunt Bauman.[33]

The ideas of multiculturalism or even interculturalism can be seen as examples of mixophilia, while the practice of perpetrating ideas about foreigners being the source of real or assumed danger is also connected with the postcolonial reclaiming of the Gothic. H. L. Malchow's *Gothic Images of Race in Nineteenth-Century Britain* demonstrates how "race"[34]

> is an inherently fluid idea whose meaning, like those of class or nationality, shifts over time and seems at once concrete and intangible. *Racism* required a demonization (I do not use the word casually here) of difference. The gothic genre of the late eighteenth century, and its various permutations thereafter, offered a language that could be appropriated, consciously or not, by racists in a powerful and obsessively reiterated evocation of terror, disgust, and alienation. But the gothic literary sensibility itself also evoked in the context of an expanding experience of cultural conflict, of the brutal progress of European nationalism and imperialism, and was in part a construct of that phenomenon.[35]

Tabish Khair in *The Gothic, Postcolonialism and Otherness* points to Otherness as a central concern of Gothic literature. He warns, however, against the reductive perception of the Other "merely in terms of negativity."[36] Building on this, his use of "Otherness" "is not just philosophical but also sociological, which is only appropriate because, whether or not literature reflects society, it is written

---

31 Heng, *The Invention of Race in the European Middle Ages*. For more on medieval cultural diversity, see Cohen, *Cultural Diversity in the British Middle Ages*.
32 Keiko Hamaguchi, in her reading of Chaucer's "Man of Law's Tale," shows how historical foreign queens influenced the representation of figure of Custance. Hamaguchi, "The Cultural Otherness in the Man of Law's Tale."
33 Bauman, *Liquid Times*, 90–91.
34 Today, one needs to be much more cautious when using the terms "race" and "racism." Discussion of the question of race does not necessarily imply racism. Contemporary studies analyze the interconnectedness of the developing discipline of racialism, the study of races, and nineteenth-century racism; see, for example Khair, *The Gothic, Postcolonialism and Otherness*.
35 Malchow, *Gothic Images of Race in Nineteenth-Century Britain*, 3.
36 Khair, *The Gothic, Postcolonialism and Otherness*, 14.

in that most social of all human creations: language."³⁷ Khair's work articulates not only the process of othering but also the unease about various versions of the Other: the Devil, ghosts, women, vampires, Jews, lunatics, murderers, non-Europeans. In short, it revolves around revivified colonial and postcolonial notions of "not us."

Khair and Malchow's exposition of the postmedieval discussions of race, however, lack a more detailed account of the work of the Count de Gobineau, a nineteenth-century scholar whose works *The Inequality of Human Races* and *The Moral and Intellectual Diversity of Races*, published in English in 1854 and 1856 respectively³⁸ suggested such a "gothic" disparity, thereby validating racism. Writing about the Nomads and Orientals of various tribes, Sir Richard Francis Burton (1821–1890) and Charles Montagu Doughty express views that were prominent in their time and propagated by such known authorities as Arthur de Gobineau. De Gobineau could not contest there being a common ancestor of all the races, as he did not want to question the Bible, but in his work he showed the white race as the only one capable of creating an informed culture and forming an ordered state. He refuted the hypotheses that "the negro, the North American savage, the Tungoose of North Siberia, might under favorable circumstances, gain all the physical and mental attributes which now distinguish the European. Such a theory is inadmissible."³⁹ De Gobineau saw human diversity as originating in the biblical parable of talents⁴⁰ and accorded European civilization the highest level of development. In his view, Europeans preserved and continued the best aspects of ancient civilizations; they perfected the ancient Indo-European culture, which he called "Aryan." H. Hotz, in his "Analytical

---

37 Khair, *The Gothic, Postcolonialism and Otherness*, 16.
38 De Gobineau, *Moral and Intellectual Diversity of Races*.
39 De Gobineau, *Moral and Intellectual Diversity*, 336. De Gobineau claims that the prevailing medieval interpretation of the "fathers" of the three races – Japeth of the European, Shem of the Asian, and Ham of the African – is a rather "arbitrary interpretation" (338). At the same time, he uses the distinction to illustrate human "species" and their varieties by assessing certain attributes; for example, the "Ishmaelitic species" is characterized by a "callous" temperament, being "moderately mental, not originative, or inventive, but speculative; roving, predatory, revengeful, and sensual. Warlike and highly destructive" (372). He then discusses the diversity of races and permanency of types, and the spreading, for example of the Arab races; he notices that "although many centuries have elapsed since their invasion, traces of Arab blood are still discernible in some portions of Roussilion, Languedoc, and Spain" (344). Moreover, he does not deem civilizational progress dependent on the fertility of the soil, nor does he perceive Christianity as a condition for advancement. De Gobineau, *The Inequality*, 64–65.
40 Hotz, "Introduction," in de Gobineau, *Moral and Intellectual Diversity*, 27.

Introduction" to de Gobineau's work, wrote: "As if to afford a still more irrefragable proof of the mental inequality of races, we find separate divisions of the same island inhabited, one by the pure, the other by a half-breed race; and the infusion of the white civilizing blood in the latter case forms a population incontestably and avowedly superior."[41] He had no doubt that the white race was the strongest and the most progressive, and he thereby concurred that the permanence of racial qualities "is quite sufficient to generate the radical unlikeness and inequality that exists between the different branches, to raise them to the dignity of natural laws, and to justify the same distinctions being drawn with regard to the physiological life of nations . . . and applicable to their moral life."[42] Both Hotz and de Gobineau deemed the intellectual and moral inequality of human races inevitable, because human races have dissimilar mental and intellectual capabilities. Proclaiming that "mankind is divided into unlike and unequal parts,"[43] de Gobineau drew parallels between the civilizational expansion and the development of different languages.[44] It is worth remembering that the nineteenth century saw the growth of linguistics and interest in the genealogy of human languages. The concept was introduced by August Schleicher in 1871, but the hypothesis of language change emerged earlier.[45]

As was the case of languages in contact, human races would likewise unavoidably mix. In de Gobineau's assessment, this had already taken place in medieval Spain. However, he opted for anti-miscegenation as the only possible solution to the chaos resulting from such combinations. Characteristically, he ascribed the economic and political unrest in the Europe of his day to the pollution of the races. Richard Burton makes a similar observations in his works, and the mournful mixing of races is a recurring subject in his *Personal Narrative*. Linking the advance of human races with the birth and flowering of religions, de Gobineau, not unlike the nineteenth-century historians Samuel Green and Arthur Gilman, toyed with the idea that Islam was not revealed but created by Mohammed, who "invented the religion most conformable to the idea of a people,

---

41 Hotz, "Introduction," in De Gobineau, *Moral and Intellectual Diversity*, 33. I am aware of a different spelling of Henry Hotz's name; however, the Kessinger reprint of the 1856 edition of the text, which I refer to here, spells his last name without the *e*.
42 De Gobineau, *The Inequality*, 133–34.
43 De Gobineau, *The Inequality*, 181.
44 De Gobineau claims that language, "while being an excellent index of the general elevation of races, is in a special degree the measure of their aesthetic capacities." *The Inequality*, 191. He concedes, however, that not every civilization speaks the language of its ancestors.
45 Jeffers and Lehiste, *Principles and Methods*, 27.

among whom idolatry had still many zealous adherents."[46] Accordingly, "thus arrayed Islamism issued from its native deserts."[47] His stereotypical portraits of Arabs were true to the spirit of his times: "the Arab nation, [as] is well known, based its empire and its intellectual culture upon fragments of races which it had aggregated by the weight of the sword."[48] Similar descriptions are offered by the twentieth-century writer and explorer T. E. Lawrence, who, in the Preface to Charles Montagu Doughty's *Arabia Deserta*, writes that

> Semites are black and white not only in vision, but in their inner furnishing: black and white not merely in clarity, but in apposition. Their thoughts live easiest amongst extremes. . . . they exclude compromise, and pursue the logic of their ideas to its absurd ends, without seeing incongruity in their opposed conclusions.[49]

In light of such arguments, a contemporary scholar is always caught in opposing declarations. On the one hand, we have to acknowledge the "centrality of the Arab Mediterranean," since "Christians acquired a rational science from the Islamic translations of Aristotle";[50] on the other, we unremittingly point to the belligerence and backwardness of the East today, as in the past. During the Middle Ages, as J. H. Parry argues, European contacts with the Arab world "had formed part of the education of a rough and primitive Europe. European art and Industry owe much to the Arabs. [For] Greek science and learning found their way to medieval Europe – in so far as they were known at all – largely through Arabic translations."[51] By the end of the Middle Ages, that dependence was slowly waning, as the age of reconnaissance, to use Parry's expression, had begun. In the golden era of the Empire, the legacy of medieval Arabic philosophy and medicine seemed to be less significant than the possibility of conquest, buttressed by the misconception of the Arab character. These false assessments of the Arabs are unmasked by contemporary novelists such as Brian Moore and Ahdaf Soueif.

---

46 De Gobineau, *Moral and Intellectual Diversity*, 433.
47 De Gobineau, *Moral and Intellectual Diversity*, 436.
48 De Gobineau, *Moral and Intellectual Diversity*, 430.
49 Lawrence, "Introduction," in Doughty, *Travels in Arabia Deserta*, xxix. The relatively new work by Anderson, *Lawrence of Arabia*, draws attention to the issue of ideologically charged language that frequently becomes a weapon in wartime, which was certainly the case in the Middle Eastern theater of World War I. Rather than using the name "the Ottoman Empire," the Allied powers talked about "Turkey" and referred to "Constantinople" instead of "Istanbul." See "Introduction," xv.
50 Malette, *European Modernity and the Arab Mediterranean*, 2.
51 Parry, *The Age of Reconnaissance*, 25–26.

Despite the obvious prejudice contained in the quotations, as I have already noted, the present work refrains from entering the debate concerning Orientalism and counter-Orientalism. The latter term has been comprehensively scrutinized by Karla Malette in her *European Modernity and the Arab Mediterranean*. Malette's study accentuates, without being overtly critical, Said's "de-historicization" of earlier texts. She contrasts the work of northern European scholars, most notably British, with their French and Italian counterparts, uncovering the gaps in Said's accusations of a seemingly uniform European misreading of the Orient. Hers is "the tale of a peculiarly Mediterranean modernity, a model of modernity created by Arabs and Europeans in concert and to which Arabs and Europeans both continue to contribute."[52] That contribution, in the nineteenth century, was provided by explorers and scholars whose writings will be analyzed below. My main presupposition is that contemporary sensibilities should not be applied to the past, and so the harsh criticism of imperial travel in Said's *Orientalism* and Kabbani's *Imperial Fictions: Europe's Myths of Orient* should be placed in the context of Victorian, rather than present-day, attitudes and ways of thinking.

Following the Muslim invasion of the Holy Land and the subsequent Crusades, the literature of earlier periods demonized the impenetrable Muslim East. Medieval romances and travel narratives conceptualized Islam in accordance with the current state of knowledge about the world, races, and religions, creating a Saracen Other that was invariably horrifying. English travelers in foreign lands in the nineteenth century faced similar anxieties. The Saracen romances of the Middle Ages and the quest romances of the Victorian age resonate in Victorian travel narratives and historical works, signposting the interest in the history of cultures and religions alongside the more predatory forms of imperial exploration. Even though it can be argued that Victorian quest romances shun realistic descriptions, such a claim does not mean that the form lacks engagement with reality. In themselves, the romances reverberate with existing ways of thinking; they are a portrayal of (medieval) knighthood and (Victorian) "gentlemanship," with their similar mores and ideals. What is noteworthy, however, is how both forms rely on adventure. The adventurous rather than solely spiritual side of the journeys was of interest to their readers. Though it is certainly true that texts as diverse as the medieval romance of *Guy of Warwick* and the Victorian travel narrative-cum-quest romance of Richard Burton's account of his journey to Medina and Mecca in 1853 were designed to serve as instructive accounts for their contemporaries, they are as factual as they are literary.

---

52 Malette, *European Modernity*, 5.

Rather than trying to distill fact from fiction in either histories or Victorian travel narratives, in the manner of Hayden White's arguments concerning the narrative foundations of historiography, I acknowledge the struggle without judging the modes of storytelling of the chosen authors. What is more, showing the connection between the medieval and nineteenth-century debates on the East allows us to better confront the mechanisms that have led, in the eyes of Said and his followers, to the Western (mis)conception of the East.[53] By breaking with Western-centrism, Robert J. C. Young's *White Mythologies* attempts the systematic critique of Western claims about the narrative power of history, which execute the said "white mythology." The chief achievement of Young's study is in drawing attention not only to Said and others but first and foremost to the fact that, by reclaiming so-called "peripheral narratives," postcolonial theory empowers different paradigms of historiography, creating polyvocal rather than univocal histories. In the present study, however, the focus is not on the history of "History" but on the nineteenth-century historical accounts of the Saracens and biographies of Mohammed inasmuch as they inform twentieth-century novels and autobiographical narratives. The crucial value of the texts selected for further analysis is their interdependence, underscoring disparate messages of allure and aversion, laying bare the medieval construction of the Western discourses of the East. Nineteenth-century historical works brought to light the auxiliary processes that fashioned the images of the spread of the medieval Saracen empires. Still, instead of investigating the factual qualities of the travel narratives and histories, I would like to concentrate on the literary aspects of the representations of the Orient, on the Orient that exists solely as a nineteenth- and twentieth-century textual construct. Social issues and historical processes, which literature has always mirrored and responded to, betray existing ideologies. They are paradigms, and identifying them can be instrumental in revealing, at least partially, their

---

[53] Adopting a contemporary perspective requires us to take a stance on claims such as "the end of the world as we know it" (Mark Steyn) and "the unmaking of America" (Mark R. Levin). The demographic dystopia presented by these two authors goes back to nineteenth-century discussions concerning the Western empires and provides the background for our understanding of contemporary preemptive and defensive wars through the idealized dream of the West imposing (rather than suggesting) a Western-style democracy in Iraq. As is shown by Rajiv Chandrasekaran in his *Imperial Life in the Emerald City* (2007), the danger of utopian thought lies not in the belief in the ideal but in the possibility of the ideal being transformed into dystopia. Ever-romantic Poles, like Americans, are very good at hurrying into war but refuse to think about what should happen after the initial euphoria. More than the Americans, the Polish contingent was not prepared for what they had to face in Iraq and Afghanistan. The experience of strangeness and "out-of-placeness" always generates anger.

own fictionality. Nineteenth-century travel narratives and histories catered to the Victorian obsession with origins and classifications, whilst twentieth-century novels and memoirs expose contemporary preoccupations with Islam, made perceptible within the framework of postcolonial studies.

It is through the development of postcolonial studies that travel writing, a genre that long resided at the margins of literary studies, has recently gained significance. Contemporary literary criticism takes pains to discuss the issues related to the discovery of new lands and the exploration of the discourses concerning colonized territories. The ideology of discovery is clearly visible in the collection of articles edited by Rosamund Allen, entitled *Eastward Bound: Travel and Travellers 1050–1550*, and in David Wallace's *Premodern Places: Calais to Surinam, Chaucer to Aphra Behn*. Paired with Billie Melman's *Women's Orients: English Women and the Middle East, 1718–1918* and Ros Ballaster's *Fabulous Orients: Fictions of the East in England 1662–1785*, all of these texts elucidate the principles of enchantment and dissimilation of the Orient throughout the centuries. Neither Nigel Leask's *Curiosity and the Aesthetic of Travel Writing 1770–1840*, nor *Voyages and Visions: Towards a Cultural History of Travel*, edited by Jaś Elsner and Joan-Pau Rubiés, examines Richard Burton's and Charles Montagu Doughty's accounts of travels in Arabia in detail, and none of the aforementioned works see the connection between the literary trope of quest and the factual mode of travel narratives. That analysis takes place in the pages of my study.

Travel writing is based on the immediacy of experience, yet it is done after the journey, when the distance traveled allows for a more profound reading of that experience. Both medieval and nineteenth-century travel writers were aware of the need to fulfill readers' expectations as to the necessary ingredients of the genre. Although my work concentrates on the postmedieval period, the paradigms of reading involve a reappraisal of medieval texts. Hence it is crucial to indicate two works on medieval travel, namely, Shirin Khanmohamadi's *In Light of Another's Word: European Ethnography in the Middle Ages*, which demonstrates the interpretative possibilities of medieval journeys and cultural contact, and Shayne Legassie's *The Medieval Invention of Travel*, which reinterprets medieval pilgrim reports to far and near shrines through the pattern of "literate labor."

Drawing on Legassie's idea of "literate labor," the present book is divided into two parts discussing, respectively, the parallels between the medieval visions of the Orient as encoded in the Saracen romances, and their nineteenth- and twentieth-century reincarnations in literature and culture. Part 1 is entitled "'For So in *Travailing* in One Country he shall sucke the Experience of many.' Reading the Orient in Nineteenth-Century Travel Narratives and Historical

Works."⁵⁴ Chapter 1 outlines the presence of the Orient in culture and art before the nineteenth century, describing the rise of the "oriental obsession," to use John Sweetman's expression, in Western art and literature during the periods that followed the Middle Ages. Charting its existence in the European imagination of the nineteenth century, it offers an evaluation of the troubled legacy of the European Middle Ages and locates the earlier texts concerning the Saracens and their lands in the liminal space between history and tourism.

Chapter 2 clarifies the formal demands of Victorian travel narrative by viewing them through the prism of the Victorian quest romance. This chapter is an analysis of Richard Burton's *Personal Narrative of a Pilgrimage to Al-Madinah and Meccah*, published in 1855. Even though for Burton the pilgrimage is a cultural rather than spiritual experience, traveling with Muslim pilgrims requires him to exhibit a particular type of behavior during the journey, in line with the demands of Islam. While rejecting the religious aspects, the traveler nevertheless expresses the romantic and romanticized conviction that individual virtues are acquired through a proximity to nature and culture. Similar views were communicated in Charles Montagu Doughty's *Travels in Arabia Deserta*, published in 1888. The writers evoke close relationships between personal and public experience as they try to convey to their readers the sense of faraway places and foreign mores. Instead of sanitizing the ideologies of the empire, or ignoring the depiction of strangeness found in both accounts, they should be acknowledged as works that tried to do justice, however unjust it might seem today, to the perception of Muslims and the East during the Victorian and post-Victorian periods. Burton and Doughty were not "traveling Orientalists" but Arabists, who, according to Melman, "allied themselves to the belief that an Arab nationalism in the peninsula would regenerate the entire Middle East under British tutelage."⁵⁵

Likewise, the historical works analyzed in Chapter 3 are Simon Ockley's *The History of the Saracens*, published originally between 1708 and 1718, and Arthur Gilman's *The Saracens*, which appeared in 1886; both were designed to foster the understanding of Islam. These two comprehensive histories will be read against Samuel Green's *The Life of Mahomet: Founder of the Religion of Islam and of the Empire of the Saracens*, from 1840, and David Pryde's chapter on the life of Mohammed in his *Great Men of European History*, published in 1881 – works that

---

54 I have retained the original spelling and capitalization as used in Hadfield, *Amazons, Savages and Machiavels*.
55 Melman, "The Middle East/Arabia," 113.

were influential in divulging the historical processes behind the dissemination of Islam and the expansion of the Saracen empires. All of these works responded to the need for a more scientific approach to the study of Muslims cultures and to the ever-growing interest in the Orient. Building on Shamsie's observation discussed above, part 1, therefore, demonstrates how the Victorian wanderlust and scholarly approaches to the Saracens and Islam equally shaped the positive attitudes (in the sense of interest) and the negative aspects (in the sense of disparagement) of "Orientalism."

Part 2, called "'The Dark Reservoir of Hurt and Hate' in Contemporary Literature in English," discusses fictional works of the late twentieth century published before 9/11 or referring to events that took place circa 9/11, which re-established the "oriental obsession" and stimulated dread and resentment, on both sides. Instead of simply examining the representations of the Orient, these three chapters investigate the metaphorical medieval enemies of Mankind: the World, the Devil, and the Flesh, as they reappear in contemporary literature, whose preoccupations are the world of immigrants, the (d)evil who is radicalized or becomes a "freedom fighter," and white women desiring (dark) Muslim men. The latter category is exemplified by two novels set in the nineteenth-century Orient. Although in most of these instances the Muslim becomes the Other, the stranger, the immigrant whose very presence seems to exude menace, Western attitudes are also dissected. The motif of the civilized West juxtaposed with the (still) barbaric East is countered by the East speaking for itself in both fictional and non-fictional texts.

Chapter 4 discusses *Fatima's Scarf*, a novel by David Caute published in 1998, which captures the late twentieth-century dissatisfaction with prescriptive multiculturalism, and *My Ear at his Heart*, Hanif Kureishi's 2004 memoir that narrates both his own experience of "othering" and that of his father, drawing on the latter's unpublished novel. *My Ear at his Heart* will be read alongside Kureishi's earlier autobiographical essay, *The Rainbow Sign* (1986). Both texts subscribe to an idea that Sarah Ahmed expresses in this way:

> the stranger is produced as a figure that is distinct from the (philosophical body) through a process of expulsion: the stranger "comes" to be as an entity precisely by a prior inhabiting of that philosophical body or that body of the community that knows.[56]

Ahmed's work associates postcolonial theories on migration and estrangement with ethical questions of the acceptance and exclusion of the Other.

Marginalization is frequently seen as the root of current Islamist movements amongst second- and third-generation immigrants, and consequently, it

---

56 Ahmed, *Strange Encounters*, 56.

also features prominently in a large portion of Western literature about homegrown jihadis. Researchers such as John Erickson, Alaa Alghamadi, and Geoffrey Nash[57] each try in a different way to outline and understand the ways in which contemporary writers, both English-speaking and non-English-speaking, respond to what Nash terms the "kulturkampf" against Islam. Muslim identities in themselves evade simple definition; yet, in order to revise both nineteenth- and twentieth-century cultural "clashes," it is important to comprehend cultural history as encompassing a sense of perspective that allows both history and culture to be observed as conditions, effects of the processes of change, assimilation, and continuity. Chapter 5, then, tackles the question of acceptance or rejection of the stranger, who is a threatening, fetishized figure, a danger to moral health and well-being on both sides of the divide, and thus crucial in analyzing the contemporary terrorist (d)evil. Two texts selected for further analysis are a memoir by Ed Husain entitled, tellingly, *The Islamist*, which came out in 2007 but reports mainly the events before 9/11, recounting Husain's radicalization and subsequent withdrawal from fundamentalist movements, and Mohamed Laroussi El Metoui's novel *Halima*, published in English in 2005, which relates the last years of the Tunisian fight for independence.

The issue of freedom movements and violence rematerializes in chapter 6, which analyzes the 1999 Booker Prize-shortlisted *The Map of Love*, by Ahdaf Soueif, and the 1997 novel *The Magician's Wife*, by Irish-born American writer Brian Moore; the former is set in late nineteenth- and twentieth-century Egypt and the latter in late nineteenth-century Algeria. Both novels show young women entangled in Arab revolutions and enthralled with Arab culture. Their stories reverse the premises of the Victorian quest romance, in which native women become lovers and helpers of the valiant white men, and they show white women falling in love with Arabia and Arab men. Postcolonialism has been instrumental in the revising of contemporary readings of historical processes and, alongside them, the problem of the (constructed) Stranger. If Julia Kristeva, in *Strangers to Ourselves*, asserts that the stranger, the foreigner, "lives within us," that "he is the hidden face of our identity," the female characters of Soueif and Moore embrace that strangeness.[58] They are not the archetypal *ajanabee*, foreigners, but ones who leave behind their prejudices in order to immerse themselves in a different culture.

---

[57] Erickson, *Islam and Postcolonial Narrative*; Alghamdi, *Transformations of the Liminal Self*; Nash, *Writing Muslim Identity*.
[58] Kristeva, *Strangers to Ourselves*, 1.

I am fully aware of the incongruities related to the concepts of the West and the East, both in the past and today; yet, flawed as they are, they help us conceptualize the issues under discussion in the present volume. This study constantly moves back and forth between the imagined world of literature and the "real" world of historical experience, between romances, medieval and Victorian, and other factual narratives – such as those of history, the social sciences and anthropology – oscillating between the popular illustration of the domestic environments in the West and the fringes of the "enlightened" world, the East. Since the very presence of Muslims in Europe jeopardized the "well-being" of the Christian countries, an ideal and idealized community was created beyond national and secular interests,[59] and that necessitated the representation of the Orient as inferior. In the present-day literature concentrating on cultural differences, religious discontent, and religious wars, one can see the traces of such depictions. The reading of the medieval Orient in the nineteenth and twentieth centuries endorses the claim that relations between the East and the West are rarely represented in black and white terms, and sheds light on this historically grey area.

---

[59] Uebel notices that "Islam, it was maintained, obstructs and clouds the clear doctrinal origins of Christianity, preventing at the source the dissemination of salvific dogma. The Crusades represent, then, a series of new beginnings – cleansings – that are simultaneously returns to origin." Uebel, "Unthinking the Monster," 270. Uebel also claims that "[g]eography vigorously determined the kind of history that Islam would generate," arguing that "[t]his emphasis on the convergence of place and time in the representation of history was reflected in [the] twelfth-century formulation of Mundus (world) and saeculum (century, age). Representing history depended upon establishing relations of mundus and saeculum, for example, plotting the movement of civilization from East to West" (271).

Acknowledgements

Scholarly books are written as answers to certain questions, and this one is an inquiry into the world of the past and its relationship to our own reality. Using the magnifying glass to scrutinize medieval and then nineteenth-century representations of Islam, I hoped to find responses to the problems of the present. But more than any other of my works, this one owes a lot to my childhood, my background, and my family. I dedicate my book to all those who believed in me even when I did not believe in myself. I am particularly grateful to Dr. Lori Amy who encouraged me to apply for a Fulbright grant. It was with Lori, then my fellow PhD student at the University of Florida, that I first saw *Father of the Bride Part II* (1995, directed by Charles Shyer). There is a scene in the movie when the Father, George Banks, played by Steve Martin, sells his house to a stereotypical Arab, a Mr. Habib, who does not speak but grunts at his wife, standing two steps behind him. When I watched this movie together with Lori and a group of friends I laughed heartily, while she, very much in love with her Pakistani boyfriend, could not hide her anger at such an partial, stereotypical, and hurtful depiction of Muslims. Little did I know that a year later I would begin noticing similar instances in literature and culture, cases that act as a foil for our fears of Barbarians. My own interest in the so-called Barbarians was inspired by the 1981 novel *Waiting for the Barbarians*, by J. M. Coetzee. The writer himself has also been a friend throughout my hours of darkness, and for all his generous advice I am continually grateful. While Marina Warner's works have always been my sources of inspiration, I would also like to express thanks for her interest in this study.

My Fulbright grant helped me finalize the project, which before I went to Cornell remained in the misty realms of Avalon, of dreams and speculation. Cornell Professor Dr. Jonathan Culler had proffered the invitation; Dr. Shawkat Toorawa was instrumental in my search for Arabic sources, and Dr. Nathalie Melas and Dr. Walter Cohen listened very patiently to all my doubts concerning the project. I am also eternally grateful to Professor Andrzej Wicher (University of Łódź) for his meticulous reading of the manuscript and always useful comments and questions. During the long period of writing the book and then falling ill, I would not have been able to finish my endeavor had it not been for my friends. My thanks go also to the then Dean of the Faculty of English, Professor Katarzyna Dziubalska-Kołaczyk, for her unwavering support and understanding of my temporary "inability to work," and to the current Dean of the Faculty of English, Professor Joanna Pawelczyk, for her belief in my ideas and for enabling me to realize my scholarly passions. I am indebted to Dr. Joanna Maciulewicz for her meticulous reading of the second version of the manuscript, Dr. Katarzyna

Bronk, Dr. Ryszard Bartnik, Dr. Joanna Jarząb-Napierała, Dr. Marta Frątczak-Dąbrowska, Dr. Jacek Olesiejko, and last, but not least, Professor Agnieszka Setecka, from the Department of English Literature and Literary Linguistics, Faculty of English, Adam Mickiewicz University. Thank you for taking over my classes when I could not teach and telling me, quoting "Deor's Lament": *That passed away, this also may.* No words can express my gratitude. Thanks also to Ms. Katarzyna Matschi for understanding my need to write and to Professors Michiko Ogura and Minako Nakayasu for their longtime friendship and constant encouragement. I would like to thank my friends from The Japan Society for Medieval English Studies, Western Branch, especially Professor Keiko Hamaguchi, for many fruitful discussions during the conferences and lectures at which we met. I was also touched by the friendship of Professor Margaret Higonnet, President of FILLM, whose words of reassurance walked me through the valley of shadows. In my world it has been a case of not only *Amor* but also *Agape vincit omnia*!

Last but not least, I would like to thank Mr. Dwight Holbrook for all his uncomfortable questions concerning the present study and Mr. Colin Phillips for his careful proofreading of the manuscript, along with Ms. Shannon Cunningham for her enthusiasm concerning the project and Dr. Juleen Eichinger, my developmental editor, whose insightful questions helped me through the meanders of contemporary theory. I am also thankful to my family: my husband Professor Jacek Fisiak, whose physical presence I miss so much but who, I hope, is still here with me; and my mother Janina Sikorska for always being there for me. Winston Churchill once compared the writing of a book to an adventure. "To begin with, it is a toy and an amusement; then it becomes a mistress, and then it becomes a master, and then a tyrant. The last phase is that just as you are about to be reconciled to your servitude, you kill the monster, and fling him out to the public."[60]

Note on the Spelling

The transliteration of numerous Arabic words differs from author to author. I have retained the original spelling of the texts I am quoting, but in my own text I give the names "Mohammed" and "Mecca" and words such as "dervish," "caliph," and "Bedouin" in their more contemporary spellings. Because I was using a bilingual edition of the Koran, this is also the spelling that dominates in my text, although I am aware that yet another translation transliterates the word as "Qur'an."

---

60 Asma, *On Monsters*, xi.

Contents

Preface —— VII

Acknowledgements —— XXV

Part 1

Introduction
"For so in *Travailing* in One Country he shall sucke the Experience of many." Reading the Orient in Nineteenth-Century Travel Narratives and Historical Works —— 3

Chapter 1
From Oriental to Orientalist: Contact and Conflict in Culture and Literature —— 13

Chapter 2
Al-Ifranij among the Believers, or the Victorian Quest Romance(d) —— 37

Chapter 3
Under Western Eyes: The Discourses of/on History —— 85

Part 2

Introduction
"The dark reservoir of hurt and hate" in Contemporary Literature in English —— 121

Chapter 4
Dar Al-Hijira, or the World Of Immigration —— 133

Chapter 5
Arabian (K)nights: On Terrorists and Tyrants —— 151

Chapter 6
Through the Looking Glass: *Ajanabee* in Arabia —— 181

Conclusion —— 213

Bibliography —— 221

Index of Names and Terms —— 233

Part 1

Introduction
"For so in *Travailing* in One Country he shall sucke the Experience of many." Reading the Orient in Nineteenth-Century Travel Narratives and Historical Works

In 1612, when Francis Bacon wrote his essay "Of Travel," he voiced firmly established opinions of the humanists of his day who saw travel "in the younger Sort, as a Part of Education."[1] Advocating learning through experience, Bacon suggested acquiring some language and customs of the places the traveler visited. He firmly believed that keeping a diary, a record of one's experiences, was of paramount importance, but insisted that the traveler should not stay in one place for too long: "More or lesse as the place deserveth, but not long: Nay, when he stayeth in one City or Towne, let him change his Lodgings, from one End and Part of the Towne, to another; which is a great Adamant of Acquaintance."[2] Today one may argue that Bacon favored a shallow rather than an in-depth education in the ways of strangers, yet we should probably think about categories of time such as "long" and "short" according to seventeenth- rather than twenty-first century standards.[3]

The Renaissance witnessed the development of navigation in parallel with the discovery of the New World. England and Europe – especially Spain – began to conceive of a larger modern domain, as they began to reconnoiter and exploit the world beyond their bounds. In 1492, Spain sponsored the Italian-born Christopher Columbus to sail westward on his first journey in search of India, Cathay, and other places that Marco Polo had described two hundred years earlier. Presently, other explorers, adventurers, and pirates also set sail for pastures new. In the winter of 1497–1498, the Portuguese Vasco da Gama became the first to sail round the Cape of Good Hope. It was also Vasco da Gama who reached Columbus's target

---

[1] The excerpt of Bacon's essay comes from the anthology edited by Hadfield, *Amazons, Savages and Machiavels*, 33. All the italicized as well as capitalized words are original. Hadfield maintained the original spelling while Pitcher, in *The Essays*, substituted Bacon's archaic idiom for a more modern one.
[2] Bacon, "Of Travel," in Hadfield, *Amazons, Savages and Machiavels*, 34.
[3] See the essay "Of Empire," in which Bacon discusses the various dangers of the empire building and offers the story of the downfall of the Ottoman monarch, Solyman the Magnificent. Edited in Pitcher, *The Essays*, 115–19.

Note: Francis Bacon "Of Travel," in: *Hadfield, Amazons, Savages and Machiavels*, 34.

and got to India in the following April. This was soon followed by the (official) discovery of Australia[4] and journeys into the African mainland, although the so called "scramble for Africa" is routinely dated to between 1876 and 1912[5] and refers to the European race to colonize and subdue the "Dark Continent," and therefore has a different – mercantile rather than educational – stimulus. The educational motivation, however, can be observed amongst the learned and well-to-do Europeans from the seventeenth century, reaching its apogee in the eighteenth century but continuing into the nineteenth, and is best exemplified in the rationale behind the "Grand Tour." Nineteenth-century traveling was connected as much with the education of young upper-class men as with the "rest-cure"[6] – the finest fictional example of which is perhaps the journey through the South of France of the dying St. Aubert with his daughter Emily at the beginning of Anne Radcliffe's *Castle of Udolpho*, published in 1794. Juxtaposing the sublime and the beautiful, both travelogues and early novels habitually utilized the motif of a journey to corroborate the assumed factuality of their narration.[7] Apart from the accounts of real expeditions,[8] they also presented voyages of a metaphorical kind. Traveling lies at the core of European representations of the world and, more specifically, the Orient. Orientalism, then, originates in the reports of medieval merchants, pilgrims, and crusaders, finally to be born in nineteenth-century exploratory expeditions supplemented by historical works. In order to comprehend the persistence of the medieval constructions of the Orient, it is important to outline the philosophies of medieval, postmedieval, and nineteenth-century travel.

Medieval travel narratives forged the vision of the world as a network of shrines, precipitating the hunger not only to see but also, as I will argue below,

---

4 The European exploration of Australia began in the seventeenth century, but its discovery is customarily attributed to the Royal Navy Lieutenant (later Captain) James Cook in 1770. In reality, he was one of many travelers to have sighted and landed on the continent prior to English settlement.
5 In his discussion of the "Scramble for Africa," Thomas Pakenham states its beginning was "Leopold's Crusade, Brussels." Pakenham, *The Scramble for Africa*, 11.
6 Steve Clark, "Introduction," in *Travel Writing and Empire*, 14.
7 See Adams, *Travelers and Travel Liars*, a work on travelers and travel liars in the so-called "long eighteenth century" that outlines the modes of travel functioning in literary texts in the times directly preceding the development of the novel, as in the era of Defoe, Fielding, and others.
8 In her monumental work entitled *Voyage into Substance*, Barbara Stafford shows the metaphorical as well as the physical aspects of eighteenth-century and later ideas on travel, expounding the development of the exploratory method. "The explorer's enterprise, like the scientist's, was predicated on the belief that he could discover a tangible (not an illusory) world exuberant with details and alive with individualities that would withstand customary patterning, generalization or schematization" (1–2).

to experience them. Renaissance journeys to the far-off universities and places of cultural importance and the eighteenth-century Grand Tour instigated the nineteenth-century tourist, explorer, and colonist. Enthused by the Grand Tour model, whose typical "pre-scripted" itinerary would include France, Italy, Greece, and sometimes Turkey,[9] the tourists trekked the well-trodden path of other pilgrims and travelers. From the eighteenth century onwards, these expeditions were an educational rite of passage for young people of means, and the perceptions and evaluations of their explorations were shared in a written form by famous and less auspicious mortals alike. In such a milieu, it is easy to imagine that the nineteenth-century travelers' tales, as well as art works and, curiously, architecture, encouraged the comparison between home and abroad, the West and the East and, eventually, Christianity and Islam. Nonetheless, instead of discussing the all too easily evoked "clash of cultures," these nineteenth-century historical works and travel narratives show an interest in what is unknown, attempting unbiased accounts, without passing judgment as to the superiority of European civilization and inferiority of the Oriental one. Victorian travelers[10] were observant and wanted to understand rather than solely disparage cultural differences.[11] What is not commonly known is that the memoirs of the Victorians echo many themes that had been expressed by their predecessors in the Middle Ages, particularly their interest in the Old and New Testament sites.

Medieval Christian writers agreed that Jerusalem and Palestine were the true locations of the biblical stories, but these places were also designated as the future scene of the apocalypse, linked with the rise of the armies of Prester John and the events of Armageddon. John Mandeville's attestation of the existence of the land of Prester John was yet another argument that validated such

---

9 I am grateful for Professor Andrzej Wicher's observation that in the seventeenth and eighteenth centuries it was hard to distinguish or draw the borders between Greece and Turkey, as both were part of the Ottoman Empire. For more on the art works inspired by the Grand Tour, see Pickles, *The Grand Tour*. John Sweetman, in his monumental *The Oriental Obsession*, analyzes the phenomenon of the "picturesque journey," the journey to visit certain places that were believed to provide apt subjects for painters (81).
10 Victoria herself sketched people and places she visited. For more, see Warner, *Queen Victoria's Sketchbook*.
11 The visual records of the places they visited are testimonies of their intentions. Here *A Glimpse of the Burning Plain*, edited by Charles Allen, and *Queen Victoria's Sketchbook*, edited by the writer and cultural historian Marina Warner, can serve as examples. Lady Charlotte Canning was the wife of Charles Canning, Governor-General of India. She was a lady of the Bedchamber to Queen Victoria from 1842 to 1855. The Cannings went to India in 1856, where Charlotte died of malaria in 1861 and was buried in Barrackpore in West Bengal. Queen Victoria drew portraits of her family members but also documented views from her travels.

revelations,[12] and indirectly, indicated a possibility of reconquering the Holy Land. Christ's famous pronouncement that he is the Alpha and Omega, the beginning and the end, was immediately linked with the sites of his life. The circular vision of the life of humanity emphasized the meaning of Jerusalem as the real and celestial city, the center of the Christian universe, connoting the spring of life and the torrent of death, simultaneously hopeful and menacing. The historical Jerusalem and the land of Palestine inspired equally contradictory emotions; the space beyond Christendom was consistently envisioned as both hazardous and bizarre. Consider the medieval travel narrative of the true-fake Mandeville, whose *Travels* were to bring closer the entirety of God's creation and contained descriptions and illustrations of the legendary "Monstrous Races." *Mandeville's Travels* thus offered a catalogue of peculiarities found in the faraway lands of the Earth.[13] The Monstrous Races were equally beguiling in the fictional *Alexander* romance, which recounted the conquests of Alexander the Great. In order to prevent the monsters from encroaching upon Christian territories, the anonymous author consigned them to the fringes of the civilized world, where only the most valiant knights would venture. Mandeville and real medieval pilgrims, like Margery Kempe (ca. 1373–after 1438), were as awestruck as they were repelled by what they saw in the distant lands, for in the medieval imagination the East denoted a culture obdurately foreign.[14]

In the Middle Ages, encounters with other nations, be they mercantile and therefore peaceful, or military and therefore hostile, generated prose and poetry

---

[12] Mandeville, *The Travels of Sir John Mandeville*, 178–185. It is said that Prester John and his Christian knights spread Christendom beyond the see: "alle Urrye, Tartarie, Ierusalem, Palestyne, Arabye, Halappee, and alle the lond of Egypte" (Middle English version of *Mandeville's Travels*, 216). In his analysis of *Mandeville's Travels*, Higgins draws attention to the fact that the *Travels'* premise is built on acceptable truths of "what is relatively familiar and credible and then builds toward what is foreign and generally harder to credit, using the former to authenticate the latter." *Writing East*, 135. The acceptance of the existence of Prester John's Kingdom, introduced to the reader with the confidential "I trowe that yee knowe wel and haue herd" (*Mandeville's Travels*, 216), validates the rather fantastic idea of his conquests of all the aforementioned lands. To this effect, the narrative resonates with the impossible late medieval dream of pan-Christianity.

[13] Mandeville's descriptions of foreign places are more akin to the fantastic than the real. It is assumed that he did not attempt to map the real geography of Europe and Asia but, like many medieval authors, wanted to show the omnipotence of God and the variety of his creation. His text is compared to one of the first geographical treatises in English, Caxton's *Mirror of the World*.

[14] Le Goff writes that the East was a great repository of marvels and magic, yet because of that association it has been framed in the "foreignness" discourse since Antiquity. Le Goff, *The Medieval Imagination*, 41.

documenting the traveler's experiences. As early as the eighth century, in the *Hodeoporicon* (i.e., a book for a journey, ca. 754), a nun tells of St. Willibald's passage to the Holy Land.[15] Travel accounts, which included descriptions of sieges, narrated the progress of the Christian armies and provided a valuable source of medieval history. Such is the *Itinerarium Peregrinorum et Gesta Regis Ricardi*, The Chronicle of the Third Crusade (1189–1192). Davis clarifies that the so-called crusading literature "is punctuated by a series of struggles that mark the stages of an army's advance, for instance the investing and eventual capture of a city such as Antioch."[16] Written in chronological order, the histories sometimes included the pilgrimage-like material detailing the veneration of Christ's life by visiting the places connected with his life. To this effect, the Holy Land, was "the Mecca" for all Christians, who were encouraged to re-enact the sufferings of Christ rather than concentrate on sightseeing. The crusaders' diaries and letters offer portrayals of the land, exposing its beauties but also its dangers, and refer to the risks of traveling to and from the Holy Land.[17] Even though the participants were bound by the spiritual dimension of their mission, their portrayals are similar to those found in medieval homiletic romances,[18] where they were depicted as holy and heroic, as the paragons of virtue. Their engagement in the Christian cause served as encouragement for others to take up the sword and the cross. In other words, seemingly neutral travel accounts advised a certain type of behavior when facing the religious Other. The crusaders and their fictional representatives in the romances, frequently forgoing the role of the pilgrim and fighting in the holy war,[19] not only gained distinction in foreign lands but also, first and foremost, were promised a glorious future in heaven, and that was the greatest enticement to travel. Because of their noble aims the crusaders

---

15 Davis, "Pilgrimage and Crusade Literature," 11.
16 Davis, "Pilgrimage and Crusade Literature," 19. Many such works were religious narratives of a biographical nature, constructed so as to fashion a hagiographic narrative of their protagonists, very much in the spirit of the romance of *Guy of Warwick*.
17 As Davis explains "[t]he absence of *libri indulgentiarum* and of guidebooks from the crusader corpus finds its explanation in the fact that these productions appear only after the ending of the ill-fated Eighth and last Crusade, when St. Louis died on St. Bartholomew's Day 1270." Davis, "Pilgrimage and Crusade Literature," 22–23.
18 In his *locus classicus*, *The Middle English Romances of the Thirteenth and Fourteenth Centuries*, Dieter Mehl classifies medieval romances into seven categories. The homiletic romances include *The King of Tars*, *Sir Gowther*, and *The Siege of Milan*, in which the conflicts with the Saracens are central elements of the plot.
19 That is the case in *Sir Isumbras* and *Guy of Warwick*.

assumed divine aid in battle, and the pilgrims expected redemption. Both dedicated their strife to the glory of God.[20]

The purgatorial perils of traveling enhanced its spiritual merits, thereby intensifying penance. The medieval renditions of pilgrimages, found in the (auto) biographical *Book of Margery Kempe* as well as in many Saracen romances such as *Sir Isumbras* and *Guy of Warwick*, impart an image of traveling as penance, and of pilgrim-crusaders battling their own weaknesses. It was believed that even saintly people were tainted by Original Sin, and since they would see themselves as representative sinners, they were in need of exemplary self-punishment; their atonement was subsumed in the elevation of the soul and the physical degradation of the body. Kempe never admits that her wanderlust could have been associated with errant *curiositas*,[21] rather than devout traveling.[22] Her experiences of hunger, cold, uncertainty, and danger, however, can be read within the medieval framework of penitence.[23] *The Book of Margery Kempe* is far from being a veritable description of pilgrimages. As an imaginary travelogue it catalogues the places related to her spiritual models (i.e., Bridget of Sweden or Catherine of Sienna) in which she emulates, in line with the demands of affective piety, the suffering of Christ in the Holy Land. Although Kempe's work is frequently scorned for its lack of information about

---

20 In the poem *L'Estoire de la guerre sainte*, ca. 1196, Ambrose the Minstrel articulated the preoccupations of medieval writers with heroism while facing the most formidable enemy. Davis, "Pilgrimage and Crusade Literature," 21.

21 Richard Newhauser offers a comprehensive historical overview of the sin of curiosity in medieval theological works: see Newhauser, *Sin Essays*. Both pilgrims and Crusaders had a glorious aim, but their intention sometimes lapsed into sinful *curiositas*, condemned by writers such as Augustine and Aquinas. Augustine's *City of God* (early fifth century) constantly stresses the superiority of heavenly love and virtue over earthly love and existence and sees the quest for fame, a good example of pride, as the daughter of the devil. Such descriptions exemplify Augustine's repudiation of the world, a recurrent theme in many medieval writings. Thus, if the hero is to be exemplary, Guy of Warwick's journeys in search of fame have to be shown not as unimportant or altogether evil but as an empty chase, which ultimately leads to the realization of the true goal, that of repentance. Still, his sojourn in the East, the seat of the sinful worldliness, is as much a warning for future travelers as it is an advertisement of the ultimate path of chivalric glory.

22 It is enough to recall Kempe's battles with her husband and the ecclesiastical authorities to be granted a formal separation and the metaphorical mantle of a pilgrim to comprehend how traveling was monitored by the authorities.

23 European *Libri Poenitenciales* reveal pilgrimage as a form of penance as early as the sixth century. Spreading from Ireland, throughout the Middle Ages, it was treated as one of the Christian obligations, always under the auspices of the Church. McNeill and Gamer, *Medieval Handbooks of Penance*.

the places she visited, her emotionalism can be read as the glorification of travel as "travail." In contrast, Chaucer's *Canterbury Tales* can be analyzed through the exchanges between pilgrims, thus providing interesting linguistic material related to the more mundane facets of *peregrinatio*.[24]

Interestingly, as Shayne Aaron Legassie holds, "[b]etween 1300 and 1500, the authors and audiences of travel writing were engaged in what amounts to a prolonged cultural debate about the individual and collective benefits of voyages to various parts of the world."[25] He points to the classical tradition and argues that it was pilgrimage to the Holy Land that reinvented travel as literate labor.[26] Instead of defaming the conscious "exoticizing" of the descriptions, one should understand that the terms postdate all medieval travel accounts. Even illiterate pilgrims were immersed in a textual and visual culture. They "experienced the places that they visited under the influence of liturgy, painting, drama, sermons, and personal reading (in much the same way modern tourists navigate cities like New York or Paris under the influence of iconic photographs, television shows, motion pictures, and novels)."[27] Medieval pilgrims were not *flaneurs*; they could not roam and ruminate; theirs was a task of looking and remembering, and perhaps, in the end, also writing.

So there were two reasons for Europeans to travel into the Orient, the first being secular, for purposes of trade, and the second religious, in the form of pilgrimages and Crusades. The pilgrims, like the Crusaders, went into the unknown territory of the legendary place noted for its "wonders," as so aptly described by Jordanus Catalani, Bishop of Columbus, around the year 1330. His *Mirabilia Descripta* is the story of a *voyage imaginaire*, focusing on the marvelous and not the real. The work was translated from the Latin by Colonel Henry Yule and published by the Hakluyt Society in 1839, a couple of decades before the appearance of the narratives of Richard Burton and Charles Montagu Doughty that will be examined in the ensuing chapters. Although *Mirabilia Descripta* contains stereotypical images of the East similar to those found in *Mandeville's Travels*, its translation and publication coincided with the rising interest in Oriental Studies.

---

24 In the Middle English *Life of St. Augustine*, travel and reading (both activities frequently highlighted by its author, John Capgrave, 1393–1464) are the two major elements that fashion a learned man, a saint. The restorative power of Christian pilgrimage is the main motif of David Lodge's *Therapy*, in which a pilgrimage to Santiago de Compostela becomes the chief event of the novel and, like the medieval pilgrimages, has a therapeutic effect on the major character.
25 Legassie, *The Medieval Invention of Travel*, viii.
26 Legassie, *The Medieval Invention of Travel*, 13.
27 Legassie, *The Medieval Invention of Travel*, 105–6.

To account for and comprehend the complex responses of the Victorians to the East, part 1 of the present study begins with a sketch of the presence of the Orient in culture and art before the nineteenth century and then charts its existence in the European imagination of the nineteenth century, when the postmedieval ideas on the strange and the fearful were habitually evoked. Far from blindly agreeing with Said that the orient is only a "tableau of queerness,"[28] I see the pitfalls of a sightless acceptance of the wonders of the East and the outright rejection of the outlandish, for in human history the encounters with the unknown always mapped new areas of human knowledge. Medieval texts thenceforth are foils for the later rewritings of the trope of a journey. Medieval Crusades and pilgrimages, as well as later voyages, all carried the connotation of spiritual healing, with the medieval insistence being on salvation, and the postmedieval on curative well as aesthetic, cultural aspects.

The connections between the precepts of Christian pilgrimage and nineteenth-century narrative accounts of the East can be traced in the work of the celebrated traveler and translator of the *Thousand and One Nights*, Richard F. Burton. His work, entitled *Personal Narrative of a Pilgrimage to Al-Madinah & Meccah*,[29] was based on a journey that took place between 1851 and 1853 into the otherwise impenetrable Muslim worlds. Equally popular was the narrative of Charles M. Doughty, *Travels in Arabia Deserta*, originally published in 1888 but written after his wanderings in Arabia between 1871 and 1879. Their narratives will be discussed in chapter 2. The nineteenth-century enterprises that endeavored to explain Islam in fact broaden the divide between the East and the West,[30] indirectly contributing to the intensification of Western anxiety about the presence of the Saracens/Muslims as a rather unpredictable military power, still threatening, or renewing their threat against, European borders. Chapter 3, therefore, surveys the histories of the Saracens by Simon Ockley (1708–1718) and Arthur Gilman (1886) and the biographies of Mohammed[31] by Samuel Green (1840) and David Pryde (1881) to show the Victorian interest the advance of the Saracens. The historical studies, though based on the principle of

---

28 Said, *Orientalism*, 103.
29 Burton also published *First Footsteps in East Africa, or an Exploration of Harar* in 1856, based on an expedition of 1854–1855.
30 The West is still fascinated by the spread and power of Islam, hence the popularity of works such as Eugene Rogan's *The Arabs*.
31 The spelling of the name varies in the sources presented. In what follows, I will use the original versions, leaving "Mohammed" in my own commentary.

the objectivity of the scientific account, emphasize the uncanny,³² while at the same time upholding the European intellectual tradition, which requires the problematization of the system of belief, at home and abroad. In contrast, Burton's and Doughty's command of Arabic, as Billie Melman has argued, reveals a genuine fascination with the Orient. Their explanations balance the observer's supposedly impartial interest in a different culture with criticism. All of these works demonstrate the processes of the aestheticizing (Burton and

---

32 In her cultural history of dirt, Katherine Ashenburg discusses the different approaches to cleanliness represented by Christians and Arabs. She quotes an Arab gardener from *A Thousand and One Nights* who says that Christians never wash, as at their birth a man in black pours water over their head and that strange ceremony frees them from ever washing again in their life. Ashenburg, *Dirt on Clean*, 49. It is a truism to claim that all religions prescribe certain forms of cleanliness, but it is perhaps worth noting that Christianity concentrated on internal, spiritual cleansing while Islam openly stated the forms of ablutions to be performed before entering a mosque and praying. Ashenburg brings up St. Jerome, who insisted that those who bathed in Christ had no need of a second bath (50). Such pronouncements were frequently used as the basis for ascetic behavior, and Christianity knows numerous saints who begin their path to God by leaving their bodies and clothes unwashed for years. In the ninth century, Andalusian Arabs were described as "the cleanest people on earth," while the Christians "Wash neither their bodies nor their clothes which they only remove when they fall into pieces" (71). Conversely, in Lady Mary Montagu's (1689–1762) letters we find an unquestioned fascination with Turkish culture, and especially women's baths, which she had visited in Sophia (125–27). Some of the letters of Lady Mary are to be found in De Maria, *British Literature 1640–1789*, 690–97. In 1679 the "Bagno" or Turkish bath opened off Newgate Street, in the small street marked on subsequent maps as "Bath Street." Sweetman, *The Oriental Obsession*, 49–50. Kaul claims that Edward Wortley Montagu's appointment as Ambassador to Turkey confirmed an overlap of trading and political interests of the period. Kaul, *Eighteenth-Century British Literature*, 123. Indeed, Lord Wortley Montagu, a Whig politician, had been appointed ambassador extraordinary from George I to Sultan Ahmet III and "representative of the Levant Company to the Sublime Porte." According to Melman, his mission failed miserably, and he was recalled back to England. Melman, *Women's Orients*, 79. The couple spent almost two years in the country and had access to places other European travelers could only dream of. Lady Wortley Montagu's letters are an unprecedented source of knowledge about Turkish women's lives in this period. She had insight into places and spaces from which her male compatriots were excluded, while her learning of Turkish and Arabic helped in her perception of the literature and culture of their hosts. Kaul praises her for widening the horizons of the English audience. Knowing the Islamic culture, she refused to be swayed by certain Christian prejudices and was courageous enough to write that slavery in Turkey was no worse "than Servitude all over the world." Kaul, *Eighteenth-Century British Literature*, 124–25. Melman discloses that Lady Wortley kept a journal, which was destroyed by her daughter and literary executor. The letters circulated in manuscript among London literati, and only selected extracts ever appeared in print. Apart from the first "real" letters to a limited audience, she later wrote letters to a wider audience and more diverse recipients, and these still remain unprinted. There are fifteen addressees of the "pseudo-letters," twelve of whom were female. Melman, *Women's Orients*, 79.

Doughty) and rejecting as well as "Othering" (Ockley and Gilman) of Muslim culture. In a way, Burton's and Doughty's preoccupation with incongruity, along with that of Ockley, Pryde, and Gilman, reecho the medieval uneasiness about racial and religious difference. By discussing these nineteenth-century travel narratives and historical works, I would like to sketch the history of ideas that played an important role in the European reading of the Orient, which originated in the Middle Ages and paved the way for the late twentieth-century reappraisal of medieval thought through the amplification of the anxiety concerning religious fundamentalism.

Chapter 1
From Oriental to Orientalist: Contact and Conflict in Culture and Literature

Before the auspicious year 1683, when the combined armies of the Holy Roman Emperor Leopold I of the Hapsburg Dynasty and the Polish king, Jan III Sobieski, defeated the Turks and repelled the threat of the Ottoman Empire invading Europe, both the interest in and fear of "all things oriental" was stimulated by the presence of Muslims in Spain. Islam adjoined Europe and, in the case of Moorish Spain (in the eighth to the fifteenth century), Sicily (from the tenth to the twelfth century), and the Turkish-occupied Balkan area, along with Greece (from the fifteenth to the nineteenth century) was actually part of it. Christianity, which had taken root in Europe, had originated in the Near East, in a country where the Dome of the Rock nevertheless came to epitomize Muslim belief. The builders of Rome, the heartland of European classicism before the intellectual rediscovery and reassessment of Greece in the eighteenth century, had also built extensively in the deserts of Asia Minor, Syria, and North Africa. More often than not historians assert, as Caroline Finkel and Stephen Turnbull do,[1] that the beginnings of the Ottoman dynasty lay in central Asia, but the tribe was driven west by the Mongols in the thirteenth century. The Ottomans subsequently settled in Anatolia and by 1389, under a succession of vigorous rulers from the time of Osman (r. 1299–1326), had extended their power over the Balkan peninsula. One of the greatest Ottoman successes was the capture of Constantinople in 1453. It is worth adding that in Constantinople, formerly Latin Byzantium, Roman power had had an Eastern counterpart. In 1453, the shock waves of the capture of Constantinople by the Ottoman Turks spread over Europe to distant England, and a London chronicler recorded: "Also in this yere . . . was the Citie of Constantyn the noble lost by Cristen men and wonne by the Prynce of Turkes called Mahomet." He notices that "The Turks, who were gradually overthrowing the empire of the Arabs in the east, were becoming formidable to the Christians also towards the end of the fourteenth century."[2] The Ottomans overwhelmed the forces of the Mamluk sultans of Syria and Egypt in 1512 and took possession of Cairo. And so once again in its turbulent history of religious

---

[1] Finkel, *Osman's Dream*; Turnbull, *The Ottoman Empire*.
[2] Quoted in Thomas Wright, *Early Travels in Palestine*, xxvii.

wars, Europe faced the Muslim threat, bigger and stronger than the armies seen before.[3] The years between 1422 and 1606 indeed mark the greatest successes of the Ottoman Army.[4] Ottoman Sultan Süleyman, called by the Europeans "the Magnificent" (r. 1520–1566), led the Turks to Belgrade, conquered Hungary and by 1529 "stood outside Vienna."[5] The grand Turkish Army, whose reputed atrocities terrified God-fearing Christians, became the new archenemy of Christendom. The monstrous Turk became the scourge of God. Paradoxically, it was fear as well as interest that stimulated the exchange of goods and ideas. Manifestations of the Muslim presence in the drama, music, literature, architecture, and general culture of Europe from the Renaissance until the mid-nineteenth century will be the subject matter of the present chapter. In what follows, I will survey a wide array of sources, from accounts of merchants such as Sir John Chardin and the political essays of Michel de Montaigne and Jean-Jacques Rousseau, through the work of poets such as George Gordon, Lord Byron, as well as histories and travel accounts written by both Muslim and Christian travelers. All of these sources point to the complex and continual encounters between the East and the West.

A good indication of such complexity is recorded in William Shakespeare's *Othello*, set in Venice and Cyprus, which reiterates the struggles with the Turks. From the early Middle Ages, Venice served as a focal point on the textile trading routes. Even today, Venetian architecture still holds traces of the Muslim presence. In Shakespeare's time, the military power of the Ottoman Empire undoubtedly inspired awe, but Europe remained fascinated with Constantinople as a city in which the cultural and architectural traditions of the Romans, Byzantine-Christians, and Muslims merged.[6] Constantinople has always been an

---

3 Fynes Moryson traveled to the Ottoman Empire in 1617, and in *An Itinerary* (1617) he is devastatingly critical of the Turks, whom he considers sex-obsessed Orientals (frequently given to the sin of sodomy). He sees the Ottoman Empire as tyrannical, its subjects as born slaves, and the country as ridden with corruption. Moryson in Hadfield, *Amazons, Savages and Machiavels*, 167–78. Another fragment describing his travels in Jerusalem can be found in Mancall, *Travel Narratives from the Age of Discovery*, 379–86.
4 Turnbull, *The Ottoman Empire*, 22–29.
5 Finkel, *Osman's Dream*, 115–51.
6 The story of the conquest of Istanbul is recorded in *History of Mehmed the Conqueror*, written by Tursum Beg, fragments of which are to be found in an anthology of writings about the Mediterranean: Cooke, Göknar, and Parker, *Mediterranean Passages*. The Siege of Constantinople ended when the city surrendered to Mehmed II on May 29, 1453. Mehmed now called himself not only King, Khan, and Sultan but also Roman Caesar, "thus connecting his Muslim rule to great imperial precedents and making it the imperial capital" (157–61). It was he who turned the Hagia Sophia into a mosque. His son Cem Sultan (1459–1495) had a love affair with Philippine de Sassenage. He was cheated and taken prisoner by his brother and

important trading post for both the East and the West. Notwithstanding the danger, the king of France, Francis I, who led the Franks between 1512 and 1547, managed to keep the Turks at bay and in 1535 established special trading agreements with the Ottomans.[7] John Sweetman maintains that "antagonism seems to lie at the heart of the encounters between the Orient and the Occident. In England we have only to think of damask (Damascus), muslin (Mosul), or fustian (Fustat)" to recall just a few terms.[8] What is more, one of the earliest examples of the European interest in the East was the import of Turkish carpets. In the fourteenth century, woven Islamic hangings were prized in Arras, and "a cope from Mamluk Egypt inscribed in Arabic with the words 'the learned Sultan'" was found in St. Mary's church, in Danzig, Poland, early in the same century.[9] Hans Holbein's painting of *The Ambassadors*, completed in 1533, is usually used as proof of the popularity of Turkish carpets at the court of Henry VIII, as the two men in the painting pose with "the rugs beneath their feet."[10] Such paintings demonstrate how trade with the Ottomans had spread into many European countries during the Renaissance period.[11] Eastern ornamental art had become quite

---

then sent to France. One of his companions left a memoir in which he describes the strange customs of the Christians (206). As of July 2020, Hagia Sophia is once again a mosque.

7 Sweetman, *The Oriental Obsession*, 10. Sweetman lists other people who went to Constantinople and India, such as Peter Mundy (ca. 1596–1667) in 1628–1634. Sweetman includes a number of portraits of eminent Englishmen in Eastern clothes, for example Sir Anthony van Dyck (1599–1641) (29). Equally fascinating to Europeans was the Mughal Empire in India, the dynasty consolidated under Akbar the Great (1556–1605). For more, see Gascoigne, *A Brief History of the Great Moghuls*; Dalrymple, *The Last Mughal*. This fascination would continue up to the fall of Delhi in 1857. Meanwhile, the diplomatic exchange of gifts raised awareness of Eastern artefacts.

8 Sweetman, *The Oriental Obsession*, 3.

9 Sweetman, *The Oriental Obsession*, 5. Sweetman also notes: "According to the twelfth-century Arab geographer al-Idrīsī, woollen carpets were being made in his day at Chinchilla and in Murcia, both in Spain, and exported to 'all countries'" (5).

10 The striking patterns of these carpets have become so familiar to Europeans in the intervening five hundred years that it is hard to imagine a time when they had the force of novelty. In England, the history of the oriental carpet begins "somewhat abruptly" in 1518 with a request for carpets from Venice by Cardinal Wolsey. John North's reading of the picture, however, brings out the themes of the political and religious unrest, which broaden its cultural context. North, *The Ambassadors' Secret*.

11 In the nineteenth century, the Isfahan carpets shown by Count Czartoryski at the 1878 Paris Exhibition were indeed wrongly taken to be of Polish manufacture. Sweetman, *The Oriental Obsession*, 4.

popular at aristocratic courts, projecting splendor and worldliness to those living in them, and Holbein's portrait of the French Ambassadors remains proof of this trend.[12]

It is no wonder that, following the Renaissance drive to survey the world, European trading companies searched to establish contacts with the Levant. In the sixteenth century, Europe moved ever eastward in search of safe routes to Asia to claim its real or imagined riches, while the Turkish Empire was spreading westwards toward Europe. Christianity and Islam never ceased to perceive themselves as enemies, but the defeat of the Turks at Vienna marked the onset of a different kind of relationship, proffering the space for Orientalism – in a positive sense, implying attraction[13] or perhaps absorption – to be born. Because of the development of trade, less fantastic and more real reports of the Orient began to appear in the Renaissance and post-Renaissance periods.

Such was the account of the journey of George Sandys (1577–1644), who in 1615 published his *Relation of a Journey begun Anno Dom. 1610. Foure Bookes Contayning a description of the Turkish Empire, of Aegypt, of the Holy Land, of the Remote parts of Italy, and lands adioyning*.[14] Sandys was a man of his times; educated in the classics, he held firm beliefs that the people of Antiquity were more civilized and had better knowledge of the world than his contemporaries. His work abounds in learned allusions to Greco-Roman authors such as Homer, Ovid, and Juvenal.[15] Sandys is a keen observer not only of people but also of nature. While traveling through Egypt, he provides a very interesting description of the crocodile and the dolphin.[16] What transpires in the narrative are his

---

[12] North, *The Ambassador's Secret*, gives a fascinating reading of the famous painting, discussing each and every detail as relevant and connected with various political issues of the day. The love of all things Eastern is later ridiculed by Maria Edgeworth in *The Absentee*; see part 2 of the present work.

[13] I am conscious of Bartlett's discussion of the word "fascination" as used by Roger Bacon (c.1214–1292), who talks about its cognate, the Latin *fascinatio*, which should be translated as "hostile enchantment." In Bartlett's delineation, "*Fascinatio* springs from a strong 'desire to do harm' and the most familiar form of it is the so-called evil eye." Bartlett, *The Natural and the Supernatural*, 141.

[14] Fragments of this work are to be found in Hadfield, *Amazons, Savages and Machiavels*, 152–65.

[15] In Hadfield, *Amazons, Savages and Machiavels*, 158.

[16] Hadfield, *Amazons, Savages and Machiavels*, 153. According to Thomas Wright, Sandys "often erred on the side of credulity. Before the end of the century came the well-known Henry Mundresll, who, on account of the brevity of his narrative and the extreme accuracy of his descriptions, has been selected to conclude the present volume." Wright, *Early Travels in Palestine*, xxviii–xix.

attempts to present his observations in terms of dissimilarity and not lack. He does not judge but simply offers an explanation of the absence of wines in Egypt.[17]

Equally unbiased is the narrative of a voyage to Persia and India by Sir John Chardin (1643–1713) entitled rather predictably, *Travels in Persia and India 1673–1677*,[18] which stimulated interest in the Orient both as a tourist attraction and as a possible market for European goods. His work, published in 1686, was an attempt to establish contacts with the East through trade. Chardin was a well-educated son of a French jeweler who journeyed to Persia and India and later published a report of the coronation of the new Persian Shah, Soleyman. In 1671, he embarked on a second journey to Persia. After nearly two years of arduous travel through Turkey, the Crimea, and the Caucasus, he arrived in Isfahan. This time his sojourn in Persia lasted four years, after which he returned to France in 1677. Several years later, however, he fled to England to avoid the French persecution of the Huguenots. Appointed Jeweler to the Crown, he was subsequently knighted by King Charles II. The Royal Society for Natural Philosophy, established in 1661, counted Chardin as one of its members from 1682. He begins his story by recounting previous attempts to enter into trade with Persia. He claims that "The English went for the first time into Persia, about the Year 1613."[19] He sketches the reception of the English agents and gives details of the conferences with the French and English envoys to Persia.[20] The dates Chardin provides are significant because the periodization of history is different in Europe and in Asia. David Morgan, for example, views "Medieval Persia" as lasting from 1040 until 1797, which would mean Chardin's visit fell during the Persian "High" Middle Ages.

---

17 In a similar fashion, Sir John Chardin, whose account is discussed below, is admiring of the development of the sciences (such as arithmetic) in Egypt but is much more critical of the Jews, replicating anti-Semitic theories popular in the England of his day. He also points out that "[w]ine and intoxicating Liquors are forbid the Mahometans; yet there is scarce any one that does not drink of some sort of strong Liquor. The Courtiers, gentlemen, and Rakes, drink Wine, and as they all use it, as a Remedy against Sorrow, and that one Part drink it to put them to Sleep, and the other to warm and make Merry . . ., they make Faces in drinking of it, as if they were taking a Medicine, and till they are heated, the Wine is too cool for 'em, they must have some Brandy, and the Stronger it is, the better they like it." Chardin, *Travels in Persia*, 242. Interestingly, Burton would make a similar observation: "During the whole time of my stay I had to content myself with a single bottle of Cognac, coloured and scented to resemble medicine." Burton, *Personal Narrative*, 2:21.
18 The original title was in French: *Journal du Voyage . . . de Chardin en Perse et aux Indes Orientales* (London, 1686).
19 Chardin, *Travels in Persia*, 100.
20 Chardin, *Travels in Persia*, 103–11.

Because Chardin was primarily a tradesman rather than a gentleman of leisure, his reflections concern business, and in this way, he manages to avoid unjust comparisons between Islamic and European society. Unlike many of his predecessors, contemporaries, and followers, Chardin understands and respects the Muslim lack of distinction between the Church and the state.[21] For Persians, the secular rulers of the Christian world are unjust tyrants who place worldly over godly matters and who were sent to the Earth as punishments to their impious subjects. Chardin concedes that "[t]he supreme throne of the world belongs only to a *mujtahid*, a man possessed of sanctity and knowledge above the common rule of men. It is true that since the *mujtahid* is holy and by consequence peaceful, there must be a king to wield the sword, to exercise justice, but this he must do only as the minister and subordinate of the former."[22] Incidentally, Chardin's views are strikingly similar to Ayatollah Khomeini's reasons for establishing the Islamic government in Iran in the twentieth century.[23]

Chardin renders Persia as different but worth knowing about, without either false modesty or unjustified superiority on the part of the Europeans. He admires Persian crafts: "On the 9th, I went to the House of the King's Goldsmiths, which is in the Royal Palace, to see them make some Gilt Plates in the Form of Tiles, which were to cover the Dome of the Mosque of Iman-Reza, at Metched, which an Earthquake had flung down, as I before related." He also appreciates their hard work, noticing that "[a] thousand Men, as was said, were employ'd in repairing this Mosque; and they work'd at it with so much Dilligence and Application, that it was to be finish'd by the latter end of December."[24] While he is aware that the Persians do not know a lot about Europe, he respects their willingness to learn: "The Persians have so little knowledge yet of the World, that they frequently ask, if there be any horses in Europe" and continues "[s]eeing all the Europeans carry from Persia as many as they can. They imagine that we transport them into our own Country, whereas it is to make use of them in the Indies, where there are only little Horses, and those ugly ones, as well as few in Number."[25] Besides, he holds their manners in high esteem:

---

21 Morgan explains that although the caliph was recognized as the head of the Islamic community, he had "few of the powers of the pope: for example, he had no authority (at least in this period) in the matter of defining doctrine." Morgan, *Medieval Persia*, 27.
22 Morgan, *Medieval Persia*, 147. Morgan used the 1911 French version of Chardin's work, while the Dover edition used here (ed. Sir Percy Sykes with a Preface by N. M. Penzer and an Introduction by Sir Percy Sykes), is based on the 1720 text, and the above quotation does not appear in it.
23 Khomeini, *Islamic Government*.
24 Chardin, *Travels in Persia*, 112.
25 Chardin, *Travels in Persia*, 117.

> The Persians are the most Civiliz'd People of the East, and the greatest Complimenters in the World. The Polite Men amongst them, are upon a level with the Politest Men of Europe. Their Air, their Countenance, is very well composed, Lovely, Grave, Majestical, and as Fond as may be; they never fail complimenting one another about the Precedency, either going out or coming into a House, or went they meet, but 'tis over presently.[26]

Interestingly, Simon Ockley, in one of the earliest histories of the Saracens, had noticed that "[t]he Persian nobility, perceiving that the Saracens were every way too strong for them, and had now made themselves masters of the borders of their country, and were very likely to seize more of it, began to be very uneasy."[27] And indeed, Persia was conquered after defeats at Qadisiyya, ca. 637, and Nihāwand, in 642.[28] The Arabs, however, were not prepared for such a difficult country, which retained its own language. As Morgan explains, this was most probably because the country was swallowed whole and "there was no remaining Persian state to which Persians under Muslim rule could look for help or sympathy. They were therefore thrown back on self-reliance, and perhaps made a greater effort to preserve elements of their past than they otherwise have done."[29] Under Arab rule, Persia was Islamicized, yet it persisted as a multireligious territory. According to Muslim law, religious minorities like the Jews and the Christians, who were both considered "People of the Book," were given freedom to worship, even though what such toleration granted was contempt and second-class status. In Persia, Zoroastrianism was accorded the same position as Judaism and Christianity, and, curiously, Zoroastrians[30] were not forced to face the difficult choice between Islam and the sword.[31]

Chardin, however, is not interested in Zoroastrianism but in the differences between Christian Europe and Muslim Persia. Rather than demeaning the country in which he has to live and work, at least for some time, he tries to understand the Persians and their way of life. Unlike Richard Burton's occasional disparagement of Arab cuisine, Chardin does not observe anything extraordinary. He

---

26 Chardin, *Travels in Persia*, 189.
27 Ockley, *History of the Saracens*, 145.
28 Morgan, *Medieval Persia*, 14.
29 Morgan, *Medieval Persia*, 14.
30 According to Warner, Zoroastrianism predates Islam by a millennium and survived the success of the new faith, Islam. The religion is based on two opposing divinities, Ahura Mazda, the source of light and good, who contends with Ahriman, the principle of darkness and evil. Warner, *Stranger Magic*, 129.
31 Morgan, *Medieval Persia*, 15. The Islamization of the ancient Persia, now Iran, seems to be an ongoing process. In Jafar Panahi's film *Taxi Teheran* (2015), a young girl is discouraged by her teacher from using Persian (and therefore un-Islamic) names for characters in her story.

notices that the Persians drink a lot of tea and coffee and that there are houses in which to do it:

> These Houses, which are spacious and large Rooms, and rais'd in different Figures, are generally in the finest parts of the Cities, because there is the Rendezvous, and place of Diversion for the inhabitants. There are many, where there are Basons of Water in the Middle, especially in the great Towns. These great Rooms have Estrades, or galleries, quite round about, three Foot high, and three or four Foot deep, more or less according to the bignes [sic] of the Place, made of Wood or Stone to sit upon after the Eastern Manner; they open them at Day-break, and it is then, and in the Evening, that have the most Company; they serve you very exactly there with Coffee, very quick, and with abundance of Respect; there the converse; for there is the Place for News, and where the Politicians criticize upon the Government, with all the Freedom in the World, and without being disturb'd.[32]

In England, coffee-houses were commercialized sometime in the seventeenth century. Sweetman states that the first one in London was opened after 1650 in St. Michael's Alley, Cornhill. "This was the 'Pasque Rosee's Head,' named after the servant whom a Turkey merchant had brought back with him to England. By 1700 there were probably about 3,000 coffee-houses in London."[33] As it transpires, Chardin is unashamedly attracted to Persian culture. To this effect, he leaves his readers with a very colorful image of Persia, stressing the gentility of the people as well as their industry: "I have kept for ten years Linen wash'd in the Indies with cold Water, and without Soap, and when we sat our Linen by it, we found that European Linen look'd but dark and brown in comparison of it, and one may judge how much of its whiteness it had lost with lying so long in a Trunk."[34] His was a genuine interest in both the nation and the establishment of fair trade relations.

All in all, Chardin's is an uncommon account, especially in light of the growing depreciation of Islam with the onset of the European sieges of North African cities, in order to conquer and, ultimately, colonize Muslim lands. Algiers, for example, was attacked by the English in 1621, 1661, 1665, and 1669, and by the French in 1665, 1672, 1682, and 1688.[35] Throughout the fifteenth and sixteenth centuries, North Africa became a rather problematic "contact zone," to use Mary Louise Pratt's expression.[36] In the seventeenth century, however, came a turnaround: the lands of the Christians, in Arabic *bilad al-nasara*, were visited by the Muslims. The long hated "ifranij" or Franks, as all Christians were

---

32 Chardin, *Travels in Persia*, 241. All capital letters original.
33 Sweetman, *The Oriental Obsession*, 49.
34 Chardin, *Travels in Persia*, 276.
35 Matar, *In the Lands of the Christians*, xxvi.
36 I am referring to the well-known text by Mary Louise Pratt, *Imperial Eyes*.

called by the Muslims, were observed in their own environment. Given that the concept of "Europe" did not exist among Arabs, both Christian and Muslim Arabs were simply curious about other places, the *ruum*, "the Qura'nic name for the Byzantines and other Europeans."[37]

For Muslims, Christian lands were the lands of unbelievers, by definition *dar al-harb*, the house of war, which was always seen in opposition to *dar al-Islam*, the house of submission to Allah. In Islam, there is nothing in between. It is, therefore, even more revealing to inquire into the motivation of the Muslim travelers and to scrutinize their observations concerning the Europeans. Nabil Matar provides fragments by Ahmad bin Qasim, the Andalusian Morisco who went to France and Holland in 1611–1613 and wrote *The Protector of Religion against the Unbelievers*; Ilyas Hanna al-Mawsuli traveled through Italy, France, Spain, and Portugal in 1668 and recorded his reflections in *The Book of the Travels of the Priest Ilyas, son of the Cleric*. Mohammad bin Abd al-Wahab al Ghassani was sent to Spain in 1690 as an envoy to negotiate the release of Moroccan prisoners and wrote *The Journey of the Minister to Ransom the Captive*, and finally Abdullah bin Aisha went to France in 1699 and wrote letters to the member of the French court.[38] It is undeniably true that apart from the military interest connected with "the gospel of jihad" – that is, with the forceful surrender of the infidels to Islam – the Muslim objectives were mostly trade and diplomacy. "Travelers, merchants, envoys, ambassadors, and clergymen journeyed to London and Rome, Cadiz and Malta, Madrid and Moscow."[39] Strikingly, the Moroccan jurist Al-Hasan bin Masood al-Yusi encouraged his coreligionists to travel "in quest of learning."[40] Matar, perhaps slightly idealistically, asserts that while European travelers to the Orient always made negative comparisons, Muslim travelers "recognized the limits of their knowledge about Europeans and tried to learn."[41] He admits, however, that for the Muslims, the European world was one of wealth and advancement. Europe was powerful and affluent,

---

[37] Matar, *In the Lands of the Christians*, xviii. Samuel Green, in his *Life of Mahomet*, imparts: "Geography they did not so well understand, their means being exceedingly limited. Yet their public libraries could boast of globes, voyages, and itineraries, the production of men who travelled in order to increase their geographical knowledge, loaded their shelves." Green, *Life of Mahomet*, 300.

[38] Matar, *In the Lands of the Christians*, xxii–xxiii.
[39] Matar, *In the Lands of the Christians*, 2003, xv.
[40] Matar, *In the Lands of the Christians*, xxv.
[41] Matar, *In the Lands of the Christians*, xxxviii.

tempting the faithful with its ways of life in a manner the Muslims did not dare admit could be perceived as pleasurable and fulfilling.[42]

Further contacts with the East were buttressed by the East India Company, which was set up as a corporation to trade with the East and operated between 1600 and 1874. Trading provided a more commonplace knowledge of the East, and in the late seventeenth and early eighteenth centuries the travelers brought not only miscellaneous artifacts but also fashion, thereby contributing to the creation of the new, yet still fabulous, picture of the East. Sweetman notes that "[p]articularly in court circles, it was welcomed – as it had been for generations – as a break from formal conventions."[43] The urbane English court of the Restoration readily accepted the Oriental "fancy-dress." Indeed, the heightened interest in newly opened theaters, the popularity of the so-called "Turk plays,"[44] balls, and galas, as described by Maria Edgeworth in her *Absentee*, brought about the vogue for Turkish costumes. Consequently, the epoch produced a number of portraits of eminent English people dressed *á la turque*. The attraction, or rather the trend for oriental costume is also one of the motifs in Defoe's *Roxana*, which appeared in 1724.[45] The title heroine bears a stereotypical oriental name, and the early editions of the novel were equipped with a print of Roxana in an oriental dress.[46] It comes as no surprise, then, that the letters of Lady Mary Wortley Montagu (1689–1762),[47] the wife of the English Ambassador to Turkey between 1717 and 1718, show her enthrallment with Turkish life, the landscapes of the Bosphorus, and Turkish practices such as inoculation for smallpox. Published in 1763, the letters contributed to the circulation of the tales of the seraglio,[48] as they offered an

---

42 *Other Routes: 1500 Years of African and Asian Travel Writing*, ed. Tabish Khair et al. likewise demonstrates that Asian and African travelers have always been interested in discovering the lands beyond their homelands. Their writings encompass a plethora of genres comparable to those of Western travelers.
43 Sweetman, *The Oriental Obsession*, 49.
44 *Three Turk Plays from Early Modern England*, ed. Vitkus.
45 *Roxana, or the Fortunate Mistress or, a History of the Life and Vast Variety of Fortunes of Mademoiselle de Beleu, afterwards called the Countess of Wintselsheim in Germany Being the Person known by the Name of the Lady Roxana in the time of Charles II*.
46 The archetypal Turk returns in this period: "The attitude of Europeans of this period to the Turks – that they were both of the European continent yet not of it – reflected both the accessibility and the strangeness of the Muslim world. There were also Turkish tents. A building with this name was erected at Vauxhall gardens by 1744: like many of the Vauxhall buildings it seems to have been couched in a kind of pageant Gothic style with a stress on fantasy and impermanence." Sweetman, *The Oriental Obsession*, 68.
47 A selection of her letters can be found in DeMaria, *British Literature 1640–1789*, 690–98.
48 Ballaster, *Fabulous Orients*, 179–92.

insight into the lives of Turkish women that no man would be privileged to observe. Concurrently, they paved the way for the cultural preoccupations of English neoclassicism.

More than previous centuries, the cultural background of the eighteenth century was influenced by classical literature, of the Romans and Greeks, but writers and philosophers sought inspiration in the "savage" and oriental models as well. The latter also informed the nascent interest in the Gothic toward the end of the period. The oriental model, stemming from travel narratives, was augmented by architecture designed to replicate oriental patterns. No less a figure than Sir Christopher Wren (1632–1723) himself was fascinated by Oriental architecture, as was his pupil and follower Nicholas Hawksmoor (1661–1736). Green alludes that Wren derived the Gothic architecture from the "Mahometans," and their crescent arch, "a symbol of one of the deities anciently worshipped throughout the heathen world, [which] was first adopted by the Arabs of Syria, and invariably used in all the edifices erected during the supremacy of the Ommiades."[49] Additionally, the eighteenth century with its interest in the past began the debate about whether or not Gothic architecture originated from the Saracens.[50]

In music, the internationally recognized Wolfgang Amadeus Mozart's *Piano Sonata no. 11 in A minor*, written in 1783, included a very popular last movement called the Turkish Rondo, which imitated the Turkish Janissary march. Mozart's *Abduction from the Seraglio*, which premiered 1782, confirms the same inquisitiveness. The curiosity about the world beyond "the Grekkishe see," known from the medieval romance of *Sir Isumbras*, was promoted by Alexander Pope's translations of Homer's *Odyssey*. It was Joseph Spence who, in *An Essay on Pope's Odyssey*, published in 1726, coined a new word – "orientalism" – with reference to Homer's most sublime and spirited passages, where he, in Spence's view, most accurately approaches the style of the Old Testament prophets.[51]

But it was the introduction of the *Arabian Nights* sometime between 1704 and 1717 that endorsed the significance of the Orient. Such was the recognition of the *Arabian Nights* that Lady Mary Wortley Montagu, for example, assumed that the readers of her letters were familiar with Galland's translation and "even with a few travel books."[52] The tales of the *Arabian Nights*, originally translated from the French of Antoine Galland,[53] over the course of some hundred years

---

49 Green, *Life of Mahomet*, 305.
50 Sweetman, *The Oriental Obsession*, 76.
51 Sambrook, *The Eighteenth Century*, 217.
52 Melman, *Women's Orients*, 82.
53 Ballaster, *Fabulous Orients*, 3–4.

underwent a number of different translations and adaptations, including the famous one by Richard Burton prepared in the years 1885 to 1888. "Aladdin, or the Wonderful Lamp" – one of the most well-liked of the stories – became a pantomime at London's Covent Garden in 1813.[54] The French version was followed by an anonymous chapbook, the "Grub Street" edition entitled *Arabian Nights Entertainment*, likewise a reworking of Galland. According to Marina Warner, "[t]he stories began appearing in 1705, and continued to flourish; 445 instalments, three times weekly, over three years, were published in the journal, the *London News*, from 1723–1726." Galland became an admirer and probably the first advocate of Middle Eastern culture,[55] even though he "embroidered" the original, and it is even possible that the much-loved stories of "Ali Baba and the Forty Thieves" and "Aladdin and the Wonderful Lamp" might be his inventions.[56] Warner argues that Galland masquerades as an Arab story teller, yet "[i]t is possible to see, through the lens of Galland's authorship, how mischievously he is guying the improbabilities and outlandishness of fabulous conventions, not least the far-flung exoticism of its magical cosmos."[57] To show the appeal of the stories, Ros Ballaster cites the example of Mary Hays, who in her *Memoirs of Emma Courtney*, published in 1796, has her heroine feel herself transported by the narrative of the *Arabian Nights*. Emma is indeed enchanted by the stories to which she listens.[58] The mentioning of the *Arabian*

---

[54] Fitzgerald's translation of *The Rubáiyát of Omar Khayyam* of 1859 in itself "made an immense contribution to the European vision of Persia." Sweetman, *The Oriental Obsession*, 30. There are also numerous film versions of the tales, such as Pier Paolo Pasolini's (1974), and Steve Barron's (2000), the latter with a screenplay by Peter Barnes.
[55] Warner, *Stranger Magic*, 13, 15.
[56] Warner, *Stranger Magic*, 16–17.
[57] Warner claims that both Galland and the later adapters saw the imaginary Moorish Kingdom as Cathay, thereby creating a "Chinese Islam." Warner, *Fantastic Metamorphoses*, 145–46. Such is illustrated by Walter Crane's "Alladin" (1883), to be found in Warner, *Fantastic Metamorphoses*, 147. The first adaptation for the English stage, in 1788, features "imprisoned spirits," "immobilized zombie-like psyches," which for Warner are associated with the issues of slavery. These early stagings do not offer a/the true picture of the Ottoman Empire but are closer to home. De Gobineau, writing about differences between races as unchangeable, notes that the *Arabian Nights* is "a book which is apparently trivial, is a mine of true sayings and well-observed facts – we read that some negroes regard Adam and his wife as black, and since these were created in the image of God, God must also be black and the Angels too, while the prophet of God was naturally too near divinity to show a white skin to his disciples." De Gobineau, *The Inequality*, 119.
[58] Ballaster, *Fabulous Orients*, 4. The whole quotation from Hays reads: "When myself and my little cousins had worried ourselves with play, their mother, to keep us quiet in an evening, while her husband wrote letters in an adjoining apartment, was accustomed to relate (for our entertainment) stories from the *Arabian Nights*, *Turkish Tales*, and other works of like marvelous import. She recites them circumstantially, and these I listened to with ever new delight:

Nights in diverse literary works gives evidence to the ongoing fame of the tales. Karla Malette sees the story of Scheherazade not as reflecting back on ancient Arabic literature but as an amalgamation of "Persian, Sanskrit, and Greek forbears, the heroine who entered the Arabic literary tradition more than a millennium ago and who left so remarkably few manuscript traces of her passing." Through the translations and renditions, Scheherazade's story was transformed into a textual monument, "by circumambulating the comparatively humble memorial to her in Arabic letters."[59] Rewritten, adapted, reconfigured, *Arabian Nights* is nonetheless a testament to the European curiosity about the literary renditions of the Orient.

Riding on the wave of the nineteenth-century popularity of the *Arabian Nights*, Edward W. Lane, another surveyor of the day, and Richard Burton both produced their own translations of the text,[60] which reflected their personal attitudes to the East, and so did Galland, who, in Raba Kabbani's view, was solely concerned with the violence of the East.[61] In contrast to Kabbani's derision, Warner quite blatantly calls Sir Richard Burton and Edward W. Lane ardent Arabophiles[62] – an epithet that Kabbani readily discards, arguing, very much in the spirit of Edward Said, only more irately, that both Lane (whose *An Account of the Manners and Customs of the Modern Egyptians* appeared in 1835) and Burton are products of Western "Orientalism," misjudging, misunderstanding and, in fact, debasing the East.[63] It is true that Burton in his *One Thousand and One Nights*, translated in 1850 and published in 1885, does sexualize the East, looking at Oriental women with a mixture of reverence and lust, which, according to Kabbani, is particularly conspicuous in the notes to his translation.[64] Yet, embarking on the project of translation springs from authentic interest in the text, a fact disregarded by both Kabbani and Said, for whom every Orientalist

---

the more they excited vivid emotions, the more wonderful they were, the greater was my transport: they became my favourite amusement, and produced, in my young mind, a strong desire of learning to read the books which contained such enchanting stores of entertainment." Hays, *Memoirs of Emma Courtney*, 14.

59 Malette, *European Modernity and the Arab Mediterranean*, 199.

60 Borges, *The Total Library*, 93–105, gives an interesting overview of translators and their versions of the *Arabian Nights*. His take on Burton's writing against Lane is certainly of interest.

61 Rana Kabbani maintains that Galland met Chardin and read his writings on Persia, which influenced his translations. Kabbani, *Imperial Fictions*, 52–53. Appreciating his sensitivity towards other cultures and his apparent studiousness, Kabbani nevertheless deems Chardin a biased traveler (52).

62 Warner, *Stranger Magic*, 18.

63 Kabbani, *Imperial Fictions*, 48–58.

64 Kabbani, *Imperial Fictions*, 81–96.

work of the eighteenth and nineteenth centuries misrepresents the Orient, and the translations of the *Arabian Nights* and travel narratives are a particular bone of contention.

Such mistrust is not shared by Robert Irwin and Marina Warner, who see the English translators as promoters of the Eastern cultures. In his companion to the *Arabian Nights*,[65] Irwin refers to a superstition current in the Middle East in the late nineteenth century, at the time when Burton was writing his translation, that anyone who read the whole text of the *Arabian Nights* would die. Both Irwin and Warner discuss the Arabic title *Alf Layla wa-Layla*, which was literally *Tales of a Thousand and One Nights*, rather than the accepted *Arabian Nights*.[66] Warner draws attention to the Chinese box structure and open-endedness of the stories, noting that the collection contains wonders of all kinds. *Aja'ib*, in the literature of the Middle East, signifies marvels, wonders, astonishing things – it "describes a genre that ranges from fantastic travel impartial yarns to metaphysical myths."[67] The *Arabian Nights* contain such stories so as to produce the condition of *ajab*, astonishment. Additionally, Warner comments on *homo narrans*, the person to whom the story is told, who reveals no ethnic divisions. For her, the text unveils "a polyvocal anthology of world myths, fables and fairy tales. But the book is also a masterwork of Arabic literature, distinctively arranged and told, with a flavor that is unmistakably its own."[68] Whatever the assessment of their value, the sheer number of different versions and translations, above all, corroborates the tales' undying renown amongst scholars.[69]

The cultures of the East influenced yet another fashionable motif that developed in the so-called long eighteenth century, namely, the tales of savages –

---

[65] Irwin, *The Arabian Nights*.
[66] Ahdaf Soueif claims that the title can be translated as "'a thousand nights'" – or even 'lots of nights.' Soueif, *Cairo*, 34.
[67] Warner, *Stranger Magic*, 6.
[68] Warner, *Stranger Magic*, 8. Irwin notices that the stories in the original manuscripts are interrupted every five pages or so by narrative breaks along the lines of "But morning overtook Sheherazade, and she lapsed into silence. Then her sister said, 'Sister, what an entertaining story!' Sheherezade replied, 'What is this compared with what I shall tell you tomorrow night!'" Irwin, *The Arabian Nights*, 3. Later manuscripts do not contain this device. Warner highlights the diversity of narrative forms: proverbial anecdotes, riddles, lyric songs, love poems, epigrams, jokes, and fables, and notes that the twenty-two manuscripts of the text that survived look like notebooks with different handwriting. Warner, *Stranger Magic*, 9, 11.
[69] In addition to a 2001 Modern Library edition of Richard Burton's translation with A. S. Byatt's "Introduction," there is also a rather curious children's version entitled *Tales from the Arabian Nights* with color plates by A. E. Jackson; *Oriental Myths and Legends*, issued in 1889; and finally, *Tales from the Thousand and One Nights*, translated by N. J. Dawood, originally published in 1955.

reworking Jean-Jacques Rousseau's model of the "noble savage," of which Aphra Behn's *Oronooko*, published in 1688, is perhaps the most notable example.[70] Behn's novella, based on her experiences in the West Indies – and later British Guiana – as the wife of a tradesman, proved to be an immensely admired text and was adapted for the English stage in 1796 by Thomas Southerne. Trade, then, once again became a driving force of cultural contact. Apart from the East India Company, eighteenth-century Britain also had contacts with Islamic Bengal, which furthered the exchange of goods as well as art, music, and literature between East and West, and promoted the building of the empire. When the third edition of *Scienza Nuova* by Giambattista Vico (1668–1744) appeared in 1744 in Italy, it was received in the already fertile ground of scientific discussions regarding various cultures and their modes of expression and expansion through language and art. Nation formation and the growth of the empire are closely linked. As Suvir Kaul shows, human civilization is driven by technological progress, which in this period was inevitably connected with the exploration and conquest of the lands beyond Europe and, consequently, the annihilation of the primal purity of the indigenous people.[71] The two contrasting models of existence – nation and empire – seem to be in constant conflict, for less advanced nations are conquered by more developed and stronger empires. These conquests irrevocably change the weaker nations' ways of life.

Such transformations are conveyed by Michel de Montaigne, who in his much-quoted essay "Of Cannibals," written around 1580, mourns the human loss of innocence, looking at the situation of America before the arrival of the Europeans. The work, however, is not only about cannibalism and savages,[72] but also about curiosity and the dread of the unknown.[73] The unknown space and its inhabitants, whose customs we do not understand, generate misconstrued notions about the Other. The geographical, albeit arbitrary, distinctions bifurcating reality into "ours" and "theirs" have always been used by travelers to designate the concepts of the familiar and the unfamiliar. The further away

---

70 Behn's biography is most frequently discussed in relation to her plays and her stay in Surinam. For more on Surinam, see Wallace, *Premodern Places*, 239–84.
71 Kaul, *Eighteenth-Century British Literature*, 5.
72 A very interesting instance of "barbarity" is given by Burton, who notices that the English are shamed for writing their names in famous places, "yet the practice is both classical and oriental. The Greeks and Persians left their marks everywhere, as Egypt shows; and the paws of Sphinx bears scratches which, being interpreted, are found to be the same manner of trash as that written upon the remains of Thebes in A.D. 1879." *Personal Narrative*, 1:431.
73 De Montaigne, *Complete Essays*, 150.

from home, the more exotic the work becomes, the less understandable the language and customs, the more "barbaric" the places. Failing to discuss de Montaigne's arguments,[74] Said blames generations of researchers and explorers in whose writings such characteristics forge negative views of the Orient, buttressing the generalizations plaguing European systems of thought and scholarship.[75] Resembling his medieval predecessors, that is, romance authors, de Montaigne is painfully aware of the ominous presence of Europe's powerful Near and Middle Eastern neighbors, yet he is able to rise above prejudice, claiming:

> each man calls barbarism whatever is not his own practice; for indeed it seems we have no other test of truth and reason than the example and pattern of the opinions and customs of the country we live in. There is always the perfect religion, the perfect government, the perfect and accomplished manners in all things. Those people are wild, just as we call wild the fruits that nature has produced by herself and in her normal way.[76]

And so, de Montaigne concedes that the "savage" nations are barbarous only in the sense of not having been fashioned by the human mind and are still "very close to their original naturalness."[77] When he talks about the Scythians, who ate their enemies as a sign of revenge, he admits: "we may call these people barbarians, in respect to the rules of reason, but not in respect to ourselves,

---

[74] Said, *Orientalism*, 54. Said perceptively traces the movement of ideas that led from the travel, historical confrontations, and Romantic promptings of the late eighteenth century to the age of Byron and Thomas Moore and beyond; these ideas supplemented a passionate curiosity and open-mindedness regarding regions and cultures not one's own, wearing down the obduracy of self and identity, with their polarizing images of a community of embattled believers facing barbarian hordes. He also shows how these ways of thinking about foreign cultures divided the world into Christians and everyone else.

[75] Contrary to this trend is the presence of Islamic art in Kórnik Castle, situated outside Poznań. Built originally in the fourteenth century, the castle was later rebuilt in the neo-Gothic style by the architect Karl Friedrich Schinkel for Tytus Działyński and his son, Jan Kanty. After Jan's death, in accordance with his will the castle fell into the hands of his brother-in-law, Count Władysław Zamoyski, who in turn bequeathed the castle to the Polish state before his death in 1924. It was Tytus Działyński in the nineteenth century who dreamt of Poland's grandeur during the time of the Partitions. He collected armor, tapestries, manuscripts, books, and the like, and displayed them in the memory chamber, as was the fashion of the epoch. Fascinated by the Orient's splendor and power, Działyński decided to turn the castle's memory halls into a Moorish hall, inspired by the Lion's Court of the Alhambra Palace (for the room that stored manuscripts and collectibles), the Mosque of Sultan Hassan in Cairo (for the portals in the entrance hall of Kórnik), and the Taj Mahal in Agra, India (for the niche in the rear elevation). The designs of the oriental carpets were copied on the hard wood mosaic.

[76] De Montaigne, *Essays*, 152.

[77] De Montaigne, *Essays*, 153.

who surpass them in every kind of barbarity."[78] Owing to the widespread acceptance of de Montaigne's thought, in the early eighteenth century the "noble savage" becomes the symbol of the new emerging discourses of geography, history, and literature.

Analogous to de Montaigne's assertions, Jean-Jacques Rousseau's *Discourse of Inequality*, issued in 1754, shows a preoccupation with the evolution of civilization that inevitably corrupts human beings. Rousseau sees past generations as living closer to nature. In effect, they did not need much to survive and had few passions, which in a way is reminiscent of what Boethius defines as true freedom – freedom from want.[79] Yet Rousseau also says that "[r]eligion commands us to believe that

---

[78] De Montaigne, *Essays*, 156. Hayden White also notices that de Montaigne talks about what we deem "wild fruit," which in fact nature produces in its own course. He points to the fact that "by the end of the Middle Ages, the Wild Man has become endowed with two distinct personalities, each consonant with one of the possible attitudes men might assume with respect to society and nature. If one looked upon nature as a horrible world of struggle, as animal nature, and society as a condition which, for all its shortcomings, was still preferable to the natural state, then he would continue to view the Wild Man as the antitype of the desirable humanity, as a warning of what men would fall into if they definitively rejected society and its norms." White, *Tropics of Discourse*, 173. White argues that the notion of the Wild Man stands over, stands against, and undercuts the notion of the "noble savage." The noble savage, as a contradiction in terms to the idea of nobility, stands in opposition to the concepts of barbarity and civility. Like Rousseau, White uses the term to expose what Rousseau was attacking – the European system of privilege, inherited power, and oppression. Conversely, as he points out, "The ignoble savage idea is used to justify the slave trade" (191). In White's delineation, the concept was created not to "redeem the savage" but to "belabor nobility," as the Wild Man has become fetishized into the rather oxymoronic "noble savage" through the encounters between the Europeans and the New World (186).

[79] Rousseau sets out his task as a study of: "original man, of his real needs, and of the fundamental principles of his duties, [which] is moreover [the] only effective means of dispersing the host of difficulties which surrounds the problems of the origin of moral inequality, the true foundation of the body politic, the reciprocal rights of its members, and a thousand similar questions, as important as they are obscure." Rousseau, *Discourse on Inequality*, 71. He claims that his book is true because it is taken from nature, and nature never lies (79). The savage man begins to discern his surroundings and makes comparisons between himself and the animals around him. In a truly ecocritical manner, Rousseau asserts that the savage man experiences passions only of the natural kind (89). "The Caribs, who of all peoples existing today have least departed from the state of nature, are precisely the most peaceful in their loves, and the least subject to jealousy, despite their living in the kind of hot climate which always seems to inflame those passions" (103). What is more: "Politicians utter the same sophisms about love of liberty that philosophers utter about the state of nature; on the strength of things that they see, they make judgments about very different things that they have not seen, and they attribute to men a natural propensity to slavery because they witness the patience with which slaves bear their servitude, failing to remember that liberty is like innocence and virtue: the

since God himself withdrew men from the state of nature they are unequal because he willed them to be."[80] Although at first glance Rousseau seems to idealize the natural man, he differentiates between the natural state and the social state. The primitive state, while closest to nature, is inevitably forgotten, as man will always be driven by the ideas of change and progress. Rousseau sees the past as the Golden Age but is not blinded by the idea. On the contrary, he recognizes social organization, and indeed all human societies, as a necessary form of existence. Rousseau's attitudes concerning progress and the development from "simple" to more "complex forms of existence" dominated eighteenth-century discourses on human societies in general. The philosophy of progress, fueled by the scientific debates of the period and related to the ambivalent philosophies of the empire, would become the great preoccupation of the Victorian age, both buttressing and hindering the advancement of the colonized nations. The eighteenth century served merely as the training ground for such ideologies.

Despite authentic attempts to grasp the intricacy of Orient through cultural absorption and business agreements, the image of the lands beyond Europe in the history of European thought remains, if not outright negative, then at least peculiar. The Renaissance geographical discoveries and explorations, followed by the seventeenth- and eighteenth-century wanderlust, did little more than corroborate the timeless strangeness of the oriental cultures. The tales of harems and seraglios, of incommensurable riches like the ones depicted in *Vathek*[81] by William Beckford,[82] published in 1786, were interspersed with those of the mercenary ferocity of

---

value of it is appreciated only so long as one possesses it oneself, and the taste for it is lost as soon as one loses it" (125).

80 Rousseau, *Discourse on Inequality*, 78.

81 Gilman, *The Saracens*, 394, maintains that that Vathek "eldest son of Motasim, assumed supreme authority in 842, and immediately issued a decree confirming the laws of Mamun regarding the nature of the Koran, thus continuing the war that had been begun against his own subjects." The Turks were mostly courtiers at Vathek's court, and they began their campaign to overcome the Muslim land. Vathek came to the throne at a difficult time, and he tried to go back to the simple rules of the Koran; wine was forbidden, as were hazard, music, dancing, and buffoonery. However, he was killed during a riot.

82 Warner sees Beckford as an important figure in the history of the reception of *The Arabian Nights*, which he began translating, and his work as an Orientalist is frequently forgotten. Warner, *Stranger Magic*, 295. *Vathek* introduces a character called Giaour (which means "infidel" in Turkish, derived from Persian). Later on, Giaour is the one who asks the caliph, Vathek, to worship his God, Fire. Warner deems Giaour a dark magician, yet she also shows the texts' links with Dante (297, 302); see also Hogg, *Private Memoirs and Confessions*. Warner sees the work's debatable authorship as inherently Arabic in nature, like the *Tales* themselves, and cites the publishing history of the text. Warner, *Stranger Magic*, 298–304. She also points to the prevalent opinions about Beckford's excess, "which chimes immediately with Said's

Byron's *The Giaour*, which appeared in 1813,[83] and awe mixed with aversion in *Childe Harold's Pilgrimage*, where "The pilgrim rested here his weary feet, / And gazed around on Moslem luxury" (Canto II, LXIV).

Sustained by the late eighteenth-century popularity of the Grand Tour, pre-Romanticism and Romanticism boasted poets who portrayed exotic places. The celebrated poet-traveler, George Gordon, Lord Byron, perhaps would not think of himself as a tourist, and yet his extensive travels and the works inspired by these travels, especially *Childe Harold's Pilgrimage*, published between 1812 and 1818, evoked interest not only in the classical past of Greece and Rome but also in the East.[84] Together with other Turkish Tales written and published between 1812 and 1816, the poem consolidated Byron's fame and congealed the unfavorable image of Islam,[85] even though the second canto of *Childe Harold* professed his admiration

---

critique of Western views of the Arab world, Beckford's own opinions and even [his] political activity [which] show[s] little sympathy with imperialist views. He was nothing if not Islamophile, and he has many advocates in Middle Eastern studies" (305–6). What is also interesting is that Beckford wrote two parodies of the Gothic romance – *Modern Novel Writing, or The Elegant Enthusiast* by "Lady Harriet Marlow" (1796) and *Azemia* (1979) by "A. M. Jenks" – the latter featuring the heroine Azemia, a native of Constantinople and giving vent to Beckford's true fascination with the Orient. Norton, *Gothic Readings*, 261.

[83] With his Turkish Tales, Byron enters into the polemic concerning Ottoman Greece. Although he is a manifest philhellenist, at the same time he seems to understand the context of Hassan's execution of his lover, who was unfaithful to him. Martin, "Heroism and History," 95. For more on Byron's Turkish Tales and the question of Ottoman Greece, see Leask, "Byron and the Eastern Mediterranean."

[84] The eighteenth and nineteenth centuries witnessed also the birth of the literary tourist with the fashion for visiting places connected with great writers such as William Shakespeare or Jean-Jacques Rousseau. Watson, in *The Literary Tourist*, explains: "The embarrassment palpable among professional literary scholars over the practice of literary pilgrimage co-exists with a marked willingness to indulge in it as a private or even communal vice, or so conference programmes ranging from the annual Wordsworth Conference in Grasmes (providing Wordsworthian walks, Wordsworthian readings *in situ*, and tours of Dove Cottage and Mount) summer conference in Dorchester (which comparably provides 'Hardy' walks) might suggest" (5–6), despite the fact that the landscapes that the literary tourists see is markedly different than the one perceived by the writer in whose footsteps they follow.

[85] In a similar manner, the turbaned Oriental included by Delacroix in the background of his 1827 painting "Greece on the Ruins of Missolonghi," the work that commemorates the Turkish victory, depicts him as a figure of some splendor, which "almost eclipses that of the woman representing Greece, the central focus of sympathy." An earlier painting such as Delacroix's "Massacre of Chios" (1824), "showing prostrate Greeks resigned to the actions of Turkish horsemen, might superficially indicate a return to the old division between the European and Saracen that had come down from the Crusades. His "Greece Expiring" (1827) makes a hero of the Turk as well." Sweetman, *Oriental Obsession*, 245.

for the Albanians and Sulinotes in their "native fastness."[86] The seemingly peaceful co-existence of different nations and religions – "The Turk, the Greek, the Albanian, and the Moor, / Here mingled in their many-hued array, / While the deep war-drum's sound announced the close of the day" (Canto II, LVII) – is always undercut by the dominance of the Turkish Empire. *Childe Harold's Pilgrimage* compellingly mourns the Turkish occupation of Greece: "Trembling beneath the scourge of Turkish hand; / From birth till death enslaved; in word, in deed, unmanned" (Canto II, LXXIV). Byron sees the Turks as powerful but proud: "The bearded Turk, that rarely deigns to speak, / Master of all around, too potent to be meek" (Canto II, LVIII). The defamation of the Turks is also evident in *The Corsair* (1814), dedicated to Thomas Moore, where Byron presents a Greek Pirate named Conrad who courageously attacks a Turkish ruler. The poem is an allegorical tale presenting the predicament of Greece as a country of freedom-loving people enslaved by Turkish Empire. Coincidentally, both poems reiterate all the Western stereotypes concerning harems and Muslim family life. Looking at the lives of women, Byron stresses their silence and enclosure: "Here woman's voice is never heard: apart, / And scarce permitted, guarded, veil'd, to move, / She yields to one her person and her heart, / Tamed to her cage, nor feels a wish to rove" (Canto II, LXI).

Similar descriptions are also brought to light in *The Giaour*, where the unfortunate titular hero falls in love with a woman walled in a harem, who is drowned as a punishment for their transgression. Having killed Hassan in revenge for his beloved's death, the Giaour wants to be absolved of murder because his enemy, the tyrant Hassan, spoke ill of Christianity:

> The very name of Nazarene
> Was wormwood to his Paynim spleen.
> Ungrateful fool! Since but for brands
> Well wielded in some hardy hands,
> And wounds by Galilean given,
> The surest pass to Turkish heaven,
> For him his Houris still might wait.
> Impatient at the Prophet's gate.
> (ll. 1040–1047)

The narrative of *The Giaour* recasts the Orient as lascivious and irrational, where women are a commodity, and a prize for the faithful awaiting them in the afterlife. The doe-eyed virgins waiting for a man in Paradise reappears in *The Bryde of Abydos* (1814), a tragic tale of the love between Zuleika and Salim. Muslim Paradise shuns women, so Zuleika "dream'd what Paradise might be / Where woman's

---

86 Sweetman, *The Oriental Obsession*, 79.

parted soul shall go / Her Prophet had disdained'd to show" (Canto II, VII). In all of the above-mentioned poems, Byron depicts Islam as a religion of bellicosity and control, which vanquishes human rights of the believers. As his interest in Greek independence is well attested in literature and history, for him, the Orient, fascinating as it was, should have been subdued by the West: "Red gleam'd the cross, and waned the crescent pale, / While Afric's echoes thrill'd with Moorish matrons wail."[87] Curiously, the unbelievably horrid wails of mothers for sons who have been conscripted is also pointed out by Burton in his *Personal Narrative of a Pilgrimage to Al-Madinah and Meccah*.[88] Moreover, Burton recalls "Eastern clatter" when he talks about the pilgrim's ship full of Turks, who are making "a hideous noise" as "the children howl because their mothers howl and the men scold and swear."[89]

As can be easily observed, Orientalism continued to be the hot-button political issue in the nineteenth century. Byron, who was active in his support of Thomas Moore and admired Moore's *Lalla Rookh*, was also obliging toward Coleridge and his *Kubla Khan*, published in 1816. Coleridge begins his poem with the famous lines: "In Xanadu did Kubla Khan / A Stately pleasure-dome decree."[90] Powered by his readings of travel literature, he imagines the East as "[a] savage place! as holy and enchanted," where fire and ice intermingle: "A sunny-pleasure-dome with caves of ice!"[91] where the dreamer "on honey-dew hath fed, / And drunk the milk of Paradise."[92] Kabbani emphasizes that Coleridge actually never traveled to the East and entered Xanadu noticeably tripping on opium.[93] In fact, the apparent incongruities are well in line with the Romantic imagination. For all the Romantic writers, whether they actually visited the places or not, the Orient was a site of ambivalent and often contradictory emotions, combining their own repressed reservations and desires. It was the culture of mysteries and temptations, courtly luxury, harems, and brothels, besides heat, excess, and street poverty. Accordingly, in *Jane Eyre*, which appeared in 1847, we first find Jane sitting cross-legged like the Turk, only to have Edward Rochester declare that he "would not

---

87 All the quotations from Byron come from Page, *Byron: Complete Poetical Works. Childe Harold's Pilgrimage*, Canto I, xxxv.
88 Burton, *Personal Narrative*, 1:117–18.
89 Burton, *Personal Narrative*, 1:186.
90 Coleridge, *Complete Poems*, 250.
91 Coleridge, "Kubla Khan," in *Complete Poems*, 251.
92 Coleridge, "Kubla Khan," in *Complete Poems*, 252.
93 Kabbani, *Imperial Fictions*, 66.

exchange this one little English girl for the grand Turk's whole seraglio; gazelle-eyes, houri forms and all."[94]

All of the above examples clearly suggest what gave rise to both "manifest Orientalism" as well as to "latent Orientalism." The former has always been present in travel narratives of the nineteenth century, which contain internalized prejudices and value judgments and describe perpetual clashes between the East and the West. This type is easily countered and refuted. Latent Orientalism is far more dangerous, because for the most part, it also remains undetected in current cultural and political discourses. As is evident from both the fictional and non-fictional texts here, nineteenth-century Orientalism has always been associated with the processes of creating Eurocentric dogmas buttressing imperial ideologies. It would be a gross simplification, however, to agree with Said, who sees colonialism as the product of Orientalism, a misconception countered by, for example, Ahmad.[95] Orientalism indeed contributed to the fashioning of the white man's myth, yet, the manifold discourses of empire gave vent to other nineteenth-century preoccupations – among others, race and "racialism." Racist as they may seem to the twenty-first-century readers, the Victorians were intent on providing scientific explanations of biological and ethnic differences between populations. The seventeenth-, eighteenth-, and nineteenth-century accounts of the Orient made the East more familiar and palatable to the West. What is more, "Ornamentalism," the term used by David Cannadine to denote imperial self-perception,[96] provides an alternative, more culture-oriented view of British colonialism.

The processes involved in what eventually became the British Empire are far too complex for such a short presentation. Suffice it to say that the politics of conquest and colonization catered to, among other things, economic needs. As early as 1798, Thomas Malthus's *Essay on Population* began the examination

---

94 Brontë, *Jane Eyre*, 269. "Yakmak" is in fact "yashmak," a curtain/veil, "houri" means a young woman/virgin with gazelle eyes, and "seraglio" means sequestered living quarters at the Ottoman courts. *Jane Eyre* contains a number of allusions to Byron (i.e., to *Corsair*), and Rochester himself bears the traits of a Byronic hero (179).
95 Ahmad, *In Theory*, 159–219.
96 I am well aware that Cannadine's *Ornamentalism* is a rather popular source; nevertheless, it does include a number of interesting aspects concerning certain domestic ideologies that were instrumental in creating the "grand narratives" of imperial Britain. I am using the expression coined by Lyotard solely to draw attention to its theoretical fallacy, as we no longer believe in the greatness of History as such. The discussion of the issues of historiography and the narrativization of history can be found in White, *The Content of the Form*, and Carroll, *The States of "Theory"*.

of the possibilities of emigration to the colonies.[97] The adventurers and pioneers who charted the unknown lands contributed to the development of geography, zoology, botany, and anthropology. But most of all, they brought hope to those who wanted to emigrate to the new lands. Nineteenth-century literature is full of allusions to various parts of the empire and the possibilities of work and settlement[98] – in short, career opportunities for those willing to undertake the risk of exploration and immigration. Some of those daredevils, like Richard Burton, were conscious of and disgruntled by the Victorian ideologies of advancement and subjugation. Thus it is not Orientalism, understood as the pursuit of knowledge of the foreign, but colonialism that, under the mask of imposed progress, encouraged exotization and exploitation. While historians, intent on tracing the expansion of the Saracens, homogenized the area under the umbrella of shared religion, the travelers tried to see its complexity, its diverse languages and cultures. Consequently, even though the Orient became a discursive nineteenth-century construct, as we can see in the ensuing chapters, it retained part of its original meaning found in Samuel Johnson's *Dictionary*, where it is not a noun, but an adjective, signifying: "Bright; shining; glittering; gaudy; sparkling." Two hundred years later, the Oxford English Dictionary added the verb "to orient," meaning "to adjust, to correct, or bring into defined relations, to know facts and principles."[99] The Orient dazzled the historian and the traveler, whose experiences of "disorientation" were only alleviated by the constant comparisons between here and there.

---

97 Although immigration was a possibility, Malthus acknowledges the emotional toll on those going into the unknown as well as those left behind. Malthus, *An Essay on the Principle of Population*, 17. He sees the Barbarians as essentially nomadic, living by "a constant expectation of plunder" (27). Malthus's thesis was that the oversupplied labor market breeds poverty, and the only way to avoid that is to curb fertility by natural means.
98 The discussion of the "gendered" Orient is slightly beyond my present scope, although the intertwining notions of gender and race are of interest to many researchers, such as Melman in *Women's Orients*, who sees that "dark places" of the world were always represented as female. Hence the metaphors of rape, which so enraged Said.
99 Spurr, *Rhetoric of the Empire*, 142.

Chapter 2
Al-Ifranij among the Believers, or the Victorian Quest Romance(d)

Claude Levi-Strauss begins his travelogue *Triste Tropiques* with a disclaimer: "I hate travelling and explorers. Yet here I am proposing to tell the story of my expeditions . . . The truths which we seek so far afield only become valid when they have been separated from this dross."[1] He goes on to disparage travel narratives with their concentration on insignificant details pertaining solely to the experiences of a given traveler in a specific time and place. It is undoubtedly true that every text and every reader is a product of a theoretical standpoint. For this reason, Roxanne L. Euben defines the theory of travel narratives as:

> a practice of inquiry in which critical distance plays an integral role, thereby shifting the emphasis from "theory" as a body of ideas subject to domestication or in need of constant chastening to "theorizing" as a reflective activity engaged in by ordinary people at particular moments in time. In this way, the particular standpoint at work in all theorizing represents not an inadequacy or the theoretical enterprise but a critical component of it.[2]

Travel writings always oscillate between fact and fiction, and their reception does as well. The celebrated (fictional) travelogue *Mandeville's Travels*, for example, originally produced in the fourteenth century, was in its time treated as a factual narrative, while postmedieval audiences deem both the book and even its supposed author[3]

---

[1] Levi-Strauss, *Tristes Tropiques*, 17.
[2] Euben, *Journeys to the Other Shore*, 11.
[3] Many scholars believe that Mandeville was a pseudonym and that the work was written by Jean de Bourgogne (or Jean à la Barbe), a physician of Liège, or by Jean d'Outremeuse (1338–1400), a citizen of Liège and composer of fabulous history. A growing number of scholars, however, contest that the book was composed, as reported in the text, by John Mandeville. Biographical details are not wholly clear, but he seems to have been born at St. Albans in the late thirteenth century, to have spent the prime of his life on the Continent, and to have completed the book by 1356 as a travel romance, rather than as an authentic account. For a lucid discussion of the whole scholarly problem and of Mandeville's artistry, see Higgins, *Writing East*; Letts, *Sir John Mandeville*.

Note: *Al-ifranij* means the Franks, in general, and this term referred to Christians. According to Ayalon, the term referred to the Franks (*Firanj*), named so after the city of *Ifransiya*, which was supposedly one of the cities of the northern Europeans. Ayalon notes that most writers of the medieval period used the term collectively "as a name for the heathens coming from across the sea." Ayalon, *Language and Change*, 6. *Among the Believers* is, of course, the title of V. S. Naipaul's travelogue, subtitled *An Islamic Journey*, originally published in 1981.

https://doi.org/10.1515/9781501513367-003

fictitious.⁴ John Mandeville, whoever he was, wrote as a response to what was happening in Christendom at the moment. The Crusade of 1270 led by Louis IX of France had ended in disaster, and Mandeville, like others, must have perceived the growing power and presence of Islam at the borders of Christendom with apprehension.⁵ Unlike earlier adventurers, who were driven by the hunger to know the world and whose travels led to the creation more than the discovery of ancient *mirabilia*, Victorian voyagers saw themselves as scholars who searched the uncharted territories to have them mapped, catalogued, and conquered. The development of the disciplines of archeology and anthropology imposed a scientific approach on travel writing.⁶ Pioneering figures such as Sir Richard Burton (*Personal Narrative of a Pilgrimage to Al-Madinah and Meccah*) and Charles Montagu Doughty (*Travels in Arabia Deserta*),⁷ whose works are examined in this chapter, were knights-errant, or perhaps, "knights-erring," who in their attempts to record their experiences usually conflated ideas on race, ethnicity, and culture. And like their medieval predecessors, they were devoted to the pursuit of their own version of the Holy Grail.

Nineteenth-century travel accounts show an affinity with the romance mode as they emulate the elements of challenge, quest and adventure. The authors and heroes of Victorian travel narratives, like the characters of Sir Isumbras and Guy of Warwick, the protagonists of medieval Saracen romances, set out into an unknown and dangerous reality of the Middle East. Still, it is assumed that the world depicted in travel narratives is more commonplace than that of the romance. The literary expression of nineteenth-century explorations is best realized in the genre known as the Victorian quest romance or, as Fraser terms it, the Victorian travel romance.⁸ Henry Rider Haggard's (1856–1925) African adventure novels, Rudyard Kipling's (1865–1936) *Jungle Book* and Arthur Conan Doyle's (1859–1930) *The Lost World* (published originally in 1912) were written to celebrate

---

4 Authors such as Orosius (fl. 417) and the encyclopedist St. Isidore of Seville (d. 636) in their works mixed fact and fable in their descriptions of men and of animals. Pliny the Elder (d. 79 CE) was also a recognizable authority on the natural world.
5 The Irish monk Fidelis talked about Egypt when he traveled to the Holy Land and Jerusalem (ca. 679–688).
6 Thompson, *Travel Writing*, 91.
7 Both Burton and Doughty were avid Orientalists, but Burton's Orientalism is coupled with his intense dislike of Africa and the black man, whom he sees as idle and ignorant; such claims are quite transparent in *First Footsteps in East Africa*. His defamation of the black race, however, has to be seen in the context of existing prejudices not only between black and white men but also between Arabs and Black Africans. Burton also eschewed any outward criticism of slavery in Arab countries.
8 Fraser, *Victorian Quest Romance*, 7.

male knowledge, courage, and prowess or, in short, old-time heroic masculinity. They appeared to counter the growing popularity of the late nineteenth-century "new woman" fiction. Fraser marks out Lord Alfred Tennyson's *Idylls of the King* (published between 1859 and 1885) and Tennyson's inspiration, Thomas Malory's *Le Morte D'Arthur*, as the staple reading of Victorian boys, but young readers of the late Victorian period, such as Rudyard Kipling himself, were also brought up on the translations of *The Arabian Nights*. Consequently, their own novels were set in exotic locales, in remote parts of the globe where European women were not welcome, and they described male investigative and sexual adventures in which the conquered land is as malleable as the subjugated native women, who then conveniently die so as not to endorse the idea of miscegenation.

As has been noted, the literary ancestry of the quest romance derives from the chivalric romances of the Middle Ages, together with nineteenth-century travel narratives. The medieval insistence on valor and moral integrity when facing a dangerous and terrifying enemy was translated into the honorable, albeit still merciless, engagement in black vs. white conflicts. Medieval chivalrous knights become Victorian gentlemen, as Mark Girouard shows, but their need for challenges remained similar to that of their medieval forerunners. Characteristically, as was the case with the Saracen romances, the Victorian quest romance was also preoccupied with religious disputes, both at home – in the form of never-ending struggle between the head (the crown) and the heart (the Church) – as well as abroad – through the inevitable clashes with Islam. What is more, the medieval Christian praise of virtue is upheld through the Victorian insistence on purity. In Victorian quest romances, white women, with a few exceptions, were excluded from real and fictional adventures. Their place was to guard the hearth, not to suffer the inconveniences of travel. The vital part of such tales is always an account of bravery against adversity and of the undeniable nobility, resourcefulness, and intelligence of the white man.[9] The Victorian travelogue, as well as its fictional counterpart, the quest romance, are protean genres amalgamating an imperialistic vision of the colonies or would-be colonies and exhibiting the Victorian nostalgia for the brave white man's world. For Pratt, the idea of discovery

> consisted of a gesture of converting local knowledges (discourses) into European national and continental knowledges associated with European forma and relations of power.... In the end, the act of discovery itself, for which all the untold lives were sacrificed and miseries endured, consisted of what in European culture counts as a purely passive experience, that of seeing.[10]

---

9 Girouard, *The Return to Camelot*.
10 Pratt, *Imperial Eyes*, 198.

Richard Burton's and Charles Montagu Doughty's oeuvres are among the most famous "products" of the Victorian discovery aesthetic, both documenting and fabricating the images of the Orient.

Indeed, one cannot but agree that European travel writing is "a one way traffic, because the Europeans mapped the world rather than the world mapping them."[11] The admission of such a position of guilt leads to the reversal of hitherto uncontested power structures.[12] Predictably, Edward Said accuses Burton of the "imperial gaze,"[13] that is, of grounding his work in "Oriental legend" instead of involving himself with the unfamiliar.[14] In Said's view, narratives such as Burton's contrived the image of the Orient as a kind of womb "out of which they were brought forth" and thus created a simulacrum, unsatisfactory and untrue. Apart from the reservations against the depiction of the Muslims and their lands, Said also belittles Burton's chronological narration, labeling it "dutifully linear," as if what he was describing was "a shopping trip to an Oriental bazaar rather than adventure." For Said, regardless of the traveler's knowledge of the language, culture, and religion, Burton's narration presents the "Englishman's East,"[15] with the Orient being a thoroughly European

---

11 Clark, "Introduction," in *Travel Writing and Empire*, 3.

12 The criticism of the genre is frequently geared toward deconstructing, in the sense of undoing, the conservatism of the texts, which quite frequently essentialize that which they are supposed to analyze. Yet the twenty-first-century gender- and race-conscious travelogues grew out of the earlier texts, which more often than not were patriarchal, racist, and profoundly uninformed.

13 Said claims that part of the construction of Orientalism was done through citing uncontested texts, such as Burton's. Said, *Orientalism*, 23. For Said, a nineteenth-century Orientalist was either a scholar or a gifted enthusiast, or both, as was the case with Burton (51).

14 As was customary, he was offered the Royal Geographical Society's help (Burton, *Personal Narrative*, 1:2), which was hard-won, as Rice reports in *Captain Sir Richard Burton*, 233.

15 Said, *Orientalism*, 193. Burton leaves for Southampton on April 3, 1853. He passes from the English fog to the splendors of the East and delights the reader with the story of a typically Arab form of intoxication. "And this is the Arab Kayf. The savouring of animal existence; the passive enjoyment of mere sense, the pleasant languor, the dreamy tranquility, the airy castle building, which in Asia stand in lieu of the vigorous, intensive, passionate life of Europe. It is the result of a lively impressible, excitable nature, and exquisite sensibility of nerve; it argues a facility for voluptuousness unknown to northern regions, where happiness is placed in the exertion of mental and physical powers; where *Ernst is das Leben*; wherever niggard earth commands ceaseless sweat of face, and damp chill air demands perpetual excitement, exercise, or change, or adventure, or dissipation, for want of something better. In the East, man wants to rest and shade; upon the banks of a bubbling stream, or under the cool shelter of a perfumed tree, he is perfectly happy, smoking a pipe, or sipping a cup of coffee, or drinking a glass of sherbet, but above all things deranging body and mind as little as possible; the trouble of conversations, the displeasures of memory, and the vanity of thought being the most

invention[16] and nothing more than that. Yet what Said ignores is the word "personal" in the title of the work, which suggests the link between travel writing and autobiography and thus a subjective rather than objective point of view.

Saidian criticism is largely based on contemporary approaches to representation, while the nineteenth-century travel narratives were influenced by the advent of realism and empirical objectivism. Within the framework of current thinking, the genre is scrutinized through poststructuralist and postmodernist critiques of language, selfhood, and historical narrative. For a contemporary – informed, not to say academic – reader, language cannot convey reality, and what is more, if the self is a fictive construct or mere multiplicity of subject positions, then the narrative is a mere impressionistic subjective account, rather than an objective one. Like autobiographical life-writing, it does not contain all of experience but presents a selection of events, impressions, and people chosen for the benefit of coherence or entertainment by the writer. Travel writing is also unavoidably self-presentation; hence the position of the author and his attitudes toward the world he observes underpin the arguments he makes. Such an "inward turn," to use Carl Thompson's expression,[17] can be related to the simple self-fashioning of the author's persona as much as to the more elaborate self-aggrandizing of the traveler. Knowing Sir Henry Morton's Stanley's life,[18] for example, one should not be surprised at his quite conscious glorification of himself as a "last action hero," whose African quests were not altogether successful. Taking into account the very fluidity of the genre, and its connection with autobiography, one has to admit that these narratives to a larger or smaller degree demonstrate some form of self-creation and fictionalization, and this argument can serve to exculpate Burton's attitudes to the East.

---

unpleasant interruptions to his *Kayf*. No wonder that 'Kayf' is a word untranslatable in our mother-tongue." Burton, *Personal Narrative*, 1:9. *Kayf* is given the name of all kinds of intoxication, says the footnote on the same page. This is the excerpt that particularly enrages Kabbani as an example not of the untranslatable experience Burton claims, "unpronounceable" or "unmentionable" for the Victorian gentleman, but as prudish and hypocritical. Kabbani, *Imperial Fictions*, 94–95.

16 Mary Louise Pratt uses the term "contact zone" in her analysis of the Victorian expansion into Africa and South America, which refers to "the space of colonial encounters" in which geographically and historically separated peoples come into contact with each other and establish not always friendly relations, marked by racial inequality and cultural conflict. As far as traveling is concerned, she considers women travelers to be less prejudiced toward native populations.
17 Thompson, *Travel Writing*, 108.
18 See, for example, Jeal's *Stanley*.

Mary Louise Pratt, in turn, asserts that travel narratives frequently aestheticize foreign landscapes:

> The sight is seen as a painting and the description is ordered in terms of background, foreground, symmetries between foam-flecked water and mist-flecked hills, and so forth. . . . It is important to note that within the text's own terms the esthetic pleasure of the sight singlehandedly constitutes the value and significance of the journey.[19]

Thus, a bone of contention is the relationship between the landscape and people and Burton's portrayal of his experiences. Pratt's analysis, however, concentrates on *The Lake Regions of Central Africa*, published originally in 1860,[20] and does not include a detailed scrutiny of *Personal Narrative of a Pilgrimage to Al-Madinah and Meccah*. Analyzing Burton's African account, she suggests that he used "conventional means which create qualitative and quantitative value for the explorer's achievement."[21] It is of no importance to her what he saw, but whether his depiction of the landscape was in line with the Victorian exploratory rhetoric. For Pratt, the aesthetic qualities of the landscape constitute the social and material value of the discovery to the traveler's home culture, at the same time as its aesthetic deficiencies suggest a need for social and material intervention by that very home culture.[22] The juxtaposition of beauty and serenity with ugliness and bustle, though, need not be seen as contrasting the ideas of "home" and "away." The peaceful countryside and the clamorous towns and cities, with their upper-class mansions and poor hovels, can be found in whatever country. Still, the legacy of contrasts is one of the crucial aspects of the present-day travel writing, infested with what Euben calls "grievances haunting contemporary politics,"[23] which are especially poignant in the relationship between the East and the West, often stereotypically referred to as the "the clash of civilizations" after the title of Huntington's 1997 book. Postcolonial critics, for instance Nicholas Thomas,[24] relentlessly try to address these issues while acknowledging the European role in the nineteenth-century colonial encounters. Post-postcolonial writers, such as Ahdaf Soueif, whose work will be analyzed in

---

19 Pratt, *Imperial Eyes*, 200.
20 Burton, *The Lake Regions of Central Africa*.
21 Pratt, *Imperial Eyes*, 212–13. Pratt gives the examples of Alberto Moravia and Paul Theroux. Burton likewise notices the problem of crime. "On one occasion a party of Arab merchants, not understanding the 'fun of the thing,' shot two Somal: the tribe had the justice to acquit the strangers, mulcting them, however, a few yards of cloth for the families of the deceased." Burton, *First Footsteps*, 148.
22 Pratt, *Imperial Eyes*, 201.
23 Euben, *Journeys to the Other Shore*, 1.
24 Thomas, *Anthropology, Travel and Government*, 11–65.

part 2 of the present study, do not simply "write with a vengeance" but embrace the colonial past, giving voice to the hitherto silent subjects by using the motif of travel, in both the literal and metaphorical sense. There is no doubt that since the late Middle Ages, European travelers have provided, or rather imposed, varied descriptions of the world, and travel writing crafted "the rest of the world for European readership."²⁵ Nineteenth-century explorers such as Burton and Doughty reproduced previously accepted attitudes of evaluation and conquest. By explaining that which was unknown and dissimilar, they prepared the ground for further colonization. Even so, Burton, like Todorov's Columbus, was not only a seer but also, possibly, a first interpreter of the new land,²⁶ and his adventures were recorded for the benefit of English-language audiences.

Sir Richard Francis Burton (1821–1890) was soldier, Orientalist, geographer, cartographer, ethnologist, writer, linguist, translator, and diplomat. Sponsored by the Royal Geographical Society, between 1851 and 1853 he embarked on a journey to Medinah and Mecca chronicled in his *Personal Narrative of a Pilgrimage to Al-Madina and Mecca*, published in 1855. The work is a geographical and ethnographic record of the Muslim Holy Land, then unknown to Christians. Highlighting differences, Burton's initial observations respond to the demands of the genre of Victorian travel narrative, catering to the expectations of the British audience. The storyline evincing the essential alteration of reality in the travelogue is a conscious operation. Burton continually tells the reader that he traveled with ink and paper and that he knew what he wanted to see and where he wanted to go: unquestionably, he had some preconceived ideas about his destinations. Yet the narrative as we know it was written after the journey, its author combining the aesthetic and descriptive methods and adding extra-literary elements, such as drawings. We do not know how much of the work has been amended from its original drafts; we can only assume that some crude illustrations and basic observations were recorded during his journey and that his inquiries into the history and culture of the place were added later. Even as a "Muslim," Burton had to be

---

25 Euben, *Journeys*, 2. The origin of the currently abhorred word "Eurocentrism" points precisely to this. For the most part, Europe still tends to think about "the West and the Rest," whereas, in fact . . . "[t]he West is also an amalgamation of multiple traditions – the Greek, Roman, Judaic, and Christian to name a few – and has been perpetually influenced by and shaped in terms of other cultures and civilizations. Indeed, crucial components of Western intellectual history may not be Western in any meaningful sense at all. . . . Europe as we know it begins not only with Greek and Roman civilizations but also with the Byzantines of Constantinople, and it was the Arabs of Andalusia who have preserved the Hellenized urban civilization of the antique Mediterranean long after it was destroyed in Europe." Euben, *Journeys*, 3–4. Neither Europe nor Arabia is ethnically pure.
26 Todorov, *The Conquest of America*, 14–35.

excessively careful what and where he was writing and drawing, because of the Islamic ban on man-made pictures and the fear of idolatry.

Immersing himself in his different disguises – a Persian wanderer, a "Darwaysh," a figure customarily respected for his austerity, and an Afghan pilgrim – Burton did not foresee that his later readers would attack him for "posing" as a Muslim. It was only by taking on the personality of an Eastern sage that he was able to discern the customs and ways of living of those around him. He also knew that a Christian might never be safe in Mecca. Islam's most sacred places would have been defiled if a Christian were to enter, and a Christian pilgrim could have been killed if he entered the abodes connected with the life of Mohammed.[27] As it transpires, Burton's familiarity with the language and Arab – or better, Muslim – ways of thinking gave him the advantage not only of continuing his journey but also, first and foremost, the chance of survival. This is noted by Jorge Luis Borges, who, admiring Burton's courage, sees him as:

> the English captain with his passion for geography and for the innumerable ways of being a man that are known to mankind. . . . Burton, disguised as an Afghani,[28] made the pilgrimage to the holy cities of Arabia; his voice begged the Lord to deny his bones and skin, his dolorous flesh and blood, to the Flames of Wrath and Justice; his mouth, dried out by the *samum*, left a kiss on the aerolith that is worshipped in the Kaaba. The adventure is famous: the slightest rumor that an uncircumcised man, a *nasráni*, was profaning the sanctuary would have meant certain death.[29]

Richard Burton, the *enfant terrible* of Victorian Britain, wrote a number of accounts of his explorations within Asia, Africa, and the Americas, sharing his extraordinary knowledge of cultures and languages. In the preface to the third edition of his *Personal Narrative*, Burton asks the readers not to criticize his apparent conversion to Islam. He pleads: "judge not; especially when you are ignorant of the case which you are judging."[30] In order to visit places sacred to the Muslims, he had to abide by the law of the land and be aware of the Muslim rites performed during the Hajj. Consequently, it took quite a long time for him to prepare for the rather perilous journey. Burton was circumcised, grew a long beard, and stained his skin with walnut juice.[31] He learned to eat with his right hand, ride a camel, and sit and even urinate like an Arab. Fawn Brodie quotes a

---

[27] Burton, *Personal Narrative*, 2:207.
[28] Burton poses as an Afghan and takes offense at being called Hindi (Indian), alluding to the "mountain of Hindu-kush whence the Afghans sallied forth to lay waste to India." *Personal Narrative*, 1:243. Being the victor, he does not want to be taken for the subjugated victim.
[29] Borges, *The Total Library*, 97.
[30] Burton, *Personal Narrative*, 1:xxi.
[31] Brodie, *The Devil Drives*, 93.

Chapter 2 Al-Ifranij among the Believers, or the Victorian Quest Romance(d) — 45

rumor concerning Burton that was circulating in London: while in Arabia, he was spotted urinating in the European manner, standing up, and had to kill a young Arab to avoid detection. Burton himself tried to clear his name, claiming that the story was "a total fabrication."[32] Nevertheless, wherever he was in Arabia, he felt in constant peril. In the Ka'abah, for example, he was forced to assert his Afghani identity quite frequently, so as not to be accused of lack of reverence in the holy place. Despite his knowledge that in the Ka'abah it was disrespectful and unsafe for the pilgrim to look at the ceiling, he was afraid that one false move might result in him blowing his cover.[33] What is more, following his return to England, he was forced to withstand attacks from unnamed critics who pilloried his conversion on the ground of morality. To them he retorted:

> I recognize no man's right to interfere between a human being and his conscience. But what is there, I would ask, in the Moslem pilgrimage so offensive to Christians. What makes it's a subject "inward ridicule"? Do they not also venerate Abraham, the Father of the Faithful? Did not Locke, and even greater names, hold Mohammedans to be heterodox Christians, in fact Arians who, till the end of the fourth century, represented the mass of North-European Christianity? Did Mr. Lane never conform by praying at a Mosque in Cairo? Did he ever fear to confess it? Has he been called an apostate for so doing? Did not Father Michael Cohen prove himself an excellent Moslem at Wahhabi-land?[34]

Burton begins his account delineating the reasons why he decided to undertake the journey. He professes to be "thoroughly tired of 'progress' and of 'civilization'" and unsurprisingly "curious to see with my eyes what others are content to 'hear with ears.'" He is explicitly interested in authentic Muslim life in a Muslim, or as he terms it "Mohammedan" country.[35] What is articulated here, and what

---

32 Brodie, *The Devil Drives*, 101.
33 Burton, *Personal Narrative*, 2:207.
34 Burton, *Personal Narrative*, 1:xxii.
35 Burton, *Personal Narrative*, 1:2; spelling original. Still in Alexandria, he secured the assistance of a sheikh (in the Arab world, a priest, elder, or chieftain) "and plunged once more into the intricacies of the Faith; revived my recollections of religious ablutions, read the Koran, and again became an adept in the art of prostration" (1:11). "After a month in Alexandria, I prepared to assume the character of a wandering Darwaysh; reforming my title from 'Mirza'" (Persian "Mister") (1:14). Burton writes that assuming a Persian identity was a mistake, and gave him a bad name, as Persians were viewed as followers of the Shi'a heresy. "A systematic concealment of doctrine, and profession of popular tenets, technically called by the Shi'ahs 'Takiyah': the literal meaning of the word is 'fear,' or 'caution'" (1:67). His story once again testifies to the many facets of Islam and Arab culture. Later he tells of a person called Haji Wali, whom he befriended on board a steamer and with whom he smoked the forbidden weed "hashish" (*Personal Narrative*, 1:44). "'I believe in Allah and his prophet, and in nothing else' was Haji Wali's sturdy creed; he rejected alchemy, jinnis and magicians, and truly he had the most unoriental distaste for tales and wonder" (1:44).

Said does not seem to notice in Burton's writings, is the inherent criticism of Victorian values, of the European enthrallment with technology and the Victorian restrictive morality that Burton constantly derided in his works. Not only his *First Footsteps in East Africa* but also his earlier "Indian adventures" testify to his interest in the sexuality of non-Europeans and manifest his criticism of Victorian morality.[36] The Industrial Revolution, which brought about many technological innovations, in Burton's lifetime caused the most radical changes in individual lives. The development of science and its impact on culture, with its overpowering belief in advancement, indisputably made Britain the most powerful nation in the world. Scientists argued that only science could grant one the knowledge of nature and human beings, but with the emergence of Darwinism,[37] science became a political issue. As much as the eighteenth century celebrated the idea of European civilization, and Romanticism valued universal freedom and civil liberties, the Victorians, in turn, venerated progress. And that is what Burton belittles.

Reading Burton's work, Rana Kabbani states that it was Burton's "urge" to be "contrary" and "different" that prompted his desire to learn Arabic,[38] and following the assertions of Kathryn Tidrick, she identifies Burton as a misfit who set out to India having made a fuss about not being able to study Arabic at Oxford, and saving himself from "academic disaster and family chastisement."[39]

---

36 For more, see Brodie, *The Devil Drives*, 41–68.
37 Darwin's *On the Origin of Species* (1859) was read as a travel book, as was his earlier travelogue, *The Voyage of the Beagle* (1839). He is not seen as an important travel writer by Fraser and Brown in *English Prose of the Nineteenth Century*, O'Gorman in *The Cambridge Companion to Victorian Culture*, or Tucker in *A Companion to Victorian Literature and Culture*.
38 Kabbani, *Imperial Fictions*, 82.
39 Kabbani singles out Burton's Indian adventures, focusing on his "sexual curiosity" and "linguistic insatiability," denigrating whatever Burton wrote and observed. Kabbani, *Imperial Fictions*, 83. She sees Burton as a colonial officer whose views on Eastern women would always be mediated through the master–slave relationship connected with Victorian prudery. Indian women were there to provide his sexual gratification. "Burton always retained his age's polarized view of women. They were either sexual beings who were whorish, or caring companions in the home, untinged by sexual ardour" (85). She voices a similar disregard concerning Burton's translations of *The Arabian Nights*, claiming that for him the tales "abound with descriptions of lecherous women who copulate with anyone, anywhere" (87). Like the Romantics, such as Byron, Burton notices the subjugation of women in Islam. For him, Muslim women (especially the poor ones of loose morals) are degraded and abused – "those who degrade it are the first to abuse it for degradation" – but he sees that "no society of French gentlemen avoids mentioning in public the name of a woman more scrupulously than do the misogynist Moslems." Burton, *First Footsteps*, 1:42. He recognizes, however, that "[p]olygamy is indispensable in a country where children are the principal wealth" (1:85).

Chapter 2 Al-Ifranij among the Believers, or the Victorian Quest Romance(d) — 47

Whatever the reasons, his grasp of the language and the beguilement with the culture of the Arabs enabled him to enter Mecca and Medina. In the nineteenth century, Al-Madinah was proclaimed "virgin territory," as Thomas L. Wooley writes in his "Preface" to the first edition of Burton's *Pilgrimage*. He exonerates Burton by saying that the purpose of the author's story seems to be to illustrate the peculiarities of the people in order to dramatize, as it were, the dry journal of the journey. The explorer's involvement with the people of the land and his frequent insertions of their tales were geared toward the preservation of "the tone of the adventures, together with that local colouring which mainly consists of '*l'education d'un voyage*.'"[40] Burton is rarely melodramatic, yet he continually declares that there are certain scenes that imprint themselves upon the traveler's memory:

> night of stormy darkness of the Cape, and African tornado, and perhaps, most awful of all, a solitary journey over the sandy Desert. Of this class is a stroll through the thoroughfares of old Cairo by night. All is squalor in the brilliancy of noon-day. In darkness you see nothing but a silhouette. When, however, the moon is high in the heavens, and the summer starts to rain light upon God's world, there is something not of earth in the view.[41]

This apparent "esthetization" of the landscape – to use Pratt's favorite expression – reveals an ungoverned admiration for the beauty of the world, an appreciation that comes with firsthand knowledge of the places, not as a tourist but as one of the people. Against Said's allegation that an Orientalist could be regarded as a special agent of Western power, always on the lookout for new territorial acquisitions,[42] it can be said that Burton tries to be an insider, even though there are moments when he does perceive the Orient through his "Western" eyes. Then he is not ashamed or afraid to utter remarks of distaste: "This was another day truly orientally lost,"[43] he writes, describing Alexandria's "Foreign Office" whose doors were bolted with no explanation offered. Burton is not uncritical about the East, but he tries to emulate the ways of the inhabitants of the area. Consequently, undeterred by closed doors, Burton waited like everyone else, and "[o]n the morrow, however, I obtained permission, in the character of Dr. Abdullah, to visit any part of Egypt I pleased, and to retain possession of my dagger and pistols."[44] The pistols and other types of weapons

---

40 Wolley, "Introduction" to Burton's *Personal Narrative*, 1:xxvi.
41 Burton, *Personal Narrative*, 1:88–89.
42 Said, *Orientalism*, 223.
43 Burton, *Personal Narrative*, 1:22.
44 Burton, *Personal Narrative*, 1:22. Burton discloses that in Arabia, generally the wound is a lesser consideration in justice and revenge than the instrument with which it was inflicted. Sticks and stones in Arabia are held to be venial weapons, "guns and pistols, swords and

would prove handy on the road, as Burton tells us: "That night I slept with my Shugduf, for it would have been mere madness to sleep on the open plain in a place so infested by banditti."[45] Irrespective of his reservations, in Cairo, Burton becomes "an Oriental" and relinquishes his English passport. Said's "Travelling Theory," an essay that tracks how theories and ideas circulate – and in particular how they are adapted, transfigured, undone, reworked, and domesticated – argues that our identities are themselves "the product of travel and the conduit by which meaning moves and changes from place to place."[46] In a way, Burton's transformations are also the product of his travels, necessitated, as I have argued above, by the impossibility to enter the Muslim world as a Christian. That is why he continues to be cautious, because as "a 'new' Moslem," especially a Frank (*ifranij*), he could have been questioned about the sincerity of his devotions. What is more, there could have been a suspicion of the forced or feigned conversion. So he was quite rightly anxious that the Egyptians might "look upon him as a spy, and let him see as little of life as possible."[47]

Teeming with life, Cairo is for Burton both an intriguing and an unsafe place, for different nations are treated with varied degrees of hostility by the Egyptians. "If you claimed that you were not Persian but "an Indian under British Protection," Burton writes, the guards could claim that they found you "without a lantern, dead-drunk, beating respectable people, breaking into houses, invading and robbing harims."[48] Equally unpleasant consequences awaited a European: "You would either have been dismissed at once, or sent to your Consul, who is here judge, jury, and jailor. Egyptian authority has of late years lost half its prestige."[49] Nonetheless, throughout his journey, he remained true to his original purpose to see the Arab world from the inside. More often than not, he does not

---

daggers, are felonious" (1:229). Burton likes the veil on women because it conceals "coarse skins, fleshy noses, wide mouths, and vanishing chins" and shows the art most to the woman's advantage, the eyes (1:229). He describes an Arab sheikh in a picturesque dress (1:234–235), and he knows all the important names for the articles of clothing. He also enumerates different types of weapons such as *yambiah*, the crooked dagger, and points out the veil that is used at the Ka'abah, quoting the poet Abd al-Rahim al Bura'i: "And Meccah's bride (i.e., the Ka'abah) is displayed with (miraculous) signs" (2:212). He sees the similarities between the face-veil and the covering of the temple. He also draws attention to the pre-Mohammedan history of the Ka'abah, which was supposedly Jewish; the Muslims simply took over the temple together with the covering (2:212–13). The temple is guarded by eunuchs.

45 Burton, *Personal Narrative*, 1:270.
46 Quoted in Euben, *Journeys*, 12.
47 Burton, *Personal Narrative*, 1:23.
48 Burton, *Personal Narrative*, 1:120–21.
49 Burton, *Personal Narrative*, 1:121.

Chapter 2 *Al-Ifranij* among the Believers, or the Victorian Quest Romance(d) — 49

praise the wonders of the East but instead concentrates on the mundane affairs that can be troublesome to the unprepared visitor; however, in Baconian fashion, he constantly stresses the educative experience of his stay, trying to provide good advice to future travelers:[50]

> In the generality of barbarous countries you must either proceed, like Bruce, preserving the "dignity of manhood": and carrying matters with a high hand, or you must warm your way by timidity and subservience; in fact, by becoming an animal too contemptible for man to let or injure.[51]

In preparation for his onward journey out of Cairo, Burton began collecting provisions as well as necessities for the trip, such as a tent, water skins, and so on. He noticed that Suez was not friendly toward Muslim pilgrims, but he could no longer reveal his English identity. He consulted an acquaintance of his, Haji Wali, about a sum that would make him "a temporary subject of the Shah." They found a dragoman, a member of a tribe Levantine and Christian and

---

[50] He tells the readers that those traveling as Orientals should always have a change of clothes, especially clothes for special occasions. He also had a goat-skin water bag, which when new has "hardly an attractive flavor of tanno-gelatine," and a roll of canvas with threads and needles, "most useful in lands where tailors abound not; besides which, the sight of a man darning his coat or patching his slippers teems with pleasing ideas of humility." Burton, *Personal Narrative*, 1:24. He also had a dagger, a brass inkstand, and a penholder together with a rosary, which could be used as a weapon, and money he had hidden in a belt. "This is the Asiatic method of concealing valuables, and one more civilized than ours in the last century, when Roderick Random and his companion 'sewed their money between the lining and the waistband of their breeches'" (1:24–25). "A pair of common native Khurjin, or saddle-bags contained my wardrobe; the bed was readily rolled up into a bundle; and for a medicine chest I bought a pea-green box with red and yellow flowers, capable of standing falls from a camel twice a day" (1:26).

[51] Burton, *Personal Narrative*, 1:22–23. Later in Cairo he provides information about the local administration. "The 'Wakálah,' as the Caravanserai or Khan is called in Egypt, combines the offices at hotel, lodging-house, and store. It is at Cairo, as at Constantinople, a massive pile of buildings surrounding a quadrangular 'Hosh' or court-yard. On the ground floor are rooms like caverns for merchandise, and shops of different kinds – tailors, cobblers, bakers, tobacconists, fruiterers, and others. A roofless gallery or a covered verandah, into which all the apartments open, runs round the first and sometimes the second story: the latter, however, is usually exposed to the sun and wind. The accommodation consists of sets of two or three rooms, generally an inner one and an outer; the latter contains a hearth for cooking, a bathing-place, and similar necessaries. The staircases are high narrow, and exceedingly dirty; dark at night, and often in bad repair; a goat or donkey is tethered upon the different landings; here and there a fresh skin is stretched in process of tanning, a smell reminds the veteran traveler of those closets in the old French. There he calls himself a Turkish pilgrim. In the spirit of a Victorian gentleman, he informs the readers that he paid quite dearly for "comfortless rooms" and for the man who washed and swept the rooms" (1:41–42).

supposedly prone to corruption;⁵² and so with the help of Shaykh Muhammad, Burton becomes an Afghani:

> The clerk filled up a printed paper in the Turkish language, apparently borrowed from the European method for spoiling the traveler; certified me, upon the Shaykh's security, to be one Abdullah, the son of Yúsuf (Joseph), originally from Kábul, described my person, and, in exchange for five piastres, handed me the document.⁵³

This is how Burton began the first of his transformations. His clandestine exploits substantiating the assertions of bribery play into Said's indignation at such representations. Elsewhere, Burton explains that Oriental hospitality necessitates leaving a present for the man who has admitted him into his house, though they would be offended at an offer of remuneration. He notices that "[s]hame is a passion with Eastern nations. Your host would blush to point out to you the indecorum of your conduct; and the laws of hospitality oblige him to supply the every want of a guest, even though he be *détenu*."⁵⁴

Recounting the generosity of the people, Burton points to the communal way of life of the Arabs, as opposed to "our solitary habits." On a steamboat to Cairo, Burton met the polite Khudabakhsh, who invited him to spend some time in his house. Burton was glad to receive such an invitation and remained there some ten days or a fortnight. "But at the end of that time my patience was thoroughly exhausted. My host had become a civilized man, who sat on chairs, who ate with a fork, who talked European politics, and who had learned to admire, if not to understand, liberty – liberal ideas!"⁵⁵ Indeed, Burton's flight from the

---

52 Burton, *Personal Narrative*, 1:128. At Suez, "the people of the country were determined that an English fleet would soon appear in the Red Sea, and this fort is by them ridiculously considered the key of Suez" (1:157). Depictions of thievery and greed abound. Burton also quotes fragments of a letter from Mr. Levick about Suez and the Suezians. Asserting that from the year 1851–1852 to 1852–1853, the number of pilgrims shrank, Levick insists that the people of Suez are a "finer and fairer race than the Cairenes" (1:176). It is typical that if anyone rises to prominence, he "publicly complains that the Christians are all in all, and that in these evil days Al-Islam is going to destruction." Levick suspects that there are secret meetings as well. He claims that the Egyptian, despite a nonchalant disposition to merriment, is prone to insurrection "when the blood is up" (1:183–84).
53 Burton, *Personal Narrative*, 1:131.
54 Burton, *Personal Narrative*, 1:36–37.
55 Burton, *Personal Narrative*, 1:35–36. Moreover, "we English have a peculiar national quality, which the Indians, with their characteristic acuteness, soon perceived, and described by an opprobrious name. Observing our solitary habits, that we could not, and would not sit and talk and sip sherbet and smoke with them, they called us 'Jangli,' wild men, fresh caught in the jungle and sent to rule over the land of Hind" (1:35–36). "This year Id [or the Eid festival, which ends the long month of fast, Ramadan] was made gloomy, comparatively speaking, by

rational, ordered, and inexorably boring British upper-class world cannot stand comparison with the strange and exciting, because largely unknown, East. Burton is, however, British born and bred, used to certain comforts, and his Britishness is exhibited in the following comment about an East Indian who: "Like the fox in the fable,[56] fulsomely flattering at first, . . . gradually becomes easily friendly, disagreeably familiar, offensively rude, which ends by rousing the 'spirit of the British lion.'"[57] The literary parallels can also be detected in the animosity between Albanians and Egyptians; as Burton reports, the Albanians, in a rather medieval manner, call the Egyptians a "race of dogs."[58] In medieval romances, the Saracens who in *The Song of Roland* "yelp like hounds"[59] are frequently disrespected with derogatory appellations of "heathen hounds" and "black dogs." Notwithstanding the criticism, the time spent in the native household is as interesting as it is exasperating for Burton, whose clarifications make us aware how different are the Western and Eastern ideas concerning guests. The very essence of Oriental hospitality, which he refers to as the "old barbarous" one, is characterized by the lack of retreat for a guest.[60] The absence of the distinction between private and public space is perhaps the most acutely felt contrast between the West and the East, with the East praising the collective –

---

the state of politics. Reports of war with Russia, with France, with England, who was going to land three million men at Suez, and with Infideldom in general rang through Egypt, and the city of Mars [he believes that Káhirah is the "City of Káhir," or Mars the Planet] became unusually martial. The government armouries, arsenals, and manufactories, were crowded with kidnapped workmen. Those who purposed a pilgrimage feared forcible detention. Wherever men gathered together, in the Mosques, for instance, or the coffee-houses, the police closed the doors, and made forcible capture of the able-bodied" (1:117–18). The streets were filled with wretches marching to be made soldiers. "The dismal impression of the scene was deepened by crowds of women, who habited in mourning, and scattering dust and mud over rent garments, followed their sons, brothers, and husbands, with cries and shrieks. The death-wail is a peculiar way of cheering on the patriot departing *pro patria mori*, and the origin of the custom is characteristic of the people" (1:118).

56 Reynard the Fox is one of the most famous medieval characters from beast fables. His story is used by Chaucer in his "Nun's Priest's Tale" and by Caxton, who translated the French version of Reynard the Fox.

57 Burton, *Personal Narrative*, 1:37.

58 Burton, *Personal Narrative*, 1:139. Elsewhere, he comments on the Greeks, who are hated in Arabia for being "clever scoundrels, ever ready to do Al-Islam a mischief," and continues: "The Maltese, the greatest of cowards off their own ground, are regarded with a profound contempt: these are the protégés which bring the British nation into disrepute at Cairo. The Italians are known chiefly as 'istruttori' and 'distruttori' – doctors, druggists, and pedagogues" (1:111). As is clear, cultural stereotypes are a universal human response to the Other.

59 *The Song of Roland*, l. 3527.

60 Burton, *Personal Narrative*, 1:36–37.

within the male community, that is – ways of life, and the West idolizing privacy and private space. No wonder Burton feels his patience severely tried, "when from the hour you rise to the time you rest, you must ever be talking or listening, you must converse yourself to sleep in a public dormitory, and give ear to your companions' snores and mutterings at midnight."[61] Interestingly, Levi-Strauss observes that in Muslim culture it is difficult to conceive of solitude, as Islam "sees life as being first and foremost a communal affair."[62]

Except for occasional grumbling, Burton nonetheless does not demean the Muslim way of life. He does, however, indicate various aberrations, such as the (ab)use of alcohol in a case involving an Albanian captain of the Irregulars, Ali Agha.[63] The adventure took place immediately before Burton's departure from Cairo. They communicated in Turkish, of which they both knew a few words. The Captain invited Burton to his quarters. "I refused to do so [to acquiesce] during the day, but wishing to see how these men sacrifice to Bacchus, promised compliance that night." He found the Captain sitting in a room in full light – "all Orientals hate drinking in any but a bright light" – but does not offer any explanation as to why it happens.[64] Instead, he explains an elaborate drinking ritual with Ali Agha, which was connected with masking the odor of alcohol (*araki*) with perfume.[65] Drunken soldiers are dangerous anywhere in the world, and so, expecting a brawl, Burton left. Because of this incident, involving the substance forbidden by Shari'a, Haji Wali urged Burton to leave Cairo and start his pilgrimage at once. This was one of the adventures in the style of the Victorian quest romance – risky, yet necessary to push the traveler onto the road again.

True to an Arab proverb – "conceal thy Tenets, thy Treasure, and thy Travelling"[66] – Burton spread the word that his destination was Meccah via Jeddah, though in reality he wanted to reach Medina first. Theft was one of the most commonly committed crimes on the road, despite being punished with the cutting off of a hand in Shari'a. That is why Burton was always troubled by the fear

---

61 Burton, *Personal Narrative*, 1:36.
62 Levi-Strauss, *Tristes Tropiques*, 400.
63 Burton, *Personal Narrative*, 1:134. He refers to the Irregulars once more when he reports the parade of the Arnaut Irregular horse, which prompts him to make a comparison with Western drills, which are never good with horses, and "whose riding-drill never made a good rider, whose horses are over-weighted, and whose swords are worthless" (1:268). In spite of calling the riders "Semi-barbarians," he does admire their skills.
64 Burton, *Personal Narrative*, 1:135.
65 Burton, *Personal Narrative*, 1:137.
66 Burton, *Personal Narrative*, 1:140.

of losing his possessions. Neither he nor his fellow travelers, however, were deterred from undertaking the Hajj. Later in the text, Burton refers to a place called Yanbu'a, which in Arabic means "a Fountain." This place shares with others the title of "Gates of the Holy City," as it lies on the road between Cairo and Meccah. In Yanbu'a, pilgrims leave behind "goods too heavy to be transported in haste, or too valuable to risk in dangerous times."[67] The leitmotif of oriental thievery, thus, is one of the recurring motifs of his adventures. Even in his oriental disguise, during his quest Burton is still a "knight of the empire," to use Girouard's expression,[68] considering valor, honor, and honesty as important qualities. Although he detects the remains of "the chivalry of the desert"[69] amongst the Arabs in Medina, he nevertheless allows himself a negative comment concerning the Madanis: "It is not to be believed that in a town garrisoned by Turkish troops, full of travelled traders, and which supports itself by plundering Hajis, the primitive virtues of the Arab would exist."[70] Mecca and Medina were equally important in the Prophet's life, leading to an ongoing rivalry between the inhabitants of the two cities. Being dispassionate toward either group, Burton cites the prejudices existing between the Madanis and the Meccans:

> The Meccans, a dark people, say of the Madani that their hearts are as black as their skins are white. This is of course, exaggerated; but it is not too much to assert that pride, pugnacity, a peculiar point of honour and vindictiveness of wonderful force and patience, are the only characteristic traits of Arab character which the citizens of Al-Madinah habitually display.[71]

He also exposes an interesting disagreement concerning the holiness of the two places: Mecca and Medina. "The general consensus of Al-Islam admits the superiority of the Bayt Allah ("House of God") at Meccah to the whole world; and

---

67 Burton, *Personal Narrative*, 1:225. On the road from Bir Abbas to Al-Madinah, Burton is constantly conscious of thieves and the necessity to guard his belongings. Such dangers were also part and parcel of medieval pilgrimages.
68 Girouard, *Return to Camelot*, 220.
69 Burton, *Personal Narrative*, 2:19. He notes that "The Hindu Pandits assert that Shiva and his spouse under the forms and names of Kapot-Eshwara (pigeon god) and Kapotesi, dwelt at Meccah" (2:174). This time Burton avoids any negative commentary and tamps down his obsession with thieves. He remarks that the Meccan pigeons, resembling those of Venice, are held as sacred. For the first time, Burton feels safe in an Arab town, with people sleeping everywhere "upon cots placed opposite their open doors" (2:177). He describes going to the mosque at Arafat and at the sacred site of the "Mountain of Mercy" (2:192).
70 Burton, *Personal Narrative*, 2:18. Burton also reports his visit to Jeddah, which for him was in the "perpetual state of commotion, owing to the perpetual passage of pilgrims, and provisions were for the same reason scarce and dear" (2:269).
71 Burton, *Personal Narrative*, 2:18–19.

declares Al-Madinah to be more venerable than every part of Meccah."[72] Traditionally, Mohammed asserted that

> "One prayer in this my Mosque is more efficacious than a thousand in other places, save only the Masjid al-Harim. It is therefore the visitor's duty, as long as he stays at Al-Madinah, to pray there *the five times per diem*, to pass the day in it reading the Koran, and the night, if possible, in watching and devotion."[73]

Notwithstanding each city's importance, the Meccans perceive themselves as superior to the inhabitants of Medina, while the latter group stresses that theirs is Al-Madinah, *the* City.[74] As Edward Rice explains, the visit to Medina grants the pilgrim the title of Zair, and only after the visit to Mecca can one use the title Haji,[75] and this is taken as the decisive argument in favor of Mecca. Still, both places have a number of important places, the must-see for the faithful.

In keeping with the demands of the genre, Burton includes a number of anthropological descriptions of the Arab races:

> The Arab may be divided into three races – a classification which agrees equally well with genesitic genealogy, the traditions of the country, and the observations of modern physiologists. The first race, indigens or autochtones, are those sub-Caucasian tribes which may still be met with in the province of Mahrah, and generally along the coast between Maskat and Hazramut. The Mahrah, the Janábah and the Gara especially show a low development, for which hardship and privation alone will not satisfactorily account. These are Arab al-Aribah for whose inferiority oriental fable accounts as usual by thaumaturgy.[76]

---

[72] Burton, *Personal Narrative*, 1:306. He continues writing about the people of Al-Madinah, which he maintains contained a few families descended from the Prophet's Auxiliaries, and points out their genealogies (2:1). "The Sanctity of the city attracts strangers, who, purposing to stay but a short time, become residents" (2:5).
[73] Burton, *Personal Narrative*, 1:305.
[74] Burton, *Personal Narrative*, 1:378.
[75] Rice, *Captain Sir Richard Burton*, 258.
[76] Burton, *Personal Narrative*, 2:76–77. Elsewhere, Burton makes ethnographical observations about "Sinaitic clans," claiming that by virtue of facial features one could not mistake a true Egyptian for any other; he calls them the "Nilotic" race (1:146). "I therefore believe the Turi Badawin to be an impure race, Syro-Egyptian, whereas their neighbor the Hijazi is the pure Syrian or Mesopotamian." Burton quotes Sir John Mandeville, who portrays the Tawarah tribes as "folke fulle of alle evylle condiciouns." In a footnote, he adds: "The Osmanlis have, as usual, a semi-religious tradition to account for the superiority of their nation over the Egyptians" (2:147). Yet he found the Tawarah still retained many characteristics of the Badawi race: "The most good-humoured and sociable of men, they delight in a jest, and may readily be managed by kindness and courtesy. Yet they are passionate, nice upon points of honour, revengeful, and easily offended, where their peculiar prejudices are misunderstood. I have always found them pleasant companions, and deserving of respect, for their hearts are good, and their courage is beyond a doubt" (1:148).

He further explains that "Oriental ethnography, which, like most Eastern sciences, luxuriates in nomenclative distinction, recognizes a fourth race under the name of Arab al-Mustajamah. These 'barbarized Arabs' are now represented by such a population as that of Meccah." Discussing the Badawi (Bedouins) of Al-Hijaz, he highlights elements such as skulls, complexion, temperament, and so on;[77] even the length of the thumb, which is long, "extending almost to the first joint of the index,"[78] just as it does in the Celtic race, is of importance for him. He contends that "[t]he Arab's dress marks his simplicity; it gives him a nationality . . . It is remarkably picturesque."[79] Clearly, in such comments the author positions himself as an outsider, a Westerner, even though he always tries to deliver a neutral image of Arabia and its peoples. To strengthen the accuracy of his observations, he provides illustrations, for example of the Badawi heads and headdresses.[80] He rarely discusses the poverty of the region,[81] but concentrates on the rituals of the nomadic life: "The ceremonies of Badawi life are few and simple – circumcisions, marriages, and funerals. Of the former rite there are two forms, *Tahrah*, as usual in Al-Islam, and *Salkh*, an Arab invention. . . . On such occasions feastings and

---

77 Burton, *Personal Narrative*, 2:79–123.
78 Burton, *Personal Narrative*, 2:83.
79 Burton, *Personal Narrative*, 2:115.
80 Burton, *Personal Narrative*, 2:80–81. He then proceeds to recount some stories of bravery, mentioning in passing that guns and pistols were introduced to the Badawi at ten times the price in England. Burton makes a racist and probably not a particularly popular comparison between Arabs and American Indians, claiming: "The Arabs plunder pilgrims; the Indians, bands of trappers; both glory in forays, raids, and cattle-lifting; and both rob according to certain rules. Both are alternately brave to desperation, and shy of danger. Both are remarkable for nervous and powerful eloquence; dry humour, satire, whimsical tales, frequent tropes; boasts, and ruffling style; pithy proverbs, extempore songs, and languages wondrous in their complexity. Both, recognizing no other occupation but war and the chase, despise artificers and the effeminate people of cities, as the game-cock spurns the vulgar roosters of the poultry-yard. The chivalry of the Western worlds, like that of the Eastern wilds, salutes the visitor by a change of cavalry, by discharging guns, and by wheeling around him with shouts and yells. The 'brave' stamps, a red hand joins his mouth to show that he has drunk the blood of a foe" (2:118–19).
81 Burton quite frequently brings up his financial arrangements and difficulties. Outside Mecca one finds "Sittna Hawwa, the Mother of Mankind," which is Eve's tomb. *Personal Narrative*, 2:273. "On leaving the graveyard I offered the guardian a dollar, which he received with a remonstrance that a man of my dignity should give so paltry a fee. Nor was he at all contented with the assurance that nothing more could be expected from an Afghan Darwaysh, however pious" (2:275). Burton later found out that he was mistaken for Pasha Al-Madina (2:276). When visiting the mosque at Al-Kuba, he worried more and more about the state of his purse, or rather pouch (1:411), as the pilgrimaging in Arabia is, as always, costly. Doughty also draws attention to Eve's grave (which is now in Jeddah). *Arabia Deserta*, 2:536–39.

merrymaking take place as at our christenings."[82] What he is alluding to in the above quotation is both male and female circumcision, the latter, as WHO reports, still practiced in Africa and countries around the world.[83] Marked as a particularly atrocious ritual,[84] Female Genital Mutilation has been performed to assure their chastity, as female sexual desire was supposed to be ten times stronger than that of the male.[85] Apparently, the issue was included in the first version of his *Personal Narrative of a Pilgrimage to Al-Madinah and Meccah*, but his editor, as Rice holds, withdrew the material as too controversial.[86]

Describing the Bedouin society, Burton does not forgo a condescending comment that "[i]n their leonine society the sword is the greater administrator of law," as if adhering to the Latin saying that when arms speak, laws are silent (*inter arma enim silent leges*), and observes that inter-group relations are either *Ashab, Kiman*, or *Akhwan*. *Ashab* means "comrades bound by oath of an alliance offensive and defensive, they intermarry and are closely connected." He clarifies that *Kiman* denotes foes, or tribes between whom the blood feud exists; and *Akhwat* refers to the ties of brotherhood between the stranger and the Badawi, the latter asserting "an immemorial and inalienable right to the soil upon which his forefathers fed their flocks."[87] His narrative exposes his learning, as Burton definitely sees the alien culture as an "inside observer," and such a *contradictio in adjecto* points to the constant negotiations in his recounted adventures. In spite of all his attempts at open-mindedness, he can be patronizingly arrogant at times, and his generalizations concerning the "Orientals" weaken his apparent comprehension of Arabia.

When looking at The Apostle's Well in Al-Madinah, Burton suggests that the Arabs are curious and proud about water and their wells, and they even

---

82 Burton, *Personal Narrative*, 2:111. He adds, "During Wahabi rule it was forbidden under pain of death, but now the people have returned to it. The usual age for Taharah is between five and six; among some classes, however, it is performed ten years later."
83 See the novel *Lyrics Alley* by Aboulela. In Ahdaf Soueif's *The Map of Love*, analyzed below, an Egyptian character conscious of the stereotypical representations of Egyptian culture is certain that an American journalist cum her cousin will ask about "the fundamentalists, the veil, the cold peace, polygamy, women's status in Islam, female genital mutilation . . . " (6).
84 https://www.who.int/news-room/fact-sheets/detail/female-genital-mutilation.
85 Rice, *Captain Sir Richard Burton*, 259.
86 Rice, *Captain Sir Richard Burton*, 259–60. Sexuality was one of the taboo topics in Victorian Britain. Closely linked with the idea of respectability, on the one hand, and pornography on the other, it was rarely discussed by non-professionals. Burton's interest in the sexual mores of different societies would have shocked his Victorian readership. For further discussion see Marcus, *The Other Victorians*, and Mason, *The Making of Victorian Sexuality*.
87 Burton, *Personal Narrative*, 2:113.

take the trouble to weigh the produce of their wells; the lighter the water, "the more digestible and wholesome it is considered." Arabian viewpoints concerning medicine are for both Burton and Doughty a source of information about the culture. While still in Cairo, Burton presented himself as a physician, which afforded him the possibility of closer encounters with the Egyptians. Even though based on a lie, because Burton had no medical training, he used common knowledge of the basic ailments and the medicaments he brought with him from England. His "medical practice" gave him the freedom to observe the people among whom he lived, and thus he dutifully describes his first success in curing the slaves of a neighbor, an Arab slave dealer. The slaves were mostly Abyssinian women, whom Burton characterizes as:

> the steatopygous Abyssinian breed, broad-shouldered, thin-flanked, fine-limbed, and with haunches of a prodigious size. None of them had handsome features, but the short curly hair that stands on end being concealed under a kerchief there, there was something pretty in the brow, eyes, and upper part of the nose, coarse and sensual in the pendent lips, large jowl and projecting mouth, whilst the whole had a combination of piquancy with sweetness.[88]

The use of the adjective "sensual" brings to the fore the Orientalist feminization of the East, recapped in travel narratives and refashioned in Victorian quest romances. In the former, Arabia is weak, irrational, and voiceless, a land to be taken by the strong, rational, and outspoken masculine explorers. In the latter, the Oriental and African female characters, once their help and (presumably sexual) services are no longer needed, sacrifice their lives for the great white men. It has to be stressed, however, that the images of the feminized East in imperial discourse are reinforced by the existence of slavery. The discussion of slavery – without, however, passing judgement on its horrors or merits – is reiterated in *Personal Narrative* a number of times. In the nineteenth century, slavery was the norm in the Orient, as it was in America at the time. Yet Burton's remarks seem to play into the present-day criticism of his work that pinpoints the theme of sexualizing the Orient through bondage. The anticlimactic question "Why don't you buy me?"[89] posed to Burton to end his flirting, does nothing to alter his attitudes

---

[88] Burton, *Personal Narrative*, 1:59. Burton supplements his narrative with a lot of details. He also hears dogs fighting in the streets, deeming them superior to and stronger than the dogs in Cairo (1:301–2).

[89] Burton, *Personal Narrative*, 1:60. Burton offers his views on slavery in Egypt: "England has already learned that slaves are not necessarily the most wretched and degraded of men. Some have been bold enough to tell the British public that, in the generality of Oriental countries, the serf fares far better than the servant, or indeed the poorer orders of freemen. . . . The laws of Mahomet enjoin his followers to treat slaves with the greatest mildness, and the Moslems are in general scrupulous observers of the Apostle's recommendation. Slaves are considered

toward the female slaves. He sees their condition in the context of the scholarly attitudes to Hispano-Arabic medieval poetry prevalent at the time. He comprehends that the influence of Arabic poetry on the European notions of chivalry and "love" was insurmountable,[90] and asserts that the spiritualizing of sexuality is a universal human feature attested throughout the centuries. Nevertheless, he takes a rather malicious satisfaction in writing that in medieval Christian Europe "[c]ertain 'Fathers of the Church' . . . did not believe that women have souls. The Moslems never went so far."[91] Finding himself in a male-dominated society, Burton nonetheless portrays the "native" women whenever he can. In Mecca, for example, he reports an encounter with a young woman of about eighteen, whose complexion, as he sees it, is "somewhat citrine-coloured," with "soft and clear, symmetrical eyebrows, the most beautiful eyes, and a figure of grace." He likes her because she does not reveal any "elegant barbarisms"[92] such as bending of the toe. Unwittingly, though he ran away from Europe, his views on beauty are very much the creation of his Western upbringing. During his stay in the house of Shaykh Hamid he is happy, though he never sets eyes on a woman: "unless the African slave girls be allowed that title. Even these at first attempted to draw their ragged veils over their sable charms, and would not answer the simplest questions; by degrees they allowed me to see them, and they ventured their voices[93] to reply to me; still they never threw off a certain appearance of shame."[94] Here and elsewhere, he regards even free women as a marketable commodity, noticing

---

members of the family, and in houses where free servants are also kept, they seldom do any other work than filling the pipes, presenting the coffee, accompanying their masters when going out, rubbing his feet when he takes his nap in the afternoon, and driving away the flies from him. When a slave is not satisfied, he can legally compel his master to sell him" (1:61). Burton reports that he tried to get a servant but that the person he had chosen, known as Ali the Berberi, stabbed his fellow servant and was punished by law with dismissal and four hundred lashes to his feet. Burton makes a summary of the costs of living in Cairo, and it turns out to be quite an expensive place (1:65). He finally found a servant whose "swarthy skin and chubby features made the Arabs always call him an Abyssinian slave," which was good for his disguise (1:64).

90 For more on this topic, see Nykl, *Hispano-Arabic Poetry*.
91 Burton, *Personal Narrative*, 2:92.
92 Burton, *Personal Narrative*, 2:197.
93 Burton, *Personal Narrative*, 1:297. Burton reports that a boy, Mohammed, reported seeing a very pretty woman – who was not veiled – fanning herself. He wanted to "shame" her by asking her to marry him (1:303).
94 He embarks on a discussion of other people traveling through the orient like a certain Miss Martineau, who visited a "harim" (Burton's spelling) in Egypt and wept over "the degradation of her sex," drawing "sundry strong and unsavory comparisons between the harim and certain haunts of vice in Europe" (2:91).

that "[t]he youth in Al-Hijaz is not married till his father can afford to buy him a bride."[95]

Apart from his observations concerning Arab women, other important aspects of Burton's *Personal Narrative* are his comments concerning religion and education. While watching the activities of a mosque, Burton ironically scrutinizes the system of education, noticing that boys of four and five are made to chant the Koran without understanding it, and that the main principle of education is "the Green Rod . . . of the Trees of Paradise."[96] Although usually supportive and sympathetic, in this instant Burton is far from admiring of the educational methods, which are based on solely memorizing the material rather than analyzing and understanding it.[97] The Koranic schools and their principles of learning have never ceased to mystify Western travelers, since, at the time, European schools and universities already prided themselves in being at the forefront of logical thinking and self-development through discussion. In contrast, Burton reports that in Arabia young boys are taught to intone the Koran, and later "at the university they are taught a more exact system of chanting." The technique, habitual in Muslim countries, is called "Hafs."[98] Though critical of the system, Burton nonetheless does not agree with Dr. Bowring, who dismisses the Mohammedan schooling for priesthood; Burton is more open-minded, seeing that:

> both [the systems of the law] are eminently adapted for the Oriental mind. When the people learn to appreciate ethics and to understand psychics and aesthetics, the demand will create a supply. Meanwhile they leave transcendentalism to their poets and philosophers, and they busy themselves with preparing for heaven by practicing the only part of their faith now intelligible to them – the Material.[99]

Burton's scrutiny of the demands of Islam as regards the clergy is tainted by his intense dislike of Christian missionaries who encouraged racial segregation, on the one hand endorsing the idea of white supremacy while on the other hand courting the notion of the intrinsic equality of whites and blacks in the eyes of

---

95 Burton, *Personal Narrative*, 2:111. He also repeatedly talks about pilgrims' costumes (2:139): "the *Izar* wrapped round the loins from waist to knee, and, knotted or tucked in at the middle, supports itself."
96 Burton, *Personal Narrative*, 1:103. Burton pictures the Azhar, the grand collegiate mosque of the city; it is also a center of study, with about 150 professors bearing the title "Teacher in Al Azhar" (1:103). The teaching and reciting of the Koran is one of the fundamental differences between the educational systems of the West and the East. For the primacy of oral transmission, see Schoeler, *The Genesis of Literature in Islam*.
97 Burton, *Personal Narrative*, 1:105.
98 Burton, *Personal Narrative*, 1:107.
99 Burton, *Personal Narrative*, 1:109–10.

the Christian God. Burton's criticism is deeply rooted in his atheism. For him the Hajj is not a religious but a cultural experience, and adventure as much as a quest to understand Islam. Consequently, his narrative is saturated with what we might now call sightseeing details. In the vicinity of Medina, he enumerates the Mosque of Kuba, the Cemetery Al-Bakia, and the martyr Hamzah's tomb at the foot of Mount Ohod.[100] It is believed that in the Mustrah resting place, the Prophet sat for a few minutes on his way to the battle of Ohod. In order to honor that event, "[d]evout Moslems visit Ohod every Thursday morning after the dawn devotions in the Harim; pray for the Martyrs; and after going through the ceremonies, return to the Harim in time for midday worship."[101] True to his calling, he reports the visit to the saint's cemetery, and the Al-Aqsa Mosque, which is deemed to be the one in which the Prophet prayed on the first Friday after his flight from Mecca.[102] Mecca, the birthplace of the Prophet, boasts the Black Stone or Ka'abah where "[t]he Prophet used to weep when he touched the Black Stone, and said that it was the place for the pouring forth of tears."[103] The site is supposedly that of an ancient temple attributed to the prophet Ibrahim (Abraham). It holds the most sacred relic of Islam, the stone sent from the heavens[104] that came to earth together with Adam.[105] Burton, not unlike Victorian historians, discerns:

---

[100] Burton, *Personal Narrative*, 1:398.
[101] Burton, *Personal Narrative*, 1:424. He amends his narrative with observations concerning various cultural characteristics: "The citizens delight in speaking of dates as an Irishman does of potatoes, with a manner of familiar fondness; they eat them for medicine as well as food" (1:402). He juxtaposes this remark with the comment on "[t]he Nebek, Lote, or Jujube, [which] is here a fine large tree with a dark green leaf, roundish and polished like the olive; it is armed with a short curved, and sharp thorn, and bears a pale straw coloured berry, about the size of the gooseberry, with red streaks on the side next the sun. Little can be said in favor of the fruit, which has been compared successively by disappointed 'Lotus Eaters' to a bad plum, an unripe cherry, and an insipid apple" (1:405). Doughty also writes about the things he tastes, as we shall see, stressing the differences. He notes, for example, the diet of the nomads, marveling at the fact that they like to eat wolf meat; the wolf, according to Doughty, was eaten in medieval Europe. "The Aarab think the flesh medicinal." Doughty, *Arabia Deserta*, 1:327; spelling original. Doughty finds yet another strange victual to be the locust that the women collect and fry: "early locust, toasted, is reckoned a sweet-meat in town and in the desert" (1:204, 336). Dates, which are an important part of the desert diet, feature in Burton's as well as Doughty's narratives, and the latter describes the date harvest (1:538–40). Curiously, Doughty also clarifies that dogs are not particularly liked by the Arabs and are mistreated, like the starveling hounds following the nomads (1:337).
[102] Burton, *Personal Narrative*, 2:45.
[103] Burton, *Personal Narrative*, 2:164.
[104] Bokhari and Seddon, *Complete Illustrated Guide*, 13, 19.
[105] Bokhari and Seddon, *Complete Illustrated Guide*, 159.

"Al-Islam, grown splendid and powerful, determined to surpass other nations in the magnificence of its public buildings."[106] In Mecca, the mosque is guarded by attendant Eunuchs and closed immediately after night prayers, but in Ramadan and the pilgrimage season, "when pious visitors pay considerable fees there to pass the night in meditation and prayer," then the mosque is open for them.[107] In the mosque, Burton once more put himself in danger, because when other pilgrims were praying, he was sketching the floor plan on his white ihram, knowing that if caught, he could easily be killed.

Besides seeing the places of the cult, the true pilgrim, the Haji, must partake of all the difficulties of voyaging in hostile environment, and Burton himself is privy to all the perils of nightly desert journeys, as "there is nothing more disagreeable than the Sariyah or night-march, and yet the people are inexorable about it."[108] To counter this unexcited statement, Burton quotes the Prophet, who said, "Choose early Darkness (daljah) for your Wayfarings," arguing that "the Calamities of the Earth (serpents and wild beasts) appear not at Night."[109] The pilgrims are scorched by the sun, they travel by night and rest during the day, but that is what "the Arabian traveler must expect."[110] In view of the Holy City, however, he behaves like a genuine Muslim, emulating, even if not wholeheartedly, the manners of the other pilgrims. "We halted our beasts as if by word of command. All of us descended, in imitation of the pious of old, and set down, jaded and hungry as we were, to feast our eyes with a view of the Holy City."[111] What is more, the panorama inspired many poetic exclamations that, as Burton asserts, are perfectly in order when Arabs are "under the influence of strong passion or religious enthusiasm."[112]

The Hajj or Greater Pilgrimage is essential, obligatory by Koranic order for every Muslim. Richard Barber maintains that the origins of the Hajj can be traced to the centuries before the beginning of Islam, because Mecca stands on "the two great routes which connect the Arabian coast with the hinterland." Some five hundred years before Mohammad's time there was a great fair and pilgrimage,

---

106 Burton, *Personal Narrative*, 1:364.
107 Burton, *Personal Narrative*, 1:333. Burton uses the expression "the blessed month Al-Ramazan."
108 Burton, *Personal Narrative*, 2:67.
109 Burton, *Personal Narrative*, 2:67.
110 Burton, *Personal Narrative*, 1:251.
111 Burton, *Personal Narrative*, 1:279.
112 Burton, *Personal Narrative*, 1:280. "The Shaykh, whose manners had changed with his garments, from the vulgar and boisterous to a certain staid courtesy, took my hand, and led me up to the Majlis (parlour), which was swept and garnished, with all due apparatus, for the forthcoming reception-ceremony" (1:290).

"the pilgrimage providing a kind of sacred truce among the warring tribes of the area during which it was possible to trade in safety."[113] Barber concurs with Muslim sources that Mohammed himself made the pilgrimage nine years after *hejira* in AD 631. The Hajj is therefore described in the Koran, and it is much more formal – including a number of rituals prescribed for each place and stage – than any Christian pilgrimage has ever been. Although the pilgrims usually travel much longer, the actual pilgrimage lasts ten days of the twelfth lunar month. The journey ends with Id al Adga, the Feast of Sacrifice; then, "hundreds of thousands of pilgrims flock to the sanctuary to perform the reformed or de-paganized rituals instituted by the Prophet during the final year of his life."[114] The ceremonies performed during the Hajj seem to alleviate the tedium of the long journey, and they include, for instance, circling the temple seven times and kissing the stone. The rite is called *The Tawaf*, and it is followed by *The Sal*, the seven-fold running between the hillocks of Safa and Marwa, the standing on the Plain of Arafat, and the "Tawáf" or circumambulation of the House of Allah at Mecca; the latter must never be performed at the Apostle's tomb.[115] Yet another noteworthy observance is the stoning of the three pillars representing the devil.[116] Even today, the ritual is still executed every year,[117] and it pertains to the symbolic casting out of evil from one's life. Burton's elaborate descriptions of the actions confirm the structured way in which the Muslim pilgrimage is conducted.[118] In contrast to many of his contemporaries, he understood the magnitude of the rules of the Hajj, warning his readers and prospective followers never to spit upon any part of the mosque or behave contemptuously toward any of the sacred

---

113 Barber, *Pilgrimages*, 31–32.
114 Ruthven, *Islam*, 30.
115 Burton, *Personal Narrative*, 1:305.
116 "Stoning the Jamaraat means throwing a certain number of pebbles in the specific places for stoning in Mina (the Jamaraat). It is one of the great rituals of the Hajj which the pilgrims do during a certain number of days in Mina. The Jamrah is not the pillar that is found in the middle of the basin surrounding it (the *marma*), rather the Jamrah is the basin surrounding this pillar. If a person's pebbles fall inside the basin that is allocated for stoning, then his stoning is valid and is acceptable, according to scholarly consensus. Imam al-Shaafa'i (may Allah have mercy on him) said: 'The minimum that is required in stoning is that he should throw so that his pebbles land in the place for pebbles. If he throws a pebble and cannot see it and he does not know where it fell, he should repeat it, and it does not count until he knows that it has fallen in the place of pebbles.'" Quoted from http://islamqa.info/en/126231.
117 "Chanting 'God is great,' an estimated 2.5 million Muslims yesterday stoned pillars representing the devil on the second day of their annual Hajj or pilgrimage, a day that marks the start of the Islamic holiday of Eid al-Adha." http://metro.co.uk/2011/11/07/eid-al-adha-festival-begins-muslim-pilgrims-stone-pillars-at-mecca-210935/.
118 Burton, *Personal Narrative*, 2:222.

Chapter 2 Al-Ifranij among the Believers, or the Victorian Quest Romance(d) — 63

Muslim sites, as this might be taken to be "the act of an Infidel."[119] It is worth remembering, however, that the Christian pilgrimage is likewise connected with the counting of steps, columns, and lanterns, which is related to the "ritual commemoration of important" events in the Holy Land, followed by the formation of vivid pictures that would enable lifelong reconstruction of these experiences.[120]

While the pilgrims concentrated on the inner side of their experiences, the travelers were frequently more attuned to the outer ones. Burton's narrative is thus saturated with ethnographic detail, for instance: the place called Shuhada, an hour's ride through Wady Sayyalah, derives its name from martyrs, supposedly some "forty braves that fell in one of Mohammed's many skirmishes."[121] Mohammed erected the first mosque "at Kubá, near Al-Madinah: shortly afterwards when he entered Meccah as a conqueror. . . . He destroyed the three hundred and sixty idols of the Arab Pantheon," in this way cleansing "that venerable building from its abominations."[122] The Muslim iconoclasm is one of the most misunderstood aspects of the religion, particularly aberrant in the medieval Saracen romances, which misrepresented Islam as a pagan religion based on the worship of the trinity of idols: Mohammed, Apollo, and Terragount, in itself a perverted Christian Trinity. In the romances such as *Octavian* or *King of Tars*, angry sultans pray to their "gods" to obtain victory over the Christians, only to smash their idols when the victory is not granted. One commonplace scene informing the vision of Islam as a pagan religion was the smashing of

---

119 Burton, *Personal Narrative*, 1:314. According to Burton, from the very beginning the shape of the Apostle's tomb was a mystery. "In one place he describes the coffin: in another he expressly declares that he entered the Hujarah when it was being repaired by Kaid-Bey, and saw in the inside three deep graves, but no traces of tombs. Either, then, the mortal remains of the Apostle had, despite Moslem superstition, mingled with the dust (a probable circumstance after nearly nine hundred years internment), or what is more likely, they had been removed by the Shi'ah schismatics who for centuries had charge of the sepulcher" (1:340–41). Burton does not want to challenge the official history, but "where a suspicion of fables arises from popular 'facts', a knowledge of man and of his manners teaches us to regard it with a favouring eye" (1:341). In Chapter XVII, entitled "An Essay Towards the History of the Prophet Mosque," Burton reproduces some known facts about the dispersing of the tribes after the flood. The Israelites were supposedly straying from the worship of the one true God, and God "raised up against them the Arab tribes of Aus and Khazraj, the progenitors of modern Ansar. Both of these tribes claimed a kindred origin, and Al-Yaman as the land of their nativity" (1:347–48).
120 Legassie, *The Medieval Invention of Travel*, 110–11.
121 Some authorities consider it the cemetery of the people of Wady Sayyalah; as stated by Burton, "Others attribute these graves to the Beni Salim, or Salmah, an extinct race of Hijazi Badawin." Burton, *Personal Narrative*, 1:274.
122 Burton, *Personal Narrative*, 1:91.

the idols,[123] which not only confirmed the shallowness of Saracen beliefs but also presented the irate sultans as rather silly and impotent, like raging two-year-olds throwing tantrums. The stock figures, their stereotypical presentation, and repeated insults are multiplied in the romances in question, whereas the Christian characters of Florent (*Octavian*) and Bishop Turpin (*The Siege of Milan*) display extraordinary courage in performing many chivalric feats, including the courageous, albeit secret, penetration of the enemy's camps. These tales reflected the undying crusading spirit and continually accentuate the authority of the Christian religion, in the region that was still thought of as Christian. While Burton does not recognize the Holy Land as a Christian territory, he nevertheless highlights the Muslim aversion to idolatry and stresses that it is forbidden to decorate the temples with statues and pictures. In their place, the shrines are filled "with quotations from the Koran, and inscriptions, 'plastic metaphysics,' of marvelous perplexity."[124]

Burton was aware that during his lifetime Mohammed had fought against idolatry and had not wanted either his person or his tomb as objects of a cult. The Prophet's tomb is therefore located in some isolation from other sights. Reportedly, Mohammed himself had stressed the imperative not to venerate his grave: "O Allah, cause not my Tomb to become an Object of Idolatrous Adoration! May Allah's Wrath fall heavy upon the people who make the Tombs of their Prophets Places of Prayer."[125] It is for this reason, as Burton suggests,

> that the site should not be visited in the Ihram or pilgrim dress; men should not kiss it, touch it with the hand, or press the bosom against it, as at the Ka'abah; or rub the face with dust collected near the sepulcher; and those who prostrate themselves before it, like certain ignorant Indians, are guilty of deadly sin.[126]

---

[123] In *The King of Tars*, ll. 646–57.
[124] Burton, *Personal Narrative*, 1:94–95.
[125] Burton, *Personal Narrative*, 1:314. The Prophet's tomb was also distinguished by a large pearl rosary, "the celebrated *Kaukab-al-Durri*, or constellation of pearls, suspended to the curtain breast-high" (1:322). Burton enumerates all the different pillars, for example Ayisha's Pillar (1:335). "And lastly is the Makam Jibrail (Gabriel's Place), for whose other name, Mirbaat al-Bair, 'the Pole of the Beast of Burden,' I have been unable to find an explanation" (1:336). Burton claims that illiterate visitors believe that the trees are the descendants of the trees planted by the Prophet's daughter (1:337). "Although every Moslem, learned and simple, firmly believes that Mohammed's remains are interred in the Hujrah at Al-Madinah, I cannot help suspecting that the place is doubtful as that of the Holy Sepulcher at Jerusalem. It must be remembered that a tumult followed the announcement of the Apostle's death, when the people, as often happens, believing him to be immortal, refused to credit the report, and even Omar threatened destruction to any one that asserted it" (1:339).
[126] Burton, *Personal Narrative*, 1:305.

Chapter 2 *Al-Ifranij* among the Believers, or the Victorian Quest Romance(d) — 65

In Brodie's view, most of Burton's biographers thought that he preferred Islam to Christianity, while in fact, he was "equally harsh in attacking what he believed to be the superstitions and banalities of both religions."[127]

Burton frequently recounts religious, cultural and ethnic peculiarities. Whenever his caravan rests, he always offers reflections about his fellow pilgrims. He notices that some participants, in particular those from Turkey, in order to show their devout motivation, carry "a Hamail," which is "a pocket Koran, in a handsome gold-embroidered crimson velvet or red morocco case, slung by red silk cords over the left shoulder. It must hang down by the right side, and should never depend below the waist-belt."[128] During Christian pilgrimages, even wealthy medieval pilgrims were symbolically transformed into poor palmers carrying palms as a sign that they had visited the Holy Land. Christians who put on their penitential cloaks become equal in the eyes of God; this is not the case during most of the Islamic pilgrimage where, even though all pilgrims are dressed in white clothes, one's affluence is displayed in many ways. For Burton, the Africans, traveling on alms only, "appeared of the lowest class; their garments consist of a Búrnus-cloak and a pair of sandals; their sole weapon a long knife, and their only stock a bag of dry provisions."[129] Burnus is the cheapest type of cloak, and the Magrabis "travel in hordes under a leader who obtains the temporary title of 'Maula' the master."[130] In Burton's view, this leader is "a burly savage,"[131] full of "superficial information" because he has traveled the same road before. He then reports a number of brawls, always connected with name calling,[132] which is all the more interesting as apparently neither Burton himself nor his companions could understand the Magrabi language.[133] Undermining the peacefulness and religiosity of the pilgrims, Burton attests to the innate belligerence of Muslims, as the Magrabis, "hearing that the Persians were Rafaz (heretics) crowded fiercely round to do a little Jihad, or Fighting for the Faith."[134]

In spite of all the preaching of peace and the noble aims of such journeys, Muslim as well as Christian pilgrimages beheld disagreements between various parties. Many contemporary critics, most conspicuously Edward Said and Kamila Shamsie as well as Roxanne L. Euben, notice that there is not one Islam but

---

127 Brodie, *The Devil Drives*, 74.
128 Burton, *Personal Narrative*, 1:239.
129 Burton, *Personal Narrative*, 1:156.
130 Burton, *Personal Narrative*, 1:190–91.
131 Burton, *Personal Narrative*, 1:191.
132 Burton, *Personal Narrative*, 1:191–92.
133 Burton, *Personal Narrative*, 1:198. Burton spells the word as "Maghrabi."
134 Burton, *Personal Narrative*, 1:206; capitalization original.

many "islams" embraced by such diverse communities as Pakistan, Afghanistan, the United States, and Europe.[135] Euben disputes the homogeneity of Shari'a law, which is based on the interpretations of the Koran, markedly dissimilar within different schools (*madhhab*) "at once articulated and transfigured by way of jagged and unpredictable exchanges with other practices and peoples."[136] Accentuating the varied behavior of various nationalities, Burton's narrative reflects the religious diversity among the faithful and brings out the true flavor of the Hajj. Still, he is also an surveyor providing linguistic, historical, geographical, anthropological, and cultural elucidations of places and phenomena, which in themselves are testimonies to his scholarly passion.

In *Majarr al-Kabsh*, "the Dragging place of the Ram,"[137] for instance, Burton studied the Hijazi ape, "a hideous cynocephalus, with small eyes placed together, and almost hidden by a disproportionate snout; a greenish-brown coat, long arms, and a stern of lively pink, like fresh meat." The medieval cynocephali, as Burton avows, citing a local legend, are supposedly the Jews "transformed for having broken the Sabbath by hunting."[138] Herodotus identified the *Kynokephalos* with the dog-faced baboon,[139] and the people who are half-dog, half-man also feature in Thomas de Kent's *Roman de Toute Chevalerie*.[140] In the illustration included in the eleventh-century English anonymous work entitled *Tractatus de diversis monstris*,[141] the Cynocephali are dressed like merchants, with human hands and feet, but instead of human heads they have dogs' heads. They are depicted in the process of buying and selling something from a rather large container. The Cynocephali epitomize the distorted mirror version of the diversity of races; they embody the most terrifying qualities the medieval Christians feared. Earlier illustrations portray a Cynocephalus as an "uncivilized and ravening monster."[142] Found at the edge of the world, the dog-headed monster "is a living

---

135 An interesting example is provided by Burton, who describes the ancient – but during his visit, still ongoing – rivalries between the Medanis and the Meccans. For Burton, the Meccans gave the impression of being "more civilized and more vicious than those of Al-Madinah." Burton, *Personal Narrative*, 2:233. They are darker and have black concubines. He notices that "male children are prayed over, and then taken to the barber which gives them three gushes on a cheek, they don't know the origin of that. Meccans are covetous spendthrifts, proud and with coarse language" (2:234–35).
136 Euben, *Journeys*, 5, 7.
137 Burton, *Personal Narrative*, 2:219.
138 Burton, *Personal Narrative*, 2:220.
139 David Gordon White, *Myths of the Dog-Man*, 48.
140 David Gordon White, *Myths of Dog-Men*, 53.
141 Daston and Park, *Wonders*, 31.
142 Daston and Park, *Wonders*, 38.

excoriation of gender ambiguity and sexual abnormality."[143] Cynocephalus, standing in an upright position and having human hands and feet, is like a human being but has a dog's head, thus remaining inhuman. To St. Augustine, the dog-people are the monstrous embodiment of sin and punishment, because their existence is understood as a retribution for human depravity and degradation. They are also symbolic monsters, tantamount to unconverted pagans;[144] nonetheless, he warns Christians not to pass any judgment concerning whichever creatures created by God.[145] The Cynocephalus came to represent the Saracens "because in both the East and the West, Christian sources often referred to the Muslims as a 'race of dogs.'" What is more, "Christian writers, such as Eulogius of Cordoba (ca. 810–859), linked the Prophet himself with dogs because to Muslims, dogs are considered impure."[146]

Michael Uebel strengthens this argument, explaining that the Saracens were branded as dog-headed monsters because for medieval Christians their religion "symbolized the blurring of ideal boundaries, such as those separating rational man from animal or civilized man from barbarian."[147] The comparison to dogs, a further affinity with the Cynocephali, is one of the most extreme and spectacular representations of the so-called "wonders of the East." The medieval monster is thus seen in terms of religious orientation but also through bodily deviation, with size and blackness being outward signs of monstrosity. Hence, in the story of *The King of Tars*, for the King's black heathen son-in-law and the unformed lump of flesh that is his grandson, the only way to cure monstrosity is baptism, as in the Middle Ages the omnipotence of Christian baptism was read literally.[148] Baptism and the ensuing miraculous transformation are the focus

---

143 Cohen, "Monster Culture (Seven Theses)," in Cohen, *Monster Theory*, 9.
144 Strickland, *Saracens, Demons and Jews*, 48.
145 Augustine, *The City*, 661–62.
146 Strickland, *Saracens, Demons, and Jews*, 159.
147 Uebel, "Unthinking the Monster," 268.
148 In *The King of Tars*, the sultan comes with a huge army and a proposal of marriage; he is subsequently refused the hand of the Christian princess and is offended by his prospective father-in-law, the titular hero the King of Tars. In retaliation, following an outburst of uncontrolled rage, he attacks Christian lands, thus earning the abuse of a "black heathen hound." After all, a heathen remains a heathen: atrocious, violent and, as is the canvas of the story, desirous of white European women and fruitful European lands. The Christian maiden sacrifices herself for her people and becomes the sultan's wife and the mother of his child. Her husband is black, and the child is born unformed, like a stone. Nevertheless, the greater the sultan's and then his child's monstrosity, the more evident the power of the miracle. The repeated pontificating of the sultan's wife, coupled with the homiletic tone of the author, magnifies the transformation of the husband and of their unformed child following the child's baptism and the sultan's conversion. Not only is the child given a human form but the black

of the legend of St. Christopher, who was supposedly born as a giant Cynocephalus named Reprobus: after he converted to Christianity, was baptized, and changed his name, he was astoundingly transformed into a human being.[149] Reprobus's story was consistent with the Augustinian belief that all extraordinary creatures are most probably Noah's descendants and, if so, are not beyond redemption if they are willing to accept God.[150] The creatures of the legend, quoted by Burton, foreground the Arab antipathy toward the Jews, whom they, in turn, identified with the medieval Monstrous Races.

By drawing attention to Cynocephali, Burton's narrative provides yet another argument for the persistence of medieval models in reading the Orient. Burton was not only an adventurer but also a scholar who, trying to record his experiences as accurately as possible, reiterated the attractiveness of the Orient but always conveyed a sense of long-lasting anxiety and aversion. To this effect, as a Victorian traveler versed in Arabic, knowledgeable about Islam, and genuinely interested in Arab culture, he occasionally reminds his readers of the peculiarities of the land and people, evoking the fabled medieval wonders of the East. Analogously to other fictional and non-fictional accounts of his times as well as later ones,[151] his is a tale of people and places. What distinguishes his *Personal Narrative* are Burton's attempts to understand the Orient not in terms of lack but of difference.

---

sultan is likewise changed into a pure white human being. The steadfastness of the sultan's wife – who, even though she has officially accepted Islam and bows to her husband's idols, remained Christian – amplifies the triumph of Christianity.
149 Strickland, *Saracens, Demons and Jews*, 245.
150 Augustine, *City of God*, 661.
151 The most commonly suggested examples are Stephens, *Incidents of Travel*, and Blunt's *Secret History of the English Occupation of Egypt*. Stephens shows disgust with the Arabs, seeing them usually as naked, dirty, and poor, and he mourns Egypt and Alexandria's ruins, "into which she had been plunged by years of misrule and anarchy." Stephens, *Incidents*, 4. For Stephens, Turks have "the usual air of Turkish conceit and insolence" (53), and yet upon meeting Arabs in the desert and then having more and more encounters with them, he changes his mind and begins to discover their human traits, finding that "Arabs are not so bad as they might be" (61). His description would be of interest for the further analysis of contemporary texts. Blunt's work is heavily influenced by the British politics of the Victorian period and relations with the Ottoman Empire. Uncharacteristically, he shows greater understanding and compassion toward the poverty of the people (11–21), he appreciates the fellah (Arab peasants) hospitality (10), and sees various problems with Arabs as a result of "our ignorance of the rules and customs of the desert" (25). He is also the only British official praised by Kabbani as "a staunch defender of Eastern rights against his own nation." Kabbani, *Imperial Fictions*, 33. Even though his was a rather naive vision of Arab nationalism, it was after his meeting with the leader of the army's revolt against the despotic Khedive Tawfiq, Ahmad 'Urabi, that Blunt began his vigorous apology for the Egyptian Nationalists (156).

A similar motivation to have a firsthand experience of the Orient drove Charles Montagu Doughty (1843–1926) to spend two years in Arabia. *Arabia Deserta*, published originally in 1888, was based on his voyage into Arabia between 1876 and 1878. The second edition of his work, published in 1920, contained a preface by T. E. Lawrence, whom Doughty calls "my distinguished friend . . . leader with Feysal, Meccan Prince, of the nomad tribesmen."[152] Incidentally, Said refers to T. E. Lawrence as one of the last solitary adventurers, whose *Seven Pillars of Wisdom*, published in 1922, built "a monument to betrayed hopes (from the Arab viewpoint), and a structure of hypocrisy (his own)."[153] Doughty's original motivation, as he discloses in the preface, was to look at and decipher the inscriptions at Medain Salih; he was in fact searching for cultural references, geographical and archeological remnants of biblical history. As a result, his narrative contains commentaries on the Frankish colonies in Arabia. He refers to the ruins of Philadelphia, now Amman, ancient Rabbath, and the metropolis of Ammon.[154] About Kerak, he says it is "a small rude town and her people, of nomad speech, are perhaps of Moabitish blood and partly immigrants. It is so populous in the eyes of the dispersed nomads that they call it *el-Medina*,"[155] but he admires the ruins of the Roman city of Jerash. Doughty describes *Arabia Petrea* with its pictures and inscriptions on its walls. He is fittingly impressed by Petra. As an informed traveler, he gives many historical and geographical details to his readers while relating his excursions, and he cites fables dating back to pre-Mohammedan times. "Pity Mohammed had not seen Petra!"[156] he exclaims. His interest in the Bible might have been the reason why he chose to tell his story in fake Spenserian English. Using an antiquated idiom, he might have wanted to render classical Arabic, or perchance add some sophistication to the narrative, and by spicing his tale with archaisms, he ensures a more "literary" flavor to the story of his ramblings. For instance, when the Arabs wanted to know something about his country, Doughty, whom they renamed Khalil, said that there was a little voice "in his chest and no tale ready upon his tongue."[157]

His longing to see Arabia as the biblical land is translated by Kabbani[158] as the desire to culturally conquer Arabia. Again and again, she accuses Doughty of subscribing to the crusader's rhetoric and hostility toward Islam. It is true that Doughty sees Islam as a religion of zealots, and many a time he speculates

---

152 Doughty, *Arabia Deserta*, 1:xi.
153 Said, *Reflections on Exile*, 39.
154 Doughty, *Arabia Deserta*, 1:19.
155 Doughty, *Arabia Deserta*, 1:23.
156 Doughty, *Arabia Deserta*, 1:87.
157 Doughty, *Arabia Deserta*, 1:127–28.
158 Kabbani, *Imperial Fictions*, 165–71.

that Muslims are irrational in the matter of faith.[159] His account is also replete with examples of why he feared for his life as he mingled with Arabs. Throughout his narrative, Doughty remains an aloof Englishman proud of his nationality. Once when he is taken for a Kheybar, he boldly states several times that he is "an Engelysy," not a Muscovite spy.[160] Being a man of his times, Doughty smugly reports that he was asked, this time by the women, to tell them "of that great sheykha, the sovereign Lady," whom "Khalil affirmed to be of power more than any man in the world."[161] He feels pride when, during an evening in the company of a person who tells of big cities in Egypt with gas lights and railroads built by the "Engleys,"[162] acknowledging England's might, this person was full of admiration for technological "miracles" and wanted his son to go to a Western school.[163] Despite his European haughtiness, Doughty could not travel as a Victorian gentleman as he began the Hajj. Consequently, he posed "as a Syrian of simple fortune, and ready with a store of caravan biscuit to ride along with him; mingled with the Persians in the Hajj journey, I should be less noted whether by Persians or Arabs."[164] Such behavior incurs Kabbani's scrutiny; in her eyes, both these Westerners, Burton and Doughty, have strikingly similar visions of the Orient.[165] She dislikes Burton's disguises and devalues Doughty's "transformation" into an Arab by simply changing his dress.

Like Burton, Doughty spoke Arabic, but unlike Burton, he never pretended to be a Muslim; he remained a *Nasrâny*, a Christian, which placed him in constant danger of his life. This earned him even more respect from Lawrence, who argues that Doughty, an otherwise simple, trusting, and quiet man, "seemed proud only of being a Christian."[166] Anyone who did not like the Christian, however, could accuse him of being a cause of evil, while those who hid the Christian could possibly endanger their own life.[167] One of his friends, for example, was questioned as to the whereabouts of the *Nasrâny*, and he was "never in such trouble."[168] It was well known that Mohammed decreed that Mecca was forbidden to unbelievers, and the ban was ferociously enforced. Throughout the

---

159 Doughty, *Arabia Deserta*, 2:372. He gives more details about religion in 2:373–74.
160 Doughty, *Arabia Deserta*, 2:81–82.
161 Doughty, *Arabia Deserta*, 1:445.
162 Doughty, *Arabia Deserta*, 1:154.
163 Doughty, *Arabia Deserta*, 1:171.
164 Doughty, *Arabia Deserta*, 1:4.
165 Kabbani, *Imperial Fictions*, 172–74.
166 Doughty, *Arabia Deserta*, 1:xxvii.
167 Doughty, *Arabia Deserta*, 1:484–85.
168 Doughty, *Arabia Deserta*, 1:206.

centuries, Jews or Christians were impaled or crucified for such a transgression, the last two in 1845. "[O]fficial law in 1853," writes Brodie, gave the infidel "a choice thrice offered between circumcision and death."[169] Upon entering Mecca, Doughty notes: "I was to pass a circuit in whose pretended divine law is no refuge for the alien; whose people shut up the ways of the common earth; and where any felon of theirs in comparison with a Nasrâny, is one of the people of Ullah.[170] In this way, Doughty acknowledges the pains of exclusion, of being forever marked as an outsider, even if at times, he also communicates instances of unexpected cordiality, especially during the strenuous journeys with the caravan. Then he felt part of a group: "Moslem or Nasrâny, Khalil is now one of us."[171] Doughty was certainly aware of the risks when he reported that "the Emir was favourably minded towards me, but the company of malignant young fanatics always about him, continually traduced the Nasrâny."[172] In his narrative, most Arabs reviled Christians. The fear for his life conveyed in the account is far from hypothetical. Close to Mecca, he is captured and sentenced to die by decapitation the next morning.[173] Yet he did not die but survived to tell about his adventures of being an unwanted visitor in the Muslim lands. The threat of death from the hands of the "heathens" is yet another reenactment of the Saracen romances emulated by the Victorian quest romance. He is saved, but this last adventure, or rather misfortune, hastens the conclusion of his wanderings.

It is the prerogative of travel narratives to show the traveler's encounters with a deep-seated dissimilarity. Even if speaking the language definitely helps him comprehend the culture and mindset of the people he encounters, Doughty feels himself a wandering foreigner left at the mercy of inhospitable people.[174] Feeling alternately befriended and rejected, he listens to and records the stories and voices of the Arabia of his time, continually reminding us of the complexity of the Arabian culture, and that of its ancient history.[175] Notwithstanding acts

---

169 Brodie, *Devil Drives*, 91.
170 Doughty, *Arabia Deserta*, 2:484.
171 Doughty, *Arabia Deserta*, 1:104.
172 Doughty, *Arabia Deserta*, 2:12–13.
173 Doughty, *Arabia Deserta*, 2:501.
174 Doughty, *Arabia Deserta*, 2:408–9.
175 Doughty always tries to provide not only geographical references, such as the topography of the volcanic country around Medina, but also historical background, for example discussing the final defeat of the Wahabi power. He remarks that the Wahabi rulers taught the Bedouins Islam. *Arabia Deserta*, 2:425. He also narrates the wars of Aneyza (2:428–30) and recalls a rather ugly tale about the Kathan tribes, who, according to the Nejd Arabians, are "eaters of the flesh of their enemies; and there is a vile proverb said to be of these human butchers" (1:40).

of friendliness, Doughty lived in a constant state of alarm as he heard threats that "they would cut the Nasrâny in pieces if he ventured himself amongst them; and yet between their words and deeds is commonly many leagues' distance,"[176] and so his own sense of menace is always acute. "I had passed many days of those few years whose sum is our human life, in Arabia . . . I must needs leave the Mecca kafily at a last station before the (forbidden) city." So close was he to death that he mourned his fate: "What horror, to die like a rabbit in a hostile land."[177]

The recurrent motif of anxiety connected with the presence of a Christian amongst Moslems foregrounds the Muslim unease and stereotypical responses to Christianity being the result of their lack of knowledge about religion. To Muslims, Doughty is a stranger and a "wicked person, and of the adversaries of Ullah."[178] Doughty also accepted the reservations of Muslims toward Christians when one of his interlocutors asked whether Amm Mohamed would not be killed in the land of Christians. The Muslims bring to his attention the fact that most of them try not to "be hard with men of another religion more than God, for even of the Nasâra there be some just men and perfect in their belief, which was taught to them by the holy prophet Aysa."[179] Aysa, elsewhere referred to as Issa, is Jesus, who in the Koran is considered one of the prophets.

Because of his insistence on remaining a Christian, near the town of Aneyza and very much in the spirit of Margery Kempe's misfortunes, Doughty is left by his caravan, while the inhabitants say that "he cannot remain here, and we cannot receive him in our house."[180] The nomads:

> took me to be of that hostile heathen nation, which conspired continually to beat down the saving religion of Islam. After supper, when we have broken meat together and they heard good reported of me, they were become of my counsel. Some of them desired that I should come to the knowledge of Ullah, also being Moslem I might ever inhabit with them – then every man bringing some goat or sheep, they would gather the flock to sustain me, I should receive of them immediately a camel, and a maiden to wife.[181]

In spite of their anti-Christian attitudes, he nevertheless perceives his hosts as exhibiting a semblance of cordiality. The kindness, however, is not practiced by all the Arabs with whom he travels. From the onset of his wanderings, Doughty

---

176 Doughty, *Arabia Deserta*, 2:290–91.
177 Doughty, *Arabia Deserta*, 2:452.
178 Doughty, *Arabia Deserta*, 1:523.
179 Doughty, *Arabia Deserta*, 2:159.
180 Doughty, *Arabia Deserta*, 2:334.
181 Doughty, *Arabia Deserta*, 1:394.

realizes how risky it was to demonstrate his religious affiliation, yet foregoing danger, he insisted on the superiority of Christianity. Despite his friends' pleas to call himself a "Misslim," and with a rather typical Western narcissism, Doughty refuses to bend down to what he considers an inferior religion: "It had cost me little or naught, to confess Konfuuchu or Socrates to be apostles of Ullah; but I could not find it in my life to confess the barbaric prophet of Mecca and enter under the yoke into their solemn fools' paradise."[182] In another place, Doughty notes that

> [t]he Aarab, although they pardoned my person, yet thought me to blame for my religion. There happened another day a thing which, since they put all to the hand of Ullah, might seem to them some token of Providence which cared for me. Weary, alighting from the ráhla in blustering weather, I cast my mantle upon the next bush, and sat down upon it.[183]

It turned out that there was a venomous snake there; one of the shepherds destroyed it, but Doughty felt himself saved by Christian Providence. His moral certitude is then contrasted with the lack of backbone displayed by an Italian who "converted" in order to be left in peace. The conversion into Islam is a short process during which all one needs is the presence of a Muslim, who would attest that "there is not God but God, and Muhammad is his prophet." In the words of the Italian: "You confess, then their 'none Ilah but Ullah, and Mahound, apostle of Ullah' – which they shall never hear me utter, may Ullah confound them!"[184] In the Muslim mind, the person pronouncing those words becomes Muslim and can go on the Hajj. Doughty admits his disgust with the converts: "It amazed me that one born in the Roman country, and under the name of Christ, should waive these prerogatives, to become the brother of Asiatic barbarians in a fond religion." But the Italian man wanted to capitalize on his conversion. He was going to go back to Italy to publish his travelogue, and "once returned to Italy, he would wipe off all this rust of the Mohammedan life."[185]

It comes as no surprise that Kabbani focuses solely on Doughty's contempt for the "Mohammedan life" and the Koran,[186] expressed in such statements as: "The high sentencious fantasy of the ignorant Arabs, the same that will not trust the heart of man, is full of infantile credulity in all religious matter."[187] Doughty makes a statement about "the barbarous Arabic authors" who had no knowledge of the

---

182 Doughty, *Arabia Deserta*, 1:212.
183 Doughty, *Arabia Deserta*, 1:313.
184 Doughty, *Arabia Deserta*, 1:68.
185 Doughty, *Arabia Deserta*, 2:51.
186 Kabbani, *Imperial Fictions*, 170.
187 Doughty, *Arabia Deserta*, 1:95.

tongues or times and who "discourse with disdain ineptitude of the noblest human spirits which lived almost a thousand years before their beginning, and were not acquainted with their néby Mohammed."[188] He considers the Arabs "Naturals in [their] religion," who however, do not fathom the "stink of sin" or "the leprosy of their own souls."[189] In all of the above quotations one cannot but recognize Doughty's denigration of the faith and the faithful. Still, Doughty also directs his literary virulence at other nations. He sees, for example, Greek Christians as "less worthy and hospitable than Moslems, their formal religion is most in pattering and dumb superstition."[190] Both Burton and Doughty are representatives of the nineteenth-century European scientific milieu in which civilization was judged by technological progress. It is not surprising that when Hotz writes about the white races as vigorous and morally highly cultivated, he conversely talks about black races as feeble in mind, although physically strong, their moral manifestation "partially latent."[191] Doughty's vilification of Islam is akin to that of de Gobineau and Hotz, who affirmed that: "The conception of the Deity will be more elevated and refined, though the idea of a future state will probably be connected with visions of material enjoyment, as in the paradise of the Mohammedans."[192] In a different framework, that of ecocriticism, the West should look upon the nomads with awe. In the nineteenth century they were the only humans living close to and in accordance with nature. Doughty does not understand the pantheistic and ecological premises of the Bedouin mindset: "The nomad's fantasy is high, and that is ever clothed in religion."[193] Nevertheless, he eventually accepts their lifestyle and culture, and forgoes the constant belittling of the Bedouin convictions which enables him not only to help the ailing through his knowledge of medicine but also make friends, and he boasts of some success in both areas.[194] This is one of the few moments in his book where Doughty shows surprising resilience in his determination to fit in, while at the same time maintaining his English identity.

By November 1876, Doughty left with the caravan, witnessing euphoria matched by the celebrations of the caravans going out and those coming home.[195] Accordingly, the traveler conveys this sense of joyous anticipation:

---

[188] Doughty, *Arabia Deserta*, 1:154.
[189] Doughty, *Arabia Deserta*, 1:470.
[190] Doughty, *Arabia Deserta*, 1:24.
[191] Hotz, "Introduction," 94.
[192] Hotz, "Introduction," 95.
[193] Doughty, *Arabia Deserta*, 1:264.
[194] Doughty, *Arabia Deserta*, 2:4–5.
[195] Doughty, *Arabia Deserta*, 1:3.

"In the first evening hour there is some merrymaking of drum-beating and soft fluting, and Arcadian sweetness of the Persians singing . . . The Hajjis lie down in their clothes the few hours till the morrow gun-fire; then to rise suddenly for the march."[196] As was already mentioned, thievery is one of the most frequent but also most despised of crimes among Arabs, generating many "tales of the robbers."[197] In the melting pot of oriental nations, Doughty is constantly aware of menace not only in the form of religious fanatics but also thieves and bandits intent on killing and taking preying upon anyone journeying in the desert.[198] Even so, he values nomadic Arabia, which without gambling, banquetng, and the "many ruinous sores and hideous sinks of our great towns"[199] is a place that esteems moral certitude. The vice of drinking, increasingly a social problem in Victorian Britain, is particularly abhorrent to Muslims, who replace alcohol with the water pipe. "The Beduins love well to 'drink' the fume of a strong leaf (tobacco) till the world turn round." They are addicted to their water pipes, although they call it *"bawl iblis*, the devil's water."[200] Doughty claims that tobacco was brought to Arabia by the English cloth merchants during the time of James I and has been grown there ever since.[201] Surprisingly, in spite of such addiction, Doughty compliments the native inhabitants who are "not less frugal than Spartans, are happy in the Epicurean moderation of their religion."[202]

Paradoxically, the Bedouins recognize him as a Christian, but deem him "of one mind with the Aarab." This he found out during a colloquy with the Bedouins,

---

196 Doughty, *Arabia Deserta*, 1:8.
197 Doughty, *Arabia Deserta*, 2:155. Eventually he is robbed (2:316–17) and stripped, but even though this adventure was very frightening, he did not waiver in his resolve to continue and was soon on his way again.
198 Doughty, *Arabia Deserta*, 1:7. Doughty then witnessed a punishment (a beating) of a man and, against the better advice of his friends, tried to intervene on behalf of the thief, but was advised not to interfere with it. He notes that one station that has a reputation of being "thievish," but then concedes that the "thieves" are "the poor Beduins" (1:86). "With the Haj returning from Mecca, are brought the African slaves, for all the north-west of the Mahomedan world, but gazing all day up and down, I could not count five among them" (1:209). Like Burton, Doughty did not make any particularly negative comments about slavery. "The free negroes are commonly seen lusty and thriving; they are rich men's children by adoption, where the poor disinherited Arabs must hire themselves to every man's task as day labourers. But also of the natural stalwart condition of negro bodies, they fare well enough of a feeble diet and shoot up strongly in lean soil, where you see only pithless and languishing growths of the country Arabs" (1:554).
199 Doughty, *Arabia Deserta*, 2:401.
200 Doughty, *Arabia Deserta*, 1:247.
201 Doughty, *Arabia Deserta*, 1:247.
202 Doughty, *Arabia Deserta*, 2:401.

some of whom "had not heard of a life to come after our natural decease!"[203] And so, in the manner of Guy of Warwick, who, unmindful of the Saracen danger, always gave the sultans a harangue on the inferiority of Islam followed by a short outline of Christianity, Doughty equally expounds on "Isa ben Miriam, from the spirit of Ullah, that is higher than the heaven! Forbids all evil meaning and dealing, and bids men live in devout fear and love of the Lord which made them, with godly love of their neighbor."[204] He observes that "Beduins of the common sort are garrulous tale-bearers."[205] Concurrently, they seem strangely interested in some doctrinal aspects concerning heaven and hell, for example whether smoke drinkers (hookah users) were to go to hell to be burned by Iblis or Sheytan. Such stories are augmented by those in which he quotes the Bedouin interest in the West, even though he himself always tries to learn more about their "version" of Islam. Doughty finds out that Ramadan, for instance, is not so faithfully practiced among the Bedouin tribes.

> The month of Lent which should be kept clean and holy, is rather, say the nomads and villagers, a season of wickedness, when the worst sores break forth and run afresh of human nature. Not more than a good half of the rest are "ignorants" – this is to say they have not learned to pray, yet they cherish little less fanaticism in their factious hearts, which is a kind of national envy or Semitic patriotism.[206]

Furthermore, during Ramadan, the month-long fast, during which the devout refrain from eating and drinking from dawn to sunset: "The Arabs very impatiently suffering the thirst of the first Ramathan days, lie on their breasts sighing out the slow hours, and watching the empty daylight till the 'eye of the sun' shall have gone down from them."[207] Ramadan is one of the pillars of faith, expected to be observed by all Muslims. The evening meal is not only an occasion for a family celebration but should also be a time for religious reflection. Even today, scholars do not agree as to the origins of the practice of both fasting and retreat, whether Mohammed adopted them from the existing pagan cultures or the Christian anchorites he met in Syria. It is agreed, however, that after his prolonged meditations, he received his first revelations.[208] Although, Doughty saw Muslim devotion as genuine, he assumed that the Bedouin tribes accepted Islam

---

203 Doughty, *Arabia Deserta*, 1:445.
204 Doughty, *Arabia Deserta*, 1:446.
205 Doughty, *Arabia Deserta*, 1:468.
206 Doughty, *Arabia Deserta*, 1:521.
207 Doughty, *Arabia Deserta*, 1:521.
208 Ruthven, *Islam*, 32.

"partly fearing for themselves and partly in the hope of booty."[209] T. E. Lawrence, as well, observed the primal qualities of Bedouin belief:

> There is no human effort, no fecundity in Nature; just heaven above and unspotted earth beneath, and the only refuge and rhythm of their being is in God. This single God is to the Arab not anthropomorphic, not tangible or moral or ethical, not concerned particularly with the word or with him. He alone is great, and yet there is a homeliness, and every-dayness of this Arab God who rules their eating, their fighting and their lusting; and is their commonest thought, and companion, in a way impossible to those whose God is tediously veiled from them by the decorum of formal worship.[210]

Anthony T. Sullivan stresses Doughty's perseverance in his Victorian conviction of the absolute superiority of the West and Christianity.[211] It comes as no surprise that religious differences would be the subject matter of his numerous and sometimes quite risky adventures and colloquies with the Arabs. Usually quite critical, Doughty notices the meanness of the Bedouin life, whose poorest families had no clothes for their children.[212] In his mind, "[t]he Arabians inhabit a land of dearth and hunger, and there is no worse food than the date, which they must eat in their few irrigated valleys."[213] The poverty of the region manifests itself in the characters of its inhabitants.

Doughty's narrative, however, is filled with contradictory opinions. He sees the Arabs firstly as his friends, only to then deem them guilty of the worst of crimes, and therefore his enemies. He identifies the Bedouins as free and worthy, only to portray them as fanatical, malicious, and inhuman in the end. The latter argument, in a way, is in accord with what an old Moor tells him: "Khalil, all the Beduw are sheyatin!"[214] and more: "[E]l-Beduw! They are always affinîn, corrupt to rottenness, and whatsoever they do, it will be found good for naught."[215] More than once, Doughty brings to light the Arab and Bedouin conflicts, seeing them as rather inconsistent because they seem to share a history and a religion.[216] Surprisingly, he refrains from commenting on the Bedouin conceptualization of the past, which is one of the categories that, for Todorov, would distinguish them

---

209 Doughty, *Arabia Deserta*, 1:247.
210 Lawrence, "Introduction," xxxi.
211 "The Obstinate Mr Doughty." https://www.saudiaramcoworld.com/issue/196904/the.obstinate.mr.doughty.htm.
212 Doughty, *Arabia Deserta*, 1:301–2.
213 Doughty, *Arabia Deserta*, 1:148.
214 Doughty, *Arabia Deserta*, 1:358.
215 Doughty, *Arabia Deserta*, 1:377.
216 Doughty, *Arabia Deserta*, 1:403.

from the ancient barbarians; instead, he argues that the Bedouins cannot think about the future:

> they pray and they fast as main duties in religion, looking (as the Semitic Patriarchs before them) for the present life's blessing. There is a sacrifice for the dead, which I have seen continued to the third generation. I have seen a sheykh come with devout remembrance, to slaughter his sacrifice and to pray at the heap where his father or his father's father lies buried.[217]

Making connections between the landscape and human character, Doughty assumes that "[t]he Moors are born under wandering stars,"[218] therefore "every Arab is a wayfaring man, and made for the journey."[219] Analogously, the Bedouins "led their lives under the skies of God."[220] In a similar vein, T. E. Lawrence expounds that "[t]he Beduin has been born and brought up in the desert, and has embraced this barrenness too harsh for volunteers with all his soul, for the reason, felt but inarticulate, that there he finds himself indubitably free."[221] Doughty considers the Bedouins of "the Beny Sókhr, a strong tribe and lately formidable, having many horsemen; so that none durst pass these downs, unless by night time or riding in strong companies. The Aarab easily discouraged, whose most strength is in their tongues."[222] Concomitantly, he sees them as prone to disagreements,[223] and "always of a factious humour."[224] This view is shared by Doughty's friend Mohammed Aly, who regards the life of the Bedouins as a "hostile and necessitous," questioning Doughty's sanity in staying with them: "is [it] to such wild wretches thou wilt another day trust thy life?"[225] Such statements reverberate with inborn animosity between the nomads and the settled Arabian tribes.[226]

Both Lawrence and Doughty seem to share an opinion that the Arab mind is guileless, their innate belligerence overpowering their better natures. No wonder Doughty became increasingly weary of the skirmishes he witnessed, his exhaustion magnified by the perpetual need to affirm his position in an alien culture. His anxiety was first and foremost associated with being far from everything known and safe, in this way his covert homesickness contributed to the creation

---

217 Doughty, *Arabia Deserta*, 1:240–41.
218 Doughty, *Arabia Deserta*, 1:89.
219 Doughty, *Arabia Deserta*, 1:291.
220 Doughty, *Arabia Deserta*, 1:222.
221 Lawrence, "Introduction," xxx.
222 Doughty, *Arabia Deserta*, 1:15.
223 Doughty, *Arabia Deserta*, 1:232.
224 Doughty, *Arabia Deserta*, 1:11.
225 Doughty, *Arabia Deserta*, 1:123.
226 Doughty, *Arabia Deserta*, 1:30.

Chapter 2   Al-Ifranij among the Believers, or the Victorian Quest Romance(d) — **79**

an image the inhabitants of Arabia simultaneously friendly and treacherous, wild and civilized. Such pronounced disparities are fittingly applauded by Lawrence, whose "Introduction" is full of praise for the realism, the completeness, the understanding of the land and its people:

> If there is a bias it will be against the Arabs, for he liked them so much; he was so impressed by the strange attraction, isolation and independence of this people that he took pleasure in bringing out their virtues by a careful expression of their faults.[227]

Notwithstanding the fact that contemporary science might class them as racist, Doughty's ideas simply replicate the "racialist" ideas of de Gobineau, who, for nineteenth-century audiences, proffered the confirmation of existing convictions that of the superiority of the white race and their civilization.[228]

The remarks concerning the geography of the place, in turn, belong to the "ethnography" of nineteenth-century travel writing. Ethnography began to develop as a science in the nineteenth century, with explorers observing and writing about different cultures. Doughty reports legal proceedings and various discourses with people he met in his wanderings; he also provides pictures of the sights and the architecture as well as hand-drawn maps and rarities, like the pictures of Himayrite trade money. Burton and Doughty's approaches rebound the medieval and early modern thinking concerning the lands and peoples beyond Christendom. As Shirin Khanmohamadi argues, in the wake of colonization there was a need for new ideologies de-rationalizing other nations and rationalizing the new European empires.[229] Despite Augustinian attempts to raise pagans – and the Monstrous Races, for that matter – to the status of human beings, and therefore capable of conversion and salvation, the prevailing discourse in the nineteenth century created a divide between the infinitely superior Christians and naturally inferior non-Christians. Replicating such centuries-old ideas, Doughty does not downgrade Islam directly but implicitly shows it as a religion of violence and its culture belonging perhaps to the more embryonic state. To substantiate his claims, he offers, for instance, an account of the funeral rites – when one is dead, his kinsmen kill an ewe at his grave,[230] and he discusses the sacrifices performed in the desert – giving examples of when and what is offered. As a curiosity, he adds that "*ghrôl* or

---

[227] Lawrence, "Introduction," 1:xxix.
[228] De Gobineau, *Moral and Intellectual Diversity*, 272–311.
[229] Khanmohamadi, *In Light of Another's Word*, 29.
[230] Doughty, *Arabia Deserta*, 1:450–51.

ghrûl is a monster of the desert in which children and women believe and men also."[231]

Yet another instance of cultural inferiority is polygamy, an interest in which is shared by the two travelers. The harem life, the result of which is the separation of men and women, who practically lead unconnected lives,[232] remained an enigma for the Victorians.[233]

> Hareem are unseen, and the men's manners are the more gracious and untroubled; it may be their Asiatic society is manlier, but less virile than the European. They live-on in a pious daily assurance: and little know they of stings which be in our unquiet emulations, and in our foreign religion. . . . Women are not seen passing by their streets, in the day-time; but in the evening twilight (when the men sit at coffee) you shall see many veiled forms flitting to their gossips' houses.[234]

Fascinated by the oriental female world that was mystifyingly close but utterly inaccessible, Doughty surveys household relations. In Medina, he notices that the male inhabitants "sit all day in their coffee halls, with only a resting-while at noon. To pass daylight hours withdrawn from the common converse of men were in their eyes unmanly; and they look for no reasonable fellowship with the

---

231 Doughty, *Arabia Deserta*, 1:53. He provides a drawing of the creature done by Doolan the Fehjy at el Héjr (54).
232 He tells the story of Prince Mohammed and his childlessness, and his taking of other wives (polygamy again) as a remedy. *Arabia Deserta*, 2:25–26.
233 A very good example of such a mixture can be found in Levi-Strauss's *Tristes Tropiques*, in which he describes his trip to India and Pakistan. As an anthropologist, he tries to maintain scientific objectivity, but one cannot fail to notice that he is highly critical of the Muslim (he uses the word "Moslem") separation of the male and female spheres. As he enters a compartment in a train, where the lady is "in purdah," he writes, for instance: "although she made an attempt to isolate herself by crouching down on her bunk wrapped in her *burkah* and with her back obstinately turned towards me, the promiscuity eventually appeared too shocking and the family had to split up" (394). Later he wonders about the Muslim contempt for the arts, and gives an example of an English lady married to a Muslim who worked at the University of Lahore in the Department of Fine Arts, who told him that only women attended her lectures and that sculpture was forbidden (400). He then goes on to compare the Hindu and Muslim cultures, and admits that the "Islamic legal system is better than the Hindu system as regards mattes of inheritance" (401). Everything else he despises, including Muslim moralism and the separation of men and women, which for Muslim men results in them being "obsessed with the problem of pre-nuptial virginity and subsequent fidelity; secondly purdah, that is the segregation of women, which in one sense puts obstacles in the way of amorous intrigue, encourages it on another level by enclosing women in a world of their own." Levi-Strauss's Islam is a seraglio of intolerance, and he sees Muslims as jealous and proud (403), intent on preserving "Islamic fraternity" (404).
234 Doughty, *Arabia Deserta*, 2:349–50.

hareem. Women are for the house-service."[235] Men reenter their houses at the end of a long day to enjoy what seems to Doughty like a semblance of a family life. He concludes that "the open loving affection of our spouses-for-life" is unimaginable for the Arabs.[236] To assure their husbands of their honor, Muslim women were required to cover their entire body, including their faces and hair:

> The women go closely veiled, and live in the jealous (Hejaz or Moorish) tyranny of the husbands; their long and wide wimples are loaded with large glittering shards of mother-of-pearl shells from el-Wejh. The wives of my acquaintance, that I have seen in their houses partly unveiled, were abject-looking and undergrown, without grace of womanhood.[237]

The mystery of veiling was intriguing to the Victorians as they observed differences and similarities in their respective approaches to clothes and the position of women within marriage. In *Vanity Fair* (1848), for instance, William Makepeace Thackeray expresses the view that Victorian Men were

> Turks with the affections of our women; and have made them subscribe to our doctrine too. We let their bodies go abroad liberally enough, with smiles and ringlets and pink bonnets to disguise them instead of veils and yakmaks. But their souls must be seen by only one man, and they obey not unwillingly, and consent to remain at home as our slaves – ministering to us and doing drudgery for us.[238]

The only time Doughty notices beauty is during the journey when he spied on "a lone Beduwia wife and a young maiden, her daughter, that without knowledge of herself, were to our eyes a vision of amiable beauty in that frightful desert."[239] Doughty's statements are in agreement with the demands of physiognomy, a tool utilized by travel writers for characterization, especially the portrayal of women. As Melman specifies, nineteenth-century travel writers were not only describing their experiences but also were "*physiognomists*, that is, they used human features and expressions and the human physique to judge oriental 'nature,' whether the character of individual oriental women, or the moral state of Middle Eastern society."[240] Melman deems "the obsession with elaborate physical detail" generic, in

---

235 Doughty, *Arabia Deserta*, 2:129.
236 Doughty, *Arabia Deserta*, 1:175.
237 Doughty, *Arabia Deserta*, 1:149.
238 Thackeray, *Vanity Fair*, 216. The Victorian preoccupation with marriage is a rather complex issue and has to be analyzed in conjunction with the nineteenth-century legal acts that influenced its status, to wit, the Matrimonial Causes Act of 1857 and the Married Women's Property Act of 1870. For more, see Altick, *Victorian People and Ideas*, 50–59.
239 Doughty, *Arabia Deserta*, 1:464.
240 Said, *Orientalism*, 113.

both fictional and non-fictional works.[241] Victorian novelists and travel writers appear to be guilty of similar misconceptions concerning the "oriental character," which is invariably sexual, and this was also what Burton exposed in his unpublished material on female circumcision.[242]

Unlike Burton, Doughty never comments on the practice but divulges the colloquies with his Arab friends regarding male sexuality as they wondered how an uncircumcised man can be with his wife.[243] Doughty's self-imposed chastity was inconceivable and unhealthy to them. "Hast thou any mind to be wedded amongst us?" asks his friend Zeyd. "See, I have two wives, and billah, I will give thee to choose between them; say which hast thou rather, and I will leave her and she shall become thy wife."[244] In Victorian culture, this would have echoed earlier instances of abduction, the most famous being narrated in *Sir Isumbras*, whose wife is forcefully taken from Isumbras and made a "wife" of the Saracen sultan.[245] In the case of Doughty, the indecent proposal, shocking as it may be, comes out of an honest concern on the part of the Arabs and, in this case, well-wishing on their part. Trying to convince Doughty that a wife would follow and serve him, would even "learn your tongue as thou has learnt Araby," reflected the conceptualizations of conjugal harmony in Islam. Doughty, however, repeatedly shunned offers of marriage and therefore acceptance as a full-fledged member of a tribe, ignoring the fact that such proposals were not only acts of kindness but would have provided the best life insurance when among Arabs. For his hosts, the union between a Christian and a Muslim might even be beneficial because true worshippers could be born to them.[246] And that, "the obstinate Mr Doughty" could have never allowed to happen.

Undeniably, in contrast to Burton, Doughty represented himself purposefully as an Englishman and a Christian, even if, among the Arabs and for safety reasons, he wore oriental clothing. In keeping with Doughty's assertion that "Every man leans upon his own hand in the open desert"[247] – such are the desert rules, both were privy to the jeopardy of Eastern travel and relied on themselves and on their knowledge of the region. Venturing into the unknown, in the spirit of the Victorian quest romance, the voyagers anticipated potentially

---

241 Said, *Orientalism*, 114.
242 Rice, *Captain Sir Richard Burton*, 259.
243 Doughty, *Arabia Deserta*, 1:410.
244 Doughty, *Arabia Deserta*, 1:321.
245 Her conversion is never declared, and so she is henceforth referred to as a "Queen" rather than "Sultana," which precipitates the reunion of the couple at the end of the romance.
246 Doughty, *Arabia Deserta*, 1:322.
247 Doughty, *Arabia Deserta*, 1:347.

perilous situations. Danger is what Stephen Greenblatt associates with "desire and ignorance and fear"[248] when encountering the outlandish, whilst anxiety can only be annihilated by an unconquerable spirit. Fashioning themselves as knights-errant searching for their own Holy Grails – the genuine tomb of the Prophet, in the case of Burton; the biblical sites, in the case of Doughty – they created narratives of unprecedented cultural value. Their accounts, encompassing vast areas of historical, anthropological, and cultural knowledge, *do* portray the East, but they also underpin the Western idea of the Orient as mesmerizing in its primordial nature, yet unsophisticated in its approach to other religions and fundamentalist in its adherence to Islam. Because of the links with Victorian quest romance, however, their works can be read as personal, subjective, and literary expressions of individual experiences and views, reclaimed through the adventure mode, rather than objective and comprehensive travel accounts, presenting unchangeable truths about the land and its native peoples.

---

248 Greenblatt, *Marvelous Possessions*, 20.

Chapter 3
Under Western Eyes: The Discourses of/on History

Western curiosity about the Orient not only was present in literary works and travelogues but also was reinforced by historical works. Eighteenth-century historians, even though they believed in civilizational progress, were also fascinated by the rise and fall of empires. Suvir Kaul argues that "ideas of *translatio imperii et studii*, the transfer of imperial authority and of knowledge, were central to neoclassical historiography."[1] The work of Thomas Wright (1810–1877) is a testimony to this idea. In 1848, Wright published a collection of travelogues to the Holy Land. The work was dedicated to the Lord Archbishop of York and included, among others, fragments from the hugely popular book of travel, *The Book of Sir John Maundeville* (Wright's original spelling) and also from *The Travels of Bishop Arculf in the Holy Land A.D. 700*, *The Travels of Willibals A.D. 721–727*, *Travels of Sewulf, A.D. 1102 and 1103*, *Travels of Rabbi Benjamin, of Tudela*[2] and *The Journey of Henry Maundrell from Aleppo to Jerusalem A.D. 1697*. The editor proudly announced that his work "gives us no little insight into the history of the march of intellectual improvement to accompany these early travelers in their wanderings, as they have themselves described them to us, and [to] watch their feelings and hear their opinions." The book in itself testifies to the Victorian interest in genealogies and origins, and can be seen as one of the models upon which Victorian histories of the East are based, as the editor claims: "If the seeds of civilization ever existed in the cloister, they were seeds cast upon the barren rock, and richer soil, that they began to sprout and give promise to fruit."[3] Furthermore, it provides

---

1 Kaul, *Eighteenth-Century British Literature*, 5.
2 In 1888, Gilman (*The Saracens*, 78) cites Thomas Wright, *Early Travels in Palestine*, and brings up Wright's selection from a Jewish traveler's accounts of his travels, the famous Benjamin of Tudela. *The Saracens*, 433–34. Benjamin of Tudela gives readers a glimpse at Baghdad in its days of decline (the Fatimids were overthrown by Saladin in 1171), and Genghis Khan and the Mongol horses were already a threat. "The sons and grandsons of Jengis continued his successful career, and extended their dominions from the sea-board of China through Russia to the borders of Germany and Poland. His grandson Hulaku, who was the first sultan of Persia, overthrew the terrible Assassins, and captured Baghdad, putting the Khalif Motasim to death." According to the legend, he killed sixteen hundred thousand citizens of Baghdad. Gilman, *The Saracens*, 441.
3 Wright, *Early Travels in Palestine*, vii–viii.

Note: My title refers to Joseph Conrad's novel, published originally in 1911.

https://doi.org/10.1515/9781501513367-004

> [a] comparison of the numerous narratives to which we allude, places before our eyes the most distinct view we can possibly have of the various changes which have swept over the land of Palestine since it was snatched from the power of the Roman emperors. The more ancient are, of course, the most interesting, because they relate to a period when a far greater number of monuments of still earlier antiquity remained in existence that it has been the lot of any modern pilgrim to visit, and the traditions of the locality were then much more deserving of attention, because they were so much nearer to the time of the events to which they related.[4]

Wright sketches the Saracen presence in the Holy Land:

> the Saracens, who under Omar, obtained possession of Jerusalem in 637, by a capitulation, however, which allowed them the use of their churches on payment of a tribute, but forbade them to build new ones. This interdiction could not be in itself a great grievance, for the whole of Palestine must have been literally covered with churches when it passed under the Mohammedan yoke.[5]

While the Romantic beliefs in personal and national liberty excited an awareness of historical processes, such knowledge, buttressed by archeological findings, not only found its expression in nineteenth-century literary and cultural medievalism but also, first and foremost, revived the importance of medieval scholarship. In a climate favorable to science, the desire for origins, to use Allen J. Franzen's expression,[6] was bound together with aspirations to uncover national roots and the so-called textual beginnings of Britain. The Early English Text Society was founded by Frederick James Furnivall in 1864,[7] who with his

---

[4] Wright, *Early Travels in Palestine*, viii.
[5] Wright, *Early Travels in Palestine*, xvii. The story of Willibald. "Peace, broken immediately after the departure of Willibald, was not restored till the learned reign of the magnificent Haroun-er-Raschid (786–809), whose name, and his friendship and intercourse with the no less splendid monarch of the west, Charlemagne, have been so often celebrated in history and romance. Their friendship led to the opening of Palestine to the Christian pilgrims on much more liberal terms, and various privileges and comforts were secured for them in the holy city. Pilgrimages now became more frequent, and several are mentioned during the latter part of the eighth and the course of the ninth centuries" (xvi).
[6] Franzen, in *Desire for Origins*, stated in his thesis that it is wrong to study linguistics for the sake of innovation, and if one wants to retain a place in the mainstream of Anglo-Saxon studies, one has to engage in the debates concerning politics (xiii). Elsewhere he notes that "Anglo-Saxon language and literature recall both the oppression of philological discipline – translation and memorization – and the vague, violent primitivism that cliché has attached to Anglo-Saxon culture" (2). He notices that Anglo-Saxonists frequently see the era as the time of "natural" social organization and political order (23).
[7] See http://www.gutenberg.org/wiki/Early_English_Text_Society_(Bookshelf).

colleagues Richard Morris, Walter Skeat, and others, revived the interest in older texts by publishing their scholarly editions.[8] Their work found fertile ground in the scholarly milieu of Victorian Britain, which was booming with intellectuals devoted to scientific pursuits of histories of cultures and religions.

Eighteenth- and nineteenth-century historians such as Simon Ockley (1678–1720), Arthur Gilman (1834–1907), Samuel Green (fl. 19th c.), and David Pryde (1834–1907), whose works will be investigated in this chapter, undertook the task of tracing and explaining the origins of Islam and charting its political success. Their studies aspired to create palatable narratives about Mohammed's life and times; their texts offer persuasive, novel-like descriptions of the historical development of Islam. Highlighting the continuation of, and thus similarities in, their approaches, the histories of the Saracens and biographies of Mohammed have to be read not only in the context of nineteenth-century historiography but also within the framework of Victorian preoccupations with foreign cultures. The driving idea of technological progress left an imprint on the historians' efforts to provide their readers with objective accounts of Islam. Consequently, their endeavors display a curious mixture of admiration and resentment as they accept the greatness of Mohammed's leadership but refute his status as a prophet. The historians admit the cultural significance of Islamic biographies but reject the premises of sacred biography upon which Muslim works on Mohammed's life were founded, even though they cite the oriental sources. Punctuating their writings, however, are scorn for the revelations received by Mohammed, mistrust of the oral traditions of Islam, and an emphasis on contradictions in the Koran as well as, routinely, the cruelty of the Saracens.

In the twentieth century, Michel de Certeau noted that historiography, that is, the art of writing history, bears within its own name the paradox, almost an oxymoron, of a relationship established between two antinomic terms, between the real and discourse, between the past and our description of the past.[9] De Certeau referred to both earlier and more contemporary studies. Hayden White likewise distinguished between five levels of conceptualization connected with a historical work: chronicle, story, mode of emplotment, mode of argument, and mode of ideological implication. He sees the first two as primitive elements, the raw "unprocessed" material.[10] By analogy, the latter three we might call the processed material. White dislocated the primacy of the supposedly objective account of historical writings and equated it with the subjective narrative forms

---

8 Taken from http://users.ox.ac.uk/~eets/.
9 De Certeau, *The Writing of History*, 20–21.
10 White, *Metahistory*, 5.

of literature. His work drew heavily on the theoretical works of Northrop Frye, who linked the mode of emplotment with the forms of romance, comedy, tragedy, and satire,[11] which in fact resonates quite nicely with the nineteenth-century methods of writing specialized texts for the general public. Accordingly, the nineteenth-century histories were written for the enjoyment of an educated albeit common reader. Such accounts were meant to be a "processed" form of narrative pertaining to the explanation of the development of some past events.

Since the Orient, as I have argued earlier, held sway over the Victorian readership, one of the first and most important histories of the Saracens was reissued in 1883. This was Simon Ockley's *History of the Saracens*. The work was originally published in two volumes between 1708 and 1718. The 1883 edition was the sixth "revised, improved and enlarged," thereby affirming the rising disquiet concerning Islam in the Near and Middle Eastern regions.[12] Although Ockley's study precedes major nineteenth-century conflicts, his motivations for chronicling Saracen power and the ensuing rise of Islamic militarism reflects the prevalent approach to the topic.

> The establishment of Islamism is undoubtedly to be numbered among those stupendous events which have changed the face of society in the East; and is a subject deserving not only of the careful study of the statesman and the divine but of all who delight to search, patiently and reverently, into the ways of Providence. With the Koran in one hand, and the scimitar in the other, the impetuous and indomitable Arab achieved a series of splendid victories unparalleled in the history of nations; for in the short space of eighty years that mighty range of Saracenic conquest embraced a wider extent of territory than Rome had mastered in the course of eight hundred.[13]

Despite his declaration about the use of the original texts, Ockley mainly refers to one purportedly historical work, by Al-Wakidi, asserting that "my chief business being then with one author."[14] According to recent sources, Abu Muhammad ibn Umar (130–207/747–822), known as Al-Wakidi, was a court historian attached to the court of Harun al-Rashid in Baghdad, and his chief work, *Kitab al-Maghazi* (*The Book of Campaigns*), is one of the foundations of early Islamic history.[15]

---

11 Frye, *Anatomy of Criticism*, 7–11.
12 The Crimean War of 1853–1856, as well as the Russo-Turkish wars of the nineteenth century, especially that of 1877–1878, likewise created an environment for scholarly debates on the Saracens' earlier rise to power.
13 Ockley, *The History*, ii.
14 Ockley, *The History*, xxvii.
15 Glassé, *The Concise Encyclopedia of Islam*, 548. Glassé mentions a Katib al-Waqidi (d. 230/854), who held the title of the secretary of Waqidi and compiled Kitab al-Tabaqat al-Kabir, a biography of *Companions, Helpers and Followers* (229).

To strengthen the historicity of his thesis, Ockley also professes his indebtedness to the French interpreters of the Koran, such as Monsieur Petit de la Croix,[16] and cites a number of English scholars such as Clark, Hyde, and Huntington as well.[17] Unfortunately, contemporary historians believe Pseudo Al-Waqidi's manuscript, entitled *Futûh al-Shâm*, which most probably was the main text Ockley quoted, is a work of fiction rather than history. Samuel Green in his *Life of Mahomet: Founder of the Religion of Islam and the Empire of the Saracens*, published in 1840, lists among his sources Ockley and Gibbon but also studies a number of French histories of Islam. Green, who was a Baptist minister of Lion Street Chapel, Walworth, confesses that his interest in the "subject of Mahometanism" was stimulated by the Muslim claim that once Jesus returns to Earth, he would embrace "the religion of Mahomet," annihilate the Antichrist, and reign with his saints.[18]

To cater to the public enchantment with ancestries, Ockley discusses the origins of the Arabs: first there were the primitive Arabians who inhabited Arabia immediately after the flood (the names of their tribes are all that is left), then there appeared the pure Arabians, descended from Kaktan or Joktan, the son of Heber, spoken of in Genesis 10:25. Before the time of Mohammed, the Arabs were divided into tribes. Green also discusses the pre-Islamic Arab tribes, acknowledging that the roving tribes of the desert were a "bold, enterprising, and generous race, strong in their achievements, and like all savages, equally so in their movements."[19] Like Doughty, Green sees the Arabs as proud, though "perfectly insensible to the voice of law and humanity,"[20] which must have made them very difficult to govern. "The religion of the ancient Arabians, according to their traditions, was derived from Abraham and Ishmael," writes Ockley. "These patriarchs it was pretended built the temple of Mecca, which from its form, was called the Kaaba or Square; and was their kebla, or place towards which they turned their faces when they prayed, as the Jews turned theirs towards the temple of Jerusalem,"[21] he adds dismissively. The old beliefs and practices did not survive except for the fantastic element, which later resonated in Mohammed's explanations of various practices of faith. The tracing of similarities between pre-Islamic forms of worship and their appropriation by Mohammed is one of the features shared by all nineteenth-century historical works

---

16 Ockley, *The History*, xxvii.
17 Ockley, *The History*, xviii.
18 Green, *Life of Mahomet*, vii.
19 Green, *Life of Mahomet*, 9.
20 Green, *Life of Mahomet*, 14.
21 Ockley, *The History*, 3.

under examination here. Friday, for example, was the day when Mohammed called his followers to the mosque, but as Arthur Gilman claims, the "Arabs were used to have gatherings on that day before the prophet's time."[22]

A collection of biographies of famous people, aptly entitled *Great Men of European History*, published by David Pryde in 1881, conveys a similar image of Arabs and their religion. For him, "the majority (of Arabs) are restless rovers, owing no law but the will of their own petty chief. . . . When an opportunity occurs, they harass and plunder hostile tribes."[23] Pryde renders Arabs as filthy and monstrous Others and in an almost medieval fashion denigrates Mohammed, who "studied to appear to their superstitious minds as a prophet, austere in life, noble in sentiment, and holding frequent intercourse with Heaven."[24] Before his appearance as a prophet:

> The religion of the Arabs was idolatry of an ancient growth. At an early age they lighted upon a fountain, which they supposed was the one that had revived the exhausted boy Ishmael. From the peculiar sound of its waters welling out of the ground, they called it *Zemzem*. Near the fountain was a white stone, which they supposed to have fallen from heaven, and to be the petrifaction of an angel. Over these two sacred objects they built a temple, which was called Caaba, and which was soon crowded with idols.[25]

Recognizing the place as sanctified, where one could sense and see the manifestation of the Divine, the Arabs stormed to pray at the very spot, and because of the multitudes of visitors, as Pryde asserts, "the town called Mecca sprung up on the spot. The Caaba still stands; but from the kisses of countless sinners, the white stone has become black."[26] Green also alludes to the black stone, which was allegedly brought from heaven by the archangel Gabriel. According to popular belief, it was originally white but was given its black hue by human sins.[27]

Notwithstanding Mohammed's aversion to objects, idols, and pictures, the stone remained venerated by later Muslims, as if against one of the founding ideas of Islam, which was aversion toward idolatry, dutifully noted by Richard Burton and discussed in the previous chapter. Mohammed waged war against idolatry during his lifetime. Nonetheless, all the sources about his life reiterate

---

22 Gilman, *The Saracens*, 130.
23 Pryde, *Great Men*, 48.
24 Pryde, *Great Men*, 52.
25 Pryde, *Great Men*, 49.
26 Pryde, *Great Men*, 49.
27 Green, *Life of Mahomet*, 35–36. Green writes, with an obvious smirk, that there are several wells surrounding the site and that Muslims pour buckets of water over themselves and "think their sins are washed into the well" (38). He quotes a sketch of the pilgrimage from Burckhardt's *Travels in Arabia* to claim that no unmarried woman can go on a Hajj (54–56).

that places connected with his life were revered even before his death. One of the most famous sites is a small cavern in the red granite rock situated on the side of the mountain Hera, two or three miles to the north from Mecca. It was there that Mohammed found a quiet place to nurse his thoughts, sometimes accompanied by his first wife and first follower and believer, Kadija. Like a Christian anchorite, he secluded himself for days at a time, "brooding with ever deepening anxiety upon the weighty problems that had presented themselves to his soul."[28] His reclusiveness and meditations bring to mind the early Christian Desert Fathers as well as later medieval anchorites and mystics, for whom God was a living, breathing being, whose presence they felt on an everyday basis. Mohammed understood the idea of God in a similar way, as "acting, speaking, ruling; as one who makes his will known to men by books and apostles; as one whom man could not find out, who must reveal himself."[29] Christians and Muslims alike believe in God, the fatherly figure. Still, Mohammed also presented Allah as a ruler of heaven, eternal and everlasting: "without form or limit, including everything and including nothing; he is invoked under ninety-nine attributes which represent him as merciful and glorious, exalted and righteous; the guardian and judge, the creator and the provider."[30]

Ockley and Gilman agree that such a representation of God was perhaps not coincidental but may have conveyed Mohammed's deep-seated need for a father-figure. He had been orphaned very early in his life and had been raised in the house of Halima. It was his grandfather who named the boy Mohammed, "the raised one," a name that had not been used before. "There is such a thing as sympathetic groping for light by persons who have no communication with each other, and there is such a thing as united searching by men who find not what they want until they learn that another Galahad has actually seen the holy Grail."[31] This legend, according to Gilman, pertains to the human need to believe in extraordinary beings. The nineteenth-century philosopher and historian Thomas Carlyle saw that very same need in hero-worship.[32] From early childhood, Mohammed seemed to be earmarked as an exceptional figure; hence, the legends attest, or rather buttress, his being the chosen one. Not much is known about Mohammed's life from the age of thirteen to his early manhood, at twenty-five. The lack of attested data is a breeding ground for fabulous speculations, such

---

28 Gilman, *The Saracens*, 63.
29 Gilman, *The Saracens*, 213.
30 Gilman, *The Saracens*, 19. Beginning his story of Mohammed, he gives a subpart a rather novelistic title, "Amina's famous boy" (39).
31 Gilman, *The Saracens*, 52.
32 Carlyle, *On Heroes*.

as the tale of two men who were seen by Halima's (Mohammed's wet nurse) son to be ripping Mohammed's belly. They were supposed to be angels who took out his heart, to squeeze out of it the black drop, "which they believe is the consequence of original sin, and the source of all sinful thoughts, being found in the heart of every person descended from Adam, except only the Virgin Mary and her son Jesus."[33] Another legend, which Ockley rejects, is the "story of his being seen when very young by a monk of Bostra in Syria, called Bahira, who foretold his future grandeur."[34] And finally, the most important, albeit archetypal, event in Mohammed's life, is the miracle of literacy.

> The following account taken verbatim from Abulfeda, is the statement already alluded to. "When the apostle of God (whom God bless) was forty years old God sent him to the black and the red (i.e. to all mankind), that by a new law he might abolish the ancient laws. His first entrance upon this prophetic office was by a true night vision; for the most high God had inspired him with a love of retirement and solitude, so that he spent a month every year in Mount Hara. When the year of his mission was come he went, in the month of Ramadan, with some family into the cave. Here, as soon, as the night fell wherein the glorious God very greatly honoured him, Gabriel (upon whom be peace) came to him and said, 'Read.' And when the prophet answered 'I cannot read,' he said again, 'Read: In the name of the Lord who hath created & reciting the words as far as he taught man what he knew not, v. 5. Upon this the prophet, going to the middle of the mountain, thou art the apostle of God, and I am Gabriel,' stood still in his place looking upon Gabriel, till at length Gabriel departed, when the prophet also went away."[35]

Present-day scholarship recognizes that the *hadith*, the reports of the words and deeds of the Prophet Mohammed, were disseminated orally after his death. As Gregor Schoeler clarifies, these materials "needed up to 250 years to become 'literature'; as for Arabic poetry, which had been in existence since long before the rise of Islam, it needed up to 300 years to become 'literature.'"[36] Schoeler argues that Arabic literature has to be seen within and through the dichotomy

---

33 Ockley, *The History*, 7.

34 Ockley, *The History*, 9. "At his first setting out upon his prophetic office, he bore all affronts without seeming to resent them; and when any of his followers were injured he recommended patience to them, and for that purpose, it is said, proposed the Christian martyrs for their imitation. He was obliging of everybody; the rich he flattered, the poor he relieved with alms: and by his behavior appeared the most humane, friendly person in the world, so long as he found it necessary to wear the mask, which we shall hereafter find him, upon occasions, pulling off and throwing aside" (19).

35 Ockley, *The History*, 12. In Bede's *Historia Ecclesiastical Gentis Anglorum*, one finds the story of Caedmon, a simple shepherd who was given the gift of letters in his sleep; upon waking, he composed a poem known as "Caedmon's Creation Hymn" and then dedicated the rest of his life to God.

36 Schoeler, *The Genesis*, 1.

of the oral/written but also in the context of "aural transmission" or "audited transmission,"[37] since the first two centuries of Islam did not leave any written documentation on the events one finds in later sources.[38] What is more, the Koran was given to the faithful to be recited to them. "The system of education in Islam," Schoeler clarifies, "required that every text to be studied – including the ones that existed as actual books – be 'heard' or 'read' in the presence of the author, or an authorized transmitter, even if these texts were in fact often only disseminated through written copies."[39] Thus the Koran always demands reading and recitation, and this, although contrary to the European idea of education and thereby eschewed by Burton, is what the Koranic schools are based upon. A seminal episode is Mohammed's night journey with the archangel Gabriel, who brings him into the presence of God. In heaven, Mohammed meets Jesus, whose prayer he had solicited. He is also given the famous warning: "If you had chosen the wine, your nation would have strayed from the right way."[40] Total abstinence by Muslims, as has already been observed, puzzled Chardin during his sojourn in Persia.

All of the above-quoted incidents subscribe to the requirements of sacred biography, otherwise known as hagiography in Christian writings. The genre is defined by Thomas Heffernan as

---

37 Schoeler, *The Genesis*, 8.
38 Schoeler, *The Genesis*, 18–27, shows various documents written in the early centuries after the Prophet's death. He shows that the composition of poetry and its oral dissemination was soon perhaps not substituted but augmented with writing. He underscores the beginnings of religious scholarship, claiming that "the difference between notes and draft notes or notebooks is, in reality, a minor one: in Greek, both are indistinguishably termed hypomnēma" (49), and thus the notes are as important as the main text. He shows the development of court literature, poetry as well as annals and scholarly treatises in the form of epistles, and draws on the development of linguistics and philology as related to the study of the Koran. By the ninth century, the Arabic language can boast quite a number of important and interesting written works. Schoeler claims that it was the century of bibliophiles, "the century when large numbers of actual books came into existence and in which a broad readership arose" (107), yet the question "listening to books, or reading them?" remained, and I guess with the popularity of audiobooks today, it has remained pertinent. In the early medieval Arabic world, aural transmission persisted, "not only as an ideal but also in practice" (122); in the centuries to come, and even though the advent of literacy was unstoppable, the ideal of reading and reciting to an audience were preserved.
39 Schoeler, *The Genesis*, 36.
40 Ockley, *The History*, 21.

a narrative text of the *vita* of the saint written by a member of a community of belief. The text provides a documentary witness to the process of sanctification for the community and in doing so becomes itself a part of the sacred tradition it serves to document.[41]

Ockley, whose account is the least jaundiced, is quite conscious that he is dealing with material similar to the medieval hagiographies, whose aim was not historical but religious accuracy. Whereas the classical ideas on writing lives were concerned with two distinctive aspects of biographical writing – *praxeis*, the presentation of life in a chronological order; and *ethos*, an interpretative discussion of character – writers such as Plutarch, Suetonius and, contemporary with Suetonius, the Gospel writers would use the "miraculous anecdote indicative of character"[42] to augment their explanation of one's personality. Medieval hagiographers were, of course, acutely aware of the necessary mixture of factual and not so factual discourses. Even though hagiography had become a synonym for unreliability by Ockley's time, medievalists of the nineteenth century saw sacred biography as a kind of historical writing, imbued with vital information about medieval people and their beliefs. Fascinated with the strangeness of the medieval world, they revived and re-edited the medieval manuscripts, not because the sacred biographies were perceived as illustrating the acts of God in the world but because they were seen as auxiliary sources to research in medieval culture. Comparably, Ockley's work subscribes to the demands of classical hermeneutics in which a text's meaning was limited by "the value accorded its discourse within the culture of its first audience."[43]

Unlike medieval hagiographers, Ockley's motivation was to neither sanctify nor teach his audience about the miracles of Mohammed; nor was he interested in expounding an exemplary life, yet he unhesitatingly presented the occurrences that furthered Mohammed's steps along "the path of God." Such is the instance of the origins of the well-known Islamic creed: "There is no God but God, Mohammed is the prophet of God," which was delivered to Mohammed when he was returning from his trip to meet God. Gabriel takes Mohammed

---

41 Heffernan, *Sacred Biography*, 16.
42 Heffernan, *Sacred Biography*, 31. Heffernan argues that Christian biographers wrote out of a conviction that biography was "an *epideictic* narrative containing an encomiastic celebration of heroic virtues, they reshaped the dominant classical philosophical understanding which supported such rhetorical narratives" (151). Like Arabic writers of chronicles and Ockley's source for the life of Mohammed, Christian writers were interested not in philosophical speculation but in a straightforward eulogy of their subject, which left no margin for any doubt as to their prophetic/saintly role.
43 Hamilton, *Historicism*, 3.

through all the heavens, and there he is proffered the *Shahada*.⁴⁴ Even without an elaborate commentary, Ockley's writing exudes skepticism as to the assumptions that God turned directly to Mohammed and taught him many important things, noted in the Koran. Comparably, Green, true to his times, also depicts Mohammed as a fraud, declaring that it is "natural to suppose, that a strong colouring would be put upon every superior quality of a pretended messenger of God, sent to restore the true religion to the world."⁴⁵ He is even bold enough to write that it is impossible to determine "whether Mahomet commenced his career as a deluded enthusiast, or a designing impostor."⁴⁶

For Muslims, Mohammed's flight with Gabriel and his being given a privileged place in the hallowed pantheon are taken as definite signs that the Prophet is chosen by God to do great things for his fellow humans. Yet, as was the case of Christian saints, his was a thorny path. In the thirteenth year of his mission, Mohammed learned that his enemies in Mecca had concocted an assassination attempt and, fearing for his life, he fled "to the town then known as Yathreb, then Medinato 'l Nabi, and finally Medina."⁴⁷ In Medina, "[t]he self-sacrificing apostle started at once into the aspirant after worldly power. With wonderful skill, he set himself to gain the complete control of the wild Arabs."⁴⁸ The providential escape, known in Arabic as *Hejira* or *Hijirah*, marks the new era in the lives of Arabs, as the year from which they chronicle their past. Since Mohammed was warned by the archangel Gabriel, the flight, like all other events from the propitious history of Mohammed's life, authenticates his position as a prophet. Paradoxically, the first year of Islamic history bears a striking resemblance to the divisions of history by Christians into Before Christ and After Christ, and their concurrent disparaging of Antiquity as pagan and barbaric. According to *The Encyclopaedia of Islam*, it was not in 622, the year the escape took place, but sixteen years later that the Caliph Umar "formalized the Prophet's custom of dating events from the *Hijrah*."⁴⁹ In line with Islamic historiography, Ockley uses the date of *Hijirah* as a temporal reference to the second part of his book, which deals with the conquests of Syria, Persia and Egypt: "Hejirah 11–13, A.D. 632–634."⁵⁰ To this day, the date

---

44 Ockley, *The History*, 24.
45 Green, *Life of Mahomet*, 51.
46 Green, *Life of Mahomet*, 67–68.
47 Ockley, *The History*, 31.
48 Pryde, *Great Men*, 52.
49 Glassé, *The Encyclopaedia*, 205. It is interesting that Irwin, in his anthology of Arabic literature, uses similar dating and labeling: "Pagan Poets (A.D. 500–622)." Irwin, *Night and Horses and the Desert*.
50 Ockley, *The History*, 79.

stands for a symbolic threshold between the old and the new life of Arabs turned Muslims. What is more, *Hijirah* marks the transformation of the mundane into the miraculous, with rather unfortunate consequences for those people, like the Persians, who would be Islamicized by force.

In Pryde's view, Mohammed manipulated the illiterate Arabs through self-fashioning, positioning himself as an honorable and bold warrior as such a figure responded to their pugnacious characters. Leading an existence worthy of the colloquies with heaven, there he searched and found support for his actions; this paradigm was used when he needed a "divine" explanation for his sexual trysts with Mary the Coptic slave (addressed below). After his escape to Medina, Mohammed was handed a new revelation obliging him and his followers to spread the faith by force. Those who persisted in unbelief were to be destroyed. Thus "[t]he sword was the key of heaven and hell," and so the believers were justified in their battling and conquering *dar al-harb*, the world of unbelief. Like Ockley, Pryde also sees *hejira*, the flight, as the turning point for Mohammed. Ockley, however, underscores the divine ordinance of the new approach to faith: "Gabriel now brings him messages from heaven to the effect, that whereas other prophets had come with miracles and been rejected, he was to take different measures, and propagate Islamism by the sword."[51] For Muslims, as well as for Christians, this meant the onset of the holy war.

Gilman reasons that Mohammed saw himself as different from the previous prophets who had been sent by God. He believed that Moses showed his providence and clemency; Solomon his wisdom, majesty, and glory; and Issa – Jesus – his righteousness, power, and knowledge; but that none of these attributes or miracles had proved sufficient to conquer unbelief. Mohammed, however, thought that he was "the last of the prophets," who is sent with the sword! "Let the champions of the faith of Islam neither argue not discuss; but slay all who refuse to obey the law or to pay tribute. Whoever fights for Islam, whether he fall or conquer, will surely receive the reward. The sword is the key of heaven and hell!"[52] In the Koran, in *sura* xvii, the believers are commended to "fight for God's cause with your wealth and your persons."[53] What is more, God himself grants "permission to take up arms . . . to those who are attacked, because they have been wronged. God has power to grant them victory."[54] Mohammed considered his enemies representatives of Satan and, consequently, enemies of Allah.

---

51 Ockley, *The History*, 32.
52 Gilman, *The Saracens*, 143.
53 *The Koran*, 551.
54 *The Koran*, 336.

Ockley and Pryde, as well as Gilman, very diligently summarize Mohammed's holy wars, but Ockley also gives credit to his diplomatic efforts.[55] From here on, the account develops into a curious combination of respect and revulsion at the ways in which Mohammed handled the conversion of the world to Islam. When Mohammed converted the king of Ethiopia, "[h]e sent also to Al Mondar, king of Bahrain, who came into his religion, and afterwards routed the Persians, and made a great slaughter of them. And now all the Arabians of Bahrain had become converts to his religion."[56] While medieval Christianity did not disregard violence when it came to conversion, the Catholic Church today frequently discounts the centuries-long bloodshed. Moreover, conversion of the unfaithful, or pagans, has always been a required element of hagiography. Mohammed's wars are, then, a narrative necessity. What is derided by the historians is the framing of his own needs, aspirations, and choices into a religious law for the Prophet's followers. The tale of a gift from Makawaks, viceroy of Egypt, can serve as an example. The viceroy sent Mohammed two maidens as slaves, one of whom, fifteen-year-old Mary, caught the Prophet's eye. Still, such a present was an outright offense to Mohammed's wives, Hafsa and Ayesha. Caught between duty and desire, he is given a vision to extricate himself from the moral dilemma. This revelation is recorded in the sixty-sixth chapter of the Koran, releasing the Prophet from his oath and allowing him to take concubines if he so wished.[57] To highlight the fictionality of that fragment, Ockley cites

---

55 Gilman talks about the dispossession of the Christians of Damascus. He [Walid] took "their ancient church of St. John the Baptist, on which Roman emperors had long lavished their gold, and in which they had accumulated many relics of martyrs and saints, and on its site he employed workmen by the thousand in erecting a mosque in which, by uniting the architecture of Greece and Persia, he laid the foundation of the Saracenic style, from which some graces and ornamentation of the Gothic were to be borrowed in another age." Gilman, *The Saracens*, 322. Walid, the eldest son of Caliph Abd el Melik, who died in 705, is depicted as a stereotypical Eastern ruler: "While Walid was living in luxury at Damascus and gratifying his artistic tastes, his generals were fighting for his empire in Asia Minor, in Korassan, in Africa, and making his authority everywhere felt. They ravaged Cappadocia, Armenia, Pontus, and Galatia, and brought to Damascus the usual crowds of captives bearing rich spoils. They crossed the Oxus, drove before them the hordes of Turkestan, and captured the city of Bokhra; they went again to Samarkand and, after a siege, obliged it to pay a great tribute annually in gold and to contribute three thousand human beings every year to the slavemarts of Damascus; and they undermined the religion of the Magians, they overran Scinde, and penetrated in that direction as far as the great river of India (A.D. 708)" (322).
56 Ockley, *The History*, 51.
57 *The Koran*, 559–60. Gilman gives the same story with more details: "His [Mohammed's] long postponed desire for a son was gratified by the birth of Ibrahim, child of a Coptic maid, Mary, who had been given to him as a slave by the governor of Egypt. The wives were very jealous of

Thomas Moore's *Lalla Rookh*:[58] "And here Mohammed, born for love and guile / Forgets the Koran in his Mary's smile / Then beckons some kind angel from above / with a new text to consecrate their love."[59] After all, even today, as Glassé remarks, for Muslims "the best possession is a virtuous woman."[60] Moore is apparently more critical than Ockley, but both voice European disbelief in the rather "handy" displays of God's grace. Green, however, refrains from commenting on Mohammed's promoting "the gratification of sensual passion."[61]

Mary, as the mother of the prophet's only son, and he in turn became much displeased with them. The sixty-sixth sura was 'revealed' as a warning to the refectory spouses, who were therein told of the two wicked wives of these good men Noah and Lot, to whom it was said, on their approach to the other life, 'Enter the *fire* with those who enter!'" Gilman, *The Saracens*, 192.

58 Moore, *Lalla Rookh*, 365. This 1817 oriental romance by Thomas Moore is named for its heroine, who is the daughter of the seventeenth-century Mughal emperor Aurangzeb. The work consists of four narrative poems with a connecting tale in prose, and the story concerns the journey of the princess to marry the young king of Bukhara. She is accompanied by her court and a young poet called Feramorz, with whom she falls in love. The main story is then interspersed with the narrative poems sung by the poet: "The Veiled Prophet of Khorassan" (loosely based upon the story of Al-Muqanna), "Paradise and the Peri," "The Fire-Worshippers," and "The Light of the Harem." When Lalla Rookh enters the palace of her bridegroom, she loses consciousness, but to her happiness she discovers when she revives that her husband to be is none other than her beloved Feramorz, "a youth about Lalla Rookh's own age, and graceful as that idol of women, Crishna," as we learn from Moore (339). As is typical of the genre, Moore offers a number of observations on the forms of oriental life and culture. The Muslim warriors think of themselves as "Earth's shrines and thrones before our banner fall" (343). Moore notes the curse of Eblis, the devil, as he discusses the character of Lucifer (350–51). Eblis did not, according to the "Mahometan" tradition, acknowledge human beings, as Moore explains in a footnote. Moore writes of Greece: "The bands of Greece, still mighty, though enslaved" (357). Painting a picture of the Eastern court, he nevertheless equates luxury with weakness (360). He sees Islam as a "fierce" religion that is driven "to conquer or to perish" (373), and quotes the first fundamental commandment of Islam: "'Alla illa alla!' – the glad shout renew – Alla Akbar!" (376). In a footnote to the second tale entitled "Paradise and the Peri," Moore explains how the Persians fought against their Muslim invaders (392). In the tale about the Fire-worshippers, the Persians fight against their Muslim invaders, "the Fiends of Fire / Who groan'd to see their shrines expire, with charms that, all in vain withstood, / Would drown the Koran's light in blood" (413). Moore writes about "Iran [or Ireland], his dear-loved country made / A land of carcasses and slaves" (426). Elsewhere, he remarks on Lalla Rookh's "little Persian slave" (437). In "The Light of the Harem," Moore depicts the "burka" – "And veil'd by such a mask that shades / The features of young Arab maids" (450) – highlighting the riches of "Kublai-Khan" (451). Notwithstanding the poem's unencumbered exoticism, Moore shows some knowledge and a true fascination with the style of writing modeled on *The Arabian Nights* and the subject matter. Set in faraway lands, the tale nevertheless can be seen as an allegory of Ireland enslaved by the British.

59 Ockley, *The History*, 51.

60 Glassé, *The Encyclopaedia*, 473.

61 Green, *The Life of Mahomet*, 217.

Equally pejorative are Ockley's statements about the contradictions in the Koran.

> There are several contradictions in the Koran. To reconcile these, the Mussulman doctors have invented the doctrine of abrogation, i.e. that what was revealed at one time was revoked by a new revelation. A great deal of it is so absurd, trifling, and full of tautology, that it requires no little patience to read much of it at a time. Notwithstanding, the Koran is cried up by the Mussulmans, as inimitable; and in the seventeenth chapter of the Koran, Mohammed is commanded to say, "Verily if men and genii were purposely assembled, that they might produce anything like the Koran, they could not produce anything like unto it, though they assisted one another."[62]

For Muslims, Ockley's pronouncements could be just shy of blasphemy. Contradictions, however, are part and parcel of his work. He refers to Mohammed as "the great impostor," concomitantly calling him "founder of the Saracenic empire."[63] Correspondingly, the historian disdains the fights over succession even though he does not analyze the differences between Shi'a and Sunni Muslims.[64] Interestingly, Green puts forth the thesis that under different circumstances, Mohammed's life might have been entirely obliterated and the empire of the Saracens

> might have sunk to oblivion with the anonymous millions of his race, as the drops of rain are absorbed into the sands of his native deserts. His whole history makes it evident, that fanaticism, ambition, and lust, were his master-passions; of which the former appears to have been gradually eradicated by the growing strength of the two last.[65]

---

62 Ockley, *The History*, 65.
63 Ockley, *The History*, 79.
64 Shi'a Muslims are followers of Ali, Mohammed's son-in-law. It has to be noted that the supporters of Ali's right to Mohammed's inheritance appeared twenty years after Ali's death, and the ideology took more than one hundred years to develop. Glassé, *The Encyclopaedia*, 482. Sunni Muslims, who comprise the majority within Islam, are more orthodox in their approach, recognizing the first four caliphs, but they do not attribute any specific function or authority to the descendants of Ali (505). Count de Gobineau, who is the reputed father of contemporary "racialism," argued that Shi'ism represented a reaction of the Indo-European Persians against Arab domination – against the constricting Semitism of Arab Islam. "To nineteenth-century Europe, obsessed with the problems of national conflict and national freedom, such an explanation seemed reasonable and indeed obvious. The Shi'a stood for Persia, fighting against Arab, and later against Turkish domination. The Assassins represented a form of militant, nationalist extremism, like the terrorist secret societies of nineteenth-century Italy and Macedonia." Lewis, *The Assassins*, 136–37. For de Gobineau, the Persians, "whom the Greeks self-complacently styled outside-barbarians were, in reality, a highly cultivated people. . . . Their arts if not Hellenic still attained a high degree of perfection. Their architecture, though not of Grecian style, was not inferior in magnificence and splendor. Nay, I for one am willing to render myself obnoxious to the charge of classical heresy, by regarding the pure Persians as a people, in some respects at least, superior to the Greeks." De Gobineau, *Moral and Intellectual Diversity*, 39.
65 Green, *Life of Mahomet*, 215.

Instead, Mohammed's followers grew in numbers and strength, rooting out the Christians from Damascus, where "several battles were fought . . . in which Christians for the most part were beaten."[66] In the end, the Christians in Damascus gave way and were forced to surrender.

In a rather dramatic fashion, perhaps akin to the Whitean writing of history in a tragic mode, Ockley stresses the Saracen hate of the Christians, making a powerful utterance against their cruelty:

> Kaled (O bloody and insatiable Saracen!), when he saw these poor wretches carry away the small reminder of their plentiful fortunes, felt a great deal of regret. So mortally did he hate the Christians, that to see one of them alive was death to him. What does he do? Why, he orders his men to keep themselves and their horses in good condition, telling them, that after the three days were expired (for so long only had they a safe conduct) he designed to pursue them. And he said his mind told him that they should still overtake them all, and have all the plunder; "and," says he "they have left nothing valuable behind them, but have taken along with them all the best of their clothes, and plate and jewels, and whatever is worth carrying.[67]

Khaled eventually slaughtered the fugitives, and Ockley cites many instances in which the Christians were attacked by the Saracens, for example in a monastery.[68] Yet he also writes about Christians who, while besieging the city of Baalbec, "were bravely repulsed by the besieged, who from the walls did them a great deal of damage with their engines. The valour of the citizens, together with the extreme coldness of the weather, made the Saracens glad to draw off from the assault."[69]

Giving the Saracens their due, Ockley also points out the atrocities of war, outlining the rise of what, throughout the European Middle Ages, will be seen as the terrible, almost satanic, power of the Saracens. *The Siege of Jerusalem*,[70] which follows that of Damascus, became a prototypical narrative of the fall of a city and is the subject matter of numerous accounts in medieval histories and romances. The trope, however, was by no means new in English literature. The classical story of the fall of Troy reinterpreted in Christian writings is also re-enacted in the Old English poem "The Ruin" (eighth/ninth century). The anonymous ruminates on the results of the devastation of a Roman city, most probably Bath, wrecked after its capture by the West Saxons in 577. In this case, the classical

---

66 Ockley, *The History*, 108.
67 Spelling original, Ockley, *The History*, 151.
68 Ockley, *The History*, 165–66.
69 Ockley, *The History*, 180.
70 Malcolm Hebron writes extensively about the theme and image of the siege in medieval literature; *The Siege of Jerusalem* is one of his examples. Hebron, *The Medieval Siege*, 112–35.

tradition of the poem in praise of a city is transformed into a Christian meditation on the fall of the proud and mighty. The ruined city is also a visual reminder of the destruction of civilization, which in the medieval imagination the city represented. The cultivated, civilized land has always been seen in opposition to hostile nature; that hostility foregrounded the juxtaposition of civilized Christians against the Barbarians.[71] Their enmity can lead to only one outcome, that of war. The fictional potential of conflict, and, most commonly, the siege is shown, for example, in the medieval romance of *The Siege of Milan*.[72] Demonization of the Saracens, who are always cast in the role of antagonists, almost immediately obliterates the time gap between the medieval and Enlightenment fears visible in Ockley's narrative. As the historian explains, the treaty between the opposing forces, which included a number of articles designed to facilitate Christian–Saracen dialogue, in fact, strengthened the idea of the domination of Islam over the area, with Christianity relegated to the position of a "tolerated paganism."[73] Jerusalem was lost, forced on her knees once again:

> For though the number of the slain, and the calamities of the besieged were greater when it was taken by the Romans; yet the servitude of those that survived was nothing comparable to this, either in respect of the circumstances or the duration. For however it might seem to

---

[71] In *Landscapes of Fear*, Vito Fumagalli draws attention to the constant opposition between wilderness and cultivated land. He argues that even Paradise was conceptualized as natural but ordered. Fumagalli, *Landscapes of Fear*, 9, 13–22.

[72] Along with the literal siege, medieval literature also abounds in allegorical sieges, subsumed in personified sins attacking a human soul. The allegorical battle is perhaps best exemplified in the fifteenth-century morality play *The Castle of Perseverance*.

[73] Omar issues the articles of law: "1. The Christians shall build no new churches, either in the city or the adjacent territory; 2. They shall not refuse the Mussulmans entrance into their churches, either by night or day; 3. They should set open the doors of them to all passengers and travelers; 4. If any Mussulman should be upon a journey, they shall be obliged to entertain him gratis for the space of three days; 5. They should not teach their children the Koran, nor talk openly of their religion, nor persuade any one to be of it; neither should they hinder any of their relations from becoming Mahomedans, if they had an inclination to it; 6. They shall pay respect to the Mussulmans, and if they were sitting rise up to them; 7. They should not go like the Mussulmans in their dress; nor wear the same caps, shoes, nor turbans, nor part their hair as they do, nor speak after the same manner, nor be called by the names used by the Mussulmans; 8. They shall not ride upon saddles, nor bear any sort of arms, nor use the Arabic tongue in the inscriptions of their seals; 9. They shall not sell any wine; 10. They shall be obliged to keep to the same sort of habit wheresoever they went, and always wear girdles upon their waist; 11. They shall set no crosses upon their churches, nor show their crosses nor their books openly in the streets of the Mussulmans; 12. They shall not ring, but only toll their bells: nor shall they take any servant that had once belonged to the Mussulmans, and some say, that Omar commanded the inhabitants of Jerusalem to have the foreparts of their heads shaved, and obliged them to ride upon their panels sideways, not like the Mussulmans." Ockley, *The History*, 211–12.

be utterly ruined and destroyed by Titus, yet by Hadrian's time it had greatly recovered itself. Now it fell, as it were, once for all, into the hands of the most mortal enemies of the Christian religion, and has continued so ever since; with the exception of a brief interval of about ninety years, during which it was held by the Christians in the holy war.[74]

Trying to be dispassionate, Ockley is indisputably exasperated by the fall of Jerusalem,[75] as were all Christian historians from the Middle Ages onwards. Talking about the most venerated city in Christendom, he irrevocably loses all objectivity and becomes incensed enough to voice his opinions and sympathize with the persecuted Christians. Unexpectedly, he presents Caliph Omar Ebn Al Khattab (584–644) behaving in rather a civil way by promising the Christians he would not take or destroy their churches, which in the end, nevertheless, fell to the Muslims.

The loss of Jerusalem was for Ockley, as for writers earlier in the post-Crusading periods, a particularly ruinous retribution. Jerusalem's churches were the seat of Christianity, linked with the Old Testament and the New Testament's life of Jesus. The church where Jacob's stone lay, the one in which he slept and had a vision of the ladder, for example, became the site where the Saracens built a mosque. This was "in the place where Solomon's formerly stood, and [they] consecrated it to the Mohammedan superstition."[76] Instead of "Mohammedan faith," he uses the term "superstition," the supporters of which destroyed Christians' most sacred sites. Surprisingly, he does not dwell on the atrocities that follow the takeover; nevertheless, he alludes to the story of Constantine, the emperor Heraclitus' son, who frequently sent Christian Arabs into the camp of the Saracen army; once, one of them stumbled and swore "by Christ" and was immediately recognized as a spy, "cut to pieces in an instant."[77] Shrouded in legend, the history of the Saracens is incessantly rendered as a warning to Christians.[78]

---

74 Ockley, *The History*, 212.
75 As an example of the Muslim idea of history, Ockley quotes the dispute between Amrou, the Saracen, and the Emperor Constantine. It is Muslims who believe: "You reckon yourselves akin to us; but we have no desire to acknowledge the affinity, so long as you continue infidels. Besides you are the offspring of Esau, we of Ishmael: and God chose our prophet Mohammed from Adam, to the time that he came out of the loins of his father, and made him the best of the sons of Ishmael." Ockley, *The History*, 247–48.
76 Ockley, *The History*, 213–14.
77 Ockley, *The History*, 245. At the end of his book, Ockley cites the sentences of Ali (337–345) and traces the history of the Saracens as far as Hassan, the son of Ali, the fifth caliph after Mohammed (Hejirah 40, 41, AD 660–661) (345–54). The book ends with the Saracen's penetration of India (conquered in the East) and the victories in Spain.
78 Christians are not the only targets of the newly converted Arabs. In Medina, for example: "the stubborn Jewish colonists were butchered in cold blood, and utterly rooted out." Pryde, *Great Men*, 52. The same event as presented by Ockley reads that "[t]he Jews had many a treaty

Gilman is similarly outraged by the Saracen ban on building Christian churches:

> The Christians were bound to build no new churches, and the Moslems were always to be admitted to those then standing; the doors of their homes were ever to be open to all strangers and travelers; Moslems journeying were to be entertained free of expense for three days at a time; Jews should not interfere with the conversion of any to Islam; should rise and stand before Moslems as a sign of respect; they should adopt different dress from the Moslems, have different names, a different style of parting the hair, and different modes of talking; they could not use the Arabic tongue, sell wine, ride upon saddles, bear arms, ring the bells of their churches, set up crosses, nor take any servant that had belonged to a Moslem; they could not have windows overlooking Moslems in their houses, and were always to wear the same style of dress, and have girdles about the waist.[79]

The amalgamation of esteem and antipathy, objectivity and subjectivity, is equally perceptible in the work of later historians such as Pryde, whose study might easily be seen as the philosophy of Carlyle's hero-worship put into practice. Pryde begins his narrative by defining and listing the Barbarians invading Europe:

> About 375 the Huns appeared in Europe, from the northern plains of Asia. They were the most terrible of all the barbarians. They had squat figures, large heads, flat faces, without any beards, and with deep-sunk, bead-like eyes. They devoured their food before it was half-cooked; and they reveled in plunder, slaughter, and destruction. In fact, as the writers of that period declare, they resembled immense droves of beasts of prey ramping on their hind-legs. On the approach of these hideous savages a panic seized the nations. Even the Visigoths fled southward, and implored the Romans to admit them within the empire. The northern bank of the Danube was thronged for miles with wild figures shedding tears and uttering piteous cries.[80]

Embarking on a fairly difficult task, Pryde exculpates himself from accusations of undue selectivity, stating that he perceives Europe as "one community" and that his choice of heroes was dictated by their contribution to European history.

---

with Mohammed, and lived peaceably at Medina; till a Jew, having affronted an Arabian milkwoman, was killed by a Mussulman. In revenge for this, the Jews killed the Mussulman, whereupon a general quarrel ensued." Ockley, *The History*, 35.

79 Gilman, *The Saracens*, 249–50. Gilman sees personal fault rather than blaming the entire nation. "Having reigned ten years, Walid thus died at the age of forty-two, in the year 715, after a life of personal ease, during which his generals had filled all the surrounding nations with the fear of the Moslem arms, and had carried his renown from one end of the ancient world to the other. They had penetrated the region beyond the Oxus, bearing their victorious arms almost to the borders of China (710 AD) and promising to extend the domains of the kalif through that country to the Pacific Ocean, as they already touched the Atlantic. The greatest glory of the Omiades had been gained" (333).

80 Pryde, *Great Men*, 27–28.

Presenting eminent figures, he adopts Carlyle's views on biography. "Those events that have influenced the whole, or a great part of that community, I have regarded as emphatically European events; and to them I have given pre-eminence."[81] Such are the parameters of his work.[82] Thus, instead of concentrating on the well-known "great Englishmen," he overlooks the history of England "with the exception of King Alfred and Richard the Lionhearted." Overlooking national histories, he involuntarily evokes the concept of *respublica Christiana*, the medieval ideal of Christian countries united in their fights against God's numerous enemies both within and outside their borders.

Since he begins his discussion of the past with the portraits of the barbarians' leaders, it comes as no surprise that the archenemy of Christendom, the creator of the Saracenic empire, is portrayed as the last of them, being "one of the figures auxiliary in the dismemberment of the Roman empire." Like Green, Pryde spells the name of the Prophet as "Mahomet." Pryde's evocative image of Arabia, a land of "bleak and rugged mountains" and "dreary deserts" afflicted with an "almost insufferable climate,"[83] forms the environment in which Mohammed is born and brought up:

> Above, in a cloudless sky with the sun blazing in the middle; below, is a glaring and burning expanse of land; and ever and anon comes the simoom, as hot as the blast from a furnace, filling the air with a whirlwind of dust, and sickening and stifling animal life. It would be a land of death, were it not for the green patches, or oases, where cool fountains gurgle forth, and fragrant shrubs sweeten the air, and the date-groves cast their shades and hang out their clusters, and the nightingale lulls the weary traveler to sleep.[84]

The above-quoted observation would fit more easily into the discourse of travel narratives, but by accentuating the prohibitive nature, Pryde wants to stress the impact of nurture on Mohammed's character, for the landscapes of Arabia must have been most striking to all who visited and wrote about it. In travel narratives, nature renders the experience either familiar or strange, hence the comparisons of "here" and "there," and wherever "there" signifies the unknown, in histories, nature is used to illuminate the characters of the historical figures under scrutiny. True to the fashion of his times, Samuel Green dwells on the meaning of the word "Arabia," associating it with the apparent barrenness of the land and deriving the very name from a Hebrew word "denoting "wilderness," or "a land of deserts

---

81 Pryde, *Great Men*, ii–iv.
82 Pryde, *Great Men*, vi.
83 Pryde, *Great Men*, 48.
84 Pryde, *Great Men*, 48.

and plains."[85] He considers the south and southeastern coasts as a "ridge of dismal, barren, naked rocks, destitute of soil or herbage, and yielding to the mariner, as he passes up the Indian ocean, a picture of the most gloomy and forbidding kind."[86] He admits, however, that there are other parts "rich and delightful" with temperate air.[87]

The notion of the desolate wilderness reappears in all the travel and historical narratives concerning Arabia. Richard Burton also saw the wilderness in the desert, whose sky is "terrible in its stainless beauty," and wrote that "the Samún caresses you like a lion with flaming breath," which "chokes up and hardens the skin."[88] Elsewhere, he returns to the picture of the desert as a sublime experience,[89] recalling:

> This day's march was peculiarly Arabia. It was a desert peopled only with echoes, – a place of death for what little there is to die in it, – a wilderness where, to use my companion's phrase, there is nothing but He. Nature scalped, flayed, discovered all her skeletons to the gazer's eye. The horizon was a sea of mirage; a gigantic sand column whirled over the plain; and on both sides of our road were huge piles of bare rock, standing detached upon the surface of sand and clay.[90]

For Doughty, "The Derb el-Haj is no made road, but here a multitude of cattle-paths beaten hollow by the camels' tread, in the marching thus once in the year, of so many generations of the motley pilgrimage over this waste."[91] His last stop, the Wady Fatima, is also described as a bleak "vast wilderness."[92] Thus, he tells his readers that westward toward Jordan lies Gilead, "a land of noble aspect in these bald countries."[93] After all, Doughty was writing not for an audience that shared his experiences but for one that wanted to imagine and learn something new.

The constant juxtaposition between here and there is present in Gaston Bachelard's dialectics of *here* and *there*, which "were promoted to the rank of

---

85 Green, *Life of Mahomet*, 4.
86 Green, *Life of Mahomet*, 4, 5.
87 Green, *Life of Mahomet*, 7.
88 Burton, *Personal Narrative*, 1:149.
89 Burton, *Personal Narrative*, 1:150–51. He also evokes the images of death: "In the Desert, even more than upon the ocean, there is present death; hardship is there, and piracies, and shipwreck, solitary, not in crowds, where, as the Persians say, "Death is a Festival"; and this sense of danger, never absent, invests the scene of travel with an interest not its own" (1:149).
90 Burton, *Personal Narrative*, 2:131.
91 Doughty, *Arabia Deserta*, 1:8.
92 Doughty, *Arabia Deserta*, 2:527.
93 Doughty, *Arabia Deserta*, 1:17.

absolutism."⁹⁴ Bachelard argues that neither the terms "outside" and "inside" nor "concrete" and "vast" are symmetrical, as everything in the study of spatial relationships is given human value.⁹⁵ Immense outside areas can give people an "exterior dizziness,"⁹⁶ which is the case in the novels of Ahdaf Soueif and Brian Moore, discussed later. Colonial topographies politicized Oriental space, which is evident in Ockley, Pryde, and Gilman's works. Burton and Doughty strove to discover the untainted places, yet their narratives inadvertently entail the colonists' gaze. Indeed, in the postcolonial era it is difficult to think about foreign territories without the implication of the power that conquers, fashions and represents the subdued territories. This is in line with Henri Lefebvre's declaration that, "sovereignty implies space." Quite dejectedly, Lefebvre sees all states born out of violence rooted in (human) nature.⁹⁷ Arabia, therefore, becomes a space established and constituted by violence, and in the texts in question, it is transformed into a discursive space against which violence, whether covert or overt, is directed.

Pryde's recounting of the life of the Prophet accentuates the unruliness of his compatriots but also the unique character of Mohammed.

> The Arabs claim to be descended from Ishmael, the outcast son of Abraham; and certainly they inherit their ancestor's reckless habits. Time, which has changed the other nations of Asia, has had very little effect upon these wild men of the desert. Some indeed, have settled down in towns as traders, and send long strings of camels laden with merchandise across the wilderness.⁹⁸

Mohammed belonged to the Koreish, the chief tribe among the Arabs. When he was twelve, he went to Syria with a caravan and was amazed at the world he saw. About that time he met a Nestorian monk who "is said to have taught him some of the great truths of the Christian religion," hence the presence of Jesus and the Virgin Mary in his visions. As a grown man, he was described as having "a broad sinewy frame, a large intelligent head, a fresh-coloured face, black hair, and black flashing eyes." He was blessed with a good memory and confident and

---

94 Bachelard, *The Poetics of Space*, 212.
95 Bachelard, *The Poetics of Space*, 215.
96 Bachelard, *The Poetics of Space*, 223.
97 Lefebvre, *Production of Space*, 280. He claims that "[a]n effective examination of space – of political space and of the politics of space – ought to enable us to dissolve the antithesis between 'liberal' theories of the state, which define it as the embodiment of the 'common good' of its citizens and the impartial arbiter of their conflicts and 'authoritarian' theories, which invoke the 'general will' and a unifying rationality as justification for the centralization of power," which, in fact, outlines "the creation" of colonial empires (281–82).
98 Pryde, *Great Men*, 48.

persuasive speech, and due to his "startling" disposition, he was called "Al Amin," "the Faithful."[99] This detailed presentation of Mohammed's early life is consistent with the Victorian interest in descent. One's ancestry could provide answers to the choices one made in one's own life.

Born into a pagan material culture, Mohammed longed for spirituality. Consequently, when he was forty, he "fell into a state of religious melancholy." He started asking questions about what God is, but he was illiterate, and "no messenger came with the pure word of truth to this benighted heathen. In the course of his travels Mohammed must have had he picked up some scraps of Christian and Jewish doctrine; but those only perplexed him more."[100] Pryde assumes Mohammed's despondency, combined with fits of epilepsy, prompted his visions. When Mohammed went to meditate in the mountain cavern, he was allegedly visited by the archangel Gabriel and given the first pillar of the Muslim faith: "there is but one God."[101] Green is more skeptical about "the cave business," claiming that there are stories about the Mohammed "interviews" in the cave with some accomplices who helped him write the Koran, and that later one of them, a monk, Sergius, was killed on Mohammed's order. Green dismisses this as "a tale more likely to be the invention of prejudice than to have the support of historic testimony."[102] He acknowledges, however, that it was Mohammed's first wife, Khadijah, who declared the dream prophetic and began to spread information about Mohammed being the prophet of God. His first converts were the members of his own household. Soon after, he attracted "poor people, women, and slaves" as followers.[103] In his early life as a prophet, he was surrounded by unbelievers, who wanted him to perform miracles to prove that his was a true calling. He spent the last ten years of his life in Medina. Burton asserts that Mohammed "died on Monday, some say at nine A.M., others at noon, others a little after, on the twelfth of Rabia al-Awwal in the eleventh year of the Hijirah."[104] It is commonly believed that he died of fever, at the age of sixty-three. He left no sons as heirs to the growing empire of Islam. According to Pryde, his last words were: "To the highest companions in Paradise."[105] Ockley

---

99 Pryde, *Great Men*, 49.
100 Pryde, *Great Men*, 50.
101 Pryde, *Great Men*, 50.
102 Green, *Life of Mahomet*, 69.
103 Pryde, *Great Men*, 51.
104 Burton, *Personal Narrative*, 1:358. Burton claims that many things about the Apostle are chronicled by the Moslem authors, about his diet and domestic habits, "especially his avoiding leeks, onions, and garlic" (1:357).
105 Pryde *Great Men*, 54.

announces that, upon his death, many people thought that he would be resurrected like Jesus. Those who washed his body noticed that a mole "as large as a pigeon's egg disappeared from between his shoulders."[106]

The presence of the supernatural during Mohammed's lifetime and the miracles following his death all subscribe to the demands of sacred biography, whereas the rather noticeable tone of disbelief is, however, a typical background of the rather pejorative "staging the east" mode, to use John Ganim's expression.[107] In all of the histories in question, impartial accounts are intertwined with the subjective, outwardly biased ones. Representing Islam as "superstition," Ockley later refers to the "Mohammedan religion," consisting of two parts: faith and practice. He outlines the articles of faith without judgment as to their *raison d'être*, reminding his readers that Mohammed during his lifetime initiated the visitation of the holy places by Muslims.[108] Pryde's work reproduces two major Western stereotypes: that Mohammed is a false prophet; and that his revelation concerned the necessity to spread the religion by force. The latter undercuts Islam by portraying it as the religion of barbarity and violence and perpetrates the fear of forced conversions.[109] Both works replicate legends and myths to which they ascribe the value of historical documents.

The Victorian respect for historiography is very frequently interpreted in the context of creating the "national" narrative through the ideas of progress. Thus, Ernst Breisach elucidates how scholars

> contributed to the enhancement of history's prominence by their contributions to a historical science. Historians did not quite replace the philosophers and theologians but in many ways they surpassed them in influence, as the educated became used to calling on historiography to interpret human life, or at least to aid in approaching most problems historically.[110]

The enthusiasm shown for historical narratives furthered the demand for historical accounts of various historical phenomena, and Pryde's work was one of them. Both Pryde – and Gilman, whose *The Saracens* appeared in 1886 – thought of themselves as "reconstructors" of the past, offering their own explanation of historical processes. Gilman was an American educator whose work on the Saracens is always quoted in the context of nineteenth-century British Oriental studies. Breisach argues that by the 1880s, the sciences "enjoyed immense

---

106 Ockley, *The History*, 62.
107 Ganim, "Framing the West," 31–46.
108 Ockley, *The History*, 67–68.
109 Pryde, *Great Men*, 53.
110 Breisach, *Historiography*, 261–69.

prestige." Scientific methods guaranteed the uncovering of "certain and timeless truth."[111] Sources became increasingly important in the work of a historian,[112] and like other scientists who relied on experiment and empirical knowledge, positivist historians had confidence in the "scientific explanation of the world."[113] Furthermore, due to the general curiosity about the cultures of the East, historians began to incorporate the findings of not only archeologists but also linguists.[114]

This interest also stimulated etymological investigations. For this reason, Gilman begins with the analysis of the word "Saracens." *Saraceni* is "a name of which no philologist has yet given the signification," he writes, speculating that it might have meant "The People of the Desert" from the Arabic *sahra*, a desert, or "The People of the East," from the Arabic *sharq*, "the rising sun."[115] He also offers a lengthy scrutiny of the timeframe in the chapter aptly entitled: "The Year One":

> When we say that Queen Victoria ascended her throne in 1837, we mean if we stop to think that she began to reign 1837 years after the birth of Christ; but if we were to count back to the year one, we should find that at that time Christ was a little boy about four; which shows that there must be some error. The truth is that a mistake was made. It was not until six hundred years after the birth of Christ that the world began to date its betters and documents from that event, and there were no men of science living who could tell exactly the year when it occurred . . . [T]he Jews say that is was 3750 years before Christ;

---

111 Breisach, *Historiography*, 268–69.
112 White, *Tropics of Discourse*, 81–100. White elaborates on his theory of historical texts being essentially literary artefacts. He shows how different approaches to history create its different versions: conservatives insist on a "natural" rhythm; liberals favor the "social," educational or parliamentary debate; and radicals and anarchists adhere to the possibility of cataclysmic transformations (24–25).
113 Breisach, *Historiography*, 269.
114 In view of the above discussion, Gilman feels obliged to explain his position and his interest in the history of Islam. "One is no longer obliged thus to apologize for conducting any historical investigation, and we may study the career of the Saracens as one of the most interesting that the past can spread before us. Though the present volume is mainly devoted to the period before the Crusades lent brilliancy to the subject, and does not include the thrilling narrative of the Moors in Spain, the greatest embarrassment of the author has arisen from the amplitude of the themes. The life of the founder of Islam has alone given rise to many volumes more extensive than this one is allowed to be. And the conquests of the roving tribes of Asia as they progressed westward, might well occupy more pages than are now at command." Gilman, *The Saracens*, iv.
115 Gilman, *The Saracens*, iii. Ockley quotes Arab historians who claim that the Saracens come from Sarah, Abraham's lawful wife, being ashamed of Hagar, his slave, then continues: "But the contrary is most evident, for they were neither ashamed of Ishmael nor Hagar." Ockley, *The History*, 247. One has to give credit to Ockley that even if he did not discern between factual and more fictional accounts, he tried to use Arabic sources to support his work.

the people of Constantinople that it was 5509 years before, and so on. The Romans dated from the year of the founding of their city, but they did not even know when that event occurred; and now we find the Arabians dating from their year One, but the world cannot tell exactly when it was. We know more nearly about this than we do when our own era begins, because the Arabian year One was so many hundred years after ours. The farther we go back in our studies of history, the more misty all matters appear.[116]

Gilman, like Pryde, also attempts to provide the geographical as well as historical context of the growth of Islam: "The land of the Saracens lies four square, and comprises a territory about eight times as large as the islands of Great Britain."[117] The immensity of space in a dry, odorless desert is usually contrasted with a fragrant garden or paradise (*al-Jannah*), and such an image is akin to that of the Christian paradise, which is also populated with angels. Gilman refers to the story of angels and archangels, echoing the Gospel of St. John. One of the angels "was named Azazil, or Iblis," and he was "the first angel who rebelled against Allah, at the time of the creation of Adam, and became an evil demon corresponding with our idea of Satan. Like Satan, he was proud of his superior position, and was called the Peacock of the angels."[118] Citing the account of Solomon's ring of iron and brass engraved with the name of Allah, which gave him the command over the jinns, Gilman assures the readers that the ring forced the jinns to build the temple in Jerusalem and granted him power over winds, birds and wild beasts.[119] The jinns are ambiguous creatures; they are mentioned in the Koran, which specifies that some "are righteous, while others are not."[120] Intent on providing an objective scientific account, Gilman cannot help but be a bit ironic about all the fantastic elements in the Koran. He refers to, for example, the miracles of finding water in an ancient well covered with sand.[121] Such accounts are customarily found in sacred biographies, but Gilman neither discredits nor validates the reports. His is a coherent tale provided with a suitable geographical and cultural context strengthening his relation of events. Accordingly, he sees the Islamic Paradise, where the people living in a hot and unfertile land would have "shade, rest, water, fruit, companionship, and service . . . perennially furnished to the faithful," as Mohammed's invention. He conceptualized the afterlife as a series of

---

116 Gilman, *The Saracens*, 120–21.
117 Gilman *The Saracens*, 6.
118 Gilman *The Saracens*, 16.
119 Gilman *The Saracens*, 18–19.
120 *The Koran*, 571. Green writes about the Koran: "Remonstrances, instructions, promises, threats, blessings, and curses are all represented as coming directly from God." Green, *Life of Mahomet*, 70.
121 Gilman, *The Saracens*, 170.

spaces: "the Garden of Beauty, the Abode of Peace, the Abode of Rest, the Garden of Eden, the Garden of Resort, the Garden of Pleasure, the Garden of the Most High, and the Garden of Paradise."[122] *The Complete Guide to Islam*, however, refutes such descriptions.[123]

Granted, the Koran recurrently juxtaposes the delights of Paradise with the torments of Hell, and such images are equivalent to Christian and Jewish theology.[124] Paradise is commonly envisioned as an enclosed garden, an oasis, whereas hell is seemingly boundless and timeless in distributing its torments. Both spaces have doors, which, according to Bachelard, is one of the primal images, always pointing to the possibilities of opening and closing.[125] In the Koran, like in Christian popular imagination, doors are thresholds to other worlds (for medieval Christians, exits and entrances subsumed the circle of human life). A good departure, a good death, was important in all religions, hence their common focus on eschatology. More than Ockley or Pryde, Gilman is trying to present Islam in a framework known to his readers: Christianity. Ramadan, falling in the ninth month of the Arabian year, "is and was held to be a sort of Lent."[126] He also notices that although Muslims do not have so many different prayers as Christians do, the profession of faith is a "sort of Pater Noster": "Praise be to Allah, the Lord of creation, / The All-merciful, the All-compassionate! / Ruler of the day of reckoning."[127] Adulatory in his reading of the Muslim prayers, Gilman fuses the pre-Islamic and Islamic past of the Orient, arguing that "Judaism and Christianity existed alongside of fetishism and paganism; but the largest portion of the people worshipped the numberless divinities of the Kaaba, though admitting that there was an Allah, supreme above all others."[128]

While historical narrative aims at conveying certified information, it is on no account and cannot ever be completely objective. Claude Levi-Strauss once observed that "historical accounts are inevitably narrative,"[129] though history can be distinguished from myth by virtue of its dependency on and responsibility to the data it analyzes.[130] The nineteenth-century historian was perhaps not conscious of history being a "construct," but Ockley, Green, Pryde, and Gilman were striving to present readable as much as critical and valuable versions of

---

122 Gilman, *The Saracens*, 19–20.
123 Bokhari and Seddon, *Complete Illustrated Guide*, 144.
124 Here again we see the scholar, since in a footnote Gilman asserts that these heavens were also noted by Jewish rabbis. Gilman, *The Saracens*, 20.
125 Bachelard, *Poetics of Space*, 222.
126 Gilman, *The Saracens*, 20.
127 Gilman, *The Saracens*, 64.
128 Gilman, *The Saracens*, 62.
129 In White, *Tropics of Discourse*, 55.
130 White, *Tropics of Discourse*, 56.

the events they described – "to the best of their knowledge," one is tempted to add. Gilman's text is then frequently interspersed with claims such as: "Let us stop now at the threshold of the new era and ask what was the doctrine that Mohammed had up to this time preached, and what he was expected to bring to Medina."[131] Moreover, employing the form of a dialogue, he unintentionally underlines the narrative properties of history. By using such a style, Gilman's work caters to nineteenth-century historiography, accommodating not only various documents but also the literary and anecdotal material. Composing a narrative that is both a history and a story, Gilman's work, in a way, foreshadows the Whitean principle stating that a historical text is always, to a degree, a literary artifact.[132] It comes as no surprise that Gilman uses Moore's *Lalla Rookh*, quoting the beginning of "The Veiled prophet of Khorassan" and offering the story of the prophet Hakim, called Mokanna "the Veiled," who flourished around the year 670 and led "an obscure sect in Khorassan."[133] Such initial "disagreements" stress the lack of a unanimous form of Islam, highlighting its rapacious nature. In time, the followers of Hakim "made successful predatory excursions into their territory."[134] Shifting the focus of his narrative from politics to culture is yet another attempt at historical thoroughness, concurrently lightening the tone of discourse. Gilman also makes references to the greatest poet of Persia, Abul Casem Mansur Ferdusi,[135] "who had been compared to Homer for his fecundity, genius, and imagination."[136] Even though Gilman is always aware that he has to choose from all too many facts

---

131 Gilman, *The Saracens*, 129.
132 White shows that historical discourse can be viewed as a sign system that "points in two directions simultaneously: first toward the set of events [where] it tacitly likens the set in order to disclose its formal coherence considered as either structure or a process. Thus, for example, a given set of events, arranged more or less chronologically but encoded so as to appear as phases of a process with a discernible beginning, middle and end, may be emplotted as Romance, Comedy, Tragedy, Epic, or what have you, depending upon the valences assigned to different events in the series as elements of recognizable archetypal story-forms." White, *Tropics of Discourse*, 106.
133 Gilman, *The Saracens*, 362.
134 Gilman, *The Saracens*, 362–63. Some more stories of conquest include letters sent by Haroun al Rashid, Commander of the Faithful, to Nicephorus, "the Roman dog" (370–71). Gilman presents the end of the power of the caliphs, attributing it to the fall of the city of Baghdad in 1258.
135 Ferdousi, spelled with an "o," was one of the few Arabic authors translated into Polish in 1981. His *Księga Królewska* (*Royal Book*, which is the translation of the Polish title, trans. and ed. Władysław Dulęba) was indeed treated similarly to the other canonical works of world literature. The other interesting Polish translation is *Kitab al I'tibar. Księga pouczających przykładów Usamy ibn Munkidha: Muajjada ad-Daula abu Muzaffara Usamy ibn Murszida ibn Ali ibn Mukallada ibn Nasra ibn Munkidha al-Kinani asz-Szajzari* (*The Book of Instructive Examples* is the title that the translator, Józef Bielawski, gives to the work, 1975).
136 Gilman, *The Saracens*, 431–32.

and sources, he tried to be as comprehensive as possible, and so too was Green. Gilman's is a well-argued tale with a purpose.

In the vein of Ockley and Green, Gilman was conscious that his task was to evaluate the past in order to show its trajectory to the present. Thus, he suggests that "[t]he tribes of the desert and the Arabs of the towns and cities began to feel, before the first year closed, that Islam was not to be shaken off."[137] The famous conquests by Muslims ensue – Palestine and Mesopotamia, Damascus and Jerusalem. Gilman repeats what Ockley also examined in more detail. Gilman reminds his readers that Mohammed gave his followers advice on how to conduct their lives, but also the need and necessity to extend the presence of Islam.

> The Berbers of Africa; the barbarians of Turkestan; the lively Saracens of the Arabian Deserts; the proud Syrians with their Biblical memories; the rich and powerful Persians; the dwellers in Armenia and Mesopotamia; the Egyptians and the tribes on the borders of Kathay; the inhabitants of the peninsula of Spain; all these were not to be moulded into a homogenous nation under one religious faith in the short space of a single century. Nor was it to be expected that a series of kalifs wielding absolute power, and using the sword and the art of the poisoner to uphold their authority, could endure for any considerable length of time without giving rise to jealousies and intrigues, especially in an Oriental land where cunning and deceit, duplicity and guile, were the usual principles of action in court circles.[138]

The above quotation testifies to the inherent fear that the spread of Islam awakened, even though Gilman notes that later caliphs were incapable of properly performing the burdensome duties connected with their religious and political positions. What is more, their feisty natures made them turn against one another, so that "they have seen a powerful ally become in turn an equally powerful antagonist."[139]

Unquestionably, Gilman generates an unfavorable image of Islamic rulers, a stereotype reiterated by other historians, which Said deems "frozen once and for all in time by the gaze of western percipients."[140] Refraining from defending either Arabs or Islam, Said's criticism brings to the fore a plethora of overdetermined meanings or, rather, labels such as "Arab" or "Muslim" that cannot be used "without some attention to the formidable polemical mediations that screen the objects, if they exist at all, that the labels designate."[141] This is precisely why, instead of outright rejecting nineteenth-century historical works, we should

---

137 Gilman, *The Saracens*, 225.
138 Gilman, *The Saracens*, 423–24.
139 Gilman, *The Saracens*, 424.
140 Said, "Orientalism Reconsidered," in his *Reflections on Exile*, 201.
141 Said, "Orientalism Reconsidered," in his *Reflections on Exile*, 198–215.

reread them not only against the backdrop of Victorian historiography but also taking into account present-day cultural studies, and not as endorsements of the colonial era but as attempts to understand unfamiliar civilizations.

In light of the above, one of the most interesting pieces of information in Gilman's study, not covered by other histories evaluated here, is his telling the tale of the rise of the fabled Assassins. According to Gilman, they came into existence "[d]uring the reign of the third Prince, Melek Shas (1073–1093) as a branch of the Ismailians, who came into prominence in the person of their chief, Hasan, a man of Persian descent, known in history as 'The Old Man of the Mountains.'" The order, if one can call them that, was reputed to have always acted in secret and became quite powerful in their purportedly disreputable schemes.[142] The group was dismantled in 1258, at the time of the fall of Baghdad. Gilman plainly repeats the popular beliefs that the Assassins murdered caliphs and other eminent men, both Muslim and Christian. The group consisted of an army of particularly cruel mercenaries who used hashish (whence, probably, their name, *Hashishim*-Assassins) to enter a trance-like state in preparation for an action. "[T]he Assassins became terrible to the Crusaders, as well as to the Persians and the Saracens; but their order contained in itself the germs of disintegration from the operation of which they would have fallen had they not been overcome by the Mongols."[143] It was William of Tyre (ca. 1130 – September 29, 1186), a medieval prelate and chronicler of the Crusades, who came up with the definition of the "sect."[144] Bernard Lewis, in his history of the Assassins, likewise touches upon the etymology of the name. Hashish was known to the Arabs and, for those who were privileged to use it, associated with the delights of Paradise. In his view, different texts confirm the use of the name

---

142 Because of their extraordinary powers and their existence shrouded in mystery, their legend persisted through the ages. One attempt to bring it back was the film *Assassin's Creed*, based on a series of computer games (2016, directed by Justin Kurzel, with Michael Fassbender, Jeremy Irons, and Marion Cotillard).
143 Gilman, *The Saracens*, 434.
144 Lewis, *The Assassins*, 3. Lewis quotes Marco Polo, who passed through Persia in 1273 and claims that an old man created a beautiful garden that was to mirror the garden of Paradise: "no man was allowed to enter the garden save those whom he intended to be his ASHISHIN." Since the man kept an army of young men, "to these he used to tell tales about Paradise, just as Mahomet had been wont to do, and they believed in him just as the Saracens believe in Mahommet. Then he would introduce them into his garden, some four, or six, or ten at a time, having first made them drink a certain potion which cast them into a deep sleep, and then causing them to be lifted and carried in. So when they awoke, they found themselves in the Garden" (7).

hashishi concomitant with the sect but not to the Ismailis[145] in Persia, who refused to recognize the successor of the Fatimid Caliph al-Mustansir, imam of the time and head of the faith.[146] Such claims gave rise to "rumors and fantasies brought back from the East by medieval travelers, and from the hostile and distorted image extracted by nineteenth-century Orientalists from the manuscript writings of orthodox Muslim theologians and historians."[147] The Assassins were a fundamentalist sect in Islam, and not "nihilistic impostors" and "terrorists" or "a syndicate of professional murderers."[148] A slightly different opinion is offered by Nickolas Haydock, who brings to light the cooperation between the Assassins

---

145 For the historical context, the development of philosophy, and major players among the Ismaili dissenters, see Walker, "The Ismailis," 72–91.

146 Lewis, *The Assassins*, 49. Lewis notes that the Ismailis "were a secret society, with a system of oaths and initiations and a graded hierarchy of rank and knowledge. The secrets were well kept, and the information about them is fragmentary and confused. Orthodox polemists depict the Ismailis as a band of deceitful nihilists who misled their dupes through successive stages of degradation, in the last of which they revealed the full horror of unbelief. Ismaili writers see the sect as custodians of sacred mysteries, to which the believer could attain only after a long course of preparation and instruction, marked by progressive initiations" (48). In the thirteenth century, the Assassins became tributary to the Knights Hospitallers, as the Knights were not afraid of them. Lewis claims that the Ismaili Assassins did not invent assassinations; "they merely lent it their name" (125). "The idealization of tyrranicide became part of the political ethos of Greece and Rome, and found expression in such famous murders as those of Philip II of Macedon, Tiberius Gracchus and Julius Caesar. The same ideal appears among the Jews, in such figures as Ehud and Jehu, and most dramatically, in the story of the beautiful Judith, who made her way to the tent of the oppressor Holofernes, and cut off his head as he slept" (125–26). Regicide was also familiar in Islam – of the four Righteous Caliphs who followed the Prophet in the headship of the Islamic community, three were murdered (126). Green, similarly to Lewis, suggested that one of the caliphs, Omar, was murdered by a Persian slave, "who thought perhaps, by this means to avenge the wrongs of his miserable country." Green, *The Life of Mahomet*, 253. In the early eighth century, a man, Abu Mansur al-ijli, of Kufa, claimed to be the Imam, who taught that the prescriptions of the law have to be read symbolically, and heaven and earth were simply misfortunes experienced here on earth. According to Lewis, his followers practiced murder as a religious duty. Lewis, *The Assassins*, 128. There were many sects before the Ismailis but the Ismailis were the first to create an organization that survived, united against their enemy, the Sunni establishment. Their movement was regarded as a threat to the existing political, social and religious order. They are not isolated but can be placed in the long tradition of messianic movements. Lewis asserts that Hasan-i Sabbah managed to transform their wild desires and aimless anger into an ideology with purposive violence (139). Yet they did not manage to overthrow the existing order or hold on to any of the strongholds. Their principal lore was that of revolutionary mysticism, with what Lewis terms "the undercurrent of messianic hope and revolutionary violence" (140).

147 Lewis, *The Assassins*, 18.

148 Lewis, *The Assassins*, 19.

(who for him were a "radical branch of Shi'a Muslims" whose preferred targets were "Sunni Muslims, caliphs and power brokers") and the Christians, especially the Templars and the Hospitallers. He considers them guilty of the two attempts to murder Saladin, in 1176 and 1185.[149] As it transpires, the turbulent history of the Crusades still evokes controversies in the modern world, just as it did in the nineteenth century.

Vilifying nineteenth-century historians and Orientalists "whose main concern was to refute and condemn, not to understand or explain,"[150] Lewis addresses the issue of negative Orientalism, that of polarizing the already-divided world, in reference to the works on the Assassins. Indeed, concerned with the political aspects of the rise of Islam, Ockley, Gilman, Green, and Pryde repeat much of what has been preserved in histories, but also legends. Still, in their own way, they try to construct the logically evolving accounts to afford their readership with supposedly scientifically proven data and thereby create the ambiance for discussion rather than denigration.

One has to remember, however, that the foundations of Victorian historiography were related to the development of industry. Nineteenth-century historians both benefited from the driving force of the Industrial Revolution and were deterred by it. Throughout Europe, scholars fashioned the myth of the dominant triumphant industrialized West, concurrently legitimizing conquests of other nations by European powers. Notwithstanding the social sciences' models for comparison, the scientific view of history was an important factor in the growing divergence between the East and the West. The East, seen in terms of what it was lacking in its industrial development, had to be represented as an opposing albeit inferior force, to the more technologically advanced West. In spite of their cultural, historical, anthropological, and ethnographic interests, adventurers such as Richard Burton and Charles Montagu Doughty brought back the stories of the much less technologically advanced East. Their reports helped to shape the philosophy of expansionism. As Breisach argues: "The view of human beings as purely biological entities yielding the basis for racial histories, and the concept of the 'survival of the fittest' served other historians as the justification of imperial ventures."[151]

The four histories of the Saracens undoubtedly played a part in the development of Oriental studies in England. The eighteenth-century *History of the Saracens* by Simon Ockley and the nineteenth-century *The Saracens* by Arthur Gilman, set

---

149 Haydock and Risden, *Hollywood in the Holy Land*, 5.
150 Lewis, *The Assassins*, 18–19.
151 Breisach, *Historiography*, 271.

against two biographical works on the life of Mohammed – Samuel Green's *The Life of Mahomet: Founder of the Religion of Islam and of the Empire of the Saracens* and David Pryde's chapter on the life of Mohammed in his *Great Men of European History* – familiarized readers with the historical processes involved in the spread of Islam and the growth of the Muslim countries. Their elucidations, rationalized by systematic investigations, responded to the Victorian fascination with races, religions and the advancement of human civilizations. The literary context in their assessments was as important as the historical documents themselves. For later historians, however, their writing was not an empirical record of facts but the interpretation of events adulterated by their pro-Western bias. Furthermore, by foregrounding the political aspects of the spread of Islam, the writers aided the formation of anti-Muslim imperial ideologies exposed by twentieth-century writers and novelists whose works will be discussed in the second part of the present study. In their time, however, the historians were perceived as interpreters of the cultural background of Islam and promoters of the knowledge of the Saracens.

Part 2

Introduction
"The dark reservoir of hurt and hate"
in Contemporary Literature in English

When Pope Urban II, during his famous speech at the Council of Clermont on November 27, 1095, called for the Crusades to the Holy Land, he unleashed a torrent of events that culminated on September 11, 2001, which once again set free the "Crusades" discourse. The medieval pope, unlike President George W. Bush, referred to such an effort as a "pilgrimage" and magnanimously promised the participants a place in heaven. Yet he addressed not the penitential but the warlike instincts of the medieval aristocracy. Being the only person who could proclaim a war above all national interests, the pope skillfully played with Christian prejudices against Islam. Creating the ideology of a just war, he established a link between the Crusades and earlier evangelizing missions, fusing the necessity to take up the Cross and the sword against the pagans with the obligation to raise the sword under the signboard of the Cross against the Muslims. In order to enhance the Christian sense of duty, he emphasized that the Crusader-Pilgrims would earn a special relationship with God and that their determination would bring them nothing but glory and, perhaps, a fair share in looting the fabled Eastern riches. Thus, although the military intervention was initially a response to the plea by the Byzantine Emperor Alexius I (b. 1056, r. 1081–1118)[1] to free the Holy Land from the Muslims who blocked the trade routes and threatened European merchants, the Crusades and the pilgrimages were later represented in religious terms.

The fusion of the mercantile secular and spiritual aims is reflected in the thirteenth-century romance of *Guy of Warwick*, who travels to the East as a pilgrim to atone for his (chivalric) sins only to become a fighter for the (always just) Christian cause.[2] The Crusades and the pilgrimages were journeys in time

---

1 For the outline of the wars with Muslims in Byzantium, see *The Alexiad of Anna Comnena*. The extensive fragments from Pope Urban II's speech and other documents are published in Thatcher and McNeal, *A Source Book*, 510–44. The documents concerning trade in the medieval Mediterranean are edited and translated by Lopez and Raymond, *Medieval Trade in the Mediterranean World*.

2 Guy's story is a complicated one, because as a son of a steward he has to win his beloved Felice, the daughter of his overlord, with fame. He is consequently entangled in baronial conflicts in Europe and then in the East, and in order to free innocent Christians from prison, must

---

Note: The quotation comes from Robert Welch's novel *Groundwork*, 200. By using this quote, I would also like to pay tribute to Robert, who was our guest in Poznań in 2012.

and space; they were construed as a "voyage out," a journey into the wilderness of the unknown world and into one's consciousness, designed to overcome the fear of death and as a penance to alleviate the possible pains of the afterlife. Both the romance heroes and the Crusaders knew that theirs were battles of the spirit, and the main endeavor of the troops was to sustain devotion and morale through the frequent repetition of the higher aim of their soldierly exploits. During and after the Crusades (in life and literature, respectively), the concept of *miles Christi*, which hitherto signified an abstract idea, gained the literal meaning of those who take up the sword in the name of God. The thirteenth- and fourteenth-century romances such as *Guy of Warwick*, *Sir Isumbras*, and *Octavian* depict heroes tirelessly defending Christianity.[3] In the words of R. W. Southern, what is voiced in all such narratives is the threat of the very existence of Islam, which "called for action and discrimination between the competing possibilities of Crusade, conversion, coexistence, and commercial exchange."[4]

While Islam's power became alarming, the *respublica Christiana* seemed to be besieged by schisms, heresies and wars. Consequently, Islam came to be associated with apocalyptic revelations about the end of the world, perchance the work

---

become the champion of a sultan. His fights against the Saracens are multiplied within the story. As Mehl notices: "The rather patchwork character of the novel which in places reads like a collection of romance-clichés, certainly contributed to its popularity." Mehl, *The Middle English Romances*, 223.

3 *Guy of Warwick* and *Sir Isumbras* repeat the pattern of attack and revenge, reiterating the motifs of the Saracen viciousness, their inhumanity, their usually black champions; they also relate the prolonged battles between the Christian and the Saracen armies in the East. The early fourteenth-century Anglo-Norman romance of *Octavian* echoes the concerns of the crusading period but turns its attention to the threat of the Saracens in Europe. The romance narrates the life of Emperor Octavian's twin sons, whom he sent into exile while still infants: Florent, raised by a Parisian burgher, Clement; and the young Octavian, raised by the Eastern, meaning Byzantine, emperor. The sons are commonly associated with two sources of political power – the aristocracy and the rising middle class – but also represent West and East. The impractical Florent finds it impossible to carry on his foster father's trade, but when the Saracen armies besiege Paris, he reveals his true nobility by standing up to the terrible sultan and his monstrous champion, thereby becoming the ultimate defender of the Christian faith. By shifting focus from the more current issues of domestic disquiet and class conflicts, the anonymous author replaces the internal "enemy" with a more spectacular foreign menace. Clement's distress over his adopted son's upbringing reflects the preoccupation with social responsibilities among the rising middle class, whereas the comic scenes involving Clement – who, despite being entirely incapable of understanding the ways of chivalry, nevertheless ventures out and steals the sultan's horned horse, the unicorn, the symbol of the sultan's power – demonstrate the necessity to forgo class distinctions in time of danger. There are other parodic rewritings of the Saracen romances such as *Ralph the Collier*, but these are beyond the scope of the present work.

4 Southern, *Western Views of Islam*, 3.

of the devil, and all the more so an obscene parody of Christianity. Even Edward Said recognizes the fact that in the late Middle Ages, Islam was a "lasting trauma" for Europe.[5] And that, undoubtedly, warranted the need for unity among all Christians. Medieval literature, in particular most of the Saracen romances, reproduced the prevailing Christian belief in the so-called enemies of Mankind: the World, the Devil, and the Flesh. These adversaries preserve their significance in present-day literature and culture, as we will see in the following chapters.

Part 2 of the present study, therefore, reads contemporary fictional and nonfictional texts through the medieval tropes of World, Devil, and Flesh. Chapter 4 looks at the world of immigration in *Fatima's Scarf*, a novel by David Caute that narrates the late twentieth-century disappointment with multiculturalism, and *My Ear at his Heart*, a 2004 memoir by Hanif Kureishi, augmented by his earlier memoir, *The Rainbow Sign* from 1986. The former probes his father's experiences as Pakistani-British citizen, and the latter his own. Chapter 5 analyzes the processes of "othering" of the medieval devil in "the fetishized figures of the stranger and terrorist in a memoir of Ed Husain entitled, suggestively, *The Islamist*, which shows the author's road to and from the Islamist to Islamic movements, thereby substituting militancy with spirituality; it also explores Mohamed Laroussi El Metoui's novel *Halima*, which fictionalizes the Tunisian fight for independence. Chapter 6 is devoted to the medieval figure of the Flesh, conceptualized as desire in two twentieth-century novels: *The Map of Love* by Ahdaf Soueif and *The Magician's Wife* by Brian Moore. Both works show young women entangled in Arab revolutions and enchanted with Arabia. Their experiences undermine and transpose the narrative foundations of the Victorian quest romance-cum-travelogue in which native women become lovers and helpers of the white men. Told from the perspective of the white women, the novels portray the women's desire for Muslim men in the context of Arab unification movements of the nineteenth century and against racist imperialist ideologies.

As was the case in medieval Europe, "united we stand" has also become the motto of twenty-first-century anti-Islamic movements in America and Europe. Seeing the Muslim as monster (the Devil), is not confined to literature. The most hated monster of the present-day world is the "Islamist," a potential terrorist whose brainwashed perception of *dar al-harb* resembles that of the Saracens depicted in the medieval romances. *Britz*, a British film from 2007, written and directed by Peter Kosminsky, both contests and endorses the making of the homegrown terrorist, showing the mechanisms behind radicalization not as lying within the group of angry young men but resulting from the state's

---

5 Said, *Orientalism*, 59.

restrictive policies.⁶ Those who are supposed to be protected by these said policies are as vulnerable as the inhabitants of Heorot, invaded by the arch evil of Old English epic *Beowulf*, Grendel, the descendant of the biblical Cain. Grendel always emerged from darkness, his monstrosity asserted not only through the depiction of his being but also through his deeds. Like Grendel's, a masked terrorist's actions are atrocious, exposing the two classical etymologies of the word "monster," which in the view of St. Augustine connoted "demonstration" and according to Isidore of Seville meant "warning."⁷

These two concepts regarding monsters contributed to the persistence of the stereotype of the Other – religiously, culturally and racially different – that was created during and strengthened after the Crusades, between 1100 and 1500, and has survived throughout the centuries and is still (ab)used in the mass media. George W. Bush's famous pronouncement, that "the war on terror" was a crusade against evil, transported us all, on both sides, back to the Middle Ages, to the world in which Good and Evil were sharply outlined without dubious, shady ground in-between.⁸ Suddenly we retreated into the schismatically

---

6 A different side of the problem of radicalization is portrayed in Faulks's novel *A Week in December*, in which a young man of Pakistani origin, Hassan al-Rashid, is drawn to the radical group in the mosque and finds himself entangled in an attempted terrorist act in London. His is a search for spirituality and he feels progressively disenchanted by his wealthy parents' materialism. The myth of "Eastern spirituality" is also laid bare in Hanif Kureishi's *My Ear at his Heart*, where he confesses going to Pakistan in search of it. There he found that his family "were obsessed with cars, video recorders and stereo systems; they were not really different from us at all." Kureishi, *My Ear at His Heart*, 123.
7 Mittman, *Maps and Monsters*, 105.
8 Additionally, in relation to Bin Laden's capture, Bush used the phrase *dead or alive*, echoing the American western movie rhetoric. The catchy expression became increasingly popular, and the media held on to it whilst the public harbored fears of yet another terrorist's bomb or a letter containing a tricky white powder known as anthrax, which would destroy the shaky sense of security. This is why, in contemporary media studies, researchers talk about the "invention" of the enemy, about media-constructed wars, and about manipulating masculinity. Kathy J. Phillips, in *Manipulating Masculinity*, analyzes two versions of the myth of masculinity – that of Ovidian Apollo (from "Apollo and Daphne," which via Freud assumes that heterosexual relations with women are harmful to one's masculinity) and that of the Shakespearian Anthony (which assumes that homosexuality effeminizes a man) – and discusses how aggressive warring masculinity is created against assumed effeminization. Treating masculinity as a social construct that is also time bound, she looks at narratives about the First and Second World Wars, as well as the Vietnam War and, in an epilogue, the war in Iraq. She reminds readers that masculinity has been "[i]mbued with the militaristic psychology of imperialism, which requires a victor capable of first overcoming, then 'civilizing' his conquest," which is not unlike the dominant ideology of the Greeks overcoming the "barbarians." Phillips, *Manipulating Masculinity*, 23. She argues that such belligerent versions of masculinity promoted militarism,

divided East and West, us and them, the barbarians and the civilized, the innocent and the guilty, the saved and the damned. Like the medieval advocates of the Crusades, by promoting a war-concentrated patriotism, the US and Europe reinforced these divisions. The international campaign initially launched was called "Campaign Infinite Justice,"[9] with the ideological aim to justify further action against the Muslim East. The Bush administration subsequently tried to alter the message of these early declarations of war, arguing that America's was not a war against Islam but against terrorism, yet it was the initial "Crusade" that captivated the imagination of the Western world, as it battled not only the Enemy but was directed against socially constructed fear,[10] the main element of he terrorist enterprise. David Altheide argues that the genesis of terrorism is fixedly associated with "fear, dread, death, and entertainment."[11] The early twenty-first-century sociopolitical reality was inevitably sullied by "the war on terror," renamed the "long war" by Obama,[12] understood as "the central front in our enduring struggle against terrorism and extremism."[13]

The war on terror as a propaganda project, however, was carried out not only on the battlefield in hostile territory but also, most successfully, on the

---

racism, and Orientalism and created aggressive versions of masculinity. Medieval and contemporary heroes, such as Guy of Warwick or John Rambo, depict similar fascinations with warfare. Her reading might be well in line with the understanding of the "rape" images pinpointed by Said. She argues that military language "insinuates to soldiers that fighting is as good as sex" and uses language to promote the mythology of weapons (197). Such propaganda is not so far from the medieval delight in describing armaments, especially if it had connections with classical heroes (see *Guy of Warwick*). Phillips notes that "even President Obama may not be immune to the need to look manly." She quotes General John Mattis at a San Diego convention saying that "guys who slapped women around for five years because they didn't wear a veil . . . ain't got no manhood left anyway"; once he has dismissed the other man's manhood, he builds his own by adding breezily: "So it's a hell of a lot of fun to shoot them" (200).

9 Kearney, *Strangers, Gods and Monsters*, 112. "Al Queda [sic] was proving to be as invasive as anthrax itself – with hijacked planes sliding into buildings like 'letters into postboxes.' This was a war (in significant part) of disturbingly protean substances: a deadly game of smoke and mirrors. Nightly TV images showed grey fumes still smoldering from the subterranean bowels of Ground Zero" (114).

10 Altheide notices that Senator Kerry did not support President Bush's rationale for the war in Iraq but nevertheless pledged that America would hunt down and kill Osama Bin Laden, rather than bring him to justice. Altheide, *Terrorism and the Politics of Fear*, 4. In the previous decades, the American involvement in Afghanistan had been called an anti-terrorist Christian Crusade, and both the wars in Iraq and Afghanistan were referred to as Crusades. For a succinct outline of the conflicts in the Middle East, see Surratt, *The Middle East*.

11 Altheide, *Terrorism and the Politics of Fear*, 2.

12 Hodges, *The "War on Terror" Narrative*, 159.

13 President Barak Obama, quoted in Hodges, *The "War on Terror" Narrative*, 158.

internet, as if subscribing to the Puritan claim that pens are mightier than swords.[14] It was the first digital war using the internet and mass media,[15] although even in 1981 Edward Said was already suggesting that the media and (very obviously) the world's justification determine how the so-called general public perceives and understands the world more often than not condemning "Islam," which "ends up becoming a form of attack." This, in turn, "provokes more hostility between self-appointed Muslim and Western spokespersons."[16] The media raised popular support for the armed intervention, which became known as the Second Gulf War (2003–2011), against a country that supposedly had weapons of mass destruction and harbored terrorist training camps.[17] One of the most credible urgings of G. W. Bush, an argument that won sympathetic audiences not only in the States but also in England and other European Union countries, was his assertion that democracy itself was under attack and that to

---

14 English Puritans of the seventeenth century were said to have carried printing presses with them and to have distributed leaflets touting their supposed victories. Theirs was the first ideological media war, in many meanings of that word.

15 Keeble, in *Secret State, Silent Press*, shows the development of a new militarism in the context of the first Gulf War (1991), which he in fact calls not a war but "a series of massacres" (5) linked with the circumstances of the conservative governments coming to power. He argues that "military strategy becomes essentially a media event: an entertainment, a spectacle. Warfare, moreover, is transmuted into a symbolic assertion of US and, to a lesser degree, UK global media (and military) power. Media manipulation becomes a central military strategy. This 'mediacentrism' is a pivotal element of new militarist societies" (8). Keeble draws attention to the fetishization of weapons and the resulting "armament culture" (9), claiming that a major war was needed for the US (backed by the UK and other allies) to "assert its primacy in the 'New World Order'" (11). In the first Gulf War, the media and (so obviously) the world's justification was that they were defending an innocent Kuwait; they therefore legitimized an attack on Iraq by using "rape" rhetoric. Images of Saddam Hussein were geared to elicit sympathy with the international cause. Keeble goes on to analyze American and international politics and military operations (he refers back to the Second World War and the Vietnam War as well as the Falklands War) and their media representations. Seeing the conflict as the result of British imperialism, he delves into earlier military interventions such as the coup d'état in Egypt in 1952, Iran in 1953, and the Iraq Ba'athist coups in 1963 and 1968, as well as the question of Israeli conflicts in Palestine (88–92). The juxtaposition of the evil empire vs. the defenders of freedom is all too easily assumed, yet it is the new militarist propaganda that unalterably wins in such cases. What is striking is that we are still attached to the notions of heroism and heroic virtues, as proven in war, which in fact, as much as Pope Urban II and his crusading spirit in the Middle Ages, is still very much in vogue nowadays.

16 Said, *Covering Islam*, xv–xvi. Said uses inverted comas to denote that *dar-al-Islam* is not a consistent concept.

17 *Official Secrets*, a 2018 film directed by Gavin Hood, presents a true story of a British Intelligence Agent, Katherine Gun, who discovers the scam behind the ONZ endorsement of the war in Iraq.

fight *with* the United States and *against* Iraq and Afghanistan and the rest of the radical Islamic world was to promote the ideas on which American democracy was founded.

Threatening our well-being, the actions of "modern monsters" accelerated governmental control over individual freedoms. The US Patriot Act, passed on October 26, 2001, gave the authorities legal rights to surveillance. The State's protection of the (white Anglo-Saxon Christian) citizens soon turned into conflicts with even second- and third-generation immigrants, which is so aptly portrayed both in *Britz* and in *Bradford Riots* (the latter released in 2006, directed by Neil Biswas) and David Caute's *Fatima's Scarf*. The political situation of British Muslims generated a plethora of theoretical works on citizenship. The classics of Derek Heater and Bryan S. Turner, as well as Richard Bellamy, which delineate the notion of citizenship in the past and today and discuss civic ideals, stress Western democratic ideals and at the same time confirm their fragility.[18] Debates concerning the rights versus duties of citizens, then, are not conducted on an abstract level, referring to certain political philosophies, but are much more literal, immediately applicable to the current situation. Prompted by right-wing political movements that passed legislation legitimizing observation via telephones and social media, the question of individual rights vs. national safety reawakened and incited inquiries into the contemporary understanding of nationalism and patriotism.[19] Many countries directly threatened by terrorist attacks – for example, the USA, Great Britain, Spain, Belgium, and France – were compelled to implement defense through surveillance. Even though, as the films demonstrate, the constant invigilation of the internet can prevent terrorist attacks and help find the most dangerous terrorists, such "close watching" has a down side. As information technology is entering and revolutionizing the Middle East, Western democracies are also under examination.

In a way, the current situation is reminiscent of the later Middle Ages, when the newly established Christian culture began the formation of persecuting societies, societies based on Catholic "fundamentalism,"[20] intolerant toward

---

18 Heater, *Citizenship*; Turner, *Citizenship and Social Theory*.
19 See further: works on nationalism and particularity, such as Vincent, *Nationalism and Particularity*, and on hegemonic states, such as Peleg, *Democratizing the Hegemonic State*, as well as on fundamentalism, sectarianism, and revolution, such as Eisenstadt, *Fundamentalism, Sectarianism and Revolution*. Eisenstadt draws on the past to show how the great revolutions and social movements contributed to the birth of modernity.
20 Fundamentalism is by no means restricted to the monotheistic religions. Tabish Khair frequently talks about Hindu fundamentalism growing in contemporary India (in private conversation). Karen Armstrong in *The Battle for God* traces the origins of fundamentalist movements in Judaism, Christianity, and Islam. Oscillating between *mythos* and *logos*, Armstrong argues

other religions and moral deviation, maltreating those who thought differently (such as Galileo), prayed differently (for example, Jan Hus), wrote things that others could not understand (like Marguerite Porete), were rich enough to inspire envy (i.e., the Templars), were afflicted and blessed by a disease (the lepers), or were simply of a different faith and race (the Jews). Many medieval nations were righteous in their own self-government and characteristically un-Christian in their dealing with the Other. R. I. Moore, in his outline of the formation of a persecuting society between the years 950 and 1250, demonstrates how various fears of the devil, heretics or the Saracens played out and led to the shaping of exaggerated notions of purity and pollution in social and religious life. Medieval Europe was intolerant and judgmental but always tried to not appear so. The advent of the Renaissance did not lessen the persecution of heretics, witches, and Jews; these groups continued to be used as scapegoats in all disasters. One would think that in "the age of reconnaissance," to use J. H. Parry's expression, Europe might try to redefine its stance toward foreigners, yet – not without a good reason – it remained unmoved toward Islam, which continued to be seen as a threat.

Differences between East and West are undeniable. The Western idea of the state developed in the Middle Ages to account for the freshly created feudal organization of land and work. In the East, however, tribes, rather than nationalities and languages, were of paramount importance, with Islam as the linking ideology. These disparities were observed by both the Victorian travelers and the nineteenth-century historians whose works were investigated in part 1 of the present study. Western countries established national secular governments, and even though the famed struggle between the crown and the (papal) tiara contributed to a number of unnecessary wars, it was the secular powers and not the religious ones that governed European countries, save for the Vatican. In the postmedieval period, European states secularized their numerous institutions and curtailed the influence of the Church in civil matters, despite intense efforts by the Church to maintain its position and secure its presence in the

---

that these concepts demonstrate "complementary ways of arriving at truth," with myth being primary, timeless and constant and *logos* "the rational, pragmatic, and scientific thought that enabled men and women to function well in the world." Armstrong, *The Battle for God*, xiii, xiv. Armstrong's assertions that people in pre-modern times were less prone to act upon mythical ideas reads fundamentalism as the feature of the modern times. Criticizing Armstrong's approach, Malise Ruthven pinpoints Armstrong's lack of definition of "modernity." She challenges Armstrong's views, claiming that "[a] more fruitful approach to modern fundamentalism would focus on the empowering dimensions of myths as self-validating expressions of the sacred in a pluralistic world in which real power and authority have become diffused and anonymous." Ruthven, *Fundamentalism*, 53. For further discussion, see Ruthven, *Fundamentalism*, 52–55.

public domain.[21] In Muslim countries, one can observe the reverse process. During the (Western) Middle Ages, new territories were subdued by Mohammed and his followers. In the twentieth century, Afghanistan fell to the Taliban government. In Iran, the deposing of the Shah led to the rise of Ayatollah Khomeini in 1979. Saudi Arabia is still an extremely orthodox Wahhabi state observing Shari'a law. The recent revolutions occurring between 2010 and 2011 in Egypt, Libya, and Syria led to the establishment of the Islamic State of Syria and Iraq. The revolutions were staged by Islamic freedom fighters in order to purify Islamic territories of unbelievers and heretics and create the one and only "house of Islam."

In *dar-al-Islam*, human beings are free under the umbrella of the will of Allah. There is no other way to be free but through obedience, whereas in the West, the idea of freedom is associated with individual liberties whose premises the East repudiates. "What do you mean by being free?" asked Shafi, V. S. Naipaul's Malaysian respondent:

> Freedom for me is not something that you can roam anywhere you want. Freedom must be within the definition of a certain framework. Because I don't think we are able to run around and get everything. That freedom means nothing. You must really frame yourself where you want to go and what you want to do.[22]

Shafi, reminding Naipaul that power and success can be easily followed by injustice, failure of reason, corruption of virtue, and the possible loss of autonomy, evokes the universal experiences of mankind. Independence and imprisonment are thus embedded in human life. In so many ways, we are all born to unfreedom, and the liberty we fight for so ardently, in the great scheme of things, is nothing more than a mirage of the Saharan desert, the landscape of the mind, the *eutopos*. In Christianity, freedom is found with God and, in most radical views, is only possible when the soul leaves the prison-house of the body; so it is the Boethian freedom from want, but perhaps nowadays, it is also freedom *to* want. In Islam, one attains freedom by submitting oneself entirely to the will of God. The Muslim idea of happiness is synonymous with that of surrender to God, who stands for the ultimate good on Earth and bliss in Heaven. For Muslims, then, the concept is indisputably connected with submission to Islam and its rulers. In the Middle Ages, the Muslim territories were united under one sultan, whose task was

---

[21] The medieval example of such a struggle is best conveyed in the tug of war between Charlemagne and Bishop Turin in *The Siege of Milan*, in which Bishop Turin calls Charlemagne a heretic and excommunicates him because of the king's alleged cowardice in defending the Christian faith against the Saracens.
[22] Naipaul, *Among the Believers*, 267.

to protect the faith and the faithful.²³ The fall of the Umayyad dynasty in Egypt and the military victories of the Ottomans, however, showed the utopian foundations of the great Muslim State. The Muslim countries – inhabited by culturally and linguistically different tribe-nations, from the Pashtuns in Persia to the Ottomans in Turkey – were too widespread to be governed by one ruler. Bound with the already-existing dispute between the Shi'a and Sunni Muslims, the war for domination has plagued the lands from the Middle Ages to the twenty-first century. Conflict therefore, lies equally at the heart of Islam, as it does of Christianity.

As has been shown in the previous chapters, the Western idea of advancement is that of the secularization of science, the development of technology, the granting of individual freedom and, for the hardworking, prosperity the latter is similarly accorded to the faithful in Islam. These are the ideas that the Arabist Bernard Lewis communicates in his works, where he accentuates the power struggle between the modern and advanced West and the poor and backward East, frequently reduced to the struggle against secularism and modernism.²⁴ His assertion, though, cannot be taken at face value. Said accuses Lewis of "purely political exploits" and sees him as someone with "sublime confidence" and "unrestrained anti-intellectualism, unencumbered by critical self-consciousness."²⁵

---

23 Crone, *Medieval Islamic Political Thought*, 232, claims that the early Arabs were members of tribes and nations "rather than of social strata or classes." Later, with the appearance of more developed social structures, the idea of state structures came about.

24 What is more, works such as Mark Steyn's *America Alone* utilize yet another image, that of our own homegrown terrorism, grown – as if to say *fed* – on welfare. Steyn claims that, "While it's not true that every immigrant on welfare is an Islamic terrorist, the vast majority of Islamic terrorists in Europe are on welfare, living in radicalized ghetto cultures with nothing to do but sit around the flat plotting the jihad all day at taxpayers' expense. Muhammed Metin Kaplan used his time on welfare in Germany to set up his Islamist group, Caliphate State; the so-called 'caliph of Cologne' was subsequently extradited to Turkey for planning to fly a plane into the mausoleum of Kemal Ataturk. . . . Abu Hamza became Britain's most famous fire-breathing imam while on welfare in London, and, after being charged with incitement to murder and sent to jail, sued the government for extra benefits on top of the £1,000 a week his family already received. Abu Quatada, a leading al Qaeda recruiter, became an Islamist big shot while on welfare in Britain, and only when he was discovered to have £150,000 in his bank account did the Department for Work and Pensions turn off the spigot. Oh, and here's another Welfare Megabucks bonanza, from the *Times* of London: 'Police are investigating allegations that the four suspected July 21 bombers collected more than £500,000 in benefits payments in Britain.'" Steyn, *America Alone*, 82–84. I am usually suspicious about books with no references, but he does seem to be making a point here. What is more frightening, however, is that such voices, if persuasive enough, are equally dangerous, as they can stimulate mass hysteria and hinder any kind of racial and cultural stability.

25 Said, "Orientalism Reconsidered," in his *Reflections on Exile*, 204.

Other researchers, such as Anders Strindberg and Mats Wärn, likewise call for a more in-depth analysis of the contradictions present even within Muslim holy history. What remains unchallenged is that Islam unchangeably attaches great importance to religious conversion and the spread of the idea of utter and complete obedience to the one and only God, Allah. In the words of Sayyd Qtub, Islam "is not merely a declaration of the freedom of the Arabs, nor is its message confined to the Arabs. It addresses itself to the whole of mankind, and its sphere of work is the whole world."[26] Consequently, the two philosophies – one in which faith is an individual's private matter and religious freedom is granted by the government, and another in which religion remains a public matter with religious laws being synonymous with the state ones – can never be reconciled. That is the message of Ayatollah Khomeini's *The Islamic Government*,[27] and such ideas are also replicated in Laroussi el Metoui's *Halima* and in the first part of Ed Husain's *The Islamist*, the latter with a more up-to-date, albeit unarticulated, suggestion: "Let's agree to disagree."

The quest for purpose and fulfillment in agreement with his religion was a rocky road for Ed Husain, who had to extricate himself from fundamentalist organizations. Still, his autobiography illustrates that if there is hope in the future world – against such negative propaganda as Mark Steyn's[28] – it lies with the generation of young British, French, and American Muslims, not with the older leaders. Perhaps, against all odds, the young ones will acknowledge and accept the essential differences and will become more open-minded, like the heroines of Brian Moore's *The Magician's Wife* and Ahdaf Soueif's *The Map of Love*. What our destiny should bring, no one knows, but in order to understand the contemporary political use of the past and especially the Crusades imagery, it is our duty to unearth and study our sometimes shameful past. The necessity to retrace the symbolic systems within the discourses on the East facilitates the understanding of the specificity of the current "Islamic revolutions." Earlier texts fashioned the existing ideologies, and so the three medieval enemies of Mankind, the World, the Devil, and the Flesh retain their figurative allure in present-day literature and culture. Part 2 of the present study will thus be devoted to the tracing of the medieval concepts reincarnated in current fictional and non-fictional works: the world of immigration; the figure of the terrorist; and the desire of Christian women for Muslim men.

---

26 Qtub, *Milestones*.
27 Khomeini, *Islamic Government*.
28 Steyn, *America Alone*.

Chapter 4
Dar Al-Hijira, or the World Of Immigration

Maria Edgeworth's (1767–1849)[1] *The Absentee*, published in 1812, while criticizing the aristocratic "largesse" of the impoverished early nineteenth-century Irish gentry through the rather incompatible marriage of Lady and Lord Clonbrony (Lady Clonbrony is English and Lord Clonbrony is Irish), addresses the situation of post-1801, post-Union Ireland. At first glance, the novel is indeed about Lord Clonbrony's absence from his estate in Ireland and Lady Clonbrony's pretentiousness, stressed through the scenes of the preparation and then the execution of her "Oriental gala." The Oriental gala is almost never discussed by the critics when the novel's more serious preoccupations surface. But Edgeworth's text testifies to the fascination with the Orient, represented here through the collection of oddities suggested by the gala master, a Mr. Soho:

> You fill up your angels with *encoinieres* – round your walls with the *Turkish tent drapery* – a fancy of my own – in apricot cloth, or crimson velvet, suppose, o, *en flute* in crimson satin draperies, fanned and riched with gold fringes, en suite – intermediate spaces, Apollo's heads with gold rays – and here, ma'am, you place four *chancelières* with chimeras at the corners, covered with blue silk and silver fringe, elegantly fanciful – with my STATIRA CANOPY here – light blue silk draperies – aerial tint, with silver balls – and for seats here, the SERGALIO OTTOMANS superfine scarlet – your paws – griffin – golden – and golden tripods, here, with antique cranes – and oriental alabaster tables here and there – quite appropriate, your la'ship feels.[2]

Mr. Soho goes even further in his extravagance. He states:

> Then, for the little room, I recommend turning it temporarily into a Chinese pagoda, with this *Chinese pagoda paper*, with the porcelain border, and josses and jars, and beakers, to match; and I can venture to promise one vase of pre-eminent size and beauty – O, indubitably! If your la'ship prefers it, you can have the *Egyptian hieroglyphic paper*, with the *ibis border* to match![3]

The result, although immensely pleasing for Lady Clonbrony, is somewhat discordant.

---

[1] Edgeworth, *The Absentee*. This novel is Edgeworth's voice discussing the manifold English–Irish relationships. She portrays them through a distorted mirror, the fashionable life in London (spiced with oriental themes) versus the rural boredom of Ireland.
[2] Edgeworth, *The Absentee*, 12–13. Capital letters and emphasis original.
[3] Edgeworth, *The Absentee*, 13. Emphasis original.

> The opening of her gala, the display of her splendid reception rooms, the Turkish tent, the Alhambra, the pagoda, formed a proud moment to Lady Clonbrony. Much did she enjoy, and much too naturally, notwithstanding all her efforts to be stiff and stately, much too naturally did she show her enjoyment of the surprise excited in some and affected by others on their first entrance.

The mismatched oriental paraphernalia are appreciated by Lady Clonbrony's guests, and the whole endeavor enables her to perceive herself as the "mirror of fashion."[4] Little does she know that she herself, together with her slightly uncouth Irish husband, are the objects of curiosity and ridicule rather than praise.

Edgeworth's novel reflects the fashion for Turkish garb,[5] but the gala does not give credit to the Western interest in the East. Rather, by presenting the Orient as the "living tableau of queerness,"[6] the incongruous display denigrates the West.[7] This is so because for the eighteenth-century characters, what was the sinful World in the medieval imagination became the glamorous World of eighteenth-century public life, manifested in the fashion for oriental excess. Unsurprisingly, Eastern surfeit was a much-repeated motif of the Saracen romances, the theme transposed into later epochs. Thus Orientalism and medievalism are linked in the eighteenth century, aiding the formulations of the historical consciousness of Western Europe.[8]

---

4 Edgeworth, *The Absentee*, 28.
5 Another literary testament to the fashion is Daniel Defoe's *Roxanna* (1724).
6 Said, *Orientalism*, 103. The Romantic writer Robert Southey (1774–1843) published a long Orientalist metrical romance in 1801 called *Thalaba the Destroyer*. Southey saw his work as a continuation of the *Arabian Nights* and hoped to show Arabian and Persian life. His antiquarian research and travel journals were undertaken to authenticate the poem's exoticism. Yet he did not manage to avoid stereotypes, such as the presence of a vampire: one of the walking dead reanimated by a demon and destroyed through blood transfusion. Though dead, the corpse of the "Arabian maid" Oneiza wanders the passages of her tomb by night, possessed by a demon. The hero Thalaba and his father-in-law Moath find her there, "her lineaments changed by death to 'livid cheeks, and lips of blue.'" Ellis, *History of Gothic Fiction*, 176. The poem's Persian location was related to Southey's reading of the Hungarian and Greek sources of the vampire stories and, in a way, "reveal[ed] all exotic culture might be leveled into one primitive and superstitious discourse" (Ellis, *History of Gothic Fiction*, 177). This is yet another instance in which the East becomes feminized and human emotions chart the prevalent images of interiority.
7 Beckford's *Vathek* (1786) repeats the Faustian sin of ungoverned thirst for power and knowledge: Vathek becomes the servant of Eblis, the Devil, in order to gain access to the treasures of pre-Adamite sultans in the ruins of Istakar. He has numerous adventures in Istakar, then gains admission to the underworld of Eblis, where he realizes the vanity of the world and his own transgression. He is punished with eternal torment. His body will not be destroyed, but his heart will forever burn inside him. Norton, *Gothic Readings*, 18.
8 Ganim, *Medievalism and Orientalism*, 3.

In the Middle Ages, the external reality – the world beyond Christian domains, beyond Europe – though most certainly wicked and immoral, in the eyes of the medieval pilgrims and travelers was both disgusting and enchanting. For medieval rulers it was a place to subjugate, and for the visitors it was a place of sin, an environment in which otherwise good and honest Christians succumbed to temptations. Muslims also perceived the outer reality, the one without Islam, as a seat of various temptations and iniquity. For both groups, rejection of the sinful World was the ultimate proof of one's successful penance, and this medieval pattern is recapitulated in later literature in English. The two contemporary works selected for further analysis, David Caute's novel *Fatima's Scarf* (1998) and Hanif Kureishi's memoirs *My Ear at his Heart*, along with *The Rainbow Sign*, published in 2004 and 1986 respectively and set in the late twentieth century, narrate the uneasy transactions between the World and the Individual, between the suave and the spiritual, showing first- and second-generation immigrants in British contexts. The characters are caught between their need to adapt and thus unavoidably lose the sense of belonging to the culture of their roots and their propensity to stand out. Consequently, they become objects of dislike, if not outright derision. Depicting the pitfalls of immigration, their struggles underscore the illusive attraction of the (Western) World.

Encoded in the Augustinian vision of the celestial City of God, as opposed to the sin-ridden city of men that engendered morally unhealthy excitement and corruptible urbanity,[9] "the World" is recurrently used as a trope for the quest motif linked with the chivalric obligation to make a name for oneself and atone for one's transgressions. The trope lies at the core of the romance of *Guy of Warwick*, who has to "fare into hethen cuntre."[10] Medieval readers, like the eighteenth-century readers in Maria Edgeworth's *The Absentee*, enjoyed the tales of the exotic and strange Arabia, even though most of them never went there.[11] Such accounts were fed by an idea of what the East might have been like rather than by what it was, and that is what one finds in the story of Guy of Warwick, who is enticed by the world, only to renounce it alongside his life of affluence and hard-won glory. The romance of *Sir Isumbras* presents a reversed pattern of penitence. Punished for being happy, rich and successful,

---

[9] "The World" or "Mundus" in late medieval plays like *The Castle of Perseverance* or *Mundus et Infans* would also have the features of an exemplary bad king. In mystery plays, Herod is worldly and therefore evil; in morality plays, the king sometimes was simply presented as foolish, like Rex in *The Pride of Life*, but the gradation of wickedness was very important.

[10] *Guy of Warwick*, ll. 7396–7397.

[11] "Christopher Wren lived for some years in London in a house which was called by the sign of the Saracen's Head." Sweetman, *The Oriental Obsession*, 6.

he has to conquer his fear of poverty and of the barbarians so as to become the exemplary hagiographic hero. The climax of his redemptive journeys is set, predictably, in Jerusalem and the unnamed neighboring Saracen lands. For both Sir Isumbras and Guy of Warwick, the potent topos of a pilgrimage cum crusade is transformed into a personal crusade to conquer the hated Muslim enemy. The prevalent ideology behind such depictions is a response to the Saracen aggression; theirs is a war to end violence and bring peace to Christian lands. Having seen the World, the heroes cannot stay in the Holy Land; they have to return home to enjoy the fruits of their labors, but the healing properties of their expeditions are a lasting mark of their cleansed souls. The romances thus literalized the dangers of the World, simultaneously incorporating the advantages of the voluntary exile into their lore.

Arguing that travel can be perceived as romance, Steve Clark suggests that the "journey may be seen as a refusal, a resistance, or as an expulsion, an ignominious flight. . . . The traveler is altered, sometimes changed utterly, but primarily in the sense of being made capable of more travel."[12] Spiritual and real journeys that provide direct and indirect commentaries of the reality people live in are narrated by David Caute in *Fatima's Scarf*. The 1998 novel recounts the story of a Muslim community in the fictional Yorkshire town of Bruddersdorf, uncannily resembling Bradford and touching upon similar issues that inspired the Bradford Riots of July 7, 2001,[13] as well as earlier disputes related to the burning of Salman Rushdie's *Satanic Verses*.[14] In Caute's work, the blasphemous author is Gamal Rahman, the son of a prize-winning Egyptian novelist, who offends the Muslim community with his book *The Devil: An Interview*. Like Rushdie's *Satanic Verses*, the book is burned in a public show to demonstrate Muslim outrage. The theme of book-burning is, quite unambiguously, a fictionalized account of "the Rushdie controversy." The novel-within-the novel, *The Devil: An Interview*, apparently addresses issues similar to those touched upon in *The Satanic Verses*:

---

12 Clark, "Introduction," in *Travel Writing and Empire*, 17.
13 At the beginning of the twentieth century, Bradford had a very large South Asian population and was suffering from the so-called "white flight," the general exodus of white Bradfordians. Tensions between the two groups rose after a march, organized by the National Front, had been banned by the Home Secretary under Public Order in 1986 while the Anti-Nazi League was given permission to organize a rally in the city. A rumor spread that National Front sympathizers were gathering in a pub, and this was the spark that incited the riots so aptly depicted in the 2006 movie *Bradford Riots*, directed by Neil Biswas, which tells the story from the perspective of an Asian family.
14 There is an interesting description of Bradford in Hanif Kureishi's essay "Bradford," in Kureishi, *Dreaming and Scheming*, 57–79.

Rahman's novel holds Muslims up to a public ridicule. It also panders – very deliberately – to ancient prejudices in the Christian West. Why call Muhammad by the ancient hate-name of Mahound? In that sense Rahman's book is definitely racist. A godless takeover bid for the heritage of the Crusades.[15]

The hostility toward the text is exacerbated by Christians responding favorably to the book and provocatively wearing "I love Gamal Rahman" stickers. These actions set off the Muslims, who see themselves as yet again embarking on a "jihad" against the infidels.[16]

It's men's business, this jihad, fighting this Gamal, by his opponents called Shaytan, Rahman's book – though all Muslim women share and suffer the insults inflicted on the twelve wives of the Prophet when Rahman claimed that a thirteenth wife had turned up in Egypt in our own time – or something like that.[17]

Interestingly, the Victorian explorer Richard Burton also had noticed that Arabs thought of the English as "Shaytáns, the East knows nothing of them since the days when Osmanli hosts threatened the gates of Vienna."[18] Even though in the twentieth century the knowledge of one's opponents is much more profound, the age-old dislike still persists. Unlike in a movie by Lebanese director Nadine Labaki, *Et maintnent, on va où?* (And now where to?), in which, initially, Muslims and Christians live and work together and meet in the same café only to squabble over insignificant matters, Bruddersdorf's religious communities find it hard to deal with the issue of multiculturalism. This European philosophy of creating an open, inclusive society, originated to tackle the problem of the second generation of immigrants from Pakistan, India, the Caribbean, and Africa. Europeans in the 1990s came up with the great idea of a salad bowl, in other words, each "in its own humor," only the humor was called ethnicity. In Ali Rattansi's view, multiculturalism as a political theory is related to group identities so as to resolve the issue "of individual rights in the liberalism that underpins the constitutions of the Western nation states."[19] As social science and policy, multiculturalism focuses "on the nature of ethnicities and other group identities on the ground, the actual character of interethnic group interactions, and the range of policies that have been developed to accommodate and govern the growing cultural diversity of Western societies."[20]

---

15 Caute, *Fatima's Scarf*, 33.
16 Incidentally, book-burning is also a theme of Hanif Kureishi's novel *The Black Album*.
17 Caute, *Fatima's Scarf*, 13.
18 Burton, *Personal Narrative* 1:111.
19 Rattansi, *Multiculturalism*, 2.
20 Rattansi, *Multiculturalism*, 2–3. What Caute did not know, and yet anticipated, is that multiculturalism had failed quite miserably. A more contemporary idea, known as interculturalism, has

What makes it even more difficult is that in Caute's novel, the Muslims themselves are not united, and the Lord Mayor of Bruddersdorf, Zulfikar Zaheed, sees the crowd he is facing as "Sunnis mainly, a few Shi'ites, bearded mullahs and mustachioed youngsters, a densely woven quilt of collective indignation."[21] There are also Hindus and, of course, white Anglo-Saxons, Christians, and atheists, those whose children are supposed to profit from the much-hated "Eurocentric curricula."

The school that tries not to exclude anybody in fact isolates the title character, fourteen-year-old Fatima, who asks for permission to wear a headscarf. The hijab, the religious symbol of Islam, is forbidden in her secular multiracial school. Fatima's plea is not, however, the result of her sudden conversion, or, a sympathy with fundamentalist doctrines, but a manifestation of her teenage rebellion. What is more, struggling to retain or even regain her cultural background, she is fascinated with all that is lost in multicultural Britain. For her the scarf becomes the symbol of belonging. "Fatima studies the expressions of the Iranian girls – dignity, sweetness, discipline, faith."[22] She is in love with the much older Ali and dislikes the more modern, and therefore sinful, way of life that her sister Safia favors. Safia does not see the Koran as the ultimate guide but instead challenges her sister and her family, claiming that she prefers to read Gamal Rahman's book. She abhors her family home where her father, Izza Shah, calls her a slut. While Fatima finds Western lifestyles disgusting, Safia is clearly seduced by the World. She craves a modern lifestyle freed from the bounds of religion, a world in which it will not be immodest for a girl to drive a car, whereas Fatima fights for the hijab and is repulsed by the fact that in English schools, girls and boys mix unreservedly and girls are "exposed without a decent, modest covering."[23] After all, in the Koran the punishment for "bad" women is to be hung by their hair.[24]

In contemporary Britain, the question remains as to whether the hijab is the utmost symbol of patriarchal oppression or a sanctuary, protecting women from the *haram* of the streets. The problem is periodically brought up by French newspapers in the context of France's problems with unassimilated Moroccans and Algerians, who maltreat uncovered women, and also in the context of women who are not necessarily practicing Muslims, but who wear the hijab to avoid harassment in their own neighborhoods. The issue of full Muslim dress code is

---

been developed since. Rattansi, *Multiculturalism*, 151–64. Both terms are inextricably linked with the notion of the "hybrid" or "liquid" identities of contemporary migrants.

21 Caute, *Fatima's Scarf*, 13.
22 Caute, *Fatima's Scarf*, 25.
23 Caute, *Fatima's Scarf*, 52.
24 Caute, *Fatima's Scarf*, 59.

furthermore potentially hazardous, because the burkas restrict the vision of female drivers.²⁵ Tabish Khair sees the Muslim insistence on certain types of clothes as the ultimate expression of alterity. The stranger, after all, is supposed to be indistinguishable and therefore visibly integrated, but the overtly covered body points to its own outlandishness. In the new xenophobia, the stranger is "the person who imposes bodily constraints on himself and others, either in the shape of dress, dietary practices, or ritual-related behavior."²⁶ In effect, difference is exclusive, sameness inclusive. Multicultural guidelines are assumed to account for both, but in practice, any multiracial, multireligious and multicultural school needs strict laws against whichever display of racial, religious, and cultural symbols. Hence, in a way, the ideology designed to reflect contemporary unreserved attitudes toward other cultures and religions, and embrace an open and enlightened way of teaching, has become equally restrictive in its outcome.²⁷

In Caute's novel, the acceptance of Shari'a, however, is perceived as a backward move on the part of an inexperienced young girl who goes through an identity crisis, unknowingly shared by many of the second-generation British Muslims. Fatima's plea, then, is related to all that is troubling her adolescent self, including her sister's moving in with their adoptive brother Ali, with whom Fatima is in love. Fatima's powerlessness and adolescent rage, which would otherwise be directed at her parents, are here channeled toward the school officials. Her indignation is externalized in a scene in which Fatima calls one of her teachers, Mrs. Hassani, a whore, because she lives "in sin" with Rajiv Lal, a Hindu.²⁸ Ominously, Lal asks Nasreen (Mrs. Hassani) whether she would not be better off living in Pakistan, now that multiculturalism has failed.²⁹

The breakdown of multicultural ideals recorded by Caute is not solely attributed to the primacy of Eurocentric curricula at the price of more world-oriented teaching. Unavoidably, novels labeled as postcolonial often narrate the lives of second-generation immigrants, for whom the culture of their country of origin is no longer their culture. The most obvious explanation of nascent

---

25 Steyn claims that that mode of dress "also offers opportunities for fleeing bank robbers to disguise themselves as Muslim women." Steyn, *America Alone*, 201.
26 Khair, *The New Xenophobia*, 147–48.
27 Claude Levi-Strauss denigrates Muslim table manners and is wary of the idea of women wearing burkas, which according to him means "the heavy material with which it is made allows it to follow the exact contours of the body while at the same time concealing it as completely as possible. But this merely leads to a shifting of the threshold of anxiety, since a man is disgraced if another man as much as brushes against his wife." Levi-Strauss, *Tristes Tropiques*, 402.
28 Caute, *Fatima's Scarf*, 195.
29 Caute, *Fatima's Scarf*, 553.

religious fundamentalism is then the need to belong, to be included in a group, to have some sort of identity that is different from that of the nation that constantly denies the "darkies," to use Hanif Kureishi's expression,[30] a place in the country of their parents' choice. David Caute, however, stresses that the drive toward fundamentalism is not simply a response to religious exclusion but bound up with teenage rebellion, which questions the parents' values. Consequently, the second and third generations of British Muslims are motivated by a desire to identify themselves with the cultures of their predecessors and, unlike first-generation immigrants, are against compulsory assimilation, internalized self-rejection, and social conformity – forces at the root of the contemporary conflict between Islam and Christianity, the East and the West. They refuse to be ensnared by the West because for them it represents the transgressive World. They long for purity, associated with the non-existent imaginary homelands, and thus become easy prey for various fundamentalist movements. While Western culture is dominated by materialism, the East wants to see itself as ruled by spiritual values and deems secularization as evil. What is more, young believers envisage Christianity as too secularized to sustain true devoutness. It is

> the non-believers' religion. How to explain True Belief to a corrupted television audience; how to convey the head-to-toe, dawn-to-dusk devotion of a Muslim who bends body and soul to Allah five times a day? So what is Ramadan? A real Lent. Why do our Christian brothers and sisters congratulate themselves on trying to give up some luxury during Lent? (Indeed the Bishop himself makes a joke, no offence given or taken).[31]

Searching for their own ways of living, the Muslims in Caute's novel read Islam as the perfection of Christianity,[32] but rather than accepting the message of peace, they side with the forces declaring Gamal Rahman the ultimate monster who must die for his blasphemy. In this way they resurrect the old hatred. In the name of animosity, the young people believe that "to spill the blood of an infidel ruler is God's work, [and] the emir declares, 'Our mission is to restore the sovereignty of God on earth.'"[33] Such statement is analogous with Stephen T. Asma's argument concerning religious ideologies, which necessarily "dehumanize those who do not fit inside the sanctuary of orthodoxy." Asma further cites Ayan Hirsi Ali, a well-known Somali Muslim apostate who regards Islam's rigid belief system and moral framework regulating all spheres of

---

30 Kureishi, *My Beautiful Laundrette*, 31.
31 Caute, *Fatima's Scarf*, 29.
32 Caute, *Fatima's Scarf*, 198.
33 Caute, *Fatima's Scarf*, 377.

human life as inevitably leading to cruelty toward unbelievers, but also toward the erring faithful.[34] Ali's somewhat heretical claim that Islam in itself coerces the believers to use violence echoes Mark Steyn's "apocalyptic" assertions about the unrestrained drive of contemporary Islam toward orthodoxy, and the resultant Islamism. Steyn avers that many of the countries governed by Islamic law adopted Shari'a only in the twentieth century – for instance, Pakistan 1977, Iran 1979, and Sudan 1984.[35] In Caute's novel, the jihadists are soon mixed with "urban youths, police haters, system haters, young men reared in confrontation with skinheads,"[36] and thus the clarity of the early goals is soiled by those who are supposed to uphold them. It seems that once again, as was the case of the late medieval play entitled *The World and the Child*, the sinful World takes the best of those mesmerized by its command. Hence the World announces, "All richesse redely it runneth in me," avowing, "All pleasure worldly, both mirth and game"[37] is in his hands.[38] In Bruddersdorf, those swayed by power are indiscriminately Muslim and Christian.

The personification of the World in medieval literature, among other things, points to the never-ending clash between traditional religious ways of life marked by austerity and poverty and the inevitable change into more affluent secular existence. "Western culture knows the price of everything and the value of nothing,"[39] as one of the protagonists of Caute's novel states. In many different ways, *Fatima's Scarf* also comments on the confrontation concerning the old and the new, the need to live by well-defined rules and the impossibility of maintaining them in the contemporary reality. Nasreen Hassani, a teacher who left her Muslim husband, is a good example of such a debacle. The husband, Hassan, a violent man, was the one to bring up the issue of adultery, divorce, and rape – the latter, according to Shari'a, has to have four male witnesses before a woman can be believed, but finally, Nasreen is divorced in the Muslim way, Hassan having shouted three times

---

34 Asma, *On Monsters*, 249. Ayan Hirsi Ali's story (whose name the author misspells as "Hersi") is scrutinized by Rageh Omaar, a Somali-born British journalist who, unlike Ali, remained a devout Muslim at times at odds with his adoptive country's policies. For more, see Omaar, *Only Half of Me*. For Omaar's reading of Ayaan Hirsi Ali's memoir, see 44–60.
35 Steyn, *America Alone*, 202.
36 Caute, *Fatima's Scarf*, 533.
37 Lester, *Three Late Medieval Morality Plays*.
38 The degenerate World is frequently identified with Western Europe. Hanif Kureishi cites his father's unpublished novel, in which a Moulavi, the Muslim teacher, tells the protagonist, who suffers from a severe hangover, that Allah created Europe "with all its easy sex and drink, to test the will of the Muslims, whether they remained steadfast to their beliefs or succumbed to the temptations." Kureishi, *My Ear at His Heart*, 135.
39 Caute, *Fatima's Scarf*, 94.

that he divorces her.⁴⁰ She angrily shouts back that they are not in Pakistan and that his pronouncements are not valid in present-day Britain.⁴¹ This scene indicates the deep gulf between more progressive and secularized Muslims and the orthodox ones. The latter group buttressed its attitude with a declaration that they aim to shield "good Muslim girls" from being accosted by young Sikhs and Hindus. They maintained that the *izzat*, the honor of the family, should be protected at all costs. The *izzat* appears to be of even greater importance to the second generation of Pakistanis than to their parents.

Portraying a small, close-knit community of late twentieth-century Britain, Caute weaves together many ongoing preoccupations connected with religious practices and Muslim law. The book-burning and the Gamal Rahman hullabaloo are central to the development of the main plot, as the debate concerning the novel is placed within the web of disagreements related to libel, freedom of speech, and the freedom of artistic creation. In *Fatima's Scarf*, Sulfikar Zaeed recalls the times when Muslims "were merely picturesque 'Mohammedans' to be found in illustrated books written by intrepid explorers."⁴² This opinion is undoubtedly shared by a real-life teacher described by Hanif Kureishi in his autobiographical essay *The Rainbow Sign*: "When I was nine or ten a teacher purposefully placed some pictures of Indian peasants in mud huts in front of me and said to the class: Hanif comes from India."⁴³ Throughout the sixties, Kureishi experienced growing feelings of out-of-placeness, strengthened by his wish to suppress his Pakistani self. "The word 'Pakistani' had been made into an insult. It was a word I didn't want used about myself."⁴⁴ Kureishi sees racism as unreason and prejudice, but at the same time he understands that the groups of immigrants from Pakistan to England, the poor and the illiterate, did not give credit to the country of such a rich history and culture.⁴⁵ Under the Commonwealth Immigration Act of 1962, Pakistanis could come to Britain as workers and could stay either temporarily or permanently. The so-called "voucher system" then gave Pakistanis already in Britain the opportunity to make arrangements for their relatives and friends to join them. The system served to reinforce kinship and family ties but was adulterated by two factors in Pakistan. One was the legacy of the 1947 Partition of India, which affected Kureishi's father's family, and the foreseeable mayhem it caused, namely, the mass immigration of Pakistanis to Britain. In *My Ear at His*

---

40 Caute *Fatima's Scarf*, 483.
41 Caute *Fatima's Scarf*, 501.
42 Caute, *Fatima's Scarf*, 11–12.
43 Kureishi, *The Rainbow Sign*, 9.
44 Kureishi, *The Rainbow Sign*, 12.
45 Kureishi, *The Rainbow Sign*, 28.

Heart: Reading my Father, Kureishi reads the trauma of the Partition through his father's unpublished novel. The second factor was the construction of the Mangla Dam area, begun in 1962, which led to approximately 100,000 people losing their homes and needing to be relocated.[46] Again, many people decided to emigrate to Britain.

The disturbing experiences of moving from India to a newly created Pakistan are recounted by Kureishi's father Rafiushan, known to his family as Shanoo, in his last unfinished novel, entitled "An Indian Adolescence."[47] Rafiushan, a civil servant in the Pakistani Embassy in London, came from a Westernized family and "often talked of feeling alienated in India with its numerous eccentric religions and superstitions."[48] He viewed religion as a bar to progress: "You couldn't have a liberal, democratic political system in a society in which the families were Muslim, strictly organized around the symbolic position of the absolute father."[49] Writing helped him come to terms with the paradoxes of culture and religion, leading him throughout his adult life to write novels, stories and plays.[50] As it happens, Kureishi's "father found his own satisfaction in books, and in his burgeoning ambition as a writer."[51] Rafiushan Kureishi's final work, narrating the experiences of a youth in India, appears to be the most autobiographical, revealing the deep-seated trauma of the Partition. The buried secret of Rafiushan's young self that marked his later life was the moment of relocation, of having to say goodbye to everything he had known and loved.

No wonder the manuscript "begins with a kind of loss." There, the sixteen-year-old Shani " . . . is alone in the house in Poona with his mother, while removal men pack up the family belongings."[52] Shani comes from a well-to-do family; his father, Colonel Murad, was an Army doctor, who had just left his job to begin a new career as an owner of a soap factory. In a heartbreaking scene, Shani looks at the house for the last time, taking in the sights of his childhood, wondering what will happen to the place. "As he walked, he touched the trees –

---

46 Source: http:/www.irespect.net/Untold%20Stories/Asian/The%20Pakistani%20Community.htm.
47 After her husband's death, Hanif's mother found eighty missing pages of her husband's novel, some handwritten and some typed on A4 pages cut in half. Even though "the spelling is terrible," the text offers an interesting insight into Hanif's father's early life. Kureishi, *My Ear at His Heart*, 221.
48 Kureishi, *My Ear at His Heart*, 206.
49 Kureishi, *My Ear at His Heart*, 238.
50 According to Kureishi, his father "completed at least four novels." Kureishi, *My Ear at His Heart*, 221.
51 Kureishi, *My Ear at His Heart*, 59.
52 Kureishi, *My Ear at His Heart*, 21.

tamarind, mango, neem, peepul and the spreading Banyan. Under them he had studied, chatted, joked and ate raw mangoes with his friends, and he was sad that he was leaving them."[53] Despite the family's status and the relative painlessness of the move, as there is no reported violence in the story, Shani cannot ignore the fact that the new place was not of their choice, that it was imposed on them. The second chapter of the unpublished novel is set in Bombay, where, at six o'clock, before he goes to school and before it gets too hot, Shani runs to the beach to jog and swim. "Nevertheless, drying himself, he can't help recalling the auctioning of the family possessions. His father, with Bibi watching from the back of the auction room, holding a yellow parasol, seemed to have been reduced by it. . . . Out of his uniform he lacked authority, power and arrogance."[54] Possibly because of the ordeal of the Partition, Kureishi's father never again went to Pakistan, not even for a holiday. The price of that decision was that he did not see his mother again. "Rejoining his family would be too difficult . . . but dad had passionately complicated feelings about the place. In the early 1980s, when, at Omar's urging, I decided to go, my father was furious: betrayed, abandoned, humiliated by his envy."[55] Bullied as an adolescent in India, he treated Britain as his adoptive homeland, and there, in his adult life, he suffered under the right-wing government's domestic policies that accepted racism. In a way, Rafiushan Kureishi, Shanoo, like his fictive alter ego Shani, did not belong to either place. Surprisingly,

> it didn't make him a victim in his mind. He worked with Pakistanis and didn't endure the kind of persistent and degrading racism that some of us knew at school, the kind which made you lose faith in the rationality and justice of the British political system, which had both required immigrants and collaborated in their persecution. It seemed, at the time, that one would never recover from this disillusionment.[56]

The maltreatment of the first-generation immigrants and the isolation of the second generation of Pakistanis born in England are intertwined in both *My Ear at His Heart* and *The Rainbow Sign*. The saddest part of Hanif Kureishi's life story is that in Karachi he was as alienated as he felt in England. For his cousins, he was a "Paki," while they were Pakistani. "In England I was a playwright. In Karachi this meant little. There were no theaters; the arts were discouraged by the state – music and dancing are un-Islamic – and ignored by practically everyone else. So despite

---

53 Kureishi, *My Ear at His Heart*, 21–22.
54 Kureishi, *My Ear at His Heart*, 27.
55 Kureishi, *My Ear at His Heart*, 59.
56 Kureishi, *My Ear at His Heart*, 129.

everything I felt pretty out of place."[57] Like his father, Kureishi, a staunch supporter of atheism, saw Islam as the tyranny of the Muslim priesthood and ridiculed the Pakistanis' need to avenge themselves on their colonial oppressors by exporting heroin to the West.

> Heroin was anti-Western; addiction in Western children was a deserved symptom of the moral vertigo of godless societies. It was a kind of colonial revenge. Reversed imperialism, the Karachi wits called it, inviting nemesis. The reversed imperialism was itself being reversed . . . Oddly, since heroin and dope were both indigenous to the country, it took the West to make them popular in the East.[58]

Such ironic pronouncements, however, are a sign of the deep-seated grudge against the system that allowed for immigration but relegated the immigrant and mixed-race children to the status of second-class citizens. That is why at school, young Hanif was spoken to in a "Peter Sellers" Indian accent and addressed as "Pakistani Pete."[59]

Enoch Powell's famous "rivers of blood" speech, coupled with Duncan Sandy's words pronouncing that half-caste children "would merely produce a generation of misfits and create national tensions,"[60] did not foster a welcoming ambiance for young mixed-race Hanif to grow up in. The adolescent Kureishi battles the racist ideology of the 1960s. As a born and bred Londoner and seeing England as his mother country, he does not understand the accusations of not being able to assimilate. Nor does he comprehend Powell's recommendation that the unsuccessful and unassailable elements should be offered "voluntary repatriation."[61] Young Kureishi endures recurrent acts of psychological violence, both from his peers and from his elders. He knows the places where his school friends gather to beat up Pakistanis and dreams that he will eventually move out of the suburbs, "to make another kind of life, somewhere else, with better people." He recalls not being able to date English girls because their parents kept warning them that their reputation might be tarnished by "darkies."[62] In *The Rainbow Sign*, Kureishi brands the evil of racism as the violation of another person's dignity, it is "the failure of connection with others" but also "a failure to understand or feel what it is one's own humility consists in, what it is to be alive, and what it is to see both oneself and others as being ends not means, and as having souls."[63] In Kureishi's

---

57 Kureishi, *The Rainbow Sign*, 17.
58 Kureishi, *The Rainbow Sign*, 23–24.
59 Kureishi, *The Rainbow Sign*, 9.
60 Kureishi, *The Rainbow Sign*, 11.
61 Kureishi, *The Rainbow Sign*, 11.
62 Kureishi, *The Rainbow Sign*, 11.
63 Kureishi, *The Rainbow Sign*, 31.

case, the world of immigration, the metaphorical "hijira," is the world of constant clashes – racial, cultural, and religious.

Rafaela Dancygier has further analyzed such struggles through contemporary sociopolitical theories connected with various constituencies whose population consists mainly of immigrants. Her investigation outlines the ways in which Western countries grant citizenship rights to immigrants.[64] The deterioration of intergroup relations between various immigrant groups has also featured in religious and cultural clashes at the turn of the millennium and shortly afterwards. Dancygier defines "immigrant–native conflict" as involving "sustained confrontation between members of the immigrant and the native populations in a given locality," or, in other words, persistent disagreements from earlier periods that lead to confrontation – for example, the Bradford Riots.[65] The demographic structure of immigrant communities, which are viewed as a valid threat by Steyn, Dancygier professes to be economy-building factors – because immigrants need schools, hospitals, and kindergartens and, in due course, contribute to the tax base.[66] Dancygier also does not isolate religion as the main spark igniting the immigrant–native conflict but blames poverty, which is also the main reason for the growing political consciousness of immigrant groups. Her claims would seem contrary to those which Caute presents in his novel analyzed above, where the Bruddersdorf Muslim community is portrayed as weak, divided, plagued with doubt, and incapable of reconciling the values of the modern world with traditional Muslim ones, and so too vulnerable to find a unified voice. Nevertheless, Dancygier seem to subscribe to Caute's argument that the failure of kin-based networks contributes to the failure of communal enterprises; but she also sees outbreaks of violence against ethnic groups as a clear response to British internal policies and the media war, so aptly described by Said in his *Covering Islam*.[67] Comparably to Kureishi, Dancygier blames Thatcherite and pre-Thatcherite governments for their hostility toward Indian, Pakistani, and Bangladeshi minorities, attitudes that, in effect, contributed to the home-grown "intifada."[68] Michael Dummett

---

64 Dancygier, *Immigration and Conflict*, 110.
65 Dancygier, *Immigration and Conflict*, 21.
66 Dancygier, *Immigration and Conflict*, 29.
67 For more on immigration, see Michael Dummett, who outlines the general principles of immigration and discusses the history of immigration, showing how racism influenced the negative perception of immigrants. Particularly worth noting is the chapter entitled "How Immigration was Made a Menace in Britain." Dummett, *On Immigration and Refugees*, 89–108. An introduction to international migration with reference to different European countries is offered by Koser, *International Migration*. What is certainly interesting is that we only discuss migration to Europe and America (or Australia), but never to Africa (excluding South Africa, of course).
68 Dancygier, *Immigration and Conflict*, 64.

likewise brings up the Thatcherite paranoia about England being swamped by different cultures. The resultant Nationality Act of 1981, introduced by the Conservative Government, was designed to reduce future sources of primary immigration.[69] This is how, in the course of a couple of decades, the homegrown insurgent comes to infest the popular imagination, inciting contempt and panic. The fanatic is the product of both the East *and* the West; being an insider, s/he is at the same time an outsider, and that very fact seems to be the greatest transgression.[70] Even though they are born in the new country, second-generation immigrants carry the burden of their parents' homeland, their unfulfilled dreams and their fragile new identities. Despite the fact that their in-betweenness is of a different kind and breeds a dissimilar disillusionment, they share the fight for acceptance. Such an endeavor offers only two options: forget your roots and become truly British, or maintain your culture and religion and remain an outcast.

---

[69] Dummett, *On Immigration*, 115, 118–19.
[70] Mustafa Bayoumi tries to analyze the real-life stories of a number of Arabs and Muslims in post-9/11 America in order to elicit sympathy toward those who were wrongly accused and detained in the weeks following the first terrorist attack. In his preface, he reminds the readers how various groups, such as Jews, Germans and Japanese, were persecuted after other disasters. Rasha, born in Syria, accepted American liberal values and did not want to live in a police state. Sami, an Arab Christian who participated in the war in Iraq, has to come to terms with his origins and is an interesting example of the second-generation immigrant identity crisis. Yasmin, who fought to become her school's student body president, although admirable in her fight, is perhaps the least convincing example. She wanted to circumvent the school's law that required her, as president, to be present at various school events, including dances. Dancing, however, is forbidden in Islam. Yasmin could not participate, not even passively sitting in another room, in school dances, which as the president she should. And so Yasmin and her father consulted a Muslim lawyer and embarked on a long fight to let Yasmin become the school's president despite the prohibition. In a state school where secular values are propagated, the demand to make American schools conform to Islam is wrong. And if one cannot fulfill the responsibilities that come with the position, one should not try to change them. Similarly, Omar's account is full of anger against those who treat him as inferior. Omar claims that being Arab diminishes his opportunities for work. He wanted to be a journalist, but although he once held a temporary position at *Al-Jazeera*, no Western network wanted to hire him. The story of the Palestinian-American Akram and his trip to his homeland is a tirade against the Jews on the West Bank. Both Akram's and Lina's tales show the impossibility of returning home to Palestine and Iraq respectively. The home they yearn for does not exist anymore. Despite claiming absolute sincerity and openness, Bayoumi skillfully omits to reveal the causes for Rami's father's arrest – supposedly because his friends framed him – and does not present any reasons for an appeal or shortening of the sentence. In all the stories, there are places of indeterminacy, holes, which are not filled with information but leave the readers wondering whether Bayoumi and his respondents tell the "truth and nothing but the truth." As a result, one sees both the undeserved racism, which was Bayoumi's aim, as well as the well-deserved dislike, which certainly was not his aim. Bayoumi, *How Does It Feel to Be a Problem?*.

The figure of the foreigner in a purgatorial journey through a new country is best captured by J. M. Coetzee's *The Childhood of Jesus*,[71] a novel in which the memory of the old country is such a burden that recent immigrants are given a new language, new names, and even new birthdays to be symbolically reborn as the inhabitants of the country of their choice. Simòn and David's journeys reverberate with the Old Testament wandering of the Jews. The Israelites roam the desert for an unimaginably long time – forty years. Biblical scholars often pondered on the rationale of God's mysterious ways. To those living in the brave new world of post-communist Poland, the message has always been clear. If you cannot break with the past, the past has to break with you. What seemed like perpetual exile was simply a way to guarantee the coming of the new generation, the generation born in freedom. Those forty years gave the Jews time and space to rethink their status in the world and to change their attitudes toward nationhood. Infused with biblical allusions, Coetzee's novel captures the feeling of strangeness, of a misconstrued perception of reality, of the repeated attempts to fit in and recurring instances of being rejected, notwithstanding the fact that the unnamed Latin American country, unlike contemporary Europe, appears to be well prepared to accept the arrival of a large number of immigrants.

The deluge of barbarians that threatened Europe at the end of the Middle Ages was as mysterious as it was inexplicable, and it could only be explicated through God's wrath at mankind's sins. Similarly, the influx of immigrants in the second half of the twentieth century was seen, by popular consent, as a punishment for England's long and powerful reign over half of the world. As has been shown in Caute's novel *Fatima's Scarf* and Kureishi's memoir *My Ear at his Heart*, alongside his earlier *The Rainbow Sign*, the process of relocation is neither a peaceful nor pleasant experience, even if the country of one's choice is a hospitable one. Displacement and cultural discrepancy are only some of the problems faced by immigrants, lured by better prospects in the places they do not know and do not understand. Though it is not constructive to repeat the "poverty breeding anger" cliché, one has to admit that in order to counter the fraudulent world that does not want them, the "barbarians" revert to religion. The assumed purity of Muslim spirituality offers, albeit temporarily, relief from anxiety, providing a sense of direction and belonging, and creates new – real, rather than imagined, as Anderson claimed – communities[72] in which religion,

---

71 Coetzee, *Childhood of Jesus*.
72 Anderson's work, originally published in 1983, responded to the changing world of the post–Cold War world. He was one of the first thinkers to look at nationalism and patriotism as forces that could inspire racial hatred and ethnic cleansing. Post-Andersonian works on nationalism, such as the papers collected by McKim and McMahan in *The Morality of Nationalism*,

more than ethnicity and culture, helps the lost wanderers see and re-collect all that is important in their shattered lives. This is how "nationalism" becomes a negative idea, a trope of the right-wing politics and the banner word of those who oppose (the worldly idea of) multiculturalism. As has been indicated in the works under scrutiny in the present chapter, what seems to be cultural resilience in the case of the first generation of immigrants turns into cultural, and religious, warfare in the case of the second. It is commonly assumed that nation-states have always been reluctant to be transformed into multiethnic societies. The medieval Saracen romances portrayed characters who harbored the fear of the corrupt and corruptible World, buttressing the antithesis of the godly and the worldly, and they shaped the negative portraits of strangers still prevalent in Europe. The medieval bifurcation reverberated during the 2004 American Presidential elections, which juxtaposed the emblematic Bush's "Godly America" with the equally expressive Kerry's "Worldly America,"[73] analogous to the anti-immigrant, conservative trends opposing the progressive, pro-diversity policies in Europe. In reality, the twenty-first-century world would benefit from the amalgamation of both.

---

take up the challenge of the Andersonian reading of nationalism and try to rationalize its positive aspects, such as the need for national safety and protection of the citizens, while concurrently trying to deal with the pitfalls of extreme nationalism. Judith Lichtenberg's chapter, entitled "Nationalism, For and (Mainly) Against," exposes the dangers of nationalism. She claims that "[t]here is the nationalism of those who have succeeded in securing a state, or at least dominance within one, and the nationalism of those within this state but having a different culture who have not" (170); while Stephen Nathanson in his "Nationalism and the Limits of Global Humanism," outlines defensive arguments for national recognition and group identity, arguing that nation and culture are often central to a person's identity (176–87).

73 I was reminded of this while reading Steyn, *America Alone*, 181.

Chapter 5
Arabian (K)nights: On Terrorists and Tyrants

Joseph's Conrad *The Secret Agent* (1907)[1] was one of the first important "terrorist novels." Its central event is the attempted bombing of the London Observatory by a mentally unstable simpleton, a young man named Stevie.[2] An anarchist referred to as The Professor, a man who specializes in the production of bombs, prepares the bomb. He disdains weakness and rejoices in strength; he knows himself to be "a force. His thoughts caressed the images of ruin and destruction."[3] Unlike later works on terrorism, which outline the ideologies of inclusion and exclusion more clearly, Conrad's novel focuses on devastation as an aim in itself. His England is populated with spies, police officers, and anarchists, whose motives for destruction are not always clear.[4] This ethical ambiguity positions *The Secret Agent* as a link between early twentieth-century anarchists and freedom fighters and their more contemporary embodiments. The primary aim of the early movements was to take down the supposedly oppressive governments. By the mid-twentieth century, however, the international terrorism of the PLO, IRA or ETA (that is, the Palestinian, Irish, and Basque liberation movements)[5] could no longer be classified in black and white terms. Still, their methods to wreak havoc and engender fear were universally condemned. Adam Morton describes contemporary terrorism as "the weapon of these who have strong convictions but

---

[1] Steyn, who quotes the novel, wrongly assumes that the passage belongs to the terrorist who walks the London streets with a bomb strapped to his chest.
[2] An outline of the so-called "terrorist novel" is offered by Margaret Scanlan in the introduction to *Plotting Terror*, 15; Robert Appelbaum and Alexis Paknadel give a comprehensive account of the motif of terrorism in fiction in *Terrorism and the Novel*.
[3] Conrad, *The Secret Agent*, 200. Andrew Macdonald's *The Turner Diaries*, the text that, as it is now revealed, was written by William Pierce in 1978, is the novel about rightist extremist movements and the reputed blueprint for the Oklahoma City Bombing.
[4] Scanlan reminds us that terrorist plots in fiction have quite a long tradition. Drawing on Conrad's *Under Western Eyes* and Dostoyevski's *Demons*, she searches for parallels between the revolutionary fiction of the nineteenth and early twentieth centuries and the terrorist fiction of the second half of the twentieth century. *Novelists and Terrorists*, 2–14. She argues that after the defeat of the two archenemies of Germany and Japan, communist Russia and the Warsaw Pact bloc replaced them as the evil empire, but once that too had fallen, the need for yet another enemy was filled by Iraq, Afghanistan, and any Muslim country averse to democracy.
[5] Husain understood that the West used the term "terrorist" primarily to address the Palestinian fighters, but no authority ever spoke against Palestinian suicide bombers. Husain, *The Islamist*, 204.

little power."[6] Paradoxically, the goal of modern jihadis who inflict atrocities on civilian populations is, as it was for their early twentieth-century predecessors, the destabilizing of Western democracies. The 9/11 attacks drew attention to Islamic terrorism, adding the religious dimension to terrorists' acts. These acts enabled America to portray itself as a "victim" and thus legitimized all the necessary and unnecessary violence that followed.

Unlike their anarchist prototypes, present-day terrorist threats trade on their audience's beliefs, expectations and taken-for-granted meanings about social reality. Stereotypes concerning those who pose the threats – namely the "outsiders"[7] – has allowed the state to control its citizens, with little resistance. For David L. Altheide, the recent preoccupation with terrorism echoes the persecution of real and imagined communists during the McCarthy era.[8] In short, the politics of anxiety hinges on cultural codes, practices, and routines as well as social institutions, using the mass media to promote such a vision of the world. By offering both entertainment and knowledge, the mass media are instrumental in shaping the public perception of social and political issues. Their role is akin to both religious and secular works of the Middle Ages. Just as the medieval Saracens were depicted as the arch-barbarians, contemporary terrorists are written into the "barbarian" frame and are depicted through the accounts of criminality in literature and the media. As Altheide stresses, "fear has been transformed from natural events, catastrophes, and the 'uncontrollable phenomena' that characterized life in the Middle Ages, to the social life of the modern era. It is not the plague, typhoid, tuberculosis or polio that troubles most Americans; it is fear of crime, drugs, gangs and youth – and now terrorism."[9]

Analyzing contemporary acts of terror, researchers point to their associations with the colonial histories of America, Europe, and the East, where dispossession was a key to discontent.[10] Accordingly, Neil J. Smelser argues that the crystallization of dissatisfaction that contributes to identifying an enemy also feeds anger, and anger can easily be transformed into aggression.[11] He assumes that terrorist behavior is stimulated by political attacks, but actions

---

6 Morton, *On Evil*, 84–92.
7 Altheide, *Terrorism*, 9.
8 What is interesting is Altheide's discussion of how universities benefit from homeland defense programs. *Terrorism*, 34–37. He also notes that religion is politicized and marketed through so-called conversion books or spiritual works. After all, most American presidents declare themselves God's elect with the famous "God Bless America" utterance (38–39).
9 Altheide, *Terrorism*, 94.
10 Smelser, *The Faces of Terrorism*, 20–21.
11 Smelser, *Faces of Terrorism*, 29–34.

depend upon how well a group is organized and how immediate is the sense of opportunity to retaliate.[12] Both Altheide and Smelser evaluate the communal dimensions of the problem and make further connections between current terrorist movements and the end of European colonialism in Asia and Africa, linking contemporary radicalism with twentieth-century fights for freedom and national identity.

Whatever the motivations, terrorism is the contemporary (d)evil, one of the archenemies of mankind. The present chapter looks at the concept of religious fundamentalism and terrorism as reflected in Ed Husain's *The Islamist* and Mohamed Laroussi El Metoui's *Halima*. Although set in different temporal frames and markedly dissimilar in their approach to terrorist acts, these two works portray the lives of people entangled in an ideological struggle in their respective motherlands. In a way, they are a continuation of similar efforts narrated in the medieval Saracen romances. They stress that the world of "freedom fighters" and "jihadists" is irretrievably divided into "us" and "them," terrorists and tyrants, but they also accentuate the problem of defining terrorism, as there is a thin line between freedom fighters and terrorists.[13] This split, originating during the time of the Crusades and upheld in the periods following them, has underlaid all "clashes of civilizations," which in turn have given rise to the present-day greatest evil, religious extremism.

The medieval world perceived racial differences through religious alterity. Medieval romances clearly suggested that Saracens were pagan idolaters who refused to recognize the Christian God. True to the demands of the genre, the romances depicted decidedly evil sultans who, should they survive the attacks of valiant European knights, would ultimately admit the superiority of the Christian God. Failing to do so, their prayers would continue to be unanswered, and they would lose their battles against the Christians. If the Europeans could not beat the Saracens in reality, at least they could conquer them in fiction. To bolster the honorable Christian cause, images of Saracen armies besieging Christian towns and burning churches must have been the most frightening sign of the religious encounters, even though in reality none of the encounters between the Saracens and the Europeans depicted in medieval romances are verifiable. These acts anticipate what Bruce Hoffman calls "holy" terrorism, heightening

---

12 Smelser, *Faces of Terrorism*, 51. Smelser discusses ideologies that propagate various forms of terrorism, showing the rhetoric of fundamentalists on both sides of the divide. One of the issues raised is the exaggeration of the agency of the other, in the speeches of various politicians, including G. W. Bush (83–85), which is connected to affirmations of the legitimacy of aggression (85–87), which itself, in fact, is of the same kind as the medieval "just war" rhetoric.
13 Hoffman, *Inside Terrorism*, 1–41.

the links between terrorism and religion that originated after the Islamic revolution in Iran and that meant that no country could be immune to the "volatile mixture of faith, fanaticism and violence."[14]

Typical of the medieval post-Crusading period, the romances of *The Siege of Milan* and *The Sultan of Babylon* sketch the tug of war between the Christian God and the Saracen (d)evil. The hard-won and fictional, but nevertheless ideologically predictable, Christian victories perpetuate Western views of the East and Islam. Underscoring the superiority of Christianity, their writers show virulent anti-Islamic attitudes without the slightest attempt to offer, or understand, the Eastern point of view. In the romances, the Muslim states seems to be organized in a similar way to the Christians, but the sultans are always portrayed as tyrants worshipping the trinity of idols (Apollo, Terragaunt, and Mahound) and given to recurrent outbursts of rage. Medieval audiences did not question the accuracy of such accounts. They were accommodated within existing anti-Muslim ideologies, and, since the marvelous was frequently conflated with the bizarre and the apprehensive, they easily accepted the imagined, nonexistent, fabulous East as the seat of malevolence. Similar arguments of inherent evil were used to explain Saracen successes in what the Christians saw as the temporary takeover of Christian lands. Even though both groups were "People of the Book," devotees of each religion sought to dominate the world. Following the ultimate failure of the Crusades, the Muslim scheme was to convert the "Franks" and the "Ingreez" by whatever means, in order to create *dar-al Islam*, the house of Islam. Thus the progressive rise of the fear of the Saracens was coterminous with the rise of Islam in the Near and Middle East as a threat to southern Europe. In the later Middle Ages, Islam was identified collectively with the menacing presence of the Moriscos in Spain,[15] the Turks in southern Europe, and the Tartars in the southeast. People not only dreaded forced conversions but were also alarmed at the idea that their national identities would be endangered. Religion may be able to quench the individual fear of death, but worry about the barbarians lingers on in the collective consciousness. One needed courage to fight the devil, and, paradoxically, one needed the fear of God to oppose the malign Saracen armies, the most evident sign of evil.[16]

---

14 Hoffman, *Inside Terrorism*, 85.
15 "Marvels on the margins" were enticing but considered barbarous. In 1499, the Moors from Grenada were forcefully converted by government edict, which was later extended to Castile and then Aragon. In Spain, the prevalent image of an Arab and a Muslim was that of the unassimilated Moor hating everything that is Christian.
16 The problem of the origin and status of evil in the God-created universe was one of the questions most frequently asked by theologians and parish priests as well as their parishioners. Such

The terrifying and ruthless Saracen armies were perceived as the epitome of evil.[17] The devil was believed to lead all non-Christians, who, deprived of spiritual guidance, obeyed him blindly. Even if not outwardly impish, because of their "pagan" beliefs they were still inwardly wicked, redeemable only through conversion. As it transpires, the Saracens were constructed as wicked through a number of tautological arguments. They were malicious because they were black, and they were black because they were vicious. They were seen as evil because they were pagan, and they remained pagan because of their inborn immorality. The sheer number of literary works in which conflicts with the Saracens are a central theme accentuates the medieval attraction/disgust with Otherness and, for that matter, blackness. The Muslim champions, usually referred to and depicted in the romances as the Saracen Giants, are both unlike us – huge, terrible, fierce, cruel, and unforgiving – and like us, speaking the same language, having the same aspirations of conquering the opponent's armies and winning the hand of the sultan's daughter in marriage. They are both human – after all, the descent

---

questions were all the more pertinent after the mandatory sacrament of confession probed the minds of Christians, forcing them to identify sins and transgressions. Theologians read the Bible in order to establish the genealogy of evil, the definition of which was simple and complex at the same time, and necessary but difficult to understand through the concept of an omnipotent and merciful God. Frequently recounted in literature and art, the story of Satan's temptation of Eve, preceded by the narrative of the Fall of the Angels that appeared only in "The Apocalypse of St. John," offered only partial answers and mostly suggested gaps in the genealogical description. While most of the Old Testament implies evil as wrongdoing, genealogical narratives attempted to explain evil in terms of cosmogony. Thus, in the story of Adam and Eve, evil is seen as part of the divine plan for humanity. In the early Middle Ages, St. Augustine tried to show that evil was not a substance planted in the universe but a punishment (*poena*) for human sin (*peccatum*). He invented a new category, "nothingness" (*nihil*), and saw the history of the world in terms of sins and punishments, a world in which no one suffers unjustly. Kearney, *Strangers, Gods and Monsters*, 85.

17 Marx, *The Devil's Rights*. Later writers, according to Marx (26–27), claimed that the devil seized "power" through trickery and refuted the idea of the devil's rights of possession. Curiously, the same reading of evil and sin reappears in Julian of Norwich's late fourteenth-century *Revelations*, which explains that sin is suffering solely because it entails the absence of God. Since the twelfth century, the much-debated doctrine of devil's rights in redemption has brought forth the assumption that God is the opposite of the Devil and that, because human life is also seen as a learning process, evil is its indispensable component. As Marx clarifies, Anselm, Abelard, and other twelfth-century writers accorded "power" to the Devil – the power of his hold on humanity, "which he had by the permission of God, and this power was dependent on human kind being in a state of sin. The Devil's power was just, but this justice rested with God alone. The Devil tormented humanity in hell because God allowed him to do so, but the Devil had no rights over it" (26).

of monsters was attributed to the children of Ham[18] – and inhuman, because of their refusal to accept Christianity. The darkness of their skin was an inveterate reminder of their monstrosity. An interesting example of such a connection is to be found in the *Revelations* of the fourteenth-century mystic Bridget of Sweden. In one of her visions she described an Ethiopian, whose figure is akin to that of the devil: "Then apperyd þer an Ethiope, ferefull in sight and beryng, as þof he had byn full of envy and gretely an aungered."[19] Travel narratives, evaluated in part 1 of the present study, almost unanimously assume that the black race, most commonly identified with Arabs and Ethiopians, is given to sexual promiscuity, one of the signs of their devilish origins.[20] It comes as no surprise that in medieval literature, the notions of "Ethiopian" and "black" were equivalents.[21] The epithets used to describe the black sultan in *The King of Tars* articulate the same association. Such identification validates the roundabout argument: the Saracens are black and therefore devilish, and the devil is evil and therefore black; therefore the Saracens are devils.[22]

Timothy Beal, in "Our Monsters, Ourselves," reminds us that monsters who populate popular literature and films (*Harry Potter*, *The Lord of the Rings*) are "undead"; they keep reemerging in various configurations. For Beal, the appeal of all that is monstrous lies in the degeneration of the reality around us. When the world becomes unexpectedly horrific, we reexperience the horror of the unreal world.[23] This explains the attention we pay to the monster myths, from the Minotaur to The One who Must Not Be Named. Scrutinizing the world two months

---

18 Asma, *On Monsters*, 84–86.
19 Bridget of Sweden, *The Revelations*, 43. When Christ teaches her about the order of the world, Bridget hears him reminding her of the biblical story of Moses bringing the Jews out of Egypt (4). Egyptians are one of the dominant and therefore hated nations, and that may be the reason why the devil is so frequently represented as a dark "Ethiope," which was simply associated with dark skin and a fiery looking person, as there was no distinction between "Egyptian" and "Ethiopian."
20 According to Strickland, in *Gesta Romanorum* "the Four-Eyed, or Maritime Ethiopians always have one eye on God, one on the world, one on the devil, and the other on the flesh; in order to live right, flee the world, resist the devil, and mortify the flesh." Strickland, *Saracens, Demons, and Jews*, 53. In medieval art, Ethiopians have dark skin, woolly hair, large eyes, flat noses, and thick lips, and this is the earlier stereotype of the black race (79).
21 Strickland, *Saracens, Demons, & Jews*, 83.
22 Gowther, the devil's child, repenting his heritage and his own sins, goes against the proud sultan, who thinks that the world belongs to him. His ultimate defeat can be seen as a warning against pride.
23 Timothy K. Beal's more serious analysis is to be found in his *Religion and Its Monsters*.

after the attack on the Twin Towers,[24] Beal contemplated the effects of that act on our present and future lives.[25] If indeed this was the most horrific of all terrorist acts, then our response to it unleashed a monster far more terrible than we can imagine, the monster that has fed on our centuries-old fear of the Other. It brought back the feeling of the so-called Dark Ages, long forgotten in Enlightened Europe and America, and the necessity to avenge the dead, very much in the spirit of a medieval romance. Through the events of 9/11 and 7/7, the moral monstrosity of Osama bin Laden and his followers has been described as pathological in a manner similar to the way in which medieval authors de-rationalized the malicious sultans, and for the very same reason: to legitimize the atrocities perpetrated on the enemy. Bin Laden's death, as well as the collateral damage (the killing of civilians inhabiting the compound) at the hands of the American special forces has be seen within the perimeters of a tradition of hunting and killing various creatures from the past – the Cyclops, the many-headed Hydra, and Beowulfian dragons. Like Bin Laden, all of these monsters play on, and with, our fears. Richard Kearney ascertains that:

> [t]here can be no doubt that human beings remain utterly fascinated, as much as appalled, by hybridized creatures which flout the distinction between human and the non-human. Indeed, a thinker like Levi-Strauss will argue that myths of monsters are tokens of a universal primordial mind (*pensée sauvage*) which exists in the unconscious of each one of us – myths whose purpose it is to resolve at the level of symbolic expression contradictions which remain insoluble at the level of everyday empirical reality.[26]

The monsters exist to be annihilated, and the stories of their destruction are akin to public rites of exorcism. Hence the sultans in medieval romances are decapitated and their heads brought to the Christian camps as trophies. Their killers are exonerated by virtue of their "just war." Likewise, the apprehension and imprisonments of hostiles appeases Western righteous anger today. On the one hand, the "enemies of freedom," to use George W. Bush's expression,

---

24 In his review, Professor Wicher points out that one should not link Beal's discussion of 9/11, nor its symbol, the Twin Towers, to the title of the second part of Tolkien's trilogy, *The Two Towers* (1954).
25 Like medieval romances, contemporary culture is also populated by miscellaneous monsters. The *Alien* film series, like gothic stories of the past, are visual expressions of horror. They are also a testimony to our persistence in the collectivization of panic and the need for scapegoats at a time of crisis. In order to preserve their political, religious, and cultural unity, all nations impose mechanisms of defense against a foreign curse and pestilence. This was perhaps best seen through the politics of "sealing our borders against the Asians" during the onset and migration of the bird flu frenzy throughout Europe a couple of years ago.
26 Kearney, *Strangers, Gods and Monsters*, 120.

are either to be captured and sentenced, or, if they realize their wrong ways in time, they can amend their behavior and join the "rightful cause." On the other hand, the very same idiom is used to demonize "enemies of God" in Islamist ideology, which, ironically, is rivaled by various nationalist movements in the Middle East and Northern Africa.

One can read Ed Husain's memoir, entitled *The Islamist: Why I Joined Radical Islam in Britain, What I Saw Inside and Why I Left*, as an example of a metaphorical conversion of the prototype that one finds in the medieval *King of Tars*. Written in the post-9/11 period and based on his own experience as a young British Muslim growing up in the last two decades of the twentieth century, Husain's book touches upon the events leading up to the international crisis and is a protest against political and politicized Islam. Although Husain speaks about himself, his account can be read as the voice of those lured by the extremist groups but hesitant to espouse their ideology. In a way, this is the story of what happens when a good, obedient Muslim child goes through a teenage rebellion and loses a larger perspective. Such individuals want to be morally superior, and their drive to excel results in misery and chaos.

Mohammed Husain, born in Britain, is "British by birth, Asian by descent and Muslim by conviction."[27] For him, like for Hanif Kureishi some twenty years earlier, growing up was difficult. Britain in the 1980s was saturated with anti-Asian ideology that bred dissidents. Unlike Kureishi, who remembers the unhinged racism and discrimination experienced in his primary school,[28] Husain, because of his well-meaning teachers, did not feel discriminated against. He idealizes his parents, recalling, for example, a trip to see Santa Claus, and stresses their open-mindedness. In his early life he felt truly happy and accepted, and his friendship with the sisters of a nearby convent is the best evidence of the triumph of multiculturalism. "There was never any question of religious tension, no animosity between people of differing faiths. My mother speaks fondly of her own childhood friends, many of whom were Hindu," he writes.[29] In spite of that, his parents made the mistake of transferring him to a single-sex school, where he found himself unable to mix with the other pupils. In his previous school, his classmates had been boys and girls of diverse races and cultures, while in the new school there were no girls, and he had no English friends. Neither could he connect with the "new arrivals" from Bangladesh, formerly East Pakistan. He despised their shallowness and described

---

27 Husain, *The Islamist*, 3.
28 Kureishi, *The Rainbow Sign*, 9.
29 Husain, *The Islamist*, 3.

them as solely interested in Bollywood movies. Isolated from his classmates, Husain embraced the teachings of Sheikh Fulholy Saheb, a sage from his parents' village who had come to England and infused the boy with a moderate Muslim ethos.[30] Concurrently, he was given additional lessons by an Anglican teacher, Mrs. Rainey, so that he could understand Christianity.[31] His fellow student there was Abdullah Falik, who eventually drew him closer to the mosque. At the time, his coreligionists seemed to have had answers to all his insecurities.

At the age of fifteen, Husain was attracted to various fundamentalist Islamist texts, like those of the Indian Abul A'ala Mawdudi (1903–1979) and the Egyptian Sayyd Qutb (1906–1966). Both men were radical exponents of belligerent Islamism, for whom the primary duty of all who want to please God was to enter an organized group, dedicate one's material as well as spiritual means to the holy war, and ultimately, sacrifice one's life.[32] Multicultural and open, Husain's Britain was nevertheless the site of growing discontent and conflicts between Muslims and non-Muslims. Such ideological struggles became visualized as the everlasting tug of war between good and evil. The actions of an organization such as Jamat-e-Islami of Mawdudi, who was intent on transforming Pakistan from a Muslim into an Islamic state, were geared toward seizure of political power. At that time, Husain deemed Mawdudi's version of Islam a revolutionary doctrine that would eventually overthrow Western governments. This goal validated violence but simultaneously epitomized the only way of life for true British Muslims. Strict observance of Koranic precepts was to be the only shield against moral degeneration. Like Qtub, Husain believed in the irrevocable division between East and West, based on the conviction that there has been an ongoing war between the believers and the heathens. Alfred G. Gerteiny, in his reading of the Muslim vision of relations between Islamic and non-Islamic states, writes that:

> This perpetual conflict shall only come to an end, and the peace of God restored on earth, when God's message, as transmitted to the Prophet Mohammed through Archangel Gabriel, finally prevails. . . . This original Muslim concept of international relations, based on what Wole Soyinka, in the BBC Reith Lectures Series, called "the doctrine of submission," is not only arrogant and "contemptuous of humanity," it stands in contradiction to the other cardinal Qur'anic concept of religious "tolerance," and it clashes with the universal, humane yearning for democracy and liberty.[33]

---

30 Husain, *The Islamist*, 15.
31 Husain, *The Islamist*, 19.
32 Husain, *The Islamist*, 34.
33 Gerteiny, *The Terrorist Conjunction*, 45.

Qutb assumed that his understanding of the Koran was the only correct one. He complained that Muslims living in the West had contaminated Islam with their Westernized views and saw Islamic jihad as a defense against such pollution.[34] Ed Husain, the young adept of fundamentalism, readily accepted the revolutionary thought of his heroes, Mawdudi and Qutb. Unhappy at home and unappreciated at school, he thought he was on the way to recovering the "pure" form of Islam, while in fact, he was being led toward dangerous radicalism.

Failing to connect with his fellow students, Husain created for himself a Britain that was solely non-white and Muslim, and in the future to be governed by Shari'a law. Western democracy upheld the concepts of equality, fraternity, and liberty, and European countries cherished these ideas. Seeing the enemies of their economic position as the enemies of freedom, the European Union all too readily identified most Muslims as "Islamic terrorists" – the backward, fundamentalist, radical, frequently poor, uneducated Other – their most hated foe.[35] The enemy is always cast in the role of the intolerant stranger. Claude Levi-Strauss, in his celebrated travelogue *Triste Tropiques*, accuses Islam of intolerance, which "takes an unconscious form among those who are guilty of it; although they do not always seek to make others share their truth by brutal coercion . . . the only means they have of protecting themselves against doubt and humiliation is the 'negativization' of others," those who are of a different faith and a markedly disparate lifestyle.[36] He also intimates that "contact with non-Moslems distresses Moslems. Their provincial way of life survives, but under constant threat from other lifestyles freer and more flexible than their own, and which may affect it through the mere fact of propinquity."[37] Thus, he sees Muslims as proud of being exponents of the great principles of liberty, equality, and toleration, but he sneers at their assumption that they themselves are the only ones to do so.[38]

---

[34] Qtub, *Milestones*, 71.
[35] In 2001, Americans and Europeans were the victims under attack, soon to be the victors attacking. The issue of national defense, of nationalism and individualism, is more multifaceted than a simple good and evil, us and them bifurcation. For Western democratic societies, as well as the new democratic states of central Europe, it has been difficult to give up their hard-won liberties. Periodically, in Poland but also in England or France, one would hear voices warning against the unlimited power of the State to infiltrate and control, reminiscent of the authoritarian regimes of the past, and of police states, which become giant prisons where every citizen had duties but not rights.
[36] Levi Strauss, *Tristes Tropiques*, 403–4.
[37] Levi-Strauss, *Tristes Tropiques*, 401.
[38] See Levi-Strauss, *Tristes Tropiques*, 402, and note 234 above.

Levi-Strauss notices that the Islamic sense of fraternity "rests on a cultural and religious basis. It has no economic or social character."[39] Being part of a group is also important for teenagers and young men. In secondary school, then later at college, all of Husain's friends were all Muslim and male. Although living in Britain, he did not have a single white friend, nor a single female friend.[40] This situation is less suggestive of a failure of British multiculturalism, than of a failure of sectarian and same-sex schools to teach impressionable boys to respect differences and develop a more diverse network of acquaintances. In any religion, the relationship between ethics and virtue is always connected with the world beyond the visible. While Muslims lodge their hopes, desires, and dreams with the communal perception of happiness with God, and while their sense of morality is first and foremost associated with the divine, contemporary Christians try to reconcile the community's needs with their own. What is more, in the secular world, to be moral, to live ethically, does not require any particular belief. Young Husain repudiated such attitudes and instead found solace in the community of like-minded young British Muslims, who claimed to have returned to the fundamentals of their faith.

Husain's views at the time were influenced by his readings.[41] Because they did not comport well with his parent's idea of education, he began to lie to his parents about his activities in order to pursue his interest in the Islamist cause.[42]

---

39 Levi-Strauss, *Tristes Tropiques*, 403.
40 Husain, *The Islamist*, 59.
41 He participated in the seminar that was called, rather tellingly, "Hijab: put up or shut up." Husain, *The Islamist*, 61. For him, a woman in a miniskirt would provoke *fitna*, or moral dissension, in society. A good Muslim woman, when spoken to, should look away. The ones who were most afraid began wearing gloves (68).
42 Husain started frequenting the meetings of the Young Muslim Organization (YMO). He went to the mosque for dawn prayers and began charting his week's achievements to show to the leaders. He did not want to be a partial Muslim; he wanted to be a true Muslim. The organization counseled him that his parents will be "an obstacle to your commitment to God's work." *The Islamist*, 41. He was seventeen, and what one could read as a natural teenage rebellion became Muslim jihad. He behaves very much in the style of a fictional young character from Hanif Kureishi's story "My Son the Fanatic." After a row with his father about some leaflets that he was distributing, Husain understood that "their revulsion for my Islamism was so powerful and my commitment to ideological Islam was so uncompromising that my father had little choice but to give me an ultimatum: Leave Mawdudi's Islamism or leave my house" (44). So he left home and hid himself in a mosque. His mother called the next day and told him that they did not want to be responsible for his involvement in Islamism (47). Soon Husain, who had proved his loyalty to the Islamic Movement, was elected president of YMO. The official site of YMO offers the genesis of the movement, which now claims to have been preparing the young leaders of tomorrow. "In October 1978 young Muslim men gathered in a house in

In the end, he decided to leave home.[43] This is how he turned himself into "their son, the fanatic," to use the famous title of Hanif Kureishi's short story.[44] Husain did not recognize that he was worshipping not Allah but the god of fundamentalism, a mischievous "if not downright evil . . . demonic power who delights in setting humans at each other's throats."[45] His separation from his parents is akin to what Smelser calls renunciation or "stripping." Smelser pinpoints that in order to fully participate in a terrorist group, one has to go through the process of the "destructuring of the individual's former conception of self."[46] Individual past hardships, whatever they may be, could be used to establish a position within and strengthen the ties with the new group. If one was "shamed" or unsuccessful in one's former life, one might find solace in belonging elsewhere. Teenagers are particularly sensitive, and they frequently want to fashion themselves as loners while secretly craving acceptance. In Joseph L. Soeters's view, cultural traumas are thus the most conducive element in terrorist recruitment. Accordingly, in order to understand the process of radicalization, we have to investigate the psychological and anthropological mechanisms of engendering conflict through group functioning and ideas of purity and impurity.[47]

London to bring together a dynamic band of youth who would respond to the challenges faced by their community with deep faith, true commitment and a positive and comprehensive work plan. They believed that this was the way to success, to preserve and strengthen Muslim identity in Britain, and contribute to the global Islamic Movement whose aim is to direct the Islamic process of social change. Thus was the Young Muslim Organisation UK born!" http://www.islamicforumeurope.com/live/ife.php?doc=ymo.

43 Smelser, *Faces of Terrorism*, analyzes the motivation, social origins, and recruitment of terrorist groups described by Husain.

44 *My Son the Fanatic*, screenplay by Hanif Kureishi, directed by Udayan Prasad and starring Om Puri. Based on Kureishi's short story from the collection *Love in a Blue Time*, 119–31.

45 Ruthven, *Fundamentalism*, 3. Reading fundamentalism, Ruthven does not limit the analysis to Islamic fundamentalism but explores fundamentalist movements also within the Christian Church (7–17). In each religion, the word was at first linked with the return to the purity of the original faith (18–23).

46 Smelser, *Faces of Terrorism*, 100.

47 Soeters, *Ethnic Conflict and Terrorism*. Soeters quotes Mary Douglas's classical differentiation between grid and group. "The grid dimension refers to the social distinctions applying to individuals and can be either strongly or poorly developed. If it is strongly developed in a society or organization, then fixed rules and regulations, clear rights and duties, transparent classifications and unchallenged differences in status and symbols exist. All these lead to clearly defined social 'roles.' . . . Besides armed forces, the monastery and the Roman Catholic Church in general, are also examples of organisations with a strongly developed grid. Everyone taking part in this kind of organization or community knows their position, the rights and duties that go with it and the appropriate conduct" (17–18). The second dimension is concerned with group cohesion. "They are so-called ascriptive characteristics, attributed to humans, which

The categories of cleanliness and pollution, then, are instrumental in reading the discord within the Husain family. Rather than adopt his father's[48] views that Mohammed was a spiritual leader, Ed Husain emulated the ideology of jihad, outlined in five precepts: Allah is Our Lord, Mohammed is Our Leader, The Koran is our Constitution, Jihad is our way, and Martyrdom is Our Desire.[49] Ed Husain's personal journey through Islamism and out replicates general ideas concerning radicalization. Lack of resilience, the feeling of rejection and well-hidden though still existent racism are all factors leading to fundamentalism. According to Gerteiny, Jehadism (or jihadism) is a magnet to many ardently religious Muslims, "who are seduced by it." Swayed by Islamic jurisprudence, "[t]heir strategic objective is to accelerate the establishment of the worldwide caliphate anticipated in the Qur'an."[50] This kind of "jihadism" can be related to homicidal self-emulation (i.e., "suicide bombers"),[51] which Gerteiny labels as "apocalyptic terrorism" and which is by no means restricted to Islamic fundamentalists. Fanatics of all persuasions "blindly cling to convictions that peculiar and often phantasmagoric articles of faith are divinely ordained or revealed."[52] Husain emulated the Islamist ideology and internalized slogans such as "We act locally, but we connect globally,"[53] and "We need weapons, not food and aid. In war, we can eat our enemies," popularized by Omar Bakri,[54] leader of Hizb ut-Tahrir in Britain.

---

they cannot (much) influence. These characteristics can be summarized as the 'four R's' – race, religion, region (nation) and record" (19). Record stands for common history.
48 "Why do these people call for martyrdom when their sons are in the best universities across the West?" Husain, *The Islamist*, 52.
49 Husain, *The Islamist*, 52. Husain quotes the famous anti-homosexual motto of the new jihadists, which sounds strikingly similar to the ones promoted by the All Polish Youth Movement, the extreme right movement in Poland: "God created Adam and Eve, not Adam and Steve" (56).
50 Gerteiny, *The Terrorist Conjunction*, 26.
51 For more on the psychology of suicidal terrorism and its connection with religion, see Silke, "The Psychology of Suicidal Terrorism," in Silke, *Terrorists, Victims and Society*, 93–108.
52 Gerteiny *The Terrorist Conjunction*, 35.
53 Husain, *The Islamist*, 61.
54 The leader of Hizb ut-Tahrir in Britain (quoted by Husain, *The Islamist*, 67): "Omar Bakri, the radical cleric banned from Britain, has addressed a conference at a primary school in London in which he called for the country to become an Islamic state. Dozens of Muslims attended the rally at Sudbury Primary School in Harrow, north London, to hear Bakri preach for 40 minutes over the telephone from his exiled home in Lebanon. The 51-year-old has been living in the country since 2005, having been banned from returning to Britain after he fled his London home after the July 7 attacks. Bakri told his followers: 'The existence of the Islamic state is a necessity for justice to be established, a necessity for the people in order to keep away from personal desire and greed. I believe the way forward is Islam. It is time to go back to basics. I believe Islam is the future.'"

Even though Husain's involvement, at the time, was only to prevent Muslims from attending college discos, in the long run, the presence of Hizb ut-Tahrir was felt everywhere. But it was in the mosques, not in colleges, where one would find literature advocating violence. Posters featuring veiled women and bearded men called for a return to the pristine quality of early Islam. Indeed, as Ruthven demonstrates, Hizb ideology corresponded "to the classical concept of the Caliphate."[55] The majority of less radical Muslims felt sequestered in their conciliatory spirit and were alarmed by the organization's fundamentalist faction.

Thinking along the lines of religious rather than national (cultural and linguistic) identification, Andrew Silke distinguishes the biological factors related to individual maturation that prompt young teenagers to join paramilitary groups;[56] his examples coincide with what Husain describes in his memoir.[57] Young Husain seemed not to notice that he was living in the West, in a multicultural, open Western country that is secular and modern. Instead, he believed in a version of Islamic government that was a closed religious community, repudiating all that is worldly. No man in the world would have been able to reconcile the two. "Literalism may begin with prayer and veiling women's faces, but it leads to terrain that is far more dangerous," observes Husain.[58] What is more, the way in which the jihadi view antagonized liberal, social and even national movements and positioned itself against mainstream Islam as the only genuine ideology led Husain to abandon all hopes of ever becoming a dedicated jihadi. However, having left the Islamist groups dedicated to militancy, the young man was still far from realizing the irreconcilable differences between Islamist (militant) and Islamic (Muslim, religious) groups. In Britain, a European country hostile toward political and politicized religion, the Islamic organizations fought for religious freedom which included the un-marking of Muslim dress codes, whereas Islamist groups saw the state as autocratic and themselves as a persecuted minority that needed to fight for, however misconstrued, liberty.

---

http://www.telegraph.co.uk/news/uknews/law-and-order/4903920/Banned-cleric-Omar-Bakri-addresses-conference-at-London-primary-school.html.
55 Ruthven, *Fundamentalism*, 86.
56 Silke, "Becoming a Terrorist," in Silke, *Terrorists, Victims and Society*, 93–108.
57 Gerteiny *The Terrorist Conjunction*, 29–51. For more on the psychological aspects of social inclusion and exclusion, see Abrams, Hogg, and Marques, *The Social Psychology of Inclusion and Exclusion*.
58 Husain, *The Islamist*, 72.

Western lovers of individual and collective independence recognize two landmark texts providing the fundamentals of the idea of freedom and the relationship between an individual and the state. The first is *The Consolation of Philosophy* (hereafter *Consolation*), written by the Roman philosopher Anicius Manlius Severinus Boethius; the second is the famous *Magna Carta* of 1215, which granted civil rights to the subjects of King John "Lackland." They are still read with interest today, because their subject matter is of no less concern than when they were written. Boethius's *Consolation*[59] can be seen as a bridge between ancient philosophy and Christian thought.[60] Boethius is known to have translated and annotated the logical works of Aristotle into Latin; he was also influenced by the Greek Neoplatonists.[61] His own work, in turn, was translated into

---

[59] Anicius Manlius Severinus Boethius was born into the Roman aristocracy ca. 475/477 CE – about the same time as the last Roman Emperor, Romulus Augustus, was deposed (August 476). Boethius lived most of his life under the rule of Theodoric, an Ostrogoth educated at Constantinople, who let the old families keep up their traditions in Rome while he ruled from Ravenna. Boethius's privileged social position ensured that he was taught Greek thoroughly, and, though it is unlikely that he traveled to Athens or Alexandria, the sites of the two remaining (Platonic) philosophical schools, he was certainly acquainted with a good deal of the work that had been going on there. He was able to spend most of his life in learned leisure, pursuing his vast project of translating and commenting on philosophical texts. The Roman aristocracy was, by his day, thoroughly Christianized, and Boethius also became involved in some of the ecclesiastical disputes of his time, which concerned the schism between the Latin and the Greek Churches that was resolved shortly before his death. Boethius agreed to become Theodoric's "Master of Offices," one of the most senior officials, but he quickly fell out with many others at court – hence alluding of injustice and corruption in the *Consolation*. Boethius was accused of treason and of engaging in magic, imprisoned, and (probably in 526) executed. He wrote the *Consolation* in jail, while awaiting execution. Trying to find consolation in his innocence he condemned the crimes of others and soon turned his accusers. Boethius, *Consolation*, 11. "But you see where my innocence has brought me; instead of being rewarded for true virtue, I am falsely punished as a criminal" (13). "I can only say that the final misery of adverse fortune is that when some poor man is accused of a crime, it is thought that he deserves whatever punishment he has to suffer. Well, here am I, stripped of my possessions and honors, my reputation ruined, punished because I tried to do good" (14). Philosophy suggests that he is too angry to take in her medicine and that the sources of his trouble are within himself (16).
[60] The *Consolation* a *prosimetrum* (a prose work with verse interludes) that recounts, in polished literary language, an imagined dialogue between the prisoner Boethius and a lady who personifies Philosophy, contrasts with the rest of Boethius's oeuvre. Boethius uses his logical approach to tackle problems of Christian doctrine; Book IV, however, is a straightforward statement of Christian doctrine, a sort of confession of faith; while Book III is a brief, not specifically Christian, philosophical treatise.
[61] "In her right hand the woman held certain books; in her left hand, a scepter sign of power." Boethius, *Consolation*, 4. Although he thinks that the poetry that was his consolation will bring him consolation in his old age, he is wrong. and Lady Philosophy says that the

English, first by Alfred[62] and then by Chaucer,[63] whose "Knight's Tale" is similarly a contemplation of individual freedom.[64] Unlike the *Consolation*, which is a philosophical meditation on what makes human beings happy, free, or bound within social conventions and the requirements of religion, the famous *Magna Carta* (The Great Charter) outlines practical aspects of individual liberties.[65] Here

---

Muses "will nourish him only with their sweet poison" (4). Boethius transformed the pagan goddess into a fictional figure embodying man's limited hopes of temporal prosperity and his fears of adversity. In the introduction, Green surmises that "Fortune is, a way, and the wrong way, of regarding fate; and all men are subject to her in the sense that uncertainly and change, pleasure and anxiety, and depression are the ordinary lot of men" (xvii).

[62] King Alfred (849–899). The work draws on classical philosophy and Christianity in the way the author describes being visited by the allegorical figure of Lady Philosophy but attempts to find Christian justification for his destiny. Boethius's search for God ends with the Platonic conviction that true happiness is to be found in one immutable Good. The text discusses the nature of Fortune and Fate. Generically, the original work is a Platonic dialogue, prison literature, *consolatio*, personification allegory, Menippean satire (the alternation of prose and verse), and theodicy. Greenfield and Calder, *A New Critical History*, 46. Boethius did not intend the work to be a Christian work but wanted to counter sorrow and despair with consolation and hope and, through the use of Aristotelian logic, to appeal to human reason. The Alfredian translation no longer has five books of Latin with alternating verse, the so-called meters, but forty-two chapters with a proem and epilogue; subsequent to this prose, he translated nine meters into verse. Alfred omitted large portions of the text, added some of his own and disposed of the final chapter on divine Providence and man's free will. Alfred saw God in the Platonic Good, hence the addition of angels and devils and personified virtues. He also personified Wisdom (and not Lady Philosophy), who converses with Mind, who stresses Man's free will in all earthly activities of the human mind.

[63] Reworking the classical and contemporary Italian material of Dante, in 1391 Chaucer was simultaneously working on the translation of Boethius's *Consolation*. Chaucer refers to Boethius as Boece, the French pronunciation of the name.

[64] "He was primarily a theologian to the formation of Christian doctrine, and moral philosophy was only a part of his enterprise. Historical circumstances made the success of his undertaking almost immediate, so that one hundred years later Boethius could write as a Christian philosopher and classical scholar without apology or polemic, defining and limiting the scope of his attention and the mode of his discourse to human nature and the natural possibilities of human wisdom." Green, "Introduction" to the *Consolation*, xvi.

[65] A number of clauses pertain to the well-being of the merchant classes, for example Clause 13, granting the city of London its privileges, and Clause 41, which specifies that all merchants "may enter or leave England unharmed and without fear." The charter has a long and turbulent history. It is generally claimed that the final version comes from 1225; the document was never reissued. Reminiscent of the Anglo-Saxon laws, yet endowed with a more secular touch, its articles provide the legal basis of contemporary human rights. For example: Clause 39 says: "No free man shall be seized or imprisoned, or stripped of his rights or possessions, or outlawed or exiled, or deprived of his standing in any way, nor will we proceed with force against him, or send others to do so, except by the lawful judgment of his equals or by the law of the

we have the commonly recognized foundations of Western democracy. All such pronouncements established the rights of individuals within the society, delineating the role and duties of the ruler toward his subjects.[66]

This kind of early Western liberalism, however, is alien to Islam. The very concept of democracy is abhorrent to the leaders of Islamic states. Democracy is *haram*,[67] forbidden by Islam, illegal, for *demos kratos*, the people's rule,[68] is against God's rule on earth.[69] Ruthven draws attention to the rhetorical appeal of Islam identified with the idea of "freedom under God, from dominion of man over man."[70] In this way, *dar al-Islam* has remained the prism through which Islamic governments are perceived. In the Middle Ages as much as in the times of Ayatollah Khomeini (1902–1989) – whose *Islamic Government*, published in 1979, called for the return to a truly Islamic government as the best form of management of a Muslim state, unsurpassed by any Western systems – Islamic countries were urged to elect Islamic governments to ensure the just and moral ruling of the people. Khomeini's voice assumed the role of the messenger from God who enlightens his subjects in matters as diverse as family life and public life. Khomeini branded as "colonists" a group of his compatriots who, for him, included supporters of the Shah spreading "their poisoned cultures and thoughts and disseminated them among the Moslems, and . . . lost the formations of the proper government."[71] Khomeini's tautological explanations of why the Islamic government is the best have only one sound argument. He reckons that such government should not be despotic but constitutional; however, not in the Western meaning of the word.

> The difference between the Islamic government and the constitutional governments, both monarchic and republican, lies in the fact that the people's representatives or the king's representatives are the ones who codify and legislate, whereas the power of legislation is

---

land." Clause 40 reads: "To no one will we sell, to no one deny or delay right or justice." Here we have the commonly recognized foundations of Western democracy.

66 Clause 17 ensures that ordinary lawsuits "shall not follow the royal court around but shall be held in a fixed place," and Clause 20 grants a free man a fair trial: "For trivial offence, a free man shall be fined only in proportion to the degree of his offence, and for a serious offence correspondingly"; furthermore, "Earls and barons shall be fined only by their equals, and in proportion to the gravity of their offence" (Clause 21). The unlawful seizing of property will be rectified (Clause 52), and the fines that have been given unjustly will be remitted (Clause 55).

67 Soeters gives examples of how democracy does not work everywhere, predictably in Africa, but he also mentions the democratic Weimar Republic that gave rise to Hitler. *Ethnic Conflict*, 35.

68 Crone, *Medieval Islamic Political Thought*, contains similar ideas.

69 Husain, *The Islamist*, 196.

70 Ruthven, *Fundamentalism*, 90.

71 Khomeini, *Islamic Government*, 30.

confined to God, may He be praised, and nobody else has the right to legislate and nobody may rule by that which has not been given power by God. This is why Islam replaces the legislative council by a planning council that works to run the affairs and work of the ministries so that they may offer their services in all spheres.[72]

Muslim societies should be subject to God's laws, not human laws, hence the universal acceptance of Shari'a law in all Islamic republics. The believers in the past and today have perceived the state through the revelation of Mohammed and the Koran, in which God's will, revealed through his messengers, is the law of the people. People, who "are of dust," need the guidance of the divine because they are imperfect and frequently erring in their judgment. How, then, can those chosen to govern be sure that they do not err? That questions remains a mystery not confronted by any Islamic political writers, even though Khomeini attempted to recap the good qualities of a ruler and enumerates possible vices such as the love of glory.[73] Khomeini envisioned Western rulers in non-Islamic systems as idolaters, and their position akin to what should be God's. It is a view strikingly similar to how Burton, Doughty, Ockley, and Green saw the Eastern sultans. Calling his countrymen to unite against the Shah, Khomeini affirmed that "[t]he duty of the ulema and of all the Moslems is to put an end to this injustice and to seek to bring happiness to millions of peoples through destroying and eliminating the unjust governments and through establishing a sincere and active Moslem government."[74] In a nutshell, an Islamic government is good because it is Islamic, and because it is Islamic it is good.

The establishment of the Islamic government in Britain was the goal of young Husain and his militant friends. Although as a young man he was enchanted with thinkers such as Qtub and Mawdudi, as a more mature individual he comprehended that Mawdudi polarized Islamism and nationalism. Mawdudi's followers readily declared democracy as *dar al-kufr*, the house of disbelief, once again stressing that democratic states are not only run by infidels but also

---

72 Khomeini, *Islamic Government*, 31.
73 Khomeini *Islamic Government*, 47.
74 Khomeini, *Islamic Government*, 25, 28. This work, translated and published in the United States, is illustrated with pictures of the Ayatollah himself and shows the post-revolution killings of police officers condemned by the revolutionary forces for acts of violence during the Shah's reign. Hodges wrongly assumes that the use of examples such as the Soviet Union, Nazi Germany, and Saddam's Hussain's Iraq, is done specifically to buttress the war on terror narrative. *The "War on Terror" Narrative*, 35. The publishers of Khomeni's *Islamic Government* advertise the book as "Ayatollah Khomeini's *Mein Kampf*"; I don't think anyone could be more direct in pointing one's finger at the archetypal bad guy. Interestingly, Hodges devotes a couple of pages to discussing the shifting perception from the "War on Terror" (capitalized) to the "war on terror" (lowercase letters) (153–57).

worship men. Western states, therefore, should be seized by military power, their democracies deemed unlawful. Having gone through the fascination with radical Islam, Ed Husain warned that "[e]ven today a primary reason for Western failure in the War on Terror is this same cause: an innate inability to understand the Islamist mind. . . . It was not mere PR – they wanted to control the world, to conquer countries."[75] Nonetheless, the objectives of overpowering the Western states by military power and proclaiming their democracies unlawful was not an achievable goal.

Notwithstanding his steadfast beliefs, and throughout his "struggle with the infidels," somehow God was lost for Husain, and he felt increasingly uncomfortable with certain decisions of his fellow second-generation immigrant Muslims, isolated within their ethnic groups in a country that did not want them. Husain would have probably lingered longer in the organization were it not for the incident with Brother Saeed, a black Muslim whose knife was given the name of Abdul Jabbar. Black Christian boys were playing pool and were not allowing Muslims to play. The fact that the "inferior Christians" refused to yield the table to them so enraged Saeed that he led a crowd of two hundred people shouting *Allahu Akbar* and *Jee-had*, threatening the other boys with violence. This absolute certainty of Muslim superiority has a long tradition in the Islamic history. Ruthven claims that because the formative institutions of Islam were created during the period of its greatest victories, it is, for its adherents, "a triumphalist faith," in whose territories "non-Muslims were tolerated as long as they accepted their subordinate status." While Europe has accepted religious pluralism under the auspices of secular states, such changes were introduced gradually. The late twentieth-century neo-Islamic movements reverted to the earlier claims, safe for religious toleration granted by *Dhimma law*, unable to understand that "primitive Christian faith had been superseded by Islam, God's final revelation."[76] What was at stake in the conflict described by Husain, therefore, was not the inability to take over the pool tables but the power struggle between the two groups, framed within culture-specific perceptions of honor and shame. Reading such conflicts, Soeters addresses the question of personal vs. state violence. Both are limited in Western societies due to appropriate legislation devoted to protecting each and every citizen. It is forbidden to strike anyone in public, for example, and such a transgression in schools and colleges would

---

75 Husain, *The Islamist*, 153.
76 Ruthven, *Fundamentalism*, 27. Christians and Jews could reside in Muslim lands as *dhimmis*, under the protection of the Dhimma law. Hiro, *The Essential Middle East*, 124–25.

result in suspension or even expulsion.[77] In contrast, the Eastern perception of human life is based on the conviction that life and death are in the hands of God and fate; moreover, the survival of a community always takes precedence over the well-being of an individual. Soeters argues that in the Middle East, "during conflicts people are used to treating each other in a harsher, more violent and perhaps also more cruel manner."[78]

The incident described by Husain, which to an outsider might represent modern jihad as an outlet for teenage aggression,[79] was as much about youthful belligerence as it was about public humiliation of Muslims and their ensuing retaliation. The conflation of religious ardor with the battle for domination seemed to escalate with every such incident, culminating in Saeed stabbing to death a Christian boy of Nigerian extraction.[80] Husain, who at the time was connected with the Hizb circles[81] and very much influenced by their ideology, was deeply disturbed by such actions. On the one hand, it was a disgrace to inform the two *kafir* (i.e., strangers, non-Muslims, here the police) about fellow Muslims,[82] but on the other, he was horrified by so much viciousness that would otherwise go unpunished. Saeed was

---

[77] Soeters, *Ethnic Conflict*, 46–56. While discussing cultural differences, Soeters argues that the relevant dimension is collectivism vs. individualism. In collectivist countries, thinking in terms of groups is dominant (57–60). If societies have varied notions about violence, such notions have to be attributed to the contrastive approaches to individual life, which in "less civilized states" is less valuable (46).
[78] Soeters, *Ethnic Conflict*, 46.
[79] Soeters, *Ethnic Conflict*, 152.
[80] Husain, *The Islamist*, 150.
[81] Hizb ut-Tahrir was an organization with clear military aims. It was created in 1952 when "Taqi Nabhani" (Taqiuddin al-Nabhani, 1909–1977), its founder, had applied to the Jordanian Interior Ministry to establish "a political party with Islam as its ideology. The Hizb was, from its inception, committed to establishing an Islamic state dedicated to propagating its ideology." Husain, *The Islamist*, 83–84. Until 1990, the party operated in the Middle East, but after 1990, it spread throughout Europe. Its members were certain that the West was conspiring to reduce the number of Muslims and that Islam was in need of organized military resolutions to achieve its aims. Husain maintains that Hizb members believed that all natural events were God's will and that therefore it would be a sign of one's mistrust in God to insure their cars. To have car insurance would necessitate asking a non-Hizb member to buy it for them (101). Nabhani always taught them that there was no such thing as morality in Islam: "it was simply what God taught. If Allah allowed it, it was moral. If He forbade it, it was immoral" (102). Hizb, and other paramilitary Islamic organizations, according to Husain, were bringing back the concept of hero worship, and by mythologizing early Islamic history they tried to represent themselves as God's organizations and therefore as invincible. "God had been belittled by organized religion, particularly by literalist extremists of all persuasions" (185).
[82] Non-Muslims for Islamists were *kuffar*. "The term is used in the Koran in the context of the brutal persecution of early Muslims at the hands of pagan idolaters. To reinvent that

tried and convicted of murder, yet even in jail retained the reputation of being a "jihadi," or vigilante.

Acknowledging the danger of the militant side of Islam, Husain began also to wonder: "If God was on the Muslim side, then why had we failed to establish the Islamic state?"[83] He understood the path of alienation, confrontation and power, but did not want to follow it. He was appalled when he heard about the 9/11 bombing. He did not understand how chivalry on the battlefield could be transformed into an ideology supporting suicide missions that killed hundreds of people. This was the decisive moment in his decision to sever any ties with Muslim fundamentalists. He changed his attitude toward those around him and stopped looking at people as Muslims and non-Muslims. In so many ways, his autobiography is similar to Augustine's *Confessions*. Like Augustine, Husain shows the reader his early sins and theological errors only to demonstrate how he overcame them and found true God. Augustine traveled in order to meet important scholars of his day and gain knowledge, and so does Husain. He traveled to Turkey and Syria in order to find the true Islam. In the vein of Augustine, he refashioned himself as a true Muslim, like Augustine's true Christian. In contrast to Augustine, however, whose main error was a fascination with Manichean heresy, Husain's narrative shows the "underbelly" of a religion: through the process of misreading and ideological abuse, it becomes a despotic system for those disheartened with the West, for generations whose cultural background was neither British nor fully Muslim and who – like Hanif Kureishi – felt British while living outside Britain but were addressed as "Pakis" in Britain. Autobiographical narratives reveal a point of view, gender, class, cultural heritage, and historical specificity,[84] but Husain's work is more than just autobiography. Being more akin to what Inayatullah identifies as "trans-scientific,"[85] the book offers a framework for specific international relations. Even if genuine Islam, in Husain's view, is the religion of peace, Islamism sponsors terrorism, which has nothing to do with fighting against tyrants to maintain personal and national freedom. The honorable rationale for jihad is and should be the thing of the past, one may say.

The idea of holy war against the colonial power is the focus of Mohamed Laroussi El Metoui's (1920–2005) *Halima*,[86] a novel that depicts the nascent freedom movement in an Arab country colonized by the French. Unlike the

---

terminology and use it to refer to a population that is mainly Christian, or at least theistic, is an abject failure to understand the Koran." Husain, *The Islamist*, 222.
83 Husain, *The Islamist*, 154.
84 Inayatullah, *Autobiographical International Relations*, 5.
85 Inayatullah, *Autobiographical International Relations*, 7.
86 Metoui, *Halima*. The novel's original date of publication is not offered.

young Muslims' struggle to retain their religious and cultural identity in late twentieth-century Britain, Metoui sets his novel in the post-war period, when the fight against colonial oppression was the prerogative of the colonized nations and they often embraced the idea that the ends justify the means. *Halima*, then, narrates the growing national consciousness in pre-1956 Tunisia in the context of courtship and marriage between a country girl, the eponymous heroine Halima, and a boy from the neighborhood. Driven by Halima's spiritual strength and fearlessness, and against the custom of the seclusion of women, after the wedding the two become collaborators in the resistance movement.

Laying out the context for the story, Metoui continually emphasizes that the colonists are persecutors, intimidating the local population; they are tyrants whose crimes not only remain unpunished but are also permitted by the colonial administration. For this reason, Halima's mother has kept hidden from Halima the story of her father's death, revealing it only when Halima is about to be married and thus becomes her husband's responsibility. Until this time, her mother has simply been afraid of Halima's temper and the consequences if she were to insult, for example, the local teacher. The teacher is "well-known for his racist tendencies, his colonial fanaticism and his hatred of the local people and all Arabs."[87] He has already expelled one boy and had his father jailed for a week. The boy's single crime was a note he had kept: "Long live the martyrs of April the 9th."[88] Her father's misfortune is in itself enough to ignite an unnecessary spark of insubordination in Halima, and so in order to stop her from asking more questions, her mother solicits a neighbor, Aunt Khadija, to seek Sheikh Omar's help. He prepares a "medication" designed to keep Halima quiet. He writes something in a bowl and tells the woman that Halima should drink water from the bowl, in the morning, before she has anything to eat. The

---

87 Metoui, *Halima*, 49.

88 Metoui, *Halima*, 49. "April 9th, Tunisian Martyrs' Day, is celebrated every year at the martyrs' monument in Sijoumi. This date refers to the riots that took place on April 9th, 1938 and which led to the dissolution of the 'Neo-Destour' on April 12th, 1938." "We are here today to show our strength . . . the one that will unsettle the colonialism. . . . The Tunisian Parliament will only be created by activists' martyrdom and youth's sacrifices": these were the words of activist Ali Belhaouane, on April 8, 1938, during a protest in front of the seat of the General Residence. The demonstration was disbanded, and the Neo-Destour leaders announced that another one was planned on April 10. A huge crowd gathered in front of the courthouse on April 9 after Ali Belhaouane was convened by the investigating judge. What followed was a bloodbath; the law enforcement authorities dispersed the crowds using gunfire. Twenty-two people died, and 150 were injured; a state of siege was announced in Tunis, Sousse and Cap Bon. The April 9 events represented a major turning point in the country's path to independence. http://hellotunisia.tn/welcome/martyrs-day/.

treatment works, because Halima stops asking. Whether due to the Sheik's inscription or simply because Halima sees how painful her questions are for her mother, the writing seems to provide the solution.[89] But the girl has only internalized her feelings.

Halima's righteous anti-colonialist anger resurfaces when she finds out that her father, according to the colonial authorities, was a thief and a murderer. When her mother was pregnant with Halima, she craved a flower from a colonist's garden. Even though Ahmed, Halima's father, asked politely, the gamekeeper refused violently, treating him like dirt, which so incensed the law-abiding Ahmed that he burst out: "Cowards, thieves! It's our land. We inherited it from our ancestors. But the cowards stole it. Ah! If only I could have my revenge."[90] Such an emotional upsurge of anti-colonial pronouncements earned him the label of a troublemaker. In *The Wretched of the Earth*, Franz Fanon, the most fearless interpreter of racism and colonialism, devoted quite a lot of space to the discussion of the ways in which the colony's economy was geared toward the maximum profit channeled to the colonial center. That is why the colonial powers were only interested in educating skilled workers, preferably through religious schools, and lacked the middle class, the driving force of capitalism. "The national bourgeoisie of under-developed countries is not engaged in production, nor in invention, nor building, nor labor; it is completely canalized into activities of the intermediary type."[91] Deliberating the possible uprising in Algeria, he recognized that due to "corruption" and "brain washing," the country's revolution will have to include intellectuals supported by the "mass of starving illiterates."[92] The uprising should be accelerated through the recognition that the colonizers' wealth "is not the fruit of labor but the result of organized, protected robbery."[93] Metoui's novel captures precisely the moments of such self-realization among the oppressed native inhabitants of Tunisia.

The day after the fateful stroll close to the colonist's house, Ahmed goes back to that house, and when he is looking through the fence, the colonist shoots him. He is accused of sedition. The sheik is summoned, gendarmes search Ahmed's house, and they find nothing. The scene is one of utter chaos,

---

89 One is tempted to quote Claude Levi-Strauss, who, atypically, acknowledges that Muslim and French people are alike, exhibiting "the same bookish attitude, the same Utopian spirit and the stubborn conviction that it is enough to solve problems on paper to be immediately rid of them." Levi-Strauss, *Tristes Tropiques*, 405.
90 Metoui, *Halima*, 47.
91 Fanon, *The Wretched of the Earth*, 120.
92 Fanon, *The Wretched of the Earth*, 151.
93 Fanon, *The Wretched of the Earth*, 154.

with soldiers pointing their rifles at a pregnant woman, insensitive to her screaming that her husband is not a thief. Ahmed survives, but is severely injured and imprisoned for a crime he did not commit. When he gets out of jail, he is the labelled as a thief, and he cannot live with that. "Exasperation took hold of him and he was hit by a quartan fever that killed him only a fortnight after he returned from the hospital."[94] With the death of her husband, the mother's life is devoted solely to her daughter, but the unknown father is a muted presence in Halima's life, and the secret of his death overshadows her happiness, as mother and daughter live threatened by the unwanted presence of the French administration. They feel constantly watched and judged, their ways of life both misunderstood as well as disparaged by the colonists. Growing up, Halima is drawn to Abdelhamid, the brother of her school friend, but although they like each other before their marriage, neither can reveal their mutual attraction to anyone in their respective families for fear of being accused of immodesty. Restraint and patriotism are two distinguishing features of the novel's main protagonists both before and after their marriage. After their union, the novel is transformed from a love story into a historical-political thriller, or even terrorist novel. It tells of Halima's journey to become a "jihadi," from a young innocent village girl in awe of Tunis where she sees women without veils for the first time, to a dedicated, self-assured revolutionary.

Even though she never questions her husband, Halima notices his frequent absences and craves to earn his trust, dreaming that her husband would talk to her about more important things than domestic matters. She is sure that he was not involved in any kind of love affair: "It's the love of our beloved country, our dear and precious homeland. But these days Abdelhamid doesn't talk to me about that. . . . I have always explained to Abdelhamid that I have all the reasons in the world to fight the foreign colonists."[95] In spite of her preoccupation with the affairs of her household, and giving birth to consecutive children, she manages to extract the truth about his absences and learns of his connection with the resistance movement. She begs him to let her join and finally, becomes her husband's companion and partner in the country's struggle for freedom. Her traditional female clothing becomes a disguise and is her best weapon.

A woman dressed in a large and long dress could easily pass unnoticed, bearing arms for fighters. One finds such images in *The Battle of Algiers*, the film about Algerian independence (1966, directed by Gillo Pontecorvo with

---

94 Metoui, *Halima*, 69. Quartan fever is a type of malaria.
95 Metoui, *Halima*, 89.

Yacef Saadi, who was the real Cabash leader, and Jean Martin).[96] This is also how Halima supports the Tunisian revolution. Following a hinted-at but never mentioned miscarriage, Halima finds herself in hospital, where she befriends the nurse Suad, a fellow Destourian. Destour was a name of a Tunisian liberal constitutional party active in the 1920s and 1930s in raising the national consciousness and opposition to the French protectorate. The Destourians wanted to reinstate the suppressed Tunisian constitution of 1861 (*Dustūr*) and advocated independence from France. They were responsible for protests, strikes, and boycotts following the installation of French judges in Tunisian law courts. In 1934, some of the younger members created the Neo-Destour Party,[97] the organization with which Halima is connected. While at hospital, Halima helps a wounded oppositionist to escape from the hospital in her clothes. "Your veil served as the cape of invisibility that we find in the Thousand and one Nights stories," whispers nurse Suad, conspiratorially. "As for the shoes, although you wear a large size, they were very tight. But our brother stoically endured their pressure until he reached the waiting car."[98]

In Islam, based on the assumption of modesty, the hijab signifies the barrier between the secular and the profane, the boundary between the "forbidden space, which is hidden by the hijab," and the uncovered "permitted space." It becomes a sign of a "mobile enclosure" used to ensure the integrity not only of a wearer but also, primarily, of her masculine protector.[99] The view that Muslim female clothes signify the belief in freedom and not subjugation is strikingly similar to Fanon's argument in "Algeria Unveiled," where he tried to de-essentialize the woman's veil, seeing it as a predicament not of religious but cultural affinity and a symbol of the de-Westernization of Arab countries. An Algerian woman unveiled is the unwelcome symbol not of modernity but of the colonial past. Fanon, like Metoui, romanticizes female revolutionaries and praises their courage. Dressed in loose, long flowing robes, the women smuggled weapons and took up the arms for the good of the country. In such a context, the veil is no longer a requirement based on the ancient (not to say medieval) patriarchal rule. Yet the unveiling should not

---

96 Said discusses Pontecorvo's films in his "Reflections on Exile" essay, reporting a meeting with Pontecorvo in Rome. Although he applauded Pontecorvo's vision of the revolution, he disliked his "'fascinated' portrayal of imperialist villains." The director retorted that he needed to treat negative characters seriously so as not to turn them into "caricatured stereotypes." Said, *Reflections on Exile*, 286.
97 *The New Encyclopedia Britannica*, 4:38.
98 Metoui, *Halima*, 115.
99 Grace, *The Woman*, 16, 17, 20.

be read as the simple and simplistic discarding of the old for the new. Rather than maintaining its status as a representation of the "natural state" of femininity, which has to be protected from the corrupt, exposed, unsafe masculine world at all costs, the veil becomes part of the woman's conscious choice, indicating resistance. For Fanon, the veiling and the unveiling are political, not religious, acts. The woman behind the veil for modern-age colonizers, be they in Algeria or Afghanistan, is the sign of the old order but, in Fanon's examination, represents "the most distinctive form of a society's uniqueness."[100] Likewise, Daphne Grace in her reading of the veil and veiling underlines its importance in social and literary discourse. What has been an emblem of the inferiority and enslavement of women, "of misogyny and patriarchal denial," during the first wave of Arab revolutions in the mid-twentieth century was turned into a nationalistic symbol.[109] Like the fictional Halima's, real women's veiled bodies became "a symbol of resistance to colonization, of emerging nationhood and traditional values."[102] Such ideas were later readily transposed onto the Muslim fundamentalist movements in Western countries, which generated islamophobia and Islamism.

The call to return and uphold family values is not a uniquely Muslim prerogative. Western religious as well as numerous right-wing secular movements have been advocating the very same idea, yet they talk about moral behavior and sexual restraint, not about concealing the entire female body. In the West, veiling is frequently perceived as the most conspicuous sign of the need to control female sexuality, in a culture that reads honor and shame in terms of female virtue. Despite the prevalent assertions that "[b]y concealing her body from the stranger's gaze, the wearer proclaims that she is not a sexual object to be judged by physical appearance,"[103] the veiled woman today elicits respect among her coreligionists, coupled with fear and violence among other members of society.

Halima's traditionalism, which normally would preclude her involvement in the affairs of the world outside her home, is represented as a rightful cause, the forcefulness necessary to liberate her country from the hated tyrants. Subsequently, the novel presents instances of terrorist attacks, like the bombing of the Gabes River bridge.[104] The narrator explains how "[t]he pressure of the people increased on the oppressive colonial forces. Demonstrations, protests, sabotage and resistance activities spread in the whole country. The colonialists' rage

---

100 Fanon, "Algeria Unveiled," 161.
109 Grace, *Woman in the Muslin Mask*, 2.
102 Grace, *Woman in the Muslin Mask*, 6.
103 Ruthven, *Fundamentalism*, 75.
104 Metoui, *Halima*, 101–2.

burst forth and they became violent."[105] Uncharacteristically, the author attributes the role of terrorists to the colonial forces, claiming that:

> [t]hey thought that repression, terrorism and torture would stop the resistance movement and scare its people. So came their barbaric crimes and abominable activities, especially in the Cap Bon area, in which mercenaries caused havoc. They pulled down houses, killed women and children and destroyed food and provisions.[106]

Metoui constantly includes defamatory statements about the colonists, blaming them for all the evil in the world, including Halima's miscarriage.[107] We learn that Halima took part in a street demonstration, and even though we are not offered a more detailed description of what happened, the writer claims that the French "opposed the demonstrators with their deadly weapons and infernal cruelty."[108] He has Halima, very "unladylike," curse the soldiers, saying "May the Devil take the colonists."[109] Paradoxically, the street violence that the novel depicts is also present at home. In the hospital, Halima learns that a woman who lay close to her had a violent miscarriage due to a fist fight with her husband's other wife, who "held her by her hair and almost put her head in the fire of the brazier. Scared by the fire and losing her self-control, she had bitten her rival's breast and nearly pulled it off."[110] As a psychiatrist Fanon, studied many different forms of violence among the Algerians, attributing most of them to the war of national liberation.[111] Still, was this kind of domestic conflict described above the fault of the colonists, or is the author, perchance, voicing an unreserved yet unwanted criticism of polygamy?

Fanon, the angry young man of 1950s Algeria, argues that the colonizer who exploits and separates "the exploited from those in power" is responsible for the resultant violence; for him, "he [the colonizer] is the bringer of violence into the home and into the mind of the native."[112] Much to the chagrin of his contemporaries, Fanon seems to endorse the aggression against colonial oppression. In the struggle of the anti-colonial movements, in opposition to the "supremacy of white values," hostility, despite the imposed institutions of control,

---

105 Metoui, *Halima*, 103.
106 Metoui, *Halima*, 103.
107 *The Last Post* (directed by Jonny Campbell and Miranda Bowen, 2017), a BBC miniseries set in 1965 Aden, is a very interesting take on relations between the colonizers and the colonized.
108 Metoui, *Halima*, 104.
109 Metoui, *Halima*, 105.
110 Metoui, *Halima*, 106.
111 Fanon, *The Wretched of the Earth*, 29, 201.
112 Fanon, *The Wretched of the Earth*, 29.

apparently to prevent tribal belligerence, is inevitably "just under the skin."[113] In the hospital garden, when free to leave her bed for two hours, Halima meets an old man and hears yet another story of a family accused of trafficking arms and participating in the liberation movement. As his son worked elsewhere, the old man would not disclose his whereabouts, and in response, the gendarmes brutally kicked his wife and burned his house. Trying to protect his wife, he engaged in a fight with the police, and during the struggle his leg was injured so severely that it later had to be amputated. The old man also tells Halima about the anti-colonial actions of the previous generation – for example, about the general strike of September 11, 1924, when the police opened fire on unarmed strikers. He understood that his generation was perhaps less determined than Halima's, but their dream likewise has always been "to see the end of colonialism."[114]

Such is also Halima's heartfelt wish, even more so when her husband Abdelhamid is imprisoned for his anti-colonial, not to say terrorist, activities but is kept alive and permitted to write to her from prison. "Halima accepted her foredoomed reality. She had to kneel before the will of God and obey the strict orders of the resistance leadership. In the end, the time of victory arrived and the bells of triumph rang."[115] The novel ends on January 1, 1955, when Habib Bourguiba (1903–2000), the Supreme Mujahid, returns home. Bourguiba proclaimed the Republic of Tunisia and was its first president from 1957 to 1987. He was a tireless fighter for freedom. Having created the Neo-Destour party in 1934, he had spent some time in prison during World War II, only to come out a victorious leader of the opposition. Halima recalls that Bourguiba had been arrested on January 18, 1952.[116] In the 1950s, he was one of the political thinkers who prepared a seven-point program aimed at ending the system of French administration in Tunisia and restoring full Tunisian sovereignty as a final step to independent statehood. The year 1954 was the turning point for the French Empire in North Africa, as there were numerous protests against French rule in Morocco, Algeria, and Tunisia. The French premier went to Tunis to negotiate the takeover of power, but the bey, Muhammad VIII al-Amin, whose rule ultimately ended in 1956, did not want to give up his power and tried to disregard the Neo-Destour party. Habib Bourguiba, however, was too popular by this time, and it was he who led the Tunisian negotiating team. Tunisia was granted autonomy in 1955 and independence in 1956. Bourguiba was instrumental in securing the republican principle against the monarch, who had collaborated with the

---

[113] Fanon, *The Wretched of the Earth*, 33, 55.
[114] Metoui, *Halima*, 111.
[115] Metoui, *Halima*, 125.
[116] Metoui, *Halima*, 89.

French. The monarchy was abolished in 1957, and Habib Bourguiba became the first president of the independent Tunisia.[117] The novel shows the background of his return and the fight for liberty, but it also blurs the boundaries between terrorists and tyrants, as both groups use the same means to win their cause.[118]

Metoui's novel describes the final years of the struggle for independence, with Abdelhamid and Halima actively involved in the liberty crusade. Similar, although differently phrased, ideas about freedom for all Muslims were at the core of Ed Husain's fundamentalist journey. Disgruntled by the injustices, the fatal legacy of the encounters between the colonizers and the colonized, the colonized resort to the one thing that unites them – faith. The same pattern is recapped in the case of the second and third generations of immigrants. Excessive religiousness in the secular West, however, breeds islamophobia. Even though in the past the colonizers kept terrorism directed at them at bay, violence still occurred along ethnic and religious lines.[119] The acts of terror perceptibly deepened the gulf between the world supposedly ruled by the past and that devoted to the future. In Husain's view, Islam is the religion of peace; even so, Islamism sponsors contemporary terrorism, which has nothing to do with simply fighting against tyrants to maintain personal and national freedom. Islamism, terrorism's unfortunate twin sibling, has become a focus not only of sociology and psychology but also of contemporary literature and culture.[120] Marred by the new postcolonial order, it is now coupled with discourses on the opposing forces of secularity and spirituality. Reading terrorism as the modern-day personification of the devil thus takes us back to the original irreconcilable, albeit stereotypically presented, forces: the progressive West and the traditional East. In the ongoing matches between terrorists and tyrants, what is indisputable is the unsolvable dilemma, the moral of all those stories: namely, one man's terrorist is another man's freedom fighter.

---

117 Rogan, *The Arabs*, 371.
118 An interesting commentary concerning such boundaries is offered in the docudrama *The Road to Guantanamo*, directed by Michael Winterbottom and Matt Whitecross (2006). It is the story of four friends traveling to a friend's wedding in Pakistan. Full of youthful bravado and devoid of caution, they are caught up in the events on the Pakistan–Afghanistan border and end up in Guantanamo. Some of the scenes suggest yet another prison, located somewhere in central-eastern Europe.
119 Gerteiny notes the important difference between "domestic terrorism" and "international or transnational terrorism." *The Terrorist Conjunction*, 18.
120 There are numerous films and TV series concerning the topic, *The War Within* (2005, directed by Joseph Castelo), *24 Hours* (2001–2010), and *Homeland* (2011–2020) being perhaps most noteworthy.

Chapter 6
Through the Looking Glass: *Ajanabee* in Arabia

The works of the Polish painter and engraver Aleksander Laszenko (1883–1944) unveil the Orient through the fascinated eyes of the artist: the slightly bent figure of an Arab on a camel against the background of what looks like the rocks of the Jordanian Wadi Rum (1935); the magical entrance into an Arab town in "The Gate in Sidibel Abbes" (1932); the dreamy mirage-like vision of a North African desert town (1930); and many others that are a lasting testimony to Laszenko's sojourns in the East. The painter was born in 1883 into a Polish family in Ukraine. His first exhibition took place in 1926 and immediately earned him the reputation of being an "Orientalist" painter. Allegedly a friend of Howard Carter, the Egyptologist with whom Laszenko shared an interest in the Oriental civilizations, the artist's capacity for observation goes far beyond the surface of the Eastern landscapes. All his paintings record his unending attentiveness to the cultures of the region. In today's world, however, Laszenko's portraits of half-naked Arab women could be seen as controversial and interpreted as an example of the demonstrably Western gaze designed to "rape" and denigrate the East. In orthodox Islam, not only the process of observation but also paintings and photographs are prohibited. Seen as a forbidden encroachment upon Muslim lands and people, paintings of women exemplify all that is abhorrent in the Western world of unbelief, all that is *haram*, that is evil, sinful. Muslim women should be protected against strangers, whose glances dishonor them and expose them to possible transgressions, for example adultery or rape, the latter defined as adultery and fornication, and punishable by death under Sha-ri'a law. In the modern world, the sins of the flesh frowned upon in secular ethics are condemned in equal measure in Islam and in Christianity.

The medieval world conceptualized the Flesh as one of the enemies of Mankind, as it had needs that could lead man into temptation and transgression. In the fifteenth-century *The Castle of Perseverance*, Caro, the Flesh, features as a separate character who joins with the characters of the World and the Devil to destroy Mankind: "Behold þe Werld, þe Deuyl, and me! / Wyth all oure mythis we kyngys thre / Nyth and day besy we be / For to destroy Mankende / If þat we may."[1] In late medieval drama, more unambiguously than in earlier literature, there existed an ongoing battle between the body and the soul. To battle the urges of the flesh was first and foremost the task of every Christian; hence Sir

---

[1] *The Castle of Perseverance*, ll. 266–70.

Isumbras unquestioningly accepts his penance, relinquishes his former life, lets himself be beaten by the Saracens like a common man, and for a number of years becomes a lowly smith. Ascetic practices such as vigils, hunger, thirst, and the forgoing of personal hygiene were supposedly ways to attain the state of grace. This is how the spiritual won over the bodily, the heavenly defeated the earthly. *Solitudo carnis*, the solitude of the flesh, intimated a kind of "melancholy awareness of the shameful part of oneself, an oppressive sense of imprisonment" within one's body.[2] From the tenth century onwards, the spiritual is identified with the monastic ideal and the bodily with the material (and therefore fallen), secular world.[3] As a result, the faithful began to disparage not only sexual desires but also gluttony and drunkenness, the latter frequently attributed to the Saracen sultans, whose feasting is branded unhealthy in romances such as *The Sultan of Babylon*. The character of Caro, after all, is in charge of Gluttony and Sloth as well as "Lecherye, my dowtyr so dere."[4] Paradoxically, beautiful, well-formed bodies were a gift from God, while malformed, diseased, and incongruous bodies, even though likewise "gifts" from God, were the explicit sign of some past sin or current penance. Size and skin color also seemed to be impediments to salvation, and hence the Saracen giants in *Guy of Warwick* and *Octavian* are represented as huge, black, terrifying, boastful, rather stupid, and of course, evil.

Except for the literal meaning of being the source of sin, the body in medieval literature had a metaphorical meaning and was used to illustrate abstract notions such as the state and the nation. The healthy social and political body was a measure of the nation's well-being. The body of a king represented the *respublica*. Anthropomorphic representations of the universe occasioned the theory of the body politic, as the strong well-formed (male) body signified a salubrious moral condition, while deformity brought about unease, as illness had an ambivalent status in the medieval imagination. Depicted by John of Salisbury in his *Policraticus*, the body politic not only served to define the health of *respublica* but also accounted for the transaction between "a secular body, *corpus naturale* as distinct from the *corpus mysticum* of the Church."[5] The somatic nature of the commonwealth and the Church would deem rebellion a sacrilege.

---

2 Fumagalli, *Landscapes of Fear*, 149.
3 Fumagalli expands on the monastic penitential practices as well as "the elusiveness of perfection." *Landscapes of Fear*, 158–69.
4 *The Castle of Perseverance*, l. 999.
5 Hale, *The Body Politic*, 38–39.

Many of the ideas indicated above still apply today. Terror and terrorism, for example, are perceived as an injury done to the social body. Hence, as John O'Neil explains, there are bodily ties between individuals and institutions because "just as we think society with our bodies so, too, we think our bodies with society."[6] As has been noted, in medieval romances, bodies already not only belonged to individual figures but also represented the social and religious order. The positive constructions of well-formed and white bodies are contrasted with the negative constructions of visibly alien, dark-skinned ones. The latter, conceptualized as foreign, can easily be identified as targets of various panics surrounding health and disease. Contemporary sociology similarly tackles the question of the body within the fluctuations of marking, stereotyping, and even caricature. Bodies were, and have remained, political and are now read within the socioeconomic context.[7] "The social body constrains how the physical body is perceived," as Chris Shilling clarifies; thus in the second half of the nineteenth century, Jewish refugees were portrayed as "unclean" and "immoral," while in the 1950s the West Indians were seen as "carefree," "low-living," and "disorderly."[8] Today, the large-nosed Jew and the dark-skinned Saracen of medieval literature have been replaced by a bearded Muslim man and a veiled female figure engendering, as Tabish Khair calls it, the "new xenophobia," which relies upon the very distinguishability of the stranger. Both in medieval and contemporary society, the bodies, and therefore cultures, of others point to various urban anxieties of communal living, as "the gradual civilizing of the body has taken place in the context of changes in the major fears facing individuals and the dominant mode of social control characteristic of societies."[9] The fear of attack, however, remains the same. Currently, the imminent danger seems to be not a global war but an unwarranted individual terrorist assault. The perpetrators are either homegrown converts or darker-skinned fundamentalists, whose very aim is the destruction of the Western lifestyle, which they despise and desire at the same time. Once again, as was the case in the medieval Saracen romances, today they also wield havoc, and their guilt, whatever that might be, is as if "written on the body."

---

6 O'Neil, *Five Bodies*, 51.
7 O'Neil outlines the representations of the body in current sociological and political discourse. He also reads the body politic's presence in history and in contemporary sociological theory. *Five Bodies*, 67–90.
8 Shilling, *The Body and Social Theory*, 73, 59.
9 Shilling, *The Body and Social Theory*, 151. Shilling argues: "Fears of attack in relatively unregulated societies are increasingly replaced by social 'fears' of shame and embarrassment in modern societies, and from being forced on people externally, control comes to be self-imposed" (151).

In contrast to the medieval romances, which had dark Muslim men yearn for white Christian women, many contemporary novels habitually present Christian women as captivated by the Muslim world or as desiring Muslim men. The two novels analyzed in the present chapter offer good examples of such an inversion: Brian Moore's *The Magician's Wife* and Ahdaf Soueif's *The Map of Love*, published in 1997 and 1999 respectively. The former, set in the second half of the nineteenth century, battles the presentation of Arabs as gullible idolaters incapable of distinguishing between reality and fiction; the latter narrates a love story between a white Englishwoman and an Egyptian lawyer and nationalist at the end of the Victorian era. Characteristically, the women's romantic involvements are set in the nineteenth century, the time of colonialization and Arab nationalism, the time of the emergent discourses on races. While showing two female *ajanabee*, "foreigners," the said novels offer a more up-to-date "tourist gaze," to use John Urry's phrase.[10] Moore voices European fallacies about Arabia by portraying a woman initially prejudiced against the Orient, who learns to admire the mysterious East. Soueif presents a Western woman, captivated by Muslim culture and the strength and masculinity of Muslim men, who, against her better judgment, decides to stay in Egypt. Both women are conscious of the position and significance of white women and the female body in Arabia.

Brian Moore (1921–1999) was a Belfast-born Canadian and American writer, a screenwriter and collaborator of Alfred Hitchcock,[11] whose novels show a wide range of interests and an equally wide range of settings. *The Magician's Wife* was his last novel; in spite of very good reviews, for example by Joyce Carol Oates, it was never nominated for the Booker Prize.[12] Patricia Craig argues that "[w]hen he came to write *The Magician's Wife*, he had on his hands, once again, a story encompassing many of his primary concerns: historical recreation, a political dimension, clash of ideologies, areas of betrayal, trickery and treachery, the feminine point of view."[13] The origins of *The Magician's Wife* are to be found in Moore's reading of Flaubert's correspondence with George Sand. There he came across a note saying that a famous magician, Jean-Eugène Robert-Houdin (1805–1871), whose name was later adopted in homage by another famous magician, Harry Houdini (1874–1926), was sent to Algeria in 1857 by the Arab Bureau set up by Napoleon III. Robert-Houdin went there to frighten off the

---

10 Urry, *The Tourist Gaze*.
11 Moore wrote the screenplay for *Torn Curtain* (1966).
12 Craig, *Brian Moore*, 258.
13 Craig, *Brian Moore*, 257.

Arabs by showing them the "magic" powers of France, and in this way to discourage the "holy war."[14] The correspondence concerned Flaubert's *Salammbô*, published in 1862,[15] and his previous visit to Tunis to see the ruins of Carthage, in which the novel was set.[16] For Moore, likewise, the setting was not accidental. Denis Sampson claims that although Moore wrote the novel more than fifty years after his stay there in 1943, it must have left a lasting mark: "It was his first French city but it was also an Arab city and a divided one like Belfast."[17] Such divisions, seen on a larger scale and through the process of colonization, were also observed by Franz Fanon, who expounded that "[t]he colonial world is cut in two. The dividing line, the frontiers, are shown by barracks and police stations. In the colonies it is the policeman and the soldier who are the official, instituted go-betweens, the spokesmen of the settler and his rule of oppression."[18] Unsurprisingly, Fanon's *The Wretched of the Earth* was the main intertext of Gillo Pontecorvo's *The Battle of Algiers*, which narrates the events leading to the liberation of Algeria. Moore also understood that the partitioned colonial city is first and foremost divided by violence and counter-violence, but he wanted to capture in his novel the Arab culture at the beginning, not the end, of such discord. Talking about his wartime experiences, he was admittedly excited "by the foreign countries I was in, by the disjoined, strange life I led just behind the front lines in a time when you felt you were a living part of history."[19] It is clear that his war travels had a decisive impact on the story set in nineteenth-century Algeria. What began as an impression of the war trip to the Orient was transformed into a voyage into Europe's colonial past.

For this reason, *The Magician's Wife* is based on two journeys: one to the court of Napoleon III, the other to Algeria. Although the main hero is Henri Lambert, it is his wife Emmeline who, like Emily in Chaucer's story, is framed by what might be seen as the new "courtly love discourse," the idiom of gentility. In Chaucer's text, two knights imprisoned in the tower of the Theseus's

---

14 Craig, *Brian Moore*, 247.
15 Flaubert and Sand, *The Correspondence*. Flaubert writes to Sand: "We sent a Robert-Houdin to all the villages of France to work miracles" (152). The editors explain that Robert-Houdin was sent "to North Africa in an attempt to destroy the nefarious influence of the marabouts on the native population. His feats, announced as 'miracles,' were a great success" (153).
16 Craig, *Brian Moore*, 257.
17 Sampson, *Brian Moore*, 53.
18 Fanon, *The Wretched of the Earth*, 29.
19 Sampson, *Brian Moore*, 52. Moore felt that in Europe he was a spectator, yet he found himself drawn to the French culture and literature, which resulted in his realization that he "had a French cast of mind" (55).

castle, Palamon and Arcite, await their liberation, possibly for ransom (medieval reading), or death (classical reading). Below, in the garden, a beautiful young girl, Hippolita's younger sister Emily, walks and dreams. As the two knights both fall in love with her, their friendship is shattered, and so is her peace of mind, because Theseus contrives a fight between them to win Emily's hand in marriage. The representation of the tower as the space of imprisonment is quite straightforward and unmistakable, but the enclosed garden in which the maiden is supposedly free to roam, yet forbidden to leave, gives us an alternative vision of un-freedom. Emily's predicament seems to respond to the later claim by Jean-Jacques Rousseau that "L'homme est né libre, et partout il est dans les fers."[20] Analogously, Moore's Emmeline, the central consciousness of the narrative, is also imprisoned in the discourse of social mores. She is required to follow her husband wherever he decides to go. At Compiègne, Lambert is quite taken with the Emperor, whom he deems

> a man with vision. . . . Nine years ago he was a simple member of the National Assembly. Then, four years later, he staged his *coup d'état* and now he's Emperor Napoleon and the victor of Crimea. And by this time next year I hope he'll be the conqueror of Algeria.[21]

Little does Lambert know that the invitation to meet the Emperor is due not to the recognition of his skills but to his usefulness as a pawn in Napoleon's fight against the gullible and superstitious Algerians. Notably, in France, Lambert has also been feared, as the peasants from the vicinity of Rouen where the Lamberts live see him as someone who might be in league with the devil: "many among her husband's audience believed his inventions and illusions were a gift, granted him by that world which lies hidden behind our visible world, a world ruled by mysterious powers stronger than the Church, capable of miracles no saint could match."[22] In Algeria, despite the preliminary success of his performances, Lambert is not thought a saint. He is declared *chitan*, the devil incarnate,[23] and that is exactly what Emmeline remembers from the reception of his performances in the French countryside. Yet because of this misconception, she is not afraid to travel alone into the desert to see the Algerian *marabout*, a Muslim hermit or saint, especially in northern Africa. She is certain that if Lambert has been pronounced the devil, no one would touch the devil's wife.

---

20 "Man is born free but is everywhere in chains." Rousseau, *The Social Contract*, 45.
21 Moore, *The Magician's Wife*, 60.
22 Moore, *The Magician's Wife*, 77.
23 Moore, *The Magician's Wife*, 179.

Whilst still in France, Emmeline was reluctant to accept the invitation to the court, whereas "Henri . . . was so honoured to be here among these people that he did not see the obvious: he and Emmeline were at the lowest rung of their social ladder, ignored, shut off in cold attic quarters under the roof."[24] Lambert, then, becomes a classical fool of fortune, naively believing that what Fortune gives will never be taken away. Unknown to Lambert, such is the warning that Lady Philosophy offers Boethius. She rallies against Fortune, arguing that Fortune ensnares the minds of men:

> He who hopes for nothing and fears nothing can disarm the fury of these impotent men; but he who is burdened by fears and desires is not master of himself. He throws away his shield and retreats; he fastens the chain by which he will be drawn.[25]

The wanting and craving for material possessions as well as for dominance makes men weak.[26] Lady Philosophy reminds the desolate hero that all the gifts of Fortune are transitory,[27] and that power, however great it might be, should not be confused with happiness.[28] "Therefore, material possessions are not rightly called riches, worldly power is not true power, and public honor is not true honor," says Boethius the Christian.[29]

Predictably, blinded by his good fortune, Lambert does not see the pitfalls of his desire for success and fame. He sees the court as an earthly Paradise and is never to find out that this is where his wife has been subject to sexual abuse: "At that moment a hand touched her back, pushing askew the hoop of her crinoline and sliding down to fondle her buttocks. She turned to face the Emperor's sly concern. 'Are you cold. Madame? Do you need another wrap?'"[30] Though thoroughly disgusted with the Emperor's behavior, she is also petrified, not by fear of rape but by dread of breaking social conventions. Resembling Chaucer's Emily, she remains a slave to covenants and does not dare either to shout or, perhaps more appropriately, to slap the Emperor's face. Her husband deems the visit to Compiègne a triumph. A result of their stay at court, the Lamberts embark on a

---

24 Moore, *The Magician's Wife*, 23.
25 Boethius, *Consolation*, 9, 21–23.
26 Boethius, *Consolation*, 54.
27 Fame, even for civil officers, is of slight value. Boethius gives the example of evil Nero, who gave "the tainted seats of consulship to venerable men": the source of their power was thoroughly evil. Boethius, *Consolation*, 50.
28 Boethius *Consolation*, 50.
29 Boethius, *Consolation*, 36.
30 Moore, *The Magician's Wife*, 65.

life-changing journey to Algeria, where Emmeline feels that she "has been transported into the page of a storybook."[31]

Given that her husband is greatly intent on performing the "French miracles,"[32] he is undoubtedly a con man, paid by the colonial authorities to be precisely this. Here one is tempted to think about Fanon's pronouncement, "The white man is locked in his whiteness,"[33] which reflects Lambert's views on the Arabs. He does not see the people, the nation trying to retain autonomy. He perceives Arabia as a territory to be conquered by whatever means. Emmeline does not share his "colonial enthusiasm." For her, Africa in the sunlight is "Moorish, magical and strange."[34] European fashion and European furnishing are unfitting for such a place. She sees the French flag as oddly out of place on the Moorish building now serving as the Governor's mansion. This image is perhaps the most haunting in the whole novel, because Emmeline, like Moore himself, always places her sympathies with the subjugated nation and in favor of the preservation of the indigenous culture and religion. As Craig notices:

> One of the most striking aspects of *The Magician's Wife*, indeed, is the enticing atmosphere in which the events of the plot are located: dark narrow lanes and whitewashed Moorish houses, rosewater and orange trees and faded pink silken robes. Somehow for Emmeline Lambert, the magician's wife, her mission in Algiers – as an adjunct of her husband – must be weighed in the balance against the delicacy and integrity of the civilisation she's come face to face with, however, fragmentarily.[35]

Confrontations between different cultures in Brian Moore's novels are not as frequent as encounters between different religions. Moore studied the notions of evangelization and faith in *Black Robe*[36] and *The Catholics*.[37] *The Magician's Wife*, however, is the only novel in which he examines the precepts of Islam with so much openness and admiration. He has Colonel Deniau, whom the Lamberts have already met at Compiègne, admit that the Arab religiosity is

---

31 Moore, *The Magician's Wife*, 85.
32 Moore, *The Magician's Wife*, 87.
33 Fanon, *Black Skin, White Masks*, xiii.
34 Moore, *The Magician's Wife*, 85. "There was also a score of Arab women, most of them young, dressed in wide woolen shirts, tied at the waist with a rope and fastened at the breast with large iron pins. Their hair was plaited in long tresses and on their arms and legs they wore bracelets of silver and iron. Their faces shocked her. Many were tattooed. In their ears were large rings, and their nails were dyed red-brown with henna" (82–83).
35 Craig, *Brian Moore*, 258.
36 Moore, *Black Robe*.
37 Moore, *The Catholics*.

sound and profound.[38] Rather than belittle Islam, Moore shows it as conceivably "not more spiritual than Christianity, but stronger, frightening in its intensity, with a certitude Christianity no longer possessed."[39] In Algiers, Emmeline learns from Bou-Aziz, the new Mahdi (leader who will rule before the end of the world and restore religion and justice) that "[i]t does not matter if we worship God in mosques, in the market square, or in the lostness of the desert sands. It is the act of worship that links us to God."[40] Similarly, Colonel Deniau, for the most part functioning as the Lambert's "cultural translator," envies the Arabs' stark belief in *mektoub*, fate,[41] which implies that whatever happens is the will of God. A good Muslim should resign himself to the will of God and should hope, *inshallah*, that things will work out for him. This is the feature of Muslim culture that Richard Burton depreciates: "The expression, so offensive to English ears, Inshallah Bukra – Please God, to-morrow – always said about what should be done to-day, is here as common as in Egypt or in India. This procrastination belongs more or less to all Orientals." Such utterances, comparable to other areas of Muslim life, serve to underscore the everyday reliance upon Allah's will, "enjoined when a man should, however, depend upon his own exertions."[42] Colonel Deniau, however, expresses a different opinion. He maintains that Muslims give themselves to God wholeheartedly and, unlike Christians, do not ask for favors "for daily bread, for forgiveness of trespasses, deliverance from temptation and evil."[43] What they usually pray for is for God to guide them into the right path. Emmeline is amazed to have found people "kneeling, heads bowed, prayer five times each day for each day of their lives, prayer not of petition but of acceptance. *Everything comes from God.*"[44]

Islam, after all, means surrender. Surprisingly, in early Christianity we also find declarations that Christians should yield themselves to God, as Boethius suggests "human reason is incapable of comprehending the simplicity and perfection of divine knowledge."[45] For him "there seems to be a hopeless conflict between divine foreknowledge of all things and freedom of the human will. For

---

38 Moore, *The Magician's Wife*, 89.
39 "Human souls . . . are more free when they are engaged in contemplation of the divine mind, and less free when they are joined to bodies, and still less free when they are bound by earthly fetters. They are in utter slavery when they lose possession of their reason and give themselves wholly to vice." Boethius, *Consolation*, 104.
40 Moore, *The Magician's Wife*, 145.
41 Moore, *The Magician's Wife*, 101.
42 Burton, *Personal Narrative*, 2:21.
43 Moore, *The Magician's Wife*, 148.
44 Moore, *The Magician's Wife*, 186, emphasis original.
45 Boethius, *Consolation*, 129.

if God sees everything in advance and cannot be deceived in any way, whatever his Providence foresees will happen, must happen."[46] There can be no freedom in human decisions and actions, because the course of events has already been established in the divine mind – such arguments are the core of medieval theological disputes and show one of the common points between Christianity and Islam. In the novel, Bou-Aziz advocates submission to the will of God. Rather than proclaim the so-much-dreaded holy war, however, he calls for reform and regeneration of the faith,[47] urging his coreligionists to embark on a spiritual, not physical, jihad.

> To conquer our enemies, we must first increase our obedience to God and to the Prophet. If we do, one day our faith will be so strong that the Christian world will be powerless against it and the infidels will pass for ever from this land.[48]

That was the hope the French nestled in their hearts: that instead of instigating a military campaign, the Arabs would turn inwards to strengthen their faith. What the French do not know, however, is that Bou-Aziz sees French power as temporal and reassures the murmuring sheikhs that they are in God's hands, that their time, their victory, will come. And indeed, Algeria, which the French never considered a colony but had annexed to France and divided into *départements* like the rest of France,[49] regained independence, but only after a long, tragic and bloody revolution lasing from 1954 to 1962. Neither Napoleon III nor the fictitious characters of Henri Lambert and Colonel Deniau comprehend the specificity of Algerian – or, rather, Arab – nationalism.

As it turns out, the magician's wife understands Algeria and Algerians far better than her husband. Her initial feeling of estrangement is soon mixed with attraction, only partially ignited by Colonel Deniau. One might read their story through yet another of Moore's fascinations, Gustave Flaubert's *Madame Bovary*. Contrary to his other rewritings of Flaubert's novel (i.e., *The Doctor's Wife* and *Cold Heaven*), which both tackled the illicit love affairs of bored housewives, *The Magician's Wife* is not tainted by the sin of adultery. Here Deniau assumes the role of a guide and mentor, providing Emmeline with necessary

---

46 Boethius, *Consolation*, 104–5. As Green explains: "The author's own literal imprisonment becomes a figure of the soul's imprisonment in the body, the bondage imposed by the demands of the passions, the enslavement to Fortune and her deceitful favors." Green "Introduction" to Boethius, *Consolation*, xxiii.
47 Moore, *The Magician's Wife*, 205.
48 Instead of the Holy War, the Arabs would "turn inwards to strengthen their faith." Moore, *The Magician's Wife*, 81.
49 Rogan, *The Arabs*, 371.

information about the Arab way of life, for example the ban on alcohol. He tries to instill in her his admiration for Arabian landscapes, telling her that the famous Saharan desert epitomizes "a spiritual landscape. To enter it you must become, like it, a *tabula rasa*."[50] Deniau personifies the nineteenth-century Orientalist who likes exotic goods and exotic culture. He keeps Algerian servants, one of whom is a beautiful young girl whom Emmeline suspects is his lover, and dresses in Arab robes when it suits him, thereby embodying the Saidian claim that the allure of the Orient for Europeans always has a sexual undertone.[51] Besides, Deniau's Moorish household, which so intrigues Emmeline, is really a camouflage for his military activities. Convinced that Arabia is ripe for conquest and colonization, he nevertheless sees the possible dangers to the indigenous Arab culture in which he is so immersed. In a moment of frankness, he confesses to Emmeline the unjust nature of his undertaking and the false pretext of the French mission to "civilize" Algeria, telling her, "It is we, not the Arabs, who will benefit. And I ask myself: what will happen to their way of life?"[52] It is clearly Moore's Irishness voicing such strong criticism of colonialism, the distaste for the colonizer's ideologies, and the aversion toward the stifling presence of the colonial administration. Emmeline is equally certain that the French "should not be conquerors of these people or that we should try to make Frenchmen of them, or use their country for our gain."[53]

In reality, almost thirty years before the action of the novel takes place, in June 1830, the French had defeated the troops of Husayn Pasha and thus ended the Ottoman rule over Algeria. Their victory marked the beginning of 132 years of French rule. The Algerian population was made up of Arabs and Berbers, the latter being a non–Arab ethnic community that converted to Islam. Both groups despised Ottoman rule, just as they came to despise the French later. Resistance movements grew in strength despite various military as well as cultural conquests devised by the Arab Bureau.[54] One historical figure not mentioned by Moore, however, is Amir Abd al-Quadir (1808–1883), whose life falls within the time frame of the novel, and who was the leader of the tribes allied against the tyranny of the French.[55]

---

50 Moore, *The Magician's Wife*, 127.
51 Said, *Orientalism*, 190.
52 Moore, *The Magician's Wife*, 101.
53 Moore *The Magician's Wife*, 200.
54 Rogan, *The Arabs*, 140–46.
55 "It appears unintelligible, still it is not less true, that Egyptians who have lived as servants under European roofs for years, retain the liveliest loathing for the manners and customs of their masters. Few Franks, save those who mixed with the Egyptians in Oriental disguise are

In the novel as well as in history, the Arabs sought the protection of Allah, whereas the French were guided not by God but by perhaps an even more powerful force – Greed – and Lambert's "miracles" are orchestrated to facilitate the takeover. Following the scheme, before his performance, Henri Lambert is presented to the Arab audience as a great leader, a *marabout* who is endowed with supernatural powers, and with a sense of triumph he declares: "I am a sorcerer. I am Christian. I am French. God, whom you call Allah, protects me. As well as he will protect my country from my enemy who dares to strike a blow against France."[56] In Islam, the Messiah (al-Mahdi) is reputed to have come "at the end of time" to bring peace, justice, and unity to a world torn by "corruption, division, and strife."[57] Malise Ruthven argues that such a doctrine was a very convenient way to deal with an underground, yet divinely inspired leader, both in the turbulent beginnings of Islamic states and as a reaction to colonial oppression. During her travel to Milianah in a caravan, Emmeline begins to see that it is Colonel Deniau who is the ruthless magician, and that she and her husband are his marionettes. Despite Lambert's tricks and almost persuading the Arab audience that he cannot be killed because bullets do not harm him, the grand plan does not work because Emmeline tells Taalith, Bou-Aziz's daughter, who acts as a translator, that Henri is a mere entertainer, not a saint and performer of miracles. As a consequence, after the meeting of the sheikhs when Bou-Aziz proclaims himself the Mahdi,[58] an assassin from the crowd shoots Lambert, this time with real bullets. Lambert manages to walk a few steps before he faints. Notwithstanding Lambert's injury, Deniau sends the pair out of the country as soon as possible, so that his miracle worker will not be seen nursing a bullet wound. Emmeline's betrayal or intervention, however, is in vain. The French armies subdued the entire nation of Algeria in the following year, as we learn from the epilogue of the story.[59]

---

aware of their repugnance to, and contempt for, Europeans. Almost every able-bodied man spoke of hastening to the Jihad – a crusade, or holy war – and the only thing that looked like apprehension was the too eager depreciation of their foes. All seemed delighted with the idea of French cooperation, for, somehow or other, the Frenchmen is everywhere popular." Burton, *Personal Narrative* 1:11.
56 Moore *The Magician's Wife*, 119.
57 Ruthven, *Islam*, 53.
58 Bou-Aziz comes from the South, the Sahara, traditionally the region from which the Mahdis originate; when he proclaimed himself the next Mahdi, he took the name Muhammad b. 'Abd Allah. Moore, *The Magician's Wife*, 132.
59 Moore, *The Magician's Wife*, 215.

As has been noted already, Moore's Emmeline is at first caught up in colonial stereotypes, only to become enamored with the people and the place. While recognizing that every culture and religion is based upon various forms of limitations and restrictions, to which women are frequently subjected, she nevertheless lets herself be swayed by everything that surrounds her. When Lambert's assistant, Jules, falls ill and then dies, it is Deniau who orders Emmeline to dress in Arab fashion and take Jules's place on stage. She is asked to wear an Arab dress and to put the veil over her face. "When she had done this a masked Arab woman stared at her through the mirror as though by this simple act of disguise Emmeline Lambert was no more."[60] In this act of submission to fate, by taking on Arab dress, Emmeline symbolically strips herself of her former identity. In that very moment she is no longer an *ajanabee*; she becomes united with the place that captivated her heart. Moreover, corresponding to Fanon's dismissal of the revolutionary "unveiling of Algeria," Moore's novel suggests that the secret of Algeria lies behind the veil, while the unveiling would expose a nation not yet ready to recreate itself without its past culture and belief. The Europeans, for whom clothes are a symbol either of sexual revolution or the lack of it, are not able to recognize the difference between a woman who wears a veil of her own accord and one forced to do so by the society's pressures. Consequently, Mark Steyn sees the "unveiling" as the first and most crucial step toward the democratizing of the Arab cultures, but his is decidedly the Western perspective.[61] In the novels of Metoui and, paradoxically, Moore, it is the veiled woman who stands for Muslim strength, and it is through belief that Tunisians and Algerians achieve first national identity, and eventually, freedom. Moore's narrative demonstrates not that we are enslaved by religion but that we are prisoners to our trains of thought, our modes of thinking, customs, and cultural stereotypes; in fact, we are all un-free in our ways to freedom. More profoundly, though, Lambert fails because he is blinded by his initial good fortune. In *The Consolation of Philosophy*, Lady Philosophy suggests that Boethius is too angry to take in her medicine and that the source of his anger is his desires;[62] true happiness should be found with God, as God is the goal of everything, which is strangely akin to the Muslim notion of submission. Accepting one's fate, or the will of the divine, makes us impervious to the sudden changes of Fortune, in the words of Boethius: "What difference does it make, then, whether you desert her by dying, or she you by

---

60 Moore, *The Magician's Wife*, 150.
61 Steyn, *America Alone*.
62 Boethius, *Consolation*, 16.

leaving?"⁶³ In his misery, Lambert should perhaps remember Philosophy's ominous words, "good fortune deceives, but misfortune teaches."⁶⁴

Such an assertion could also be the motto of the account by one of the main protagonists of the Egyptian-British writer Ahdaf Soueif's *The Map of Love*, published in 1999. The novel recounts the lives of four generations of an Egyptian-British-French-American family, beginning with a late nineteenth-century narrative concerning Anna Winterbourne, a widow, who comes to the writer's native Cairo at a time of great anti-colonial turmoil. While she contends with her depression following her husband's death, she falls for and marries an Arab freedom fighter, Sharif Basha al-Baroudi. Soueif's tale moves from England to North Africa, France and America, unfolding the lives of the divided family living on three continents and struggling to connect all the disparate pieces of the jigsaw puzzle of the family's past. The novel begins with Anna's great-granddaughter Isabel and her cousin Amal (the granddaughter of Anna's sister-in-law, Layla) opening a trunk that Anna apparently had left behind in Egypt and discovering Anna's journal and letters. It is the aforemention trunk in which the past is preserved and whose contents prompt the investigation of the family history. Anna's voice then becomes the bridge between the past and the present, and her account eventually enables Isabel to discern the reasons for the rift between the two branches of her family. Anna writes in English but she communicates with her second husband and his family in French, while learning Arabic, the language which will once again become a foreign tongue to her great granddaughter Isabel Parkman. In *The Map of Love*, as in her other works, Soueif sees both the negative conservative side of Islam⁶⁵ as well as its positive liberal aspects. In the manner of Bernard Lewis,⁶⁶ she attempts to juxtapose the ostensible backwardness of the East with its rich

---

63 Boethius, *Consolation*, 27.
64 Boethius, *Consolation*, 40.
65 The 2011 revolution, which began with the slogan "bread, social justice and freedom", ousted President Hosni Mubarak (1928–2020), but did not bring the expected results. Soueif alludes to the complexity of modern Egypt in 2012, torn between conservative Muslim Brotherhood followers and the "remnant of the Mubarak regime." Soueif, *Cairo*, 223. The memoir exudes a powerful distrust towards ultra-conservative fundamentalist forces as well as towards the military rule.
66 Bernard Lewis outlines differences in the perception of time and space and shows how it influenced the development of music and literature. Lewis, *What Went Wrong?* 117–32. He also demonstrates how the lifestyle, clothing, houses, and even political organization of the state were being gradually Westernized in Turkey during Mustapha Kemal's government. Mustapha Kemal, known as Ataturk (1881–1938), whose actions led to the fall of the last dynasty of Ottoman sultans, was the first president of modern Turkey. He is now both revered as a father of the modern state and despised by the growing rightist, fundamentalist forces.

cultural traditions, imparting the complex history of the state and the nation. Within this canvas she portrays the love story of Anna and Sharif. Retaining the features of the historical novel, the narrative gains parabolic qualities, as the author, through Anna's documents, refashions the myth of Egypt's anticolonial rebirth.

The historical background, although dominated by Soueif's need to repudiate colonialism and idolize the Egyptian fight for freedom, is nevertheless historically accurate: Anna saw Egypt, which, as Mansfield holds, fell to the British in 1882,[67] a country subdued by the colonial administration. Seeing the predatory actions of the British Empire as contrary to what an "honest kingdom"[68] should stand for, she voices strong objections towards the predatory, anti-Muslim actions of the colonizers. Neither she nor her English father-in-law share the prevailing belief in the British civilizing mission. Anna's first husband died a broken man having participated in the military expedition to Sudan. From a friend, Anna learns that Kitchener's men have desecrated the body of the Mahdi, who, according to the Arabs, was a Holy Man.[69] The pillage and destruction of Sudan was inflicted as retribution for the death of General Charles George Gordon (1833–1885),[70] but Anna is not

---

[67] Mansfield, *History of the Middle East*, 114. In her memoir of the Egyptian revolution of 2011, Soueif imparts that it was Khedive Tewfiq (1852–1892) who "asked his debtor friends for help. Britain invaded, and declared Egypt a "protectorate." *Cairo*, 229.
[68] Soueif, *Map of Love*, 32.
[69] General Horatio Kitchener was appointed military vice-consul in Kastamonu Province in Turkey in 1879; in 1883, he was posted to Egypt. For Niall Fergusson, the 1880s in Sudan and Egypt stand for the hiatus of Victorian imperialism. Fergusson, *Empire*, 167. The region was the site of a religious war, which ended in the killing of General Charles George Gordon. Gordon's sad end is described by Lytton Strachey in *Eminent Victorians*, 189–267. In March 1884, Gordon was under siege in Khartoum. The British public called for action, but it was not until November that the Khartoum Relief Expedition began, under the leadership of Field Marshal Garnet Wolseley. Kitchener was an intelligence officer on the mission, and he continually pressed Wolseley to push forward more rapidly. By the time they reached the city, Gordon was dead. Fergusson, *Empire*, 268–70. See also Lawrence, *The Rise and Fall of the British Empire*, 280–87. According to Blunt, Gordon "was a man of genius, with many noble qualities, but he was also a bundle of contradictions, and the officials were probably right when they looked upon him as not being at all times quite of a sound mind." Blunt, *Secret History*, 71.
[70] Gordon was the governor of Sudan 1877–1879. The story of the war in Sudan appears in the Polish novel *W Pustyni i w Puszczy* (*In Desert and Wilderness*, 1912; serialized 1910–1912) by Henryk Sienkiewicz (1846–1916), 1905 Nobel Prize winner. The novel begins in 1884 in Port Said and narrates the story of two children: Nelly Rowlinson (age 8 and the daughter of an English engineer) and Staś Tarkowski (age 14, the son of a Polish engineer). The children are kidnapped by Arab freedom fighters, and their journey as they escape from captivity forms the main part of the story. The African landscapes and North and Central African politics form the background of the story.

consoled by such vengeance. Instead of vilifying the Orient, she embarks on a salvific journey, to see the places that her husband had seen before.

Just as Emmeline Lambert was mesmerized while looking at Algiers, Anna is equally spellbound by Egypt, its colors and splendor. Seeing Alexandria is a sublime experience for her. Her great granddaughter Isabel is also awestruck: "Egypt, mother of civilization, dreaming herself through the centuries."[71] In Cairo, Anna, inspired by the paintings she has seen in the Kensington Museum, follows the established routes, but she does not have the tourist's gaze; neither does she judge the Orient by its apparent lack of modern facilities. Unlike many of her contemporaries, Anna is smitten by Egyptian history and culture: Pompei's Pillar, the Mohammedan Cemetery, the Museum and the Catacombs[72] and tries to fit in as if Egypt has always been in her blood. Anna is delighted to take in and marvel at everything to which she is subjected, even though her experiences are a mixture of Eastern and Western cultures. She readily absorbs the pharaonic lore that once attracted archeologists and the Muslim culture that the West finds both enticing and disturbing. She is equally happy visiting the bazaar and the pyramids as she is dancing at the Khedive's ball[73] or playing croquet at the Club at Gheziragh, the symbol of the English colonial presence located on an island in the Nile, which Said in the recollection of his childhood calls "fabled." Through Anna's diary and letters supplemented by Layla' notes both Isabel and Amal salvage part of their heritage. To this effect, for Isabel, Egypt is

> [d]reaming us all, her children: those who stay and work for her and complain of her, and those who leave and yearn for her and blame her with bitterness for driving them away. And I, in my room, home after half my life has gone by, I read what Anna wrote to her father-in-law a hundred years ago, and I see the English party, lunching by the Pyramid, their Egyptian servants keeping their Egyptian petitioners at bay.[74]

Decades earlier, recognizing the economic factors of the occupation, Richard Burton had avowed that "Egypt is the most tempting prize which the East holds out to the ambition of Europe, not excepted even the Golden Horn."[75] He also had discerned that the subjugated nations both refuse to be grateful for the "benefits of British administration" and, according to him,

---

71 Soueif, *Map of Love*, 100.
72 Soueif, *Map of Love*, 61.
73 *Khedive* is the title of the ruler of Egypt, used from the times of Abbas Pasha in 1849 to the sultanate of Hussein Kamel during the First World War. Soueif, *Map of Love*, 523.
74 Soueif, *Map of Love*, 100.
75 Burton, *Personal Narrative*, 1:114.

they still long for European rule.⁷⁶ This people admire an iron-handed and lion-hearted despotism, they hate a timid and a grinding tyranny. Of all foreigners, they would prefer the French yoke, a circumstance which I attribute to the diplomatic skill and national dignity of our neighbours across the Channel. But whatever European nation secures Egypt will win a treasure. Moated on the north and south by seas, with a glacis of impassable deserts to the eastward and westward, capable of supporting an army of 180,000 men, of paying a heavy tribute, and yet able to show a considerable surplus of revenue, this country in western hands will command India, and by a ship-canal between Pelusium and Suez would open the whole of Eastern Africa.⁷⁷

Writing about Western representations of Egypt, Edward Said argues that most nineteenth-century European scholars and archeologists, save for Edward Lane, disparage the Muslim legacy, treating Egypt as a store of ancient treasures to be plundered and taken to European museums. In his view, none of the nineteenth-century Egyptologists was capable of fully comprehending its "pharaonic, Hellenistic, Coptic, Fatimid, Mameluke, Ottoman" past.⁷⁸ De Gobineau, who sneered at Arabian culture, nevertheless admitted that Europe owed a lot to the Oriental civilization, starting with the Persians and continuing with the *Arabian Nights* that inspired Southey and Moore.⁷⁹ As Karla Malette clarifies, the debate as to whether European modernity can be traced back to the Arab Mediterranean originated in the nineteenth century.⁸⁰ Traditionally, the European medical sciences acknowledge the input of Arabic scholars such as Rhazes (ca. 865–925), Avicenna (980–1037) and Averroes (1126–1198). The Arabs augmented the Greek findings and added their own observations, procedures, and remedies, and their contribution to the development of medicine is appreciated even today.⁸¹ Still, the Arab attitude to medicine in nineteenth-century accounts seems contradictory to the achievements of their predecessors.

Burton, who tried to practice medicine in Cairo, described numerous instances of the Arab disbelief in medicine, illustrating the irredeemable differences

---

76 When Burton began preparations for the journey and found an Arab servant, the youngest son of a widow, spoiled and selfish, "easily offended and as easily pacified (the Oriental), coveting other men's goods, and profuse of his own (the Arab), with matchless intrepidity of countenance (the traveler), brazen lunged, not more than half brave, exceedingly astute, with an acute sense of honour, especially where his relations were concerned (the individual). I have seen him in a fit of fury because someone cursed his father." *Personal Narrative*, 1:124–25.
77 Burton, *Personal Narrative*, 1:111–13.
78 Said, *Reflections on Exile*, 157.
79 De Gobineau, *Moral and Intellectual Diversity*, 308.
80 Malette, *European Modernity*, 3.
81 Bynum, *Medicine*, 21–23.

between the progressive West and backward East.[82] Doughty presents an equally unfavorable picture. On account of his general knowledge, he opened a (pseudo) medical practice that had nothing to do with curing diseases of the body but a lot to do with restoration of a patient's peace of mind. Even though "[t]he stranger's presence with the Aarab was not welcome to the jealous old sheikh,"[83] the Arabs enquired about his familiarity with ways of healing. Trying to practice medicine, however, Doughty was discouraged the Arab predisposition believe in miracles. "Their wild impatience looks to see marvels."[84] One of his customers was a poor woman who came to him weeping that her son is missing, pleading to "see and divine in my books what were become of her child."[85] Following some initial mishap, Doughty found out that Arabs desire not medicine but spells.[86] He met two "professors of exorcism" who were "vile and counterfeit persons,"[87] reasoning that these people held their fellow citizens in sway because of the apparent Arab gullibility. "In the Arabic border lands there is hardly a child, or almost an animal which is not defended from the evil eye, by a charm."[88] What seemed to be the most effective "medications" were amulets and incantations. Like Burton, Doughty professes that his medical practice was in good faith,[89] yet the Imam stirred people during his Friday preaching against the *Nasrâny*, the Christian.[90] The tables turn when the English medicaments are brought to Arabia by the caravan, and Doughty's medical knowledge is well spoken of. By offering his services, Doughty was able to find out about the dissemination of science amongst the Arab tribes and their ways of curing various maladies, traditionally remedied by the women in the harems. In places where Western-style hygiene does not exist, and women

---

82 Burton writes, for example, that "wounds are treated by Marham, or ointments, especially by the 'Balesan,' or Balm of Meccah; a cloth is tied round the limb and not taken out until the wound heals." *Personal Narrative*, 1:389. While in Mecca, he tried to practice as a doctor, "but a doctor is far less popular in Al-Hijaz than in Egypt" (2:229). He was also shocked by the odor of the dead animals and the possibility the spread of Asiatic cholera, which the Arabs do not seem to notice (1:384). "[A]t Meccah, the head-quarters of the faith, a desolating attack of cholera is preferred to the impiety of 'flying in the fact of Providence' and the folly of endeavoring to avert inevitable decrees" (2:224).
83 Doughty, *Arabia Deserta*, 1:409.
84 Doughty, *Arabia Deserta*, 1:255–56.
85 Doughty, *Arabia Deserta*, 1:303.
86 Doughty, *Arabia Deserta*, 2:2.
87 Doughty, *Arabia Deserta*, 2:3.
88 Doughty, *Arabia Deserta*, 1:258.
89 Doughty, *Arabia Deserta*, 2:358.
90 Doughty, *Arabia Deserta*, 2:369.

"wash their babies in camel urine believing that this will save them from insects,"[91] enchantments might be just as effective as medicine. The Arab attitudes recounted by Burton and Doughty seem to replicate the medieval prescriptions for curing various ills – immortalized in the ninth-century collection *Bald's Leechbook* – mixing herbal concoction and magic; in nineteenth-century Arabia, these seem to have been correspondingly successful.

Burton knew that it would not be prudent to advertise his services as a doctor, because Arabs commend their health to God, who is the giver and taker of disease. Muslims live by and with the will of God.[92] Accepting Allah's will, they consider their faith the strongest inoculation against adversity. Nonetheless, the Arabs feared poisoning, and so for a patient of rank, who quite obviously would have enemies, it was important to "adopt some similar precaution [sealing with one's ring] against the box or the bottle being opened."[93] In Cairo, in order to gain the trust of the Muslims, Burton began his medical "consultations," alternating them with prestidigitation and magic. It was Burton's friend, who called himself the Haji – an honorific given to those who have completed the pilgrimage to Mecca, one of the pillars of Islam – who helped the English explorer by advertising his services and referring to him as "the very phoenix of physicians."[94] Disenchanted with their lack of due (monetary) gratitude, Burton declared that when cured, a patient forgets the doctor: "An Oriental deems that he has the right to your surplus. 'Daily bread is divided' (by heaven), he asserts, and eating yours, he considers it his own."[95] In this way, he questioned oriental

---

91 Doughty, *Arabia Deserta*, 1:237.
92 For more on Arab swearing, see Doughty, *Arabia Deserta*, 1:266. One of the most interesting twentieth-century factual accounts is by Lady Joan Sharwood-Smith who, being "the colonial wife" in pre-independence Nigeria, noticed that "Allah seemed to enter into everything and the more Hausa I learnt, the more I found myself unconsciously adopting Muslim ways of speech. If I told of a death, for instance, one learnt to say Allah have mercy on him, while 'if possible' became 'if Allah wills' and, in response to the Hausa 'Goodnight' literally 'Till the morning,' one said 'Allah bring us safely'! Soon, the cracked but penetrating tones of the muezzin calling the faithful to prayer from the minaret, became one of our more familiar noises. The first call of '*Allahu Akbar-r-r*' (God is Great!) woke us each morning just before dawn, or 'as soon as a black threat could be distinguished from a white one,' to use the Muslim definition." *Diary of a Colonial Wife*, 33.
93 Burton, *Personal Narrative*, 1:57. Burton talks about the customs connected with Ramadan, which is the abstention from food from dawn to dusk. He sees the beggars as "intensely Oriental" (*Personal Narrative*, 1:82). "'My supper is in Allah's hands! Whatever thou givest, that will go with thee' chaunts the old vagrant, whose wallet perhaps contains more provision than the basket of many a respectable shopkeeper" (*Personal Narrative*, 1:82).
94 Burton, *Personal Narrative*, 1:59.
95 Burton, *Personal Narrative*, 1:51.

honesty: "Human nature feels kindness is displayed to return it in kind. But Easterns do not carry out the idea of such obligations as we do."[96] To deprecate the Arabs even further, Burton compares them with the Irish. "The Eastern pays a doctor's bill as an Oirishman does his 'rint,'[97] making a grievance of it. Your patient will show indisputable signs of convalescence: he will laugh and jest half the day; but the moment you appear, groans and a lengthened visage, and pretended complaints, welcome you."[98]

Soueif's novel offers an inverse point of view. From the very beginning of her stay in Egypt, Anna detects the unfair treatment of the natives by the English, as for example forcing Muslims to drink an alcoholic toast to His Highness, the Prince of Wales, the future Edward VII.[99] Surrounded by the English upper classes, she notices that, contrary to common convictions, high society exists in Egypt, but that society lives and entertains behind closed doors. Feeling happy for the first time since her husband died, Anna wants to enjoy and learn about Egypt. It is this thirst for new experiences that will eventually throw her into the arms of Sharif Basha. When, dressed as a man, she is mistakenly kidnapped by Egyptian freedom fighters, instead of thinking of revenge she tries to make sure that no word about her adventure would reach the British Agency and Sir Evelyn Baring, Lord Cromer, known to be conscientious and committed, though at times arrogant and condescending, especially toward the Egyptian peasants, the *fellahin*.[100] Cromer is, of course, a historical character, whose name is revealed by Wilfrid Scawen Blunt in connection with the correspondence between him and General Gordon.[101] Cromer's position in Cairo was that of unquestioned leader, a pillar of the occupying forces, and that is why Anna is afraid to divulge her secret escapade, so as not to jeopardize the British–Egyptian relations. Anna wakes up in captivity and is met by an Egyptian lady, Layla al-Baroudi, a wife of a lawyer, Husni al-Ghamrawi; Anna's "prison" is an Egyptian aristocratic home. Calmed and well looked after, Anna is told that her abductors belong to a group of young Radicals wishing to retaliate for the jailing of Husni, Layla's husband, who was arrested while participating in a peaceful

---

96 Burton, *Personal Narrative*, 1:52.
97 Although I am tempted to comment on the perception of the Irish by the Victorians, for example Thackeray, such a discussion is beyond the scope of the present work.
98 Burton, *Personal Narrative*, 1:54.
99 Soueif, *Map of Love*, 69.
100 Evelyn Baring, Lord Cromer (1841–1917), served as British Consul-General in Egypt for almost a quarter of a century, from 1883 to 1907, and was commonly known as Lord Overbearing. Mansfield, *History of the Middle East*, 97.
101 Blunt, *Secret History*, 71.

demonstration.[102] Not knowing what to do with their "prisoner," Layla asks her brother, also a lawyer, for help. This is the beginning of Anna's love story.[103] Like Anna, Sharif Basha has been married previously, but, unlike Anna's husband, his wife did not die but had been returned to her father's house. Sharif had claimed that they were not suited for each other; more importantly the girl's parents were happy to have her back, together with her dowry, once the al-Ghamrawi family was no longer in power, and the Army of Occupation destroyed Egypt's dreams of self-rule.[104] As we learn later, it is love at first sight for both Sharif and Anna. Falling in love with her most courteous and good-looking liberator strengthens and deepens the necessary romance flavor during their trip into the desert. Since Anna was apprehended when she was about to go on an expedition to Sinai to see places connected with St. Catherine of Alexandria, Sharif offers her to take her there as a recompense for the kidnapping. Analogous to Emmeline Lambert's trip into the Sahara, Anna's voyage to Sinai reveals to her a side of the country she would never be able to see as a tourist. Attired in the fashion befitting an Arab woman, she is infatuated with the desolate primal landscapes.

> A closed carriage at the door and I climbed in wearing the loose white clothing of an Arab, covered by the flowing black outer garment of an Egyptian woman of the city. My head and face were most thoroughly veiled, and my *kufiyya* and *ugal* were in the black cloth bag I carried.[105]

The disguise is not a costume to play with and discard when the party is over. She finds herself wearing the Egyptian clothing with pleasure, and this adds to her understanding of the culture. Had she traveled as Anna Winterbourne, she thinks, "I would have remained within the world I knew. I would have seen things through my companions' eyes, and my mind would have been too occupied in resisting their impressions to establish its own."[106] And in this very

---

102 Soueif, *Map of Love*, 138.
103 Sharif Basha's father is still alive, but at the time of the action of the book, he has been in retreat since 1882, and Sharif, as the oldest male in the family, undertakes his father's duties as head of the family.
104 Soueif, *Map of Love*, 151.
105 Soueif, *Map of Love*, 194. A *kuffiyya* is a scarf, the *ugal* the black cord circling the scarf. This part is a fragment of Anna's journal, in the novel printed entirely in italics.
106 Soueif, *Map of Love*, 212. Strikingly, Anna's transformation is akin to what is so frequently narrated in the conversion stories. Leila Aboulela's novel *Minaret* portrays a Sudanese woman brought up in an atheistic progressive household who, following the death of her parents and the imprisonment of her brother, motivated by the profound need to rid herself, or better, wash herself clean of her and her family's past mistakes, puts on a hijab and truly embraces Islam.

moment, she stops being a English tourist. Early in the novel, when Anna joins the picnic lunch at the foot of the great Pyramid, she learns from her fellow British:

> both HB and Mr S held that it would take generations before the Natives were fit to rule themselves as they had neither integrity nor moral fibre, being too long accustomed to foreign rule – and if foreign rule was their lot, then British rule was surely to be preferred to that of the French or Germans, who would surely have been here if we were not.[107]

In order to counter such opinions, Soueif had to invent modern characters with liberal political views, of undisputed moral integrity, education, and culture, matching or surpassing such traits of the English. In her Thomas Cook guidebook, typical of her time, Anna learns that "the people who live in the desert" are "rude, ignorant, lazy and greedy" – a scornful account, typical of condescending nineteenth-century discourse on the Arab race. The guidebook belittles the Arabs as similar in disposition to "the American Negroes in their simplicity, thoughtlessness and good humour."[108] Soueif's work is a cultural palimpsest, through which works such as these period travel guides are still glimpsed, yet Anna does not let such accounts of Egypt cloud her own views. She considers Layla her friend and almost a sister and is very much taken with Layla's mother, Zainab Hanim al-Ghamrawi; herself the heiress of an old and notable family of Minya in Upper Egypt.[109] At the same time, she feels that her time in Egypt is limited; once the sight-seeing is over, it would be improper for an upper-class woman to live alone in a hotel in Cairo. Comprehending her predicament and trying to prevent Anna from leaving the country, Sharif takes a desperate step and writes her a letter containing a proposal of marriage. He and his mother fathom what such a union entails and how much Anna will be losing. His mother warns him:

---

[107] Soueif *Map of Love*, 99–100. One finds similar ideas in slightly earlier accounts by explorers such as the American John Lloyd Stephens (1805–1852), who published *Incidents of Travel* in 1837 (published in Cairo in 1980 for the 1881–1981 centennial). Stephens shows disgust with the Arabs, seeing them as usually naked, dirty, and poor, and he mourns Egypt and Alexandria's ruins "into which she had been plunged by years of misrule and anarchy" (4). For Stephens, the Turks have "the usual air of Turkish conceit and insolence" (53), and yet upon meeting Arabs in the desert and then having more and more encounters with them, he changes his mind and begins to discover their human traits: "Arabs are not so bad as they might be" (61).
[108] Soueif, *Map of Love*, 209.
[109] Soueif, *Map of Love*, 158.

"For her, her whole life will change. Her people will be angry with her. And the British here will shun her. And even if they soften, it will be difficult for her, as your wife, to visit them or receive visits from them. She will be torn off from her own people. Even her own language she will not be able to use."[110]

Still, the besotted Sharif presses the proposal, and Anna agrees.

Paradoxically, the obstacles Anna fears most come not from his family but from the British Agency and Lord Cromer. Hence, in order to prevent any mishaps, the young couple decide to contract an Egyptian marriage first and then have it ratified at the Agency. During their meeting, Lord Cromer is visibly unsympathetic, not to say insulting. He warns Anna against polygamy, urging her to ensure in the marriage contract a clause stating that Sharif would not take another wife during his marriage to Anna,[111] a condition Sharif has already included in the Arabic documents. Edward William Lane, whose translation of the *Arabian Nights* Anna mentions while describing her abduction,[112] in his *locus classicus*, *The Modern Egyptians*, highlights that

> [t]he laws relating to *marriage* and the license of *polygamy*, the facility of *divorce* allowed by the Kur-án, and the permission of *concubinage*, are essentially the natural and necessary consequences of the main principle of the constitution of Muslim society – the restriction of the intercourse between sexes before marriage.[113]

---

110 Soueif, *Map of Love*, 281.
111 There is a very interesting comment on monogamy, polygyny, and polyandry in the preface to George Bernard Shaw's play *Getting Married*, which is his reflection on the so-called marriage debate. Defending the Christian idea of marriage, he also, however, discusses the idea of polygyny and polyandry "as not an ethical" problem but one that depends "solely on the proportion of the sexes in the population." Shaw, *The Doctor's Dilemma*, 137. He claims that "[e]xperience shews that women do not object to polygyny when it is customary; on the contrary, they are its most ardent supporters. The reason is obvious. The question, as it presents itself in practice to a woman, is whether it is better to have, say, a whole share in a tenth-rate man or a tenth share in a first-rate man. Substitute the word Income for the word Man, and you will have the question as it presents itself economically to the dependent woman" (138). He adds: "On the other hand, women object to polyandry, because polyandry enables the best women to monopolize all the men. . . . That is why all our ordinary men and women are unanimous in defence of monogamy, the men because it excludes polygyny, and the women because it excludes polyandry" (138). Shaw goes on to explain the difference between oriental and occidental polygyny, deeming the oriental version much more backward, as the "women are secluded and marriages are arranged" (140).
112 Soueif, *Map of Love*, 137.
113 Lane, *An Account of the Manners and Customs of the Modern Egyptians*, 84, italics original. Divorce in Muslim society is a simple proclamation by the husband repeated three times (163). Lane discusses the laws concerning multiple marriages and multiple divorces in more detail, and also in relation to the legitimization of children and the children of concubine-slaves (163–68).

A Muslim man can see the faces of women to whom he is related but is absolutely forbidden to see the faces of those whom he could, theoretically, marry. Anna notices that Egyptian gentlemen, "after the first look," would not look directly at her.[114] Lane quotes the Koran, which permits a Muslim man to take more than one wife provided that he will treat them all equally; if he cannot do that, he should have just one wife. Such laws allow wealthy Muslims to marry a number of official wives but also keep several concubines – slaves.[115] The women's quarters, the harem, are secluded from other parts of the house, although, as Lane notices, the wives rarely live together under the same roof.[116] Interestingly, even though the law sanctions it, Egyptian men rarely have more than one wife.[117] In the contemporary world, although Muslims are more shocked by the "sexual mores of the West," polygamy is unfashionable in the Westernized environment; nonetheless, marriage contracts often prevent the husband from taking a second wife.[118] At the beginning of the twentieth century, Anna Winterbourne was lucky to find herself in the fold of an enlightened, forward-thinking family, whose male members were not interested in polygamy but in politics.

Some decades earlier, like all European travelers to the Orient, Richard Burton also tackled the issue of polygamy, to which he is not typically averse; on the contrary, he admires the organization of social life in which a husband has to provide separate apartments for each of his wives, "unless as sometimes happens, one be an old woman and the other a child," and suggests that only in polyandry are "the quarrels about the sex . . . the exception and not the rule of life."[119] Not only polygamy itself but first and foremost the *s*-word must have been quite deplorable to his Victorian audience. Equally shocking was his

---

114 Soueif, *Map of Love*, 141.
115 Lane, *Modern Egyptians*, 85. Lane quotes the Koran, chapter iv, v. 3. He also talks about the laws concerning the marriage between a Muslim man and a Christian woman (86).
116 Lane, *Modern Egyptians*, 120–21.
117 Lane, *Modern Egyptians*, 163.
118 Glassé, *Contemporary Encyclopedia of Islam*, 415.
119 He recognizes, however, that "[p]olygamy is indispensable in a country where children are the principal wealth." Burton, *First Footsteps*, 1:85. He sees it as a result of poverty and civilizational lag. While monogamy is the growth of civilization, more primitive societies value the man with a big strong family the most. Seeing this, he also deprecates the Somali way of life: "After the early breakfast, the male portion of the community leave their houses on business, that is to say, to chat, visit, and *flaner* about the streets and mosques. They return to dinner and the siesta, after which they issue forth again and do not come home till night. Friday is always an idle day, festivals are frequent, and there is no work during weddings and mournings" (1:87–88). The women begin at dawn, superintending slaves in their housework and food preparation.

discussion of the "harem." Instead of disparaging the idea of "the harim," as he spells it, he sees it as no different from the European arrangement of a family composed of a wife and the wife's mother.[120] What is drastically dissimilar is the punishment for adultery, which in Burton's England was a cause for divorce and social ostracism but, in what he calls the Koranic law, is punishable by lapidation. The harsh sentence was perhaps the reason why the women in Al-Madinah behave "with great decency,"[121] as Burton explains, even so, he refrains from commenting on the punishments, which were seen as outrageously backward and uncivilized in the West. Instead, he pays attention to marriage customs, quoting the Arab saying that "marriage is joy for a month and sorrow for a life."[122]

Comparably to Burton, Doughty saw polygamy amongst nomad women, frequently malnourished and bearing few children, as a way to survive. "The woman's sex is despised by the old nomad and divine law in Moses." What is more, he discloses that in the "olden time of heathen ignorance" there was a custom of burying "maid-children living," the practice suggestive of the more frequent birth of girls.[123] A woman always wears the hijab, being afraid "that her husband might say the word of divorce."[124] He also notes that the daughters of the tribe are guarded in their virginity, but if they have to go into the wilderness with their flocks, no young man would ever do harm. "It were in all their eyes harrâm, a breach of the desert faith and the religion of Islam; the guilty would be henceforth unworthy to sit amongst men, in the booths of the Aarab."[125] To strengthen his tale, Doughty reports an incident involving his servant, Mohammed, who married a girl-wife. When he beat her, she ran away, and so was to be sent back to her family in disgrace. Before that happened, she approached Doughty, asking him whether he "would not receive her in marriage."[126] Like Burton, Doughty was convinced that in Arabia, the lives of women were quite insignificant, yet Victorian writers habitually used oriental metaphors to buttress their own masculinity.

---

120 Burton, *Personal Narrative*, 2:91.
121 Burton uses the expression "the Koranic law." Burton, *Personal Narrative*, 2:19.
122 Burton, *Personal Narrative*, 2:22. De Gobineau devotes some space to the issues of marriage and the Koran, claiming that Mohammed wanted girls to be married not earlier than age fifteen; he also wanted to insure their religious (and therefore moral) instruction; it is the poets who make their heroines younger than age fourteen to show them in the flower of their beauty because they are not concerned with their moral development. De Gobineau, *Inequality*, 123–24.
123 Doughty, *Arabia Deserta*, 1:239.
124 Doughty, *Arabia Deserta*, 1:465.
125 Doughty, *Arabia Deserta*, 1:322, spelling original.
126 Doughty, *Arabia Deserta*, 1:374.

The markedly inferior position of Muslim women in marriage worries Lord Cromer in Soueif's novel. Although harsh in his attitude, Cromer was simply trying to safeguard Anna's interests by laying emphasis on the need to incorporate the clause against polygamy in the marriage contract. "[T]he young women we find wandering about," Cromer cautions, "having contracted such marriages. They will tell you of their condition."[127] Anna is flabbergasted by such a request, but Sharif patiently and politely explains that that is already in the contract.[128] The Agency offers no refreshments, Lord Cromer does not shake Sharif's hand, and no pleasantries are exchanged. The marriage looks like a bargain, an unwilling sale of an English bride to a barbarous, lowly Muslim. Little does the young couple know that, like the mismatched marriage of Othello and Desdemona, their happiness is also doomed. Still, Anna suffers the criticism bravely so that their nuptial will be recognized in Britain. During the ceremony, Lord Cromer over and over again tries to warn Anna against the pitfalls of a union with a Muslim. He points to their divergent cultural and religious backgrounds, seeing race and religion as major obstacles to Anna's lasting happiness, but neither Anna nor Sharif pay attention to his admonitions. Quite the opposite: Anna almost seamlessly adjusts to her new life and a new role, and as the years pass, incessantly expresses her love for Sharif, and her new family.

Choosing to live with her in-laws, Anna fits into the household routines perfectly, spending time with her mother-in-law, her sister-in-law Layla, and Layla's young son Ahmed. When her father-in-law returns from his "retreat" – having, in reality, hidden from the colonial authorities because of some unspecified accusations against him and his family – he is a broken man. Surprisingly, the old man takes to Anna, with whom he does not have to talk as neither of them knows the other's language. It is because of him that Anna begins to learn Arabic. Anna also shares kitchen duties with her mother-in-law Zainab Hanim and takes up silk tapestry weaving; eventually, she falls pregnant. The only conflict between Anna and Sharif occurs when Anna, still very much a Western woman, goes to the bank by herself to withdraw money. Sharif is furious when he finds out. Anna is tearful, not understanding his anger. It is Layla who explains to her, "If you use your own money, Anna, you are accusing him of negligence, or of being miserly. Or you lay yourself open to the charge of having some secret expense which you cannot divulge to him."[129] They make up and

---

127 Soueif, *Map of Love*, 321.
128 The contracts signed on May 23, 1901, are written in Arabic and French and include the bride-price as well as the conditions for divorce should Sharif Basha take another wife Soueif, *Map of Love*, 319.
129 Soueif, *Map of Love*, 352.

promise to be patient with one another, alleviating their first and only quarrel. Otherwise, in Anna's diary and letters we find only the many different Arabic names for *love*, and admiration for the country and people that accepted her as their own.[130] She even refuses to go to England to give birth to their child and instead stays in Egypt, giving herself over to the attention of Egyptian ladies. Their child, Nur-al-Hayah, the light of their lives, receives the best possible care where Anna is – with her family. She does not long to celebrate Christmas in a Christian Church; she is more inclined to celebrate Ramadan. With a husband, a child, a home, and an extended family, Anna's immersion into Egyptian life is complete. It is, however, as untypical as it is romantic.

Yet another Romantic element in the novel, is the myth of the origins of a nation, which Soueif seeks to articulate against the mayhem of the early twentieth century historical events having Anna comment on the current political situation. As Anna gives birth to a child in mid-1905, Egypt is swept up in the Entente Cordiale, which granted France a free hand in Morocco and Britain a free hand in Egypt. The result of the agreement was the limitation of the power of the Khedive, who instead of becoming a true viceroy of Egypt was relegated to the role of a pawn of the colonial power.[131] In this way, the Entente agreement has cast on a shadow Egypt's freedom. Working for the benefit of her adopted country together with other ladies, Anna sets up a hospital and has high hopes for the establishment of a school of art and a university.[132] All of this finds its way into Anna's letters to her former father-in-law, Sir Charles Winterbourne, in England. Anna reports the events of Denshawai in June 1906. The persecution, unfair trials, prison sentences, and execution of the perpetrators shake her greatly. The incident, which started with clashes between British officers who were pigeon shooting and the local Denshawai villagers in Menufeyya province, led to an unforeseeable conclusion. What began as a brawl ended in the death of some officers. The whole occurrence laid bare evident anger against the British occupation in Egypt. Anna herself is engaged in the movement supporting Egypt's autonomy; writing to Sir Charles Winterbourne, she urges him to present the Egyptian cause to his friends in the British Parliament.[133] In a letter to Sir Charles of December 30, 1901, she indicates a Mr. Blunt,

---

130 Soueif, *Map of Love*, 386–87.
131 Peter Mansfield gives an outline of the British presence in Egypt between 1882 and 1914. Mansfield, *A History*, 85–113.
132 The first secular Egyptian University was funded through public donations in 1908. Soueif, *Cairo*, 9.
133 Soueif, *Map of Love*, 447–48.

who "has been much in the news here."[134] Soueif alludes to a fox hunt, in which some English gentleman rode over Blunt's land. The episode is known as "the Egyptian Garden scandal." Blunt played an important role, as his staff chased off the hunters, being afraid that their shouts and shooting would scare the very valuable Arabian horses that Blunt bred. The officers were not in uniforms, and they did trespass on Blunt's land, yet Blunt's Egyptian servants were accused of assaulting the British and consequently were imprisoned. Nevertheless, Anna sees a positive side to the incident:

> Mr Blunt, it would appear, intends to use this event to bring about a change in the law, a change that would be much favoured here, as this business of hunting across cultivated land – for every inch of land that is not desert here is cultivated – does much damage and is a cause of constant grievance to both fellaheen and landowners.[135]

Wilfrid Scawen Blunt (1840–1922) was, in fact, one of the few colonial administrators sympathetic to the Arab fight for freedom. His involvement and views were recorded in his *Secret History of the English Occupation of Egypt: Being a Personal Narrative of Events*, published originally in 1895.

In Soueif's novel, it is evident that Anna's correspondence becomes more politically conscious after her marriage to Sharif. She no longer reports facts about her domestic life but instead observes and comments on the internal politics in Egypt. Although readers are not presented with replies from her correspondents, she comes across as a well-informed, politically engaged woman who enjoys Sir Charles's accounts of various confrontations in Parliament as much as news of her friend's Caroline's family life. As Sharif's wife, Anna is strikingly more open than an Egyptian wife would be, and thus appears more progressive than she would have been in reality, even though she does witness momentous events. Before the First World War, the Arab world was the site of various political upheavals, for example, the war between Russia and Japan in

---

134 Soueif, *Map of Love*, 382.
135 Soueif, *Map of Love*, 382–83. In 1881, Blunt met an Egyptian called Arabi El Wahid (the Only One) and narrates the story in his *Secret History*. Blunt's genuine admiration for Egyptian culture and sympathy toward the Egyptian autonomy, under the slogan "Egypt for the Egyptians," earned him Arabi's friendship. Blunt's work is heavily influenced by the British politics of the late Victorian period and its relations with the Ottoman Empire. Yet he is one of the few colonial officers who saw past Britain's interests in the East. He shows greater understanding and compassion toward the poverty of the people (11–21). He appreciates the *fellah* (Arab peasants') hospitality (10) and sees various problems with Arabs as being the result of "our ignorance of the rules and customs of the desert" (25). Blunt's narrative was republished by the Arab Centre for Research and Publishing in Cairo in 1980 to mark the centenary of the Arab Revolution (1881–1981).

1905, and the Turkish revolution in 1908 coupled with the freedom as well as socialist movements in Europe and elsewhere. By 1906, Anna secretly hopes that an uprising is about to happen, and she both rejoices and worries for her husband, an engaged Egyptian nationalist. She knows that, despite his declarations that he would be happiest at home with her and Nur, he could never be fully divorced from politics. Sharif Basha understands the allure that the East holds for Europeans being a market for European goods and technology but also a vast store of religious and historical attractions. In order to reconnoiter its bounty and advance the rapport between the East and the West, he believes, Egypt has to be free "to choose those elements that most suited our own history, our traditions and aspirations – that is the legitimate commerce of humanity."[136] Sharif Basha's analysis of Egyptian–European relations was to be published in Egypt, in England and in France. Shortly after the article appears in Egypt, he is assassinated. The reasons for his demise are never openly revealed, only speculated upon. What is even more mysterious, before he died, Sharif forbade his friends and family to search for his murderers or to make use of his death, so the perpetrators are never found. His family are left with their own guesswork. Anna, dejected and alone once again, returns to England with her young daughter Nur, never to set foot in Egypt again. On the one hand, she sees her voluntary exile to her native country as fulfilling her husband's wishes; on the other, she finally realizes that she was also a victim of her blind optimism.

Anna's naive fascination with Egyptian culture and the Egyptian people leads her to ignore the dangers of the nascent freedom movements, coupled with anarchist and anti-government forces, which she likewise disregards. Unduly punished for her idealism with the loss of the husband she adored, and the country which had become her adoptive homeland, Anna becomes an emblem of the new British presence in Egypt. She is no longer an *ajanabee* but an Egyptian who has no interest in the dealings of the Agency, let alone the new Lady Cromer.[137] Anna counters prejudice with elucidations concerning the sophistication and worldliness of a matinee in a Cairo salon, held by a woman whom Anna thought was a niece of Muhammad Ali: "quite old – in age but not at all in spirit."[138] Muhammad Ali was one of the most important figures in the nineteenth-century history of Egypt and its fight against the Ottoman Empire. Although his dreams, "except for possession of Sudan," clashed with the

---

136 Soueif, *Map of Love*, 484.
137 Soueif, *Map of Love*, 383.
138 Soueif, *Map of Love*, 245.

"combined European and Ottoman pressure," as Peter Mansfield argues, "he nevertheless left his successors a cohesive semi-independent state whose strategic position gave it considerable importance in the eastern Mediterranean."[139] He was an innovator and a reformer who initiated one of the first industrialization programs outside Europe. He also created the first peasant army in the Middle East, equipping it with weapons and textiles. Recognizing the importance of education, he set up a translation bureau to publish European books and technical manuals in Arabic.[140] No wonder meeting one of his successors so impresses Anna, who sees in Egypt a thriving and organized society rather than one undeservedly called by Lord Cromer a "subject race," incapable of governing themselves.[141] The "international" modernity of the gathering indeed overwhelms Anna. She becomes convinced of the injustice of British hegemony in Egypt. When Sharif Basha is trying to raise local funds for a museum, an art school, and a university – the latter, in particular, opposed by Governor Cromer – he realizes, "Not a piastre of state money will they get as long as Cromer is in power. "The budget does not permit . . . the British Agent repeats and repeats."[142] In fact, the historical Cromer had no interest in the spread of education above the elementary level. Having spent some time in India, he was certain that higher education would produce a class of unhappy natives who would not fit into their own society. "British brains and Arab hands is Cromer's recipe for Egypt," as Sharif Basha concludes.[143] The historical Cromer thus terminated Muhammad Ali's policy of providing free education in state schools and colleges, which was readily transferred to "*kuttabbs*, the Koranic schools and *madrashas*, attached to the mosques."[144] Authoritarian in his rule in Egypt, intent on the methodical imposition of the English culture, and yet a believer in the *laissez-faire* policy,[145] Cromer did not see the dangers of religious education, which would become one of the pillars of a free Egypt. The national and nationalistic return to the religious basis of Egypt's identity incurred yet another

---

139 Mansfield, *History of the Middle East*, 85. According to Mansfield, Muhammad Ali (1769–1849) was not an Egyptian; he never spoke Arabic but in 1905 decided to make Egypt his power base (47). Mansfield credits Ali with development of the concept of an Arab nation (61). Ali established his family's hereditary rule over Egypt and the Sudan, and his dynasty would rule until 1952, when the revolution brought down the monarchy. Rogan, *The Arabs*, 83.
140 Rogan, *The Arabs*, 83.
141 Mansfield, *History of the Middle East*, 103.
142 Soueif, *Map of Love*, 261.
143 Soueif, *Map of Love*, 262.
144 Mansfield, *History of the Middle East*, 103, 104.
145 Mansfield analyzes the later Pan-Islamic movements and the issues of the Suez Canal. Mansfield, *History of the Middle East*, 106–7.

process, that of the fetishization of difference and otherness of the colonized subjects, the two concepts originating alongside the Egyptian freedom movements.

Tackling so many different aspects of the private and public lives of individuals, Soueif's novel is indeed a map, helping them, and us as readers, navigate the past, and guiding us through the present. The trunk, described as Pandora's box, also functions as the family's scrapbook, containing diaries, letters, and newspaper clippings. In this way, manifold vivid narratives are conjoined through objects and people and have to be read against and through one another. *The Map of Love* is an engrossing and enjoyable romance. It is also a cautionary parable with a historical background, containing a serious discussion regarding colonization and confronting racism. Soueif verbalizes the hitherto suppressed narratives of power relations, poverty, and economic lag, aside from the long-lasting effects of European cultural and economic conquests.[146] The typical nineteenth-century quest romance – a genre both mimicked and complicated by the author in order to convey harsh political indictments even as it narrates a lush tale of cross-cultural passion and adventure – turns into a multilayered postcolonial novel, predictably repudiating colonial representations of Egypt. The use of different literary modes to describe reality – travelogues, autobiographies, letters, and travel guides – enhances the representation of the various levels of cultural encounters. The novel, despite being dominated by Soueif's postcolonial attitudes, offers an exegesis of the British Egyptian conflict, the macrocosm seen through the microcosmic individual view. Through the voice of Anna, the Englishwoman, she inscribes the unforgiving criticism against the Empire, thereby commenting on the pervading cultural stereotypes as well as on the arrogance of the Europeans in their relations with non-Europeans.

We find analogous superciliousness in the colonial politics of France exposed in Moore's *The Magician's Wife*. Both Moore as well as Soueif created fiction in which the conventional encounters between the Occident and Orient are reversed: it is not the Arabs but the Europeans who are the barbarians. Narrated against the backdrop of historical events and featuring historical characters, the said novels undermine the power relations by awarding women dominant voices, depicting them as entranced by Algeria and Egypt respectively. For both heroines, the journey to Arabia is a life-altering experience, and both are accidentally entangled in freedom movements with which they sympathize. Their enchantment with the Orient prompts Emmeline to (almost) fall for the Moorish

---

[146] A contemporary novel by Jacky Trevane, *Fatwa: Living with a Death Threat*, published in 2005, is based on the true story of her marriage to an Egyptian and the physical and psychological abuse she had to endure once the romance was over. The book was published in 2005 but concerns events of the late 1980s.

version of Colonel Deniau, and Anna Winterbourne to become Anna Hanim Haram Sharif Basha al-Baroudi.¹⁴⁷ As they find themselves far away from home, it seems that the *Ajanabee*, the Christian women desiring Arabian men, are unmindful of St. Peter's warning: "I beseech you as strangers and pilgrims, abstain from lusts, which war against the soul" (I Peter 11).

---

147 Soueif, *Map of Love*, 324.

Conclusion

In a romantic comedy entitled *My Big Fat Greek Wedding* from 2002, directed by Joel Zwig and starring Nia Vardalos and John Corbett, the father, Gus Portokalos (played by Michael Constantine), mourns the fact that his daughter Toula (Nia Vardalos) wants to marry not a Greek (or rather, an American of Greek extraction) but a *"xeno,"* a stranger.[1] The fear or dislike of strangers, the ill-reputed barbarians; the word for the Greeks meaning anyone not speaking Greek, was bequeathed to the rest of Europe alongside the concept of democracy. As Tabish Khair aptly expounds, this ancient xenophobia may have changed meaning and form over time,[2] but the concept remains with us, unyieldingly associating the foreigner with linguistic and, more recently, racial alterity. Analyzing fluctuations of the transformation of the old into new xenophobia, Khair notices an interesting inversion: Jews were "segregated and tagged under old xenophobia, Muslims are put under pressure *not* to tag themselves or to segregate under new xenophobia."[3] The lack of, or rather the impossibility of, complete assimilation renders them permanent strangers. For Khair, "The stranger, under new xenophobia, remains a stranger but is not allowed to exhibit signs of his/her difference."[4] This does not comport with the slogan "live and let live," even though on each side there are enough good sentiments to keep peace and more than enough ill will to reinforce uproar and provoke terror. What Khair calls the new xenophobia, however, can be detected in the trope of the medieval Saracen Other depicted in the so-called Saracen romances, and in particular in *The King of Tars*. The text epitomizes the Western dream of the containment of Islam, as the black Muslim sultan, through baptism, is literally transformed into a white Christian, and as a result forces the conversion of his people to what he now recognizes as a supreme religion, Christianity. Contrariwise, Muslim jihad, from the sixth century onward, also tendered conversion and submission over death. The contemporary world inherited the categorization of "us" and "them."

Such divisions were perpetrated by medieval, nineteenth-, and twentieth-century writings, instigating a certain way of looking at the rest of the world. Both good sentiments and ill will proved to be fertile ground for fictional and

---

[1] Interestingly, Asma quotes the primate biologist Frans de Waal, who claims that the demonization of others can be observed in primate communities. In de Waal's view, chimpanzees are xenophobic. Perceiving others as monsters "brings out monstrous reactions" of brutality toward strangers. Asma, *On Monsters*, 239.
[2] Khair, *The New Xenophobia*, 30–38.
[3] Khair, *The New Xenophobia*, 37 (italics original).
[4] Khair, *The New Xenophobia*, 36.

non-fictional works; memoirs and travel narratives mostly re-inscribed the fear of the weird and wonderful, the dangerous, the unpredictable element of the Muslim world. While the earlier medieval voyages and pilgrimages were inspired by the need to fulfill one's spiritual obligations and included a visit to the holy city of Jerusalem, sadly still in the hands of "unbelievers," early modern and, later, eighteenth- and early nineteenth-century travels also encompass the educational and recreational elements. Learning about the culture as well as history and literature of these countries visited were the fixed objectives of such voyages; their mode of writing unwittingly stressed the contrasts between home and abroad, the advanced West and the underdeveloped East. In medieval as well as nineteenth-century and contemporary literature, human ignorance has frequently turned the unknown into a bogeyman, the visual representation of fear multiplied by a lack of knowledge.

From the late 1980s, militant Islamism began to replace the collapsed communism as the new "antagonist." This occurred despite the fact that the West has always bought Iranian and Saudi oil; however, Western powers approved of neither Ayatollah Khomeini's iron-fist rule nor the Saud dynasty's autocracy, and the East has long regarded Western democracies as degenerative, breeding human spiritual misery. The philosophies of mutual animosity were reanimated by politicians in the post-9/11 and post-7/7 turmoil. Reductionist as it may seem, such mindsets revealed, among others, two important issues: first, that the division between East and West has continued since the Crusades, their legacy immortalized in the contemporary so-called "holy war discourse"; and second, that Western identity is relentlessly constructed through the enemies–allies paradigm. As a result of centuries of contact and conflict, European literature and culture has been inundated with multifarious, yet mostly negative, versions of the inhabitants of the East, from the sinful medieval Saracens to the blatant nineteenth-century enemies of Christians. Muslims – not only Islamic fundamentalists – become the new savages, almost never noble, akin to various aliens threatening the civilized (human) world in contemporary science fiction.

In recent years, the demonization of Osama bin Laden and then Saddam Hussein fell within these racist frameworks, according to which "Arabs" are unanimously identified with "Islamic Fundamentalists." To some, the ongoing struggle against such images is akin to Don Quixote's duels with windmills. But we should heed Nietzsche's warning: "He who fights monsters should look to it that he himself does not become a monster. And when you gaze long into an abyss, the abyss also gazes into you."[5] Paradoxically, the dread of the cultural

---

5 Nietzsche, *Beyond Good and Evil*, 102.

and religious Other brought back the sense of a community, similar to the medieval idea of *respublica Christiana*, exemplifying the values for which Europe and America were prepared to fight.[6] Whoever they are, the strangers remain "not us," and they have to be prevented from entering Western lands. This has been the objective of European Christianity encapsulated in the powerful image of Alexander the Great, the hero of a number of medieval romances, enclosing the hateful tribes of Gog and Magog beyond the Caspian Sea. The idea of confinement reappeared with Donald Trump's proposal to build a wall on the US–Mexico border and in the recurrent pleas of Greece and Italy to tighten immigration control so as to stop the influx of migrants and refuges into the European Union. No one assumes that the medieval Saracen romances presented a verifiable portrait of Christian–Muslim relations. In showing their Christian champions triumphing over the Saracen giants, they actually revealed the West's anxiety about the Islamic deluge, stoking Europe's most primal fear – that of the barbarians. And, as the twenty-first-century "migration crisis" in Europe shows, not much has changed since the Middle Ages.

There is a correlation between the perception and representation of the Other enacted in various types of texts. Writing, of whatever kind, is never impartial. Medieval Saracen romances, thus, can be read through the forms of "Other Encounters" scrutinized in the previous chapters. Three medieval enemies of Mankind – the World, the Devil and the Flesh – have remained the most potent topoi of European culture and have proven relevant in the contemporary literature, where one can see the World through the lens of immigration, the Devil in the form of religious discontent, and the Flesh as symbolized by the corrupted West, while still opposed to the monstrous East. These concepts fueled the re-creation of the oriental obsession in the twentieth century, plainly leading to the concurrent appreciation and condemnation of Muslim cultures of the past and of today.

The fear of Islam was ultimately confronted and then assuaged after the Siege of Vienna in 1529, the climactic battle between Christian Europe and the Islamic Ottoman Empire, which marked the slow eclipse of the Saracen menace. Consecutively, Christian victories gave way to the altogether different fascination with all things oriental, undermining the confrontational model of history, at least for a while. Seventeenth-century trade inspired eighteenth-century Orientalist studies, which in turn brought about translations of Arabic literature. As the intriguing world of jinns and giants migrated to Europe, it whetted the

---

6 Even though, according to Bernard Lewis, "Islam was the first to make significant progress toward what it perceived as its universal mission, but modern Western civilization is the first to embrace the whole planet." Lewis, *What Went Wrong?* 150.

Western appetite for cultural exploration. In the years following the Napoleonic Wars, the Near and Middle East have been important to Europe on many levels – diplomatic, social, and cultural. Archeological discoveries, greater ease of travel, the heightened interest in oriental art, not to mention the imperial tendencies of European powers that saw the need to rule and direct less-developed nations, were all sparks igniting the fire. The interest in architecture brought about by the Romantic fascination with the outlandish both materialized and fabricated the Orient. Still, the sheer number of literary works, paintings, and architectural designs might involve, at least at on some level, admiration rather than depreciation, and this is what transpires from John Sweetman's work. Victorian quests encouraged colonization, yet the postcolonial enmities (in the historical sense of the period after European colonial rule) are not solely the byproduct of attempted Westernization and secularization of the Arab countries but can be traced back to early medieval disagreements between Christianity and Islam. In the nineteenth century, largely through increased travel, people were both enthralled and repelled by what they saw outside of Europe. In the late twentieth century, the same sentiments gave rise to a renewed interest in the Orient, this time imbued with the knowledge of ethnic and religious alterity.

The genres of travel narrative, history, and fiction cross-fertilize one another, and the writers, artists, and scholars of the past had a tremendous influence on the present-day blooming in the field of Middle-Eastern and Asian or Oriental studies. Even if much British art and literature of the nineteenth century is Orientalist and not oriental, and thus blatantly reestablishes the inaccurate image of the Orient, eminent Victorians such as Richard Burton and Charles Montagu Doughty were among the lucky few who, being able to speak Arabic, could immerse themselves in Arab life, saturating themselves with the culture and religion.[7] Still, Edward Said and Rana Kabbani are dismissive of their efforts, describing such accounts as subjective and non-engaged. The critics accuse Burton and Doughty of writing about Hijaz, for example, without acknowledging that the culture changed through the centuries. "In the Hejaz you can speak about Muslims, modern Islam and primitive Islam without bothering to make distinctions."[8] Although the stereotypes are still embedded in the current perceptions of the East, they are now recognized for what they are in the historical works and travel narratives of the nineteenth century and can serve not only as elucidations of the Orient but also as examples of Victorian literature – in particular, the quest romance.

---

[7] Due to more extended and intimate contacts, Islam in the nineteenth century becomes "real for Western artists and insistent for some." Sweetman, *The Oriental Obsession*, 114.
[8] Said, *Orientalism*, 235.

The nineteenth-century personal narratives, to borrow the term from Burton, can thus be read both as historical accounts based on real journeys and as fiction, romanticizing the encounters with the secretive East. Trying to refrain from ideologizing either of the discourses, the present study has attempted to vindicate the travelers Burton and Doughty – as well as the historians Samuel Green, Arthur Gilman, and David Pryde and also their eminent predecessor, Simon Ockley – not as "imperial" travelers and historians respectively, but as explorers interested in topography, history, and ethnography. If, as L. P. Hartley asserts, "the past is a foreign country," then the historians in question responded to the Victorian interest in race and descent in dissimilar cultures. Their studies, scrutinizing the origins of civilizations and religions, and preoccupied with tracing cultural differences, strengthened the supposedly objective scientific impact of these travel reports but also pointed to dislocation as an inherent aspect of the experience of the foreign. Whereas travelers gave accounts of their own experiences, historians tried to rediscover the past as a lost country,[9] conjectured as well as "re-membered." Stressing the similarities in the development of the East and the West, they also noticed divergences, involuntarily denigrating Islam in their works. Said and Kabbani have attempted to expose and devalue Orientalist myths and anti-Islamic clichés by showing the mechanisms of such falsifications, arguing that, even if unintentionally, the writings contributed to colonial expansion.

Nonetheless, because of the involvement of the Royal Geographical Society, the surveyors' aims were, at least initially, those of discovery and description. Doubtless, Burton and Doughty transformed the genre of travelogue to account for the danger to which they were constantly subject. Akin to the Victorian quest romance, their narratives were the product of nineteenth-century *Arabia deserta* lore, which attracted adventurers – or, rather, Orientalists and Arabists – who believed in their mission of the discovery of a hitherto unknown culture. Though Billie Melman recognizes the educative nature of such journeys, Said sees only the vulturine side, always geared toward occupation and subjugation, in this way fusing the interests of the scholar with those of the colonist.[10] What Said fails to notice, however, is the genuine interest and scholarship of Burton and Doughty, which produced Burton's accounts of his pilgrimage to the "forbidden" cities of Islam and Doughty's "biblical" travels. Doughty was a pioneer

---

9 The quotation was taken partly from Marina Warner's novel *Indigo*: "Dule [the Caliban character] developed an idea of the past that was foreign to the people among whom Sycorax had been born and raised: it was a lost country for him which he wanted to rediscover, whereas for her the past abided, rolling into the present, an ocean swelling and falling back, then returning again." Warner, *Indigo*, 95.
10 Said, *Orientalism*, 235.

ethnographer, and Burton positioned himself as an Arabophile and a rebel against Victorian morality. Hence, the vilification of their research and writings, and a claim that their "Orientalism" encompasses "the antiquarian study of Oriental languages, societies, and peoples, but that as a system of thought it approaches a heterogenous dynamic, and complex human reality from an uncritically essentialist standpoint,"[11] is only partially deserved. Indeed, they are the product of their times, but their aims were to see and understand, not to observe and devalue. Despite the seeming return to stereotypical representations, the rereading of the East has its merits, as it demonstrates, far from the inertia of Western scholarship, the very opposite: the ongoing critique of the premises of Orientalism and the ensuing instability of the East–West juxtaposition.

Rather than refute the adversative depictions, contemporary literature acknowledges the frustrations and challenges of the existing disagreements. Writers such as David Caute and Hanif Kureishi depict failed multiculturalism, whereas Ed Husain's and Mohamed Laroussi El Metoui's works uncover the uncomfortable aspects of Islamism, especially in relation to Arab freedom fighting. What is more, Husain's memoir can be read as a coming-of-age novel that narrates the psychological aspects of teenage rebellion and subsequent radicalization. Though markedly different from Kureishi's take on British racism of the 1960s and 1970s, Husain's experiences of alienation within British society also bring out the fiasco of religious tolerance and multiculturalism.[12] Metoui's narrative, anchored in the history of Tunisian liberation movements and charged with highly emotional responses to the French occupation, elucidates the historical experience of colonialism. Colonialism also lies at the core of the novels of Ahdaf Soueif and Brian Moore, both of which outline pivotal historical moments in the nineteenth-century histories of the East. Their works lay bare the self-interested myths of the Orient as pretexts for exercising and maintaining colonial power. Yet, instead of fossilizing the image of the mysterious impenetrable territory, whose inhabitants are religious fanatics always ready to kill Christians, the novels show people of a different culture protecting their beliefs and their way of life. Soueif and Moore exemplify the most modern trends in cultural studies, assuming cultures as hybrid and heterogenous. Therefore, even though the events of the past are seen as frozen, the reading of history is almost constantly changing. Autobiographical accounts and literary texts hitherto

---

11 Said, *Orientalism*, 333.
12 Said's negativity is deeply ingrained in his own life experiences, offered in the form of a memoir – aptly entitled *Out of Place* – of a Palestinian, born and raised in Egypt, given the Western name Edward, brought up to experience alienation and upper-class dissociation from the land and its people. He felt like a stranger in the country of his parent's choice: too Western for Arabs and too Arab for Westerners. Said, *Out of Place*.

marginalized as unreliable are now treated on a par with so-called historical sources, and as auxiliary to our understanding of the historical processes.

Unlike most recent works on Islam and its representations in medieval literature, the aim of the present study has not been to exclusively reiterate the forms of such depictions; instead it has tried to consider the manifold ways in which the medieval constructions of the Orient in crusading literature migrated and were transformed in postmedieval writings. There is no denying that contemporary culture is shaped by medieval traditions of reading the stranger, but placing the discourses of the West against those of the East forms a dialogic relationship between the monstrous "Others" on both sides of the divide. Rigorous investigations of these encounters enable us to resist the reductionist politics of Orientalism with its insistence on the antithetical representation of the rational, secular, and progressive West in contrast to the irrational, traditional, and backward East. Looking at the myriad texts concerning the East, one cannot fail to notice that the European (re)discovery of the Orient occurred on many levels and within diverse traditions that informed the culture and literature of the periods in question. Written works are like realist paintings: they capture reality through the very subjective vision of an individual, a vision that in the very moment of inception is the essence of the place and combines an image and interpretation. Moreover, their insights are influenced by the cultural and historical writings of their times. Peter Burke in his *Varieties of Cultural History* states that subsequent stages in the development of culture have occurred on a historical axis, observable only from the position of the present, which was the observed past's future.[13] Obvious as it may sound, Burke's statement points to the essential unknowability of the present, which can only be understood from the perspective of the future. The transactions between the past and the present in nineteenth- and twentieth-century European accounts of the Orient constituted an attempt to show correspondences between the medieval visions of the Orient, encoded in romances, and the nineteenth-century travel narratives and histories, alongside twentieth- and early twenty-first-century novels and memoirs. The confluence of history, geography, and literature asserts the prominence of sociopolitical contexts in both the fictional and non-fictional works in question. Not only do they expose their respective attitudes toward the Orient and the Occident but they also encode the transformations of the discourses on the East, thereby reformulating historical descriptions of peoples and cultures.

In the TV version of Paul Scott's adaptation of *The Raj Quartet*, entitled *The Jewel in the Crown*, a British official tells an Indian that British rule in India is based on two pillars, contempt and fear: contempt on the part of the British;

---

[13] Burke, *Varieties of Cultural History*, 3–5.

fear on the part of the Indians. Today's world has reversed that claim. It is the East that is full of contempt for the decadent West and the West lives in fear of terrorist attacks.[14] Each side's grievances hinder the possibility of communication, forming the dark reservoir of hurt and hate. "He who experiences grief / Will never more have clear memory," Honorat Bovet tells us, quoting Boethius.[15] When Francis Bacon wrote about travel as "Travail," he did not necessarily refer his readers to the French word *travaille*, meaning "to work." Yet one travails/travels in time and space – and both have an educational aspect, as the pilgrim enters the space of the sacred, the scholar and the explorer the space of the unknown, and finally the tourist the space of the profane. All such passages are absolutely necessary if we are to build bridges toward a safer future.

---

14 Interestingly, Charles Dance, who plays one of the British Secret Service agents in *The Jewel in the Crown* (1984), is also cast as one of the British officials who has to leave India in 1947, in an adaptation of Salman Rushdie's novel *Midnight's Children* (directed by Deepa Mehta, 2013).
15 Bovet, *Medieval Muslims, Christians, and Jews in Dialogue*, 115.

Bibliography

Aboulela, Leila. *Lyrics Alley*. London: Phoenix, 2010. Reprint, 2011.
Aboulela, Leila. *Minaret*. London: Bloomsbury, 2005. Reprint, 2006.
Abrams, Dominic, Michael A. Hogg, and José M. Marques, eds. *The Social Psychology of Inclusion and Exclusion*. New York: Psychology Press, 2005.
Augustine. *Concerning the City of God Against the Pagans*. Translated by Henry Bettenson. Introduction by John O'Meara. London: Penguin, 1972. Reprint, 1984.
Adams, Percy G. *Travelers and Travel Liars 1660–1800*. New York: Dover Publications, 1962. Reprint, 1980.
Adamson, Peter, and Richard C. Taylor. *The Cambridge Companion to Arabic Philosophy*. Cambridge: Cambridge University Press, 2005. Reprint, 2008.
Ahmad, Aijaz. *In Theory: Classes, Nations, Literatures*. London: Verso, 1992. Reprint, 1994.
Ahmed, Sara. *Strange Encounters: Embodied Others in Post-coloniality*. London: Routledge, 2000.
Alghamdi, Alaa. *Transformations of the Liminal Self*. Bloomington: iUniverse, 2011.
Allen, Charles, ed. *A Glimpse of the Burning Plain: Leaves from the Indian Journals of Charlotte Canning*. Foreword by Lord Harewood. London: Michael Joseph, 1986.
Allen, Rosamund, ed. *Eastward Bound: Travel and Travelers 1050–1550*. Manchester and New York: Manchester University Press, 2004.
Altheide, David L. *Terrorism and the Politics of Fear*. Lanham, MD: Altamira Press, 2006.
Altick, Richard. *Victorian People and Ideas*. New York: W. W. Norton, 1973.
Anderson, Benedict. *Imagined Communities*. London: Verso, 1983. Reprint, 2006.
Anderson, Scott. *Lawrence of Arabia: War, Deceit, Imperial Folly and the Making of the Modern Middle East*. London: Atlantic Books, 2013. Reprint, 2014.
Appelbaum, Robert and Alexis Paknadel. "Terrorism and the Novel, 1970–2001." *Poetics Today* 29, no. 3 (2008): 387–536.
The Arabian Nights: Tales from A Thousand and One Nights. Translated with a Preface and Notes by Sir Richard F. Burton. Introduction by A. S. Byatt. New York: The Modern Library, 1997. Reprint, 2001.
Armstrong, Karen. *The Battle for God in Judaism, Christianity and Islam*. London: Harper Perennial, 2000. Reprint, 2004.
Ashenburg, Katherine. *The Dirt on Clean: An Unsanitized History*. New York: North Point Press, 2007.
Asma, Stephen T. *On Monsters: An Unnatural History of Our Worst Fears*. Oxford: Oxford University Press, 2009.
Ayalon, Ami. *Language and Change in the Arab Middle East*. New York, Oxford: Oxford University Press, 1987.
Bachelard, Gaston. *The Poetics of Space: The Classic Look at How We Experience Intimate Places*. Translated by Maria Jolas. Foreword by John R. Stilgoe. Boston: Beacon Press, 1964. Reprint, 1994.
Bacon, Francis. *Essays and Ancient Fables of Francis Bacon*. New York: Walter J. Black, 1932.
Bacon, Francis. *The Essays*. Edited with an Introduction by John Pitcher. London: Penguin, 1985.
Bacon, Roger. *Opus Maius of Roger Bacon*. 2 vols. Translated by Robert Belle Burke. Philadelphia: University of Pennsylvania Press, 1928.

Ballaster, Ros. *Fabulous Orients: Fictions of the East in England 1662–1785*. Oxford: Oxford University Press, 2005. Reprint, 2007.
Barber, Richard. *Pilgrimages*. Woodbridge, Suffolk: The Boydell Press, 1991. Reprint, 1998.
Bartlett, Robert. *The Natural and the Supernatural in the Middle Ages*. Cambridge: Cambridge University Press, 2008.
Bauman, Zygmunt. *Liquid Times: Living in an Age of Uncertainty*. Cambridge: Polity, 2007. Reprint, 2012.
Bayoumi, Mustafa. *How Does It Feel to Be a Problem? Being Young and Arab in America*. London: Penguin, 2008. Reprint, 2009.
Beal, Timothy K. *Religion and its Monsters*. London: Routledge, 2002.
Beckford, William. *Vathek*. In *Three Gothic Novels*, edited by Peter Fairclough, 149–255. Harmondsworth, Middlesex: Penguin, 1968. Reprint, 1986.
Beg, Tursum. "History of Mehmed the Conqueror." In *Mediterranean Passages: Readings from Dido to Derrida*, edited by Miriam Cooke, Erdağ Göknar, and Grant Parker, 157–58. Chapel Hill: University of North Carolina Press, 2008.
Bharat, Meenakshi. *Troubled Testimonies. Terrorism and the English Novel in India*. New Delhi: Routledge, 2016.
Bharat, Meenakshi. *Shooting Terror. Terrorism in Hindi Films*. Oxford: Routledge, 2020.
Blunt, Wilfried Scaven. *Secret History of the English Occupation of Egypt: Being a Personal Narrative of Events*. Arab Centre for Research and Publishing, 1895. Reprint, 1981.
Boehmer, Elleke. *Colonial and Postcolonial Literature*. Oxford: Oxford University Press, 1995.
Boehmer, Elleke, and Stephen Morton, eds. *Terror and the Postcolonial*. London: Wiley-Blackwell, 2010. Reprint, 2015.
Boethius. *The Consolation of Philosophy*. Translated with an Introduction and Notes by Richard Green. London: Macmillan, 1962.
Bokhari, Raana, and Mohammad Seddon. *The Complete Illustrated Guide to Islam*. London: Hermes House, 2009.
Bone, Drummond, ed. *The Cambridge Companion to Byron*. Cambridge: Cambridge University Press, 2004.
Borges, Jorge Louis. *The Total Library: Non-fiction 1922–1986*. Edited by Eliot Weinberger. Translated by Esther Allen, Jill Levine, and Eliot Weinberger. London: Allen Lane/ Penguin, 2000.
Bovet, Honorat. *Medieval Muslims, Christians, and Jews in Dialogue: The Apparicion Maistre Jehan de Meun of Honorat Bovet*. Edited and translated by Michael G. Hanly. Tempe: Arizona Center for Medieval and Renaissance Studies, 2005.
Breisach, Ernst. *Historiography: Ancient, Medieval and Modern*. Chicago: University of Chicago Press, 1983. Reprint, 1994.
Bridget of Sweden, *The Revelations of Saint Birgitta*. Edited by William Patterson Cumming. EETS o.s. 178. London: Oxford University Press, 1929. Reprint, 1996.
Brodie, Fawn. *The Devil Drives: A Life of Sir Richard Burton*. London: Eland, 1967. Reprint, 2002.
Brontë, Charlotte. *Jane Eyre*. Edited by Margaret Smith with an Introduction and Revised Notes by Sally Suttleworth. Oxford: Oxford University Press, 1969. Reprint, 2000.
Burke, Peter. *Varieties of Cultural History*. Cambridge: Polity Press, 1997.
Burton, Richard F. *First Footsteps in East Africa or, an Exploration of Harar*. 2 vols. New York: Dover Publications, 1856. Reprint, 1987.
Burton, Richard F. *The Lake Regions of Central Africa*. New York: Dover Publications, 1860. Reprint, 1995.

Burton, Richard F. *Personal Narrative of a Pilgrimage to Al-Madinah and Meccah. Volumes I and II*. New York: Dover Publications, 1855. Reprint, 1964.
Bynum, William. *Medicine: A Very Short Introduction*. Oxford: Oxford University Press, 2008.
Byron, George Gordon. *Byron. Poetical Works*. Edited by Frederick Page. A New Edition Revised by John Jump. Oxford: Oxford University Press, 1904. Reprint, 1970.
Cannadine, David. *Ornamentalism: How the British Saw Their Empire*. London: Penguin, 2001. Reprint, 2002.
Capgrave, John. *Ye Solace of Pilgrimes*. Oxford: Henry Frowde Oxford University Press, 1911.
Carlyle, Thomas. *On Heroes, Hero-Worship, and the Heroic in History*. Oxford: Oxford University Press, 1841. Reprint, 1924.
Carroll, David, ed. *The States of "Theory": History, Art, and Critical Discourse*. Stanford: Stanford University Press, 1994.
Caute, David. *Fatima's Scarf*. London: Totterdown Books, 1998.
Clark, Steve, ed. *Travel Writing and Empire: Postcolonial Theory in Transit*. London: Zed Books, 1999.
Chardin, John. *Travels in Persia, 1673–1677*. New York: Dover Publications, 1927. Reprint, 1988.
Chaucer, Geoffrey. *The Canterbury Tales: Nine Tales and the General Prologue: Authoritative Text, Sources and Backgrounds, Criticism*. Selected and edited by V. A. Kolve and Glending Olson. New York: W. W. Norton, 1989.
Comnena, Anna. *The Alexiad of Anna Comnena*. Translated by E. R. A. Sewter. London: Penguin, 1969.
Coetzee, J. M. *The Childhood of Jesus*. London: Vintage, 2013. Reprint, 2014.
Cohen, Jeffrey Jerome, ed. *Cultural Diversity in the British Middle Ages*. New York: Palgrave Macmillan, 2008.
Cohen, Jeffrey Jerome, ed. *Monster Theory: Reading Culture*. Minneapolis: University of Minnesota Press, 1996.
Coleridge, Samuel Taylor. *The Complete Poems*. Edited by William Keach. London: Penguin, 1997.
Conrad, Joseph. *The Secret Agent*. London: Wordsworth Classics, 1907. Reprint, 2000.
Cooke, Miriam, Erdağ Göknar, and Grant Parker, eds. *Mediterranean Passages. Readings from Dido to Derrida*. Chapel Hill: University of North Carolina Press, 2008.
Craig, Patricia. *Brian Moore: A Biography*. London: Bloomsbury, 2002; Reprint, 2005.
Crone, Patricia. *Medieval Islamic Political Thought*. Edinburgh: Edinburgh University Press, 2005.
Dalrymple, William. *The Last Mughal: The Fall of a Dynasty, Delhi, 1857*. London: Bloomsbury, 2009.
Dancygier, Raphaela M. *Immigration and Conflict in Europe*. Cambridge: Cambridge University Press, 2010.
Daston, Lorraine, and Katherine Park. *Wonders and the Order of Nature*. New York: Zone Books, 2001.
Davis, J. G. "Pilgrimage and Crusade Literature." In *Journeys Toward God. Pilgrimage and Crusade*, edited by Barbara N. Sargent-Baur, 1–30. Kalamazoo, MI: Medieval Institute Publications, 1992.
De Certeau, Michel. *Heterologies: Discourse on the Other*. Translated by Brian Massumi. Foreword by Wład Godzich. Minneapolis: University of Minnesota Press, 1997.
De Certeau, Michel. *The Writing of History*. Translated by Tom Conley. New York: Columbia University Press, 1988.

De Gobineau, Arthur. *The Inequality of Human Races*. Preface by George L. Mosse. New York: Howard Fertig, 1999.
De Gobineau, Arthur. *The Moral and Intellectual Diversity of Races: With Particular Reference to Their Respective Influences in the Civil and Political History of Mankind*. Translated with an Introduction and Notes by H. Hotz. Philadelphia: J. B. Lippincott, 1856.
DeMaria, Robert, ed. *British Literature 1640–1789: An Anthology*. London: Blackwell, 1996. Reprint, 2008.
De Montaigne, Michel. *The Complete Essays of Montaigne*. Translated by Donald M. Frame. Stanford, CA: Stanford University Press, 1958. Reprint, 1966.
Doughty, Charles Montagu. *Travels in Arabia Deserta*, 2 vols. New York: Cosimo Classic, 1888. Reprint, 2010.
Douglas, Mary. *Purity and Danger*. London: Routledge, 1966. Reprint, 2002.
Dummett, Michael. *On Immigration and Refugees*. London: Routledge, 2001. Reprint, 2010.
Edgeworth, Maria. *The Absentee*. Edited with an Introduction and Notes by W. J. McCormack and Kim Walker. Oxford: Oxford University Press, 1812. Reprint, 1988.
Eisenstadt, S. N. *Fundamentalism, Sectarianism and Revolution: The Jacobin Dimension of Modernity*. Cambridge: Cambridge University Press, 1999.
Ellis, Markman. *The History of Gothic Fiction*. Edinburgh: Edinburgh University Press, 2000.
Elsner, Jaś, and Joan-Pau Rubiés, eds. *Voyage and Visions: Towards a Cultural History of Travel*. New York: Reaktion Books, 1999.
Erickson, John. *Islam and Postcolonial Narrative*. Cambridge: Cambridge University Press, 1998.
Euben, Roxanne L. *Journeys to the Other Shore: Muslim and Western Travelers in Search of Knowledge*. Princeton, NJ: Princeton University Press, 2006. Reprint, 2008.
Fanon, Franz. "Algeria Unveiled." In *The New Left Reader*, edited by Carl Oglesby. New York: Monthly Review Press, 1969.
Fanon, Franz. *Black Skin, White Masks*. Translated by Richard Philcox. New York: Grove Press, 1952. Reprint, 2008.
Fanon, Franz. *The Wretched of the Earth*. Preface by Jean-Paul Sartre. Translated by Constance Farrington. London: Penguin, 1965. Reprint, 2001.
Faulks, Sebastian. *A Week in December*. London: Vintage, 2009.
Ferdousi. *Księga Królewska [The Royal Book]*. Translated and edited by Władysław Dulęba. Warszawa: Państwowy Instytut Wydawniczy, 1981.
Fergusson, Niall. *Empire: How Britain Made the Modern World*. London: Penguin, 2003. Reprint, 2004.
Finkel, Caroline. *Osman's Dream: The Story of the Ottoman Empire 1300–1923*. London: John Murray, 2005. Reprint, 2006.
Flaubert, Gustave, and George Sand. *The Correspondence*. Translated by Francis Steegmuller and Barbara Bray. London: The Harvill Press, 1999.
Four Middle English Romances: Sir Isumbras, Octavian, Sir Eglamour of Artois, Sir Tryamour. Edited by Harriet Hudson. TEAMS Middle English Texts Series. Kalamazoo, MI: Medieval Institute Publications, 1996.
Franzen, Allen J. *Desire for Origins: New Language, Old English, and Teaching the Tradition*. New Brunswick: Rutgers University Press, 1990.
Fraser, Hilary, and Daniel Brown. *English Prose of the Nineteenth Century*. London: Pearson Education, 1997. Reprint, 2002.
Fraser, Robert. *Victorian Quest Romance: Stevenson, Haggard, Kipling and Conan Doyle*. Plymouth: Northcote House in association with the British Council, 1998.

Friedman, John Block. *The Monstrous Races in Medieval Art and Thought*. New York: Syracuse University Press, 1981. Reprint, 2000.
Frye, Northrop. *Anatomy of Criticism: Four Essays*. Princeton, NJ: Princeton University Press, 1957. Reprint, 1971.
Fumagalli, Vito. *Landscapes of Fear: Perceptions of Nature and the City in the Middle Ages*, translated by Shayne Mitchell. Cambridge: Polity Press, 1994. Reprint, 2007.
Ganim, John M. "Framing the West, Staging the East." In *Hollywood in the Holy Land: Essays on Film Depictions of the Crusades and Christian–Muslim Clashes*, edited by Nickolas Haydock and E. L. Risden, 31–46. Jefferson, NC: McFarland, 2009.
Ganim, John M. *Medievalism and Orientalism*. London: Palgrave, 2005.
Gascoigne, Bamber. *A Brief History of the Great Moghuls*. New York: Carroll and Graf Publishers, 1971. Reprint, 2002.
Gerteiny, Alfred G. *The Terrorist Conjunction: The United States, The Israeli–Palestinian Conflict and Al-Qā'ida*. Westport, CT: Praeger Security International, 2007.
Gikandi, Simon. *Maps of Englishness: Writing Identity in the Culture of Colonialism*. New York: Columbia University Press, 1996.
Gilman, Arthur. *The Saracens: From the Earliest Times to the Fall of Baghdad*. London: T. Fisher Unwin, 1886.
Girouard, Mark. *The Return to Camelot: Chivalry and the English Gentlemen*. New Haven, CT: Yale University Press, 1981.
Glassé, Cyril. *The Concise Encyclopedia of Islam*. London: Stacey International, 1989. Reprint, 2008.
Grace, Daphne. *The Woman in the Muslin Mask*. London: Pluto Press, 2004.
Green, Samuel. *The Life of Mahomet: Founder of the Religion of Islam and of the Empire of the Saracens*. London: T. Tegg, 1840.
Greenfield, Stanley B., and Daniel G. Calder, eds. *A New Critical History of Old English Literature*. New York: New York University Press, 1986.
Griffiths, Ralph. *The Fourteenth and Fifteenth Centuries*. Oxford: Oxford University Press, 2003.
Hadfield, Andrew, ed. *Amazons, Savages and Machiavels: Travel and Colonial Writing in English, 1550–1630*. Oxford: Oxford University Press, 2001.
Hale, David G. *The Body Politic*. The Hague: Mouton, 1971.
Hamaguchi, Keiko. "The Cultural Otherness in the Man of Law's Tale." *The Chaucer Review* 54, no. 4 (2019): 411–40.
Hamilton, Paul. *Historicism*. London: Routledge, 1996.
Haydock, Nickolas, and E. L. Risden, eds. *Hollywood in the Holy Land: Essays on Film Depictions of the Crusades and Christian–Muslim Clashes*. Jefferson, NC: McFarland, 2009.
Hays, Mary. *Memoirs of Emma Courtney*. Edited with an Introduction and Notes by Eleanor Ty. Oxford: Oxford University Press, 1996. Reprint, 2000.
Heater, Derek. *Citizenship: The Civic Ideal in World History, Politics and Education*. London: Longman, 1990.
Hebron, Malcolm. *The Medieval Siege: Theme and Image in Middle English Romance*. Oxford: Clarendon Press, 1997.
Heffernan, Thomas J. *Sacred Biography: Saints and Their Biographers in the Middle Ages*. Oxford: Oxford University Press, 1988.
Heng, Geraldine. *The Invention of Race in the European Middle Ages*. Cambridge: Cambridge University Press, 2018. Reprint, 2019.

Higgins, Iain Macleod. *Writing East: The Travels of Sir John Mandeville*. Philadelphia: University of Pennsylvania Press, 1997.
Hiro, Dilip. *The Essential Middle East: A Comprehensive Guide*. New York: Carroll and Graf, 1996. Reprint, 2003.
Hodges, Adam. *The "War on Terror" Narrative: Discourses and Intertextuality in the Construction and Contestation of Sociopolitical Reality*. Oxford: Oxford University Press, 2011.
Hoffman, Bruce. *Inside Terrorism*. New York: Columbia University Press, 2006.
Hogg, James. *The Private Memoirs and Confessions of a Justified Sinner*. Cologne: Könemann, 1999.
Horgan, John. "Leaving Terrorism Behind: An Individual Perspective." In *Terrorists, Victims and Society*, edited by Andrew Silke, 8–23. Chichester: Atrium, 2003. Reprint, 2006.
Howard, Philip, N. *The Digital Origins of Dictatorship and Democracy: Information Technology and Political Islam*. Oxford: Oxford University Press, 2011.
Hulme, Peter, and Tim Youngs, eds. *The Cambridge Companion to Travel Writing*. Cambridge: Cambridge University Press, 2002. Reprint, 2011.
Huntington, Samuel P. *The Clash of Civilizations and the Remaking of the World Order*. New York: Simon and Schuster, 1997.
Husain, Ed. *The Islamist: Why I Joined Radical Islam in Britain, What I Saw Inside and Why I Left*. London: Penguin, 2007.
Inayatullah, Naeem, ed. *Autobiographical International Relations*. London: Routledge, 2011.
Irwin, Robert. *The Arabian Nights: A Companion*. London: Penguin, 1994. Reprint, 1995.
Irwin, Robert, ed. *Night and Horses and the Desert: An Anthology of Classical Arabic Literature*. New York: Anchor Books, 1999.
Jeal, Tim. *Stanley: The Impossible Life of Africa's Greatest Explorer*. London: Faber and Faber, 2007. Reprint, 2008.
Jeffers, Robert J., and Ilse Lehiste. *Principles and Methods for Historical Linguistics*. Cambridge, MA: The MIT Press, 1979. Reprint, 1980.
Johnson, Samuel. *The History of Rasselas, Prince of Abissinia*. Edited with an Introduction by D. J. Enright. London: Penguin, 1976. Reprint, 1986.
Jordanus, Catalani, Bishop of Columbus. Mirabilia Descripta: *The Wonders of the East*. Translated with a Commentary by Colonel Henry Yule. London: Elibron Classics, 2005.
Kaul, Suvir. *Eighteenth-Century British Literature and Postcolonial Studies*. Edinburgh: Edinburgh University Press, 2009. Reprint, 2010.
Kabbani, Rana. *Imperial Fictions: Europe's Myths of Orient*. London: SAQI, 1986. Reprint, 2008.
Kaylor, Noel Harold, and Richard Scott Nokes, eds. *Global Perspectives on Medieval English Literature, Language and Culture*. Kalamazoo, MI: Medieval Institute Publications, 2007.
Kearney, Richard. *Strangers, Gods and Monsters: Interpreting Otherness*. London: Routledge, 2003. Reprint, 2009.
Keeble, Richard. *Secret State, Silent Press: New Militarism, the Gulf and the Modern Image of Warfare*. London: University of Luton Press, 1997.
Khair, Tabish. *The Gothic, Postcolonialism and Otherness: The Gothic, Postcolonialism and Otherness*. London: Palgrave Macmillan, 2009. Reprint, 2015.
Khair, Tabish. *The New Xenophobia*. Oxford: Oxford University Press, 2016.
Khair, Tabish, Martin Leer, Justin D. Edwards, and Hanna Ziadeh, eds. *Other Routes: 1500 Years of African and Asian Travel Writing*. Oxford: Signal Books, 2006.

Khanmohamadi, Shirin A. *In Light of Another Word: European Ethnography in the Middle Ages.* Philadelphia: University of Pennsylvania Press, 2014.
Khomeini, Ayatollah Ruhollah. *Islamic Government.* Translated by Joint Publications Research Service. Arlington, VA: Manor Books, 1979.
The King of Tars. Edited by Judith Perryman. Heidelberg: Carl Winter Universitätsverlag, 1980.
The Koran: With Parallel Arabic Text. Translated with Notes by N. J. Dawood. London: Penguin, 1956. Reprint, 1990.
Koser, Khalid. *International Migration: A Very Short Introduction.* Oxford: Oxford University Press, 2007.
Kristeva, Julia. *Strangers to Ourselves.* Translated by Leon S. Roudiez. New York: Columbia University Press, 1991.
Kureishi, Hanif. *My Beautiful Laundrette and the Rainbow Sign.* London: Faber and Faber, 1986.
Kureishi, Hanif. *The Black Album.* London: Faber and Faber, 1995.
Kureishi, Hanif. *Dreaming and Scheming: Reflections on Writing and Politics.* London: Faber and Faber, 2002.
Kureishi, Hanif. *Love in a Blue Time.* New York: Simon and Schuster, 1997. Reprint, 1999.
Kureishi, Hanif. *My Ear At His Heart: Reading My Father.* London: Faber and Faber, 2004.
Kureishi, Hanif. "My Son the Fanatic." In Hanif Kureishi, *Love in a Blue Time*, 119–31. New York: Simon and Schuster, 1997. Reprint, 1999.
Lane, Edward William. *An Account of the Manners and Customs of The Modern Egyptians.* London, New York and Melbourne: Ward, Lock, 1835. Reprint, 1890.
Lawrence, James. *The Rise and Fall of the British Empire.* London: Abacus Press, 1994. Reprint, 2011.
Lawrence, T. E. "Introduction." In Charles Montagu Doughty, *Travels in Arabia Deserta*, 2 vols., xxv–xxxv. New York: Cosimo Classic, 1888 Reprint, 2010.
Lazarus, Neil. *The Postcolonial Unconscious.* Cambridge: Cambridge University Press, 2011.
Leask, Nigel. "Byron and the Eastern Mediterranean: Childe Harold II and the 'Polemic of Ottoman Greece.'" In *The Cambridge Companion to Byron*, edited by Drummond Bone, 99–117. Cambridge: Cambridge University Press, 2004.
Leask, Nigel. *Curiosity and the Aesthetics of Travel Writing 1770–1840.* Oxford: Oxford University Press, 2002. Reprint, 2004.
Lefebvre, Henri. *The Production of Space.* Translated by Donald Nicholson-Smith. London: Blackwell Publishing, 1991. Reprint, 2005.
Legassie, Shayne Aaron. *The Medieval Invention of Travel.* Chicago: University of Chicago Press, 2017.
Le Goff, Jacques. *The Medieval Imagination.* Translated by Arthur Goldhammer. Chicago: University of Chicago Press, 1992. Reprint, 1988.
Lester, G. A., ed. *Three Late Medieval Morality Plays.* London: A. & C. Black, 1981. Reprint, 1999.
Letts, Malcolm. *Sir John Mandeville: The Man and His Book.* London: The Batchworth Press, 1949.
Levi-Strauss, Claude. *Tristes Tropiques.* Translated by John Weightman and Doreen Weightman. London: Penguin, 1955. Reprint, 2011.
Levinas, Emmanuel. *Totality and Infinity: An Essay on Exteriority.* Translated by Alphonso Lingis. Pittsburgh, PA: Duquesne University Press, 1961. Reprint, 2011.
Lewis, Bernard. *The Assassins: A Radical Sect in Islam.* New York: Basic Books, 1968.

Lewis, Bernard. *What Went Wrong? The Clash Between Islam and Modernity in the Middle East.* New York: Harper Perennial, 2002. Reprint, 2003.
Lodge, David. *Therapy.* London: Penguin, 1995.
Lopez, Robert S., and Irving W. Raymond. *Medieval Trade in the Mediterranean World.* Illustrative documents translated with Introductions and Notes by Robert S. Lopez and Irving W. Raymond. New York: Columbia University Press, 1955. Reprint, 1961.
The Macro Plays: The Castle of Perseverance, Wisdom, Mankind. Edited by Marc Eccles. Early English Text Society. Oxford: Oxford University Press. 1969.
Malchow, H. L. *Gothic Images of Race in Nineteenth-Century Britain.* Stanford, CA: Stanford University Press, 1996.
Malette, Karla. *European Modernity and the Arab Mediterranean.* Philadelphia: University of Pennsylvania Press, 2010.
Malthus, Thomas. *An Essay on the Principle of Population.* Edited with an Introduction and Notes by Geoffrey Gilbert. Oxford: Oxford University Press, 1993. Reprint, 2008.
Mancall, Peter, ed. *Travel Narratives from the Age of Discovery: An Anthology.* Oxford: Oxford University Press, 2006.
Mandeville, John. *The Travels of Sir John Mandeville: The Fantastic 14th Century Account of a Journey to the East.* Minneola, NY: Dover Publications, 1964. Reprint, 2006.
Mandeville, John. *Mandeville's Travels.* Edited by M.C. Seymour. Oxford: At the Clarendon Press. 1967.
Mansfield, Peter. *A History of the Middle East.* London: Penguin, 1991. Reprint, 2004.
Marx, C. W. *The Devil's Rights and The Redemption in the Literature of Medieval England.* Cambridge: D. S. Brewer, 1995.
Mason, Michael. *The Making of Victorian Sexuality.* Oxford: Oxford University Press, 1994.
Marcus, Steven. *The Other Victorians. A Study of Sexuality and Pornography in Mid-Nineteenth-Century England.* New York: Basic Books, 1964. Reprint, 1966.
Martin, Philip W. "Heroism and History: *Childe Harold* I and II and the Tales." In *The Cambridge Companion to Byron*, ed. Drummond Bone, 77–98. Cambridge: Cambridge University Press, 2004.
Matar, Nabil, ed. *In the Lands of the Christians: Arabic Travel Writing in the Seventeenth Century.* New York: Routledge, 2003.
McKim, Robert, and Jeff McMahan, eds. *The Morality of Nationalism.* Oxford: Oxford University Press, 1997.
McNeill, John T., and Helena M. Gamer, eds. *Medieval Handbooks of Penance: A Translation of the Principal* Libri Poenitentiales. New York: Columbia University Press, 1938. Reprint, 1990.
Mehl, Dieter. *The Middle English Romances of the Thirteenth and Fourteenth Centuries.* London: Routledge and Kegan Paul, 1968.
Melman, Billie. "The Middle East/Arabia: The 'Cradle of Islam.'" In *The Cambridge Companion to Travel Writing.* Edited by Peter Hulme and Tim Youngs, 105–21. Cambridge: Cambridge University Press, 2002. Reprint, 2011.
Melman, Billie. *Women's Orients: English Women and the Middle East, 1718–1918: Sexuality, Religion and Work.* London: Macmillan, 1992. Reprint, 1995.
Metlitzki, Dorothee. *The Matter of Araby in Medieval England.* New Haven, CT: Yale University Press, 1977.
Metoui, Mohamed Laroussi El. *Halima.* Translated by Hafedh Boujmil. Introduction and bibliography by Lora Lunt. Tunis: Nirvana, 2005.

The Middle English Breton Lays. Edited by Anne Laskaya and Eve Salisbury. TEAMS Middle English Text Series. Kalamazoo, MI: Medieval Institute Publications, 1995.
Mittman, Asa Simon. *Maps and Monsters in Medieval England*. New York: Routledge, 2006. Reprint, 2008.
Moore, Thomas. *Lalla Rookh: Moore's Poems with Notes*. Chicago: The Henneberry Company, n.d.
Moore-Gilbert, Bart. *Postcolonial Theory: Context, Practices, Politics*. London: Verso, 1997. Reprint, 2000.
Moore, Brian. *Black Robe*. London: Flamingo, 1985. Reprint, 1994.
Moore, Brian. *The Catholics*. London: Flamingo, 1972. Reprint, 1996.
Moore, Brian. *The Doctor's Wife*. London: Flamingo, 1976. Reprint, 1994.
Moore, Brian. *The Magician's Wife*. London: Flamingo, 1997. Reprint, 1998.
Morgan, David. *Medieval Persia 1040–1797*. London: Pearson Education, 1988.
Morton, Adam. *On Evil*. New York: Routledge, 2004.
Moryson, Fynes. *An Itinerary . . . Containing His Ten Years Travell*, (1617). In *Amazons, Savages and Machiavels. Travel and Colonial Writing in English, 1550–1630*, edited by Andrew Hadfield, 167–78. Oxford: Oxford University Press, 2001.
Naipaul, V. S. *Among the Believers: An Islamic Journey*. London: Picador, 1981. Reprint, 2003.
Nash, Geoffrey. *Writing Muslim Identity*. London: Continuum, 2012.
Nietzsche, Friedrich. *Beyond Good and Evil*. Translated by R. J. Hollingdale with an Introduction by Michael Tanner. London: Penguin, 1973. Reprint, 2003.
The New Encyclopedia Britannica. Vol. 4. Chicago: Encyclopedia Britannica, 1911. Reprint, 1997.
Newhauser, Richard. *Sin Essays on the Moral Tradition in the Western Middle Ages*. Burlington, VT: Ashgate Variorum, 2007.
North, John. *The Ambassadors' Secret: Holbein and the World of the Renaissance*. London: Phoenix, 2002. Reprint, 2004.
Norton, Rictor, ed. *Gothic Readings: The First Wave, 1764–1840*. London: Leicester University Press, 2000.
Nykl, A. R. *Hispano-Arabic Poetry and its Relations with the Old Provencal Troubadours*. Baltimore: J. H. Furst, 1946. Reprint, 1970.
Ockley, Simon. *The History of the Saracens: Lives of Mohammed and His Successors*. London: George Bell and Sons, 1883.
O'Gorman, Francis. ed. *The Cambridge Companion to Victorian Culture*. Cambridge: Cambridge University Press, 2010.
Omaar, Rageh. *Only Half of Me: British and Muslim: The Conflict Within*. London: Penguin, 2006. Reprint, 2007.
O'Neil, John. *Five Bodies: The Human Shape of Modern Society*. Ithaca, NY: Cornell University Press, 1985. Reprint, 1986.
Page, Frederick, ed. *Byron: Complete Poetical Works*. Oxford: Oxford University Press, 1970.
Pakenham, Thomas. *The Scramble for Africa 1876–1912*. London: Abacus, 1991. Reprint, 2009.
Parry, J. H. *The Age of Reconnaissance: Discovery, Exploration and Settlement*. London: Phoenix Press, 1963. Reprint, 2000.
Peleg, Ian. *Democratizing the Hegemonic State: Political Transformation in the Age of Identity*. Cambridge: Cambridge University Press, 2007.
Phillips, Kathy J. *Manipulating Masculinity: War and Gender in Modern British and American Literature* London: Palgrave Macmillan, 2006.

Pickles, Sheila, ed. *The Grand Tour*. London: Penhaligon, 1991.
Pratt, Mary Louise. *Imperial Eyes: Travel Writing and Transculturation*. London: Routledge, 1992. Reprint, 2006.
Pryde, David. *Great Men of European History: From the Beginning of the Christian Era Till the Present Time*. Edinburgh: William P. Nimmo, 1881.
Qtub, Sayyid. *Milestones*. Edited by A. B. al-Mehri. Birmingham: Maktabah Booksellers and Publishers, 2006.
Rattansi, Ali. *Multiculturalism: A Very Short Introduction*. Oxford: Oxford University Press, 2011.
Rice, Edward. *Captain Sir Richard Burton: A Biography*. Cambridge: Da Capo Press, 1990. Reprint, 2001.
Rogan, Eugene. *The Arabs: A History*. London: Penguin, 2009. Reprint, 2010.
Rousseau, Jean-Jacques. *A Discourse on Inequality*. Translated with an Introduction and Notes by Maurice Cranston. London: Penguin, 1984.
Rousseau, Jean-Jacques. *The Social Contract*. Translated with an Introduction and Notes by Christopher Betts. New Haven, CT: Yale University Press, 1994. Reprint, 2008.
Rushdie, Salman. *The Satanic Verses*. New York: Henry Holt, 1988. Reprint, 1997.
Ruthven, Malise. *Fundamentalism: A Very Short Introduction*. Oxford: Oxford University Press, 2007.
Ruthven, Malise. *Islam: A Very Short Introduction*. Oxford: Oxford University Press, 1997. Reprint, 2000.
Said, Edward. "Afterword (1995)." In Edward Said, *Orientalism: Western Conception of the Orient*. 329–54. London: Penguin. 1991. Reprint, 2003.
Said, Edward. *Covering Islam*. London: Vintage, 1981. Reprint, 1997.
Said, Edward. *Orientalism: Western Conceptions of the Orient*. London: Penguin, 1995.
Said, Edward. *Out of Place: A Memoir*. London: Granta Books, 1999. Reprint, 2000.
Said, Edward. *Reflections on Exile and Other Essays*. London: Granta Books, 2000, Reprint, 2012.
Sambrook, James. *The Eighteenth Century: The Intellectual and Cultural Context of English Literature, 1700–1789*. London: Longman, 1986. Reprint, 1997.
Sampson, Denis. *Brian Moore: The Chameleon Novelist*. Toronto: Doubleday Canada, 1998. Reprint, 1999.
Sargent-Baur, Barbara N., ed. *Journeys Toward God: Pilgrimage and Crusade*. Kalamazoo, MI: Medieval Institute Publications, 1992.
Scanlan, Margaret. *Plotting Terror: Novelists and Terrorists in Contemporary Fiction*. Charlottesville: University Press of Virginia, 2001.
Schoeler, Gregor. *The Genesis of Literature in Islam: From the Aural to the Read*. In Collaboration with and translated by Shawkat M. Toorawa. Edinburgh: Edinburgh University Press, 2009. Reprint, 2011.
Shamsie, Kamila. *Offence: The Muslim Case*. Calcutta: Seagull Books, 2009.
Sharwood-Smith, Joan. *Diary of a Colonial Wife: An African Experience*. London: Radcliffe Press, 1992.
Shaw, George Bernard. *The Doctor's Dilemma, Getting Married and The Shewing up of Posnet*. London: Constable, 1927.
Shilling, Chris. *The Body and Social Theory:* London: Sage Publications, 1993. Reprint, 1994.
Sikorska, Liliana. *Being (Non)Human, or on the Topography of "Monsters" Medieval and Modern* Poznań: Agder Academy Publications, 2016.

Silke, Andrew, ed. *Terrorists, Victims and Society: Psychological Perspectives on Terrorism and its Consequences*. Chichester: Atrium, 2003. Reprint, 2006.
Smelser, Neil J. *The Faces of Terrorism: Social and Psychological Dimensions*. Princeton, NJ: Princeton University Press, 2007.
Soeters, Joseph L. *Ethnic Conflict and Terrorism: The Origins and Dynamics of Civil Wars*. London: Routledge, 2005. Reprint, 2008.
Soueif, Ahdaf. *The Map of Love*. London: Bloomsbury, 1999. Reprint, 2000.
Soueif, Ahdaf. *Cairo. Memoir of a City Transformed*. London: Bloomsbury, 2012. Reprint, 2014.
Southern, R. W. *Western Views of Islam in the Middle Ages*. Cambridge, MA: Harvard University Press, 1962.
Spurr, David. *The Rhetoric of the Empire*. Durham, NC: Duke University Press, 1993.
Stafford, Barbara. *Voyage into Substance: Art, Science, Nature, and the Illustrated Travel Account 1760–1840*. Cambridge, MA: MIT Press. 1984.
Stephens, John Lloyd. *Incidents of Travel in Egypt, Arabia, Petrea, and the Holy Land*. New York: Dover Publications, 1837. Reprint, 1996.
Steyn, Mark. *America Alone: The End of the World As We Know It*. New York: Regency Publishing, 2006.
Strachey, Lytton. *Eminent Victorians*. London: Penguin, 1918. Reprint, 1986.
Strickland, Debra Higgs. *Saracens, Demons, and Jews: Making Monsters in Medieval Art*. Princeton, NJ: Princeton University Press, 2003.
Surratt, Robin, ed. *The Middle East*. Washington, D.C.: CQ Press, 2005.
Sweetman, John. *The Oriental Obsession: Islamic Inspiration in British and American Art and Architecture 1500–1920*. Cambridge: Cambridge University Press, 1988.
Tales from the Thousand and One Nights. Translated with an Introduction by N. J. Dawood. London: Penguin, 1955. Reprint, 1975.
Tales from the Arabian Nights. With Color Plates by A. E. Jackson. London: Ward, Lock, n.d.
The Romance of Guy of Warwick. Edited by J. Zupitza. Oxford: Oxford University Press. Early English Text Society, 1875. Reprint, 1966.
Thackeray, William Makepeace. *Vanity Fair*. Edited with an Introduction by J. I. M. Steward. London: Penguin, 1968. Reprint, 1985.
Thatcher, Oliver J., and Edgar H. McNeal, eds. *A Source Book for Medieval History*. New York: Charles Scribner's Sons, 1905.
Thomas, Nicholas. *Colonialism's Culture: Anthropology, Travel and Government*. Cambridge: Polity Press, 1994.
Thompson, Carl. *Travel Writing*. London: Routledge, 2011.
Three Middle English Charlemagne Romances: The Sultan of Babylon, The Siege of Milan, The Tale of Ralph the Collier. Edited by Alan Lupack. TEAMS Middle English Text Series. Kalamazoo, MI: Medieval Institute Publications, 1990.
Three Turk Plays from Early Modern England: Selimus, A Christian Turned Turk and The Renegado. Edited by Daniel J. Vitkus. New York: Columbia University Press, 1893. Reprint, 2000.
Todorov, Tzvetan. *The Conquest of America*. Translated by Richard Howard. New York: Harper Collins, 1987.
Tucker, Herbert F., ed. *A Companion to Victorian Literature and Culture*. London: Blackwell, 1999.
Turnbull, Stephen. *The Ottoman Empire 1326–1699*. Oxford: Osprey, 2003.
Turner, Bryan S., ed. *Citizenship and Social Theory*. London: Sage, 1993. Reprint, 2000.

Uebel, Michael. "Unthinking the Monster: Twelfth-Century Responses to Saracen Alterity." In *Monster Theory: Reading Culture*, edited by Jeffrey, Jerome Cohen, 264–91. Minneapolis: University of Minnesota Press, 1996.

Urry, John. *The Tourist Gaze: Leisure and Travel in Contemporary Societies*. London: Sage, 1990.

Vincent, Andrew. *Nationalism and Particularity*. Cambridge: Cambridge University Press, 2002.

Walder, Denis. *Post-colonial Literatures in English: History, Language, Theory*. London: Blackwell, 1998.

Walker, Paul E. "The Ismailis." In *The Cambridge Companion to Arabic Philosophy*, edited by Peter Adamson and Richard C. Taylor, 72–91. Cambridge: Cambridge University Press, 2005. Reprint, 2008.

Wallace, David. *Premodern Places: Calais to Surinam, Chaucer to Aphra Behn*. London: Blackwell, 2004; Reprint, 2006.

Warner, Marina. *Fantastic Metamorphoses, Other Worlds*. Oxford: Oxford University Press, 2002. Reprint, 2004.

Warner, Marina. *Indigo, or, Mapping the Waters*. New York: Simon and Schuster, 1992.

Warner, Marina, ed. *Queen Victoria's Sketchbook*. London: Papermac, 1979. Reprint, 1981.

Warner, Marina. *Stranger Magic: Charmed States and the Arabian Nights*. London: Chatto and Windus, 2011.

Watson, Nicola J. *The Literary Tourist*. London: Palgrave Macmillan, 2006.

Welch, Robert. *Groundwork*. Belfast: The Blackstaff Press, 1997.

White, David Gordon. *Myths of the Dog-Man*. Foreword by Wendy Doniger. Chicago: University of Chicago Press, 1991.

White, Hayden. *The Content of the Form: Narrative Discourse and Historical Representation*. Baltimore: Johns Hopkins University Press, 1987. Reprint, 1990.

White, Hayden. *Metahistory: The Historical Imagination in Nineteenth-Century Europe*. Baltimore: Johns Hopkins University Press, 1973. Reprint, 1975.

White, Hayden. *Tropics of Discourse: Essays in Cultural Criticism*. Baltimore: Johns Hopkins University Press, 1978. Reprint, 1985.

White, Hayden. *The Content of the Form: Narrative Discourse and Historical Representation*. Baltimore and London: The Johns Hopkins University Press, 1987. Reprint, 1990.

Wright, Alexa. *Monstrosity: The Human Monster in Visual Culture*. London: I. B. Tauris, 2013.

Wright, Thomas, ed. *Early Travels in Palestine*. Mineola, NY: Dover Publications, 1848. Reprint, 2003.

Young, Robert J. C. Colonial Desire: Hybridity in Theory, Culture and Race. London: Routledge, 1995. Reprint, 2006.

Young, Robert J. C. *Postcolonial Criticism. An Historical Introduction*. London: Blackwell, 2001. Reprint, 2004.

Young, Robert J. C. *White Mythologies*. London: Routledge, 1990. Reprint, 2010.

Index of Names and Terms

Acre VII, VIII
Alexander, romance 6, 215
Alexius I, Emperor 121
Apollo 63, 124, 154
Arabian Nights 23, 24, 25, 26, 30, 39, 46, 98, 134, 151
Augustine, St. 8, 9, 67, 68, 124, 155, 171
Assassins (the sect) 85, 99, 114–116

Bacon, Francis VII, 3, 49, 220
Bacon, Roger 16
Bayoumi, Mustafa 147
Barbarians XXV, 28, 35, 52, 73, 78, 99, 103, 113, 124–125, 136, 148, 152, 211, 213, 215
Beckford, William 30–31, 134
Beduin (see also Badawi) 54–56, 63, 75, 76, 78
Behn, Aphra XX, 27
Blunt, Wilfrid Scaven 68, 195, 200, 207–208
Boethius, Ancius Manlius Severinus 29, 165–166, 187, 189, 190, 193–194, 220
Brontë, Charlotte 34
Burton, Richard Francis. XI, XV, XVI, XVIII, XXI, 9, 10–12, 17, 19, 24–27, 33, 35, 38, 40, 41, 42, 43-68, 70, 74, 79, 82–83, 90, 93, 105 -107, 116, 137, 168, 189, 192, 196–200, 204, 205, 21–218
Byron George Gordon, Lord Byron 14, 28, 31–34, 46

Cannibals XIII, 27
Caute, David X, XII, 123, 127, 135, 136–147, 218
Castle of Perseverance, the (drama) 101, 135, 182
Catalani, Jordanus, Bishop of Columbus 9
Chardin, John 14, 17–20, 25, 93
Chaucer, Geoffrey XIV, XX, 9, 51, 166, 185, 187
Coetzee, J.M. 25, 148
Coleridge, Samuel Tylor 33
Constantinople VII, XII, 13, 14, 31, 49, 110, 165

Crusade(s) VII, VIII, XXIV, 4, 7, 8, 9, 10, 31, 38, 69, 109, 114, 116, 122, 124–125, 131, 136–137, 153, 154, 179, 192
Cynocephali 66, 67, 68
Cyprus 14

Delacroix, Eugène 31
Dogheads, see Cynocephali 66, 67, 68
Doughty, Charles Montague 69–82
Doyle, Arthur, Conan 38

Edgeworth, Maria 16, 22, 133–135

Fanon, Franz 173, 175–178, 185, 188, 193
Flaubert, Gustave 184–185, 190

Galland, Antoine 23, 24, 25
De Gobineau, Arthur XV, XVI, XVII, 24, 74, 79, 99, 197, 205
Gilman, Arthur XVI, XXI, 10, 12, 30, 85, 87, 90, 91, 96–98, 103, 106, 108–114, 116, 217
Gordon, Charles George (General) 195, 200
Grand Tour, The 4, 5, 31
Green, Samuel XVI, XXI, 10, 21, 23, 87, 89, 90, 95, 98, 99, 104, 133, 107, 110–113, 115–117, 168, 217
Gordon, George, Lord Byron see Byron

Hawksmoor, Christopher 23
Haggard, Henry Rider 38
Hajj 43, 53, 60, 61, 62, 66, 70, 73, 75, 100
Hays, Mary 24, 25
Hijab 138, 161, 175, 201, 205
Hijaz 54, 55, 59, 63, 66, 198, 216
Holy Land, The VII, VIII, XVIII, 6,7,8,9,13, 16, 43, 63, 64, 65, 85, 86, 116, 121, 136
Homer 16, 23, 112
Houdin, Jean-Eugene Robert-Houdin 184, 185
Hotz, Henry X, XVI, 74
Husain, Ed XXIII, 123, 131, 151, 153, 158–171, 179, 218

https://doi.org/10.1515/9781501513367-011

Index of Names and Terms

Interculturalism XIV, 137
Ismailis 115
Isumbras, Sir (romance) 7, 8, 23, 38, 82, 122, 135–136, 182

Jerusalem VII, 5,6,14, 38, 64, 85–86, 89, 101, 102, 110, 136, 214
Jihad/Jihadi XXIII, 21, 61, 130, 137, 141, 152, 153, 160, 161, 163, 164, 170, 171, 174, 190, 192, 213
Jews XV, 17, 19, 66–68, 71, 89, 102–103, 109, 115, 128, 147–148, 156, 169, 213, 220
Johnson, Samuel, Dr. 35

Kempe, Margery 6, 8, 72
Khair, Tabish XIV, XV, 22, 127, 139, 183, 241
Khomeini, Ayatollah 18, 129, 131, 167, 168, 214
King of Tars (romance) 7, 63, 64, 67, 156, 158, 213
Kipling, Rudyard 38, 39
Kureishi, Hanif XXII, 123, 124, 135, 136, 137, 140–149, 158, 161–162, 171, 218

Laroussi, Mohammed El Metoui XI, XXIII, 131, 153, 171, 172–179, 193, 218
Lane, Edward William 25, 45, 197, 203, 204
Lawrence, T. E. XVII, 69, 70, 77, 78, 79
Levi-Strauss, Claude 37, 52, 80, 111, 139, 157, 160–161, 173

Mahomet / Mahometan XXI, 13, 17, 21, 23, 57, 89, 90, 95, 98–99, 104, 105, 107, 110, 114, 115, 117
Malory, Thomas 39
Malthus, Thomas 34, 35
Mandeville, John 5, 6, 9, 37, 38, 54
Mecca X VIII, XXI, XXVI, 7, 10, 33, 38, 42, 43, 44, 47, 48, 52, 53, 54, 55, 56, 58, 60–63, 66, 69, 70, 71, 73, 75, 89, 90–91, 95, 198–199
Medina 18, 43, 47, 52, 53, 54, 60, 69, 71, 80, 95, 96, 102, 103, 107, 112
Miles Christi 122

Mirabilia Descripta 9
Mohammed/Mohamedan XVI, XIX, XXI, XXVI, 10, 44, 45, 48, 54, 58, 62–64, 69, 70, 73, 74, 76, 86–100, 102, 103, 104, 106, 107, 108, 110, 112–113, 117, 129, 142, 187, 163, 168, 196, 205
Montaigne, Michel de XIII, 14, 27, 28, 29
Moore, Brian XVII, XXIII, 106, 123, 131, 184, 185–200, 211, 218
Moore, Thomas 28, 32, 33, 98, 112
Mozart, Wolfgang Amadeus 23
Mughals, or Moghuls 43, 98
Multiculturalism X, XIV, XXII, 123, 137, 138, 139, 149, 158, 161, 218

Nietzsche, Friedrich 214

Obama, Barack 125
Octavian (romance) 63, 64, 122, 182
One Thousand and One Nights, see also *Arabian Nights* 10, 25, 26, 175
Othello, by William Shakespeare 1 4, 206
Orientalism XI, XII, XVIII, XII, 4, 10, 16, 23, 25, 28, 33, 34, 35, 38, 40, 47, 81, 82, 113, 116, 123, 135, 130, 134, 191, 216–219
Ottoman Empire, The XVII, 3, 5, 13–16, 24, 31–32, 34, 68, 130, 133, 191, 197, 208–210, 215
Outremer VII

Palestine 5, 6, 13, 85, 86, 113, 126
Petra, *Arabia Petrea* 69
Persia/Persians 17, 18, 19, 20, 24–25, 27, 30, 44–45, 48, 65, 70, 75, 85, 93, 96–99, 105, 112–115, 130, 134, 197
Polygamy 56, 80, 177, 203–206
Pope, Alexander 23
Powell, Enoch 145
Pryde, David XI, 10, 12, 87, 90, 95, 96, 97, 102, 103, 104, 106–108, 110, 111, 116–117, 217

Qtub, Sayyid 131, 159, 160, 168

Race VIII, XIV, V, XVI, XVII, XVIII, 4, 6, 24, 34, 38, 40, 50, 51, 54–55, 66–68, 74, 79, 89, 99, 117, 128, 145, 156, 158, 163, 184, 202, 206, 210, 217
Romance (medieval) XI, XIII, XVIII, XX
Romance (Victorian Quest) VII, XVIII
Rome 13, 21, 31, 88, 115, 165, 175
Rousseau, Jean-Jacques 14, 27, 29, 30, 31, 186

Saracens XIII, XIX, XX, XXI, XXII, 7, 10, 19, 23, 30, 35, 51, 67, 68, 85–91, 96–103, 108–114, 116–117, 122, 128–129, 152, 153–156, 182
Said, Edward XI, XII, XVIII, XIX, 10, 25, 28, 30, 34–35, 40, 41, 46, 47, 48, 50, 65, 69, 81–82, 113, 123, 125–126, 130, 134, 146, 175, 191, 195, 196, 197, 216, 217–218
Sandys, George 16
Scott, Paul 219
Shamsie, Kamila VII, IX, XII, 65
Siege of Jerusalem (romance) 100
Siege of Milan, the (romance) 7, 64, 101, 129, 154
Soueif, Ahdaf XVII, XXIII, 26, 42, 56, 106, 123, 131, 184, 194–212, 218

Southey, Robert 134, 197
Stanley, Henry Morton 41
Sultan of Babylon, the (romance) 154, 182

Tennyson, Alfred (Lord) 39
Terragount 63, 154
Terrorism VII–VIII, X–XII, 125, 130, 151–154, 162–163, 171, 177, 179, 211
Thackeray, William Makepeace 81, 200
Turkish Empire see the Ottoman Empire
Turkish art 15
Tyre, William of 114

Venice 14, 15, 53
Vienne, battle of IX

Of Warwick, Guy, (romance) VIII, XI, XVIII, 7–8, 38, 76, 121–122, 125, 135–136, 182
Welch, Robert 121
Wortley, Lady Mary Montague 11, 22–23
Wren, Christopher 23, 135

Xenophobia 139, 183, 213

Zoroastrians 19

www.ingramcontent.com/pod-product-compliance
Lightning Source LLC
Chambersburg PA
CBHW031425150426
43191CB00006B/394